A 327.116
537 456

Alliance Politics

D1336059

SOAS LIBRARY
WITHDRAWN

SOAS, University of London

18 0856133 4

A volume in the series

CORNELL STUDIES IN SECURITY AFFAIRS

edited by Robert J. Art, Robert Jervis, *and* Stephen M. Walt

A full list of titles in the series appears at the end of the book.

SOAS LIBRARY

Alliance Politics

Glenn H. Snyder

Cornell University Press

Ithaca and London

Copyright © 1997 by Cornell University

All rights reserved. Except for brief quotations in a review, this book, or parts thereof, must not be reproduced in any form without permission in writing from the publisher. For information, address Cornell University Press, Sage House, 512 East State Street, Ithaca, New York 14850.

First Published 1997 by Cornell University Press
First printing, Cornell Paperbacks, 2007

Printed in the United States of America

Cornell University Press strives to utilize environmentally responsible suppliers and materials to the fullest extent possible in the publishing of its books. Such materials include vegetable-based, low-VOC inks and acid-free papers that are also either recycled, totally chlorine-free, or partly composed of nonwood fibers.

Library of Congress Cataloging-in-Publication Data

Snyder, Glenn Herald.
Alliance politics / Glenn H. Snyder.
p. cm. — (Cornell studies in security affairs)
Includes index.
ISBN 13: 978-0-8014-8428-5 (cloth : alk. paper)

1. Europe—Politics and government—1871–1918. 2. Alliances—Case studies.
I. Title. II. Series.
JZ1314.S65   1997
327.1'16'09409034—dc21   97-20958

Cloth printing   10 9 8 7 6 5 4 3 2 1

To Otty

who waited so long . . .

Contents

Preface

This book has been some time in progress. It had its inception, I believe, while I was researching and writing a book with Paul Diesing, *Conflict among Nations*, published nearly twenty years ago. That book centered on crisis diplomacy between adversaries. I became aware then of the extent to which international conflict was colored by alliance relations, especially in multipolar systems. I could not fully explore those relations in the time and book space we had available but vowed to do it later in a spinoff article or two. This rather large book is that spinoff.

In recent years it seemed that the international system was reshaping itself to conform to my theoretical focus. So I was primed to have at least a final chapter that applied my ideas and historical findings to a post–cold war multipolar world. That turned out not to be possible for the very mundane reason that the book was already too long. So another vow, another spinoff . . . or perhaps some like-minded reader will take up the never-ending task. I hope that what I have discovered, in logic and in the pre-1914 history, will be sufficiently germane to a future multipolar system to serve as at least a point of departure for informed speculation about such a system. Of course, there are bound to be many differences.

The project got fully under way during 1981–82 when I was granted a fellowship at the Woodrow Wilson International Center for Scholars, Smithsonian Institution. In that stimulating and congenial environment, the main theoretical ideas took shape and I began my fascinating voyage through late nineteenth-century diplomatic history. A Guggenheim Fellowship in 1990–91 provided much-needed free time at a later stage of the research. Sabbaticals from SUNY-Buffalo and the University of North Carolina also helped along the way.

Among several individuals who helped, Robert Jervis deserves special mention. Not only did he read and comment extensively on the entire manuscript and some of its revisions; he has been a steady source of stimulation and encouragement for many years. Others who read portions of the manuscript at various stages are Robert Art, Jack Donnelly, David Goldfischer, William Keech, Duncan MacRae, Timothy McKeown, Eric Mlyn, James L. Richardson, and Bernard Steunenberg. George Rabinowitz gave invaluable help on some of the modeling. My daughter, Abigail, and her husband, Richard Keller, brought their methodological skills to bear. My wife, Otty, spent countless hours typing notes and helped me clarify my ideas in conversation. Eugenia Herman gave helpful suggestions for improving my style, grammar, and punctuation. Carol Nichols provided cheerful secretarial assistance. My graduate students at SUNY-Buffalo and UNC contributed much more than they realize.

Parts of the book draw on previously published articles. Chapters 6 and 9 include material from "The Security Dilemma in Alliance Politics," *World Politics*, July 1984. Some of Chapter 1 appears as "Process Variables in Neorealist Theory," in a special issue of *Security Studies*, Spring 1996. I have also made some use of articles published in *Journal of International Affairs*, Spring/Summer 1990, and in *International Organization*, Autumn 1991. I thank the editors and publishers of these journals for permission to use this material.

It goes without saying that I am grateful to all the institutions and persons mentioned and do not hold them responsible for the final product: I hope it fulfills in some measure whatever promise they saw in me and the project.

GLENN H. SNYDER

Chapel Hill, North Carolina

Alliance Politics

[1]

Alliances in a
Multipolar International System

International politics, indeed all politics, involves an interplay of conflict and cooperation. In the scholarly study of international politics we have tended to focus on one or the other of these processes while recognizing some admixture. Thus we have theories about deterrence, crises, and war in which the leitmotif is how states try to get their way in conflicts with others, and cooperation is a secondary theme. We also have theories about regimes, order, international organizations, and other forms of cooperation, and about the conditions that facilitate cooperation among states whose interests are partially in conflict.

But one central phenomenon has tended to be bypassed by this great outpouring of theory, possibly because it does not fit neatly into either category. That is the military alliance. Alliances obviously are cooperative endeavors, in that their members concert their resources in the pursuit of some common goal. The goal, however, is the prosecution of conflict with an outside party.[1] Scholars interested in international cooperation have tended to focus more on the resolution of conflict between adversaries than on its prosecution; students of national security policy have been drawn more to the prosecution of conflict by such means as armaments, crises, and wars than to cooperative measures such as alliances. Hence the hybrid phenomenon of alliance has received less attention than it deserves.

Another reason, perhaps, why alliances have been understudied is that it is so difficult to separate them from everything else. George Liska, in a work that remains the leading treatment after three decades, put it succinctly: "It is impossible to speak of international relations without referring to alliances; the two often merge in all but name. For the same reason, it has always been difficult to say much that is peculiar to alliances on the plane of general analysis."[2] Writing in 1962, before the flowering of the subdiscipline of international political economy, Liska no doubt meant international *security* relations; now the thought is even more forbidding. It becomes still more so when one considers another Liska aphorism: "Alliances are against, and only derivatively for, someone or something."[3] Alliances can hardly be studied apart from the enmities that precipitate them. If the theory is to cover informal as well as formal varieties of alignment, as realistically it must, then any relationship other than outright indifference falls within its purview. There is apparently an unbroken continuum between firm, formal alliance and "good relations," and from "cool relations" to intense hostility. Any interaction between states, friendly or hostile, no matter how minor, may create expectations and feelings of alignment or opposition or both. Confronting such a protean phenomenon, many a would-be alliance theorist may have decided to retreat to something more manageable—another analysis of NATO, perhaps.

Besides Liska's, there have been only two attempts to create anything approaching a comprehensive theory of alliances. Ole Holsti, Terrence Hopmann, and John Sullivan published a useful study in the behavioral vein in 1973.[4] Stephen Walt's 1987 book contains valuable theoretical insights, especially in linking alliances to "balancing" and "bandwagoning," but his empirical analysis is mostly limited to the Middle East from 1955 to 1979.[5]

We have, in addition, a number of partial theories, each focusing on a particular aspect of alliances or approaching them from a distinctive perspective. For example, the theory of collective goods was in vogue during the 1970s and early 1980s and became quite well developed as an explanation why the United States carried a larger share of the arms burden in NATO than its European allies did. But this theory was rarely extended to other alliances, especially to pre-bipolar alliances, or to other dimensions of alliance policy.[6] Statistically oriented scholars, led by J. David Singer, have spread the broadest historical-empirical net, but their studies are limited to testing correlations between aggregates—for example, between alliance commitments and involvement in war—thus missing the political processes of alliance making and maintenance.[7] There have been several attempts to apply sociological coalition theory, most interestingly to the U.S.–Soviet–China triangle during the 1970s.[8] The theory of "structural balance," which posits a tendency toward a positive product in triadic relationships (three positives, or two negatives and a positive), has proved quite fruitful in the analysis of pre-1914 alliance diplomacy.[9] N-person game theory, apparently the most promising formal approach, had little application until the late 1980s.[10] There have been interesting formalizations from a broadly "rational choice" perspective.[11] Some of the best theoretical writing about alliances, although necessarily brief, is to be

[2]

found in textbooks, notably those by Morgenthau and Haas and Whiting.[12] But these various efforts are not cumulative; they remain partial and idiosyncratic. Clearly, the theoretical study of alliances lags well behind the study of crises, wars, and other manifestations of conflict between adversaries.

This book attempts to fill the alliance theory void by deductive reasoning from certain essentials of the international system, by borrowing from several social science theories, and by empirical generalization from international history. Systemic reasoning concentrates on the multipolar system, on the ground that multipolarity has been the structural norm during most of international history, that deviations from this norm during bipolar and unipolar periods can be quite easily accommodated from a multipolar base, and that the international system in the foreseeable future is most likely to be multipolar. The theories borrowed from, outside the international relations literature, include microeconomics, game theory, and sociological coalition theory. With a few rudimentary exceptions, I do not present these theories in mathematical form but rather use them as a source of logical insights to be stated verbally. The historical cases, taken from the period 1879 to 1914, serve to illustrate and assess the deductive theory and to elaborate on the theory inductively.

I make no claim for the theory's applicability to the post–cold war world, which many believe is evolving toward a multipolar structure. The presence of nuclear weapons, not to speak of other recent developments such as the rise of ethnic and religious conflict, will make the new multipolarity quite different from that of a century ago. Thus, at minimum, the reader may consider this a work in theoretical history. It may also qualify as a study in comparative systems, however, since I make some comparisons with a bipolar system along the way. And the logic of the theory probably will still be present in a future multipolar world, even though it will have to be heavily qualified to reflect other causal factors.

The analysis centers on two phases in the life of an alliance: its formation and its subsequent "management." Management refers to the joint and unilateral processes by which alliance members try to keep the alliance alive and advance their own interests within it. The dominant theoretical theme in both phases is that of bargaining. In the formation phase, prospective allies bargain over the alliance terms: the scope of their commitments, the amount of forces to be contributed in what contingencies, and the like. During the subsequent management phase, they may bargain over levels of preparedness, war plans, or the amount of support to be provided in crisis confrontations with the adversary, or they may entirely renegotiate the original contract.

The protean character of alliances and alignments makes a clear definition essential. In offering one, I have in mind the need to bound the subject in a way suitable for the purposes of this book, as well as to capture some features of common usage. *Alliances are formal associations of states for the use (or nonuse) of military force, in specified circumstances, against states outside their own membership.* Thus I take it that an alliance, properly speaking, can be the result only of a formal agreement of some sort that makes explicit the contingencies in which military cooperation will occur. This definition differentiates alliances from tacit "alignments" based solely on common interests, although the latter can be as consequential as formal arrangements and are prominent in our later analysis. Alliances are associations with a military or security purpose. This sets them apart from associations or regimes with economic or other purposes, such as OPEC or the European Union. Alliances occur between "states." This excludes connections between governments and nongovernmental entities such as revolutionary groups.

Finally, alliances are aimed at states outside their own membership. This "other" orientation points to a fundamental difference between alliances and most other international institutions or regimes. The latter generally seek some common goal that is hindered by conflicts among the group members themselves. They attempt to achieve a collective good by a set of rules that, at least partially, overrides the normal competitive compulsions in an anarchic system.* Alliances, by contrast, do not override or modify anarchy; rather, they are instruments for prosecuting conflict-in-anarchy, for meeting an external threat more effectively than could be done by their members individually. Alliances, of course, usually reduce conflict among their members, but that is a by-product. Their primary function is to pool military strength against a common enemy, not to protect alliance members from each other.[13]

It is incumbent on any author, especially when his work claims to be theoretical, to state his working assumptions. Every theory requires simplifying assumptions if it is to be manageable, coherent, and useful, but of course the assumptions should stay as close to reality and good sense as possible. My assumptions, as best I can discern them, are as follows. I assume, first, that statesmen are rational, meaning simply that they choose means that are consistent with their ends, given the information available to them. I assume that the primary interest of states, as seen by their leaders, is to survive, and derivatively, to maintain security against attack. The alliances I am writing about are those made for purposes of military security. That is not to imply that there are not occasionally alliances made to serve some other purpose, say, economic, but they lie outside the purview of this book. Economic dimensions of military alliances, however, are taken account of in the case study chapters. In order to simplify the

---

*The term "anarchic" means simply the absence of a systemwide government.

theoretical reasoning in this chapter and in chapter 2, I assume a unitary state; unfortunately, my available time and space does not permit an intensive study of internal political influences. Nevertheless, I note these influences in the case studies of alliance formation when they have a significant effect and summarize them in Chapter 5. As noted above, I assume a multipolar international system. The analysis concerns only alliances among great powers in such a system, and predominantly defensive alliances.

From the perspective of individual states, alliances are primarily instruments of national security policy. Thus they are functionally more akin to other aspects of security policy than they are to other international associations. Security and security policy are among those essentially contested concepts which, like "power" and "interest," have such complex implications that they may never attain a generally accepted definition. The best that can be done is to define them in a way that suits the purpose at hand. For the purpose of this book, I define security simply, and rather narrowly, as *a high confidence of preserving, against external military attack, values presently held.* National security policy, then, is any policy primarily designed to maintain or increase that confidence. Values presently held include, as basic prior values, the territorial integrity and political independence of the state. The security of these values (which subsume all the derivative values that independence makes possible, such as the value of a particular domestic political system) might be called "political security." Another set of values includes the potential costs of war in terms of lives, economic costs, and so on; security against these costs commonly goes under the heading of "physical security." The definition admits values placed on the independence of other states, either for the strategic resources they command or for their intrinsic political, economic, or cultural attributes. The definition does not exclude the security of other governments against internal violent overthrow, to the degree that such security has high strategic or intrinsic value for the state.[14] It pointedly excludes security against value losses inflicted by nonmilitary means, such as economic deprivation, environmental degradation, or the drug trade. The definition thus stands against the current tendency to bring almost any kind of threat to any value within the rubric of "national security." That does not mean, of course, that such threats are unimportant, only that analytical clarity for the purpose of this book demands the exclusion of all but military threats.

As a first approximation, we can say that the principal means to national security are armaments, alliances, military action, and settlement of conflicts with adversaries. The first three are methods for increasing capabilities or blocking the adversary from increasing its. They may also communicate a future intention to resist attack. The fourth, conciliation of opponents, may moderate an adversary's possibly aggressive intentions. Within limits, all four are substitutable for each other. Thus alliances are substitutable for preparedness within limits posed by the adversary's capabilities and the perceived reliability of the allies. Armaments are substitutable for allies within the limits of national resources. Military action to prevent an opponent increasing its resources by expansion may reduce potential arms or alliance requirements. Accommodating an adversary may be cheaper than the various forms of resistance, provided it does not stimulate the adversary to make further demands. Each method, of course, involves different kinds of costs: armament sacrifices domestic welfare values; alliance risks loss of autonomy, including having to fight for interests that are not one's own; military action obviously sacrifices lives and other material assets; and conciliation sacrifices some values in order to increase the security of other values.

ALLIANCES AND ALIGNMENTS

The terms "alliance" and "alignment" are often employed interchangeably,[15] but it is useful to stipulate somewhat different meanings. The broader and more fundamental term is alignment, defined as expectations of states about whether they will be supported or opposed by other states in future interactions.* Alignment includes alignment "against" as well as "with"; it identifies potential opponents as well as friends. Such expectations may arise from a variety of specific sources, but in general they stem from the perceived interests, capabilities, and observed behavior of other states, including their alliance pledges. They may only be vague estimates of likelihood rather than certainties or even probabilities. Thus two states that are threatened by the same adversary will each expect defensive help from the other, since they have a common interest in preventing the adversary from gaining power. Each knows that expansion by the adversary at the other's expense will increase the danger to itself; consequently, each

---

*This definition is similar to Liska's but different from the one advanced by George Modelski in his review of Liska's book. Modelski defines alignment as "all types of political cooperation," and alliance as "military collaboration," apparently including in the latter the tacit expectation of collaboration I have labeled "alignment." See Modelski, "Study of Alliances." An alternate definition of alignment might include the "intentions" as well as the "expectations" of states. Quite conceivably, what alliance partners or adversaries expect of each other might be different from the other's actual intent. Could a supporting alignment be said to exist if the parties expected each other's support but neither had any intention of providing it? In my judgment, yes. The reality of alignment, that which will determine a party's behavior (in addition to its own interests), is its beliefs about what the other will do, not what the other intends. Thus I assume alignment is sufficiently defined by the term "mutual expectations." Of course, expectations will change as contrary intentions are revealed.

has some incentive to come to the other's defense and some reason to expect assistance if attacked. Expectations of support may also stem from common ideologies or similar ethnic makeups. They may arise in addition from inequalities of resources and military strength. For example, a small state lying between two powerful ones can reasonably expect to be defended by one against the depredations of the other. Expectations of support may be created by various behavioral means, such as joint military planning or diplomatic statements and agreements of various kinds, up to and including formal alliances. The aggregate of all such expectations throughout the international system constitutes a "pattern of alignment." This pattern is usually somewhat vague because of the uncertainty of some of the expectations that generate it. The pattern is clearer or vaguer depending on the extent to which it is verbalized, the depth of conflicts and degrees of inequality, and whether the lines of conflict and commonality on different issues tend to be reinforcing or cross-cutting.

The pattern of alignment in Europe in the 1870s (before the Austro-German alliance of 1879 set off a competition in formal alliances) serves as an illustration. There were two central axes of enmity—between France and Germany over Alsace-Lorraine, and between Austria-Hungary and Russia over the Balkans. In addition, France and England were at odds over colonial issues, and Austria-Hungary and Italy had a conflict over Italian claims to the South Tyrol irredentum. England and Russia confronted each other in the "Great Game" of imperial rivalry from Constantinople to China. Cutting across these enmities were several affinities of interest, ideology, and ethnicity. The three eastern monarchies were linked by a common ideology, as were the western democracies, Britain and France. Yet Britain had strategic interests in common with Austria and Italy in the Mediterranean and had no conflicts with Germany. There was a real ethnic affinity between Germany and Austria and a more speculative one between Germany and Great Britain. Finally, there were important inequalities of strength, ranging from Germany and Britain as the strongest states to Austria-Hungary and Italy as the weakest.

This pattern, obviously, was more cross-cutting than reinforcing. The lack of clear-cut lines of cleavage on grounds of interest, ideology, and inequality meant that the formal agreements made in subsequent decades contributed significantly to both amity and enmity in the system.

Alignments constantly change with changing patterns of power, interests, and issue priorities. Power relations change only slowly, the pattern of common and conflicting interests more frequently. Alignments also change as the attention of states shifts from one issue to another. For example, during the latter part of the nineteenth century there was an oscillation of European powers' attention between the European and colonial arenas. On colonial issues, the dominant alignment was England versus

Russia and France. On the continent, the lineup tended to be Germany and Austria versus Russia and France; England usually sided with Germany until the early 1900s, when it switched to the Franco-Russia side as it liquidated its colonial conflicts with the latter. England's switch coincided with and was facilitated by Russia's shift from an imperial to a continental orientation after its defeat in the 1904–5 war with Japan. Whereas Russia had been supported by Germany against England in the Far East, its change to a continental focus brought it into conflict with Austrian and German interests in the Balkans and the Near East.

Formal alliances are simply one of the behavioral means to create or strengthen alignments. Thus alliances are a subset of alignments—those that arise from or are formalized by an explicit agreement, usually in the form of a treaty. The formalization adds elements of specificity, legal and moral obligation, and reciprocity that are usually lacking in informal alignments. The contract specifies, with varying explicitness, the identity of the opponent, what acts by the opponent will call for an alliance response, and what that response will be. The expectations that arise from an alliance are thus more narrowly and specifically bounded than is the case with less formal alignments. Only a portion of the allies' interests, perhaps not even all their common interests, are selected for joint support. This very selectivity, with the specification of the means of joint action, probably enhances the parties' confidence in the agreement, since it underlines their seriousness and the limited nature of their liability.

On the other hand, formal alliance commitments usually have a political penumbra, or "halo," extending beyond the narrow contingency (e.g., attack by an enemy state) which activates the commitment to military assistance. Allies expect their partners to support them on a variety of issues short of war, including diplomatic crises, even though there is nothing in the alliance treaty requiring it. To withhold such support, at least when it does not run drastically counter to the partner's own interests, is likely to weaken the solidarity of the alliance. The content of and reasons for this halo effect become clearer in our case study chapters. For now, we simply remark that the making of an alliance has political and psychological implications that go well beyond the obligations contained in the formal *casus foederis*.

Formal alliances introduce a sense of obligation not present in tacit alignments. The sense of obligation arises, first, from the legal status of the contract as a treaty, although not all alliance agreements take the treaty form. It stems also from the moral convention that promises should be kept. These normative elements are enhanced by the solemnity of ceremonies attending treaty signing and ratification, by the stature of the individuals participating, and (in democracies) by the involvement of parliaments and public opinion.[16] The element of reciprocity adds further strength to the agreement.[17] Reciprocity means the implicit understanding that each party's obligation is conditional on its partner's honoring its commitment. Thus a failure to live up to the agreement may forfeit all the alliance's benefits. A related factor is the engagement of the parties' reputations. Reneging will severely damage the credibility of one's future promises, to the present ally or to others. Despite these special features, the political reality of alliances is not different in kind from that of tacit or informal alignments; it lies not in the formal contract but in the expectations that are supported or created—not only between the partners but also among all interested bystanders, including especially opponents.

Just how much alliances add to or change existing expectations is a matter of some debate. A well-known piece of "realist" conventional wisdom is that since alliance treaties are unenforceable, an alliance will be viable only to the extent that it reflects the interests of its members. The logical consequence of this view is that alliances have no independent effect at all. States will act according to their interests, whether they are allied or not. Thus alliances are either unnecessary or invalid.[18] They are unnecessary, that is, redundant, when the allies' interests are shared; they are merely bluffs when allies' interests diverge.

Reality, as always, lies somewhere between these logical extremes. Alliance promises are often made and kept even though they are not fully consistent with the parties' interests. States with identical or highly shared interests make alliances despite their apparent redundancy.

What accounts for this seeming discrepancy between logic and reality? The logic is defective on several counts. Consider first the claim of redundancy. Even when allies fully share each other's interests, they may not be sure of this fact; an alliance would enhance their confidence in each other's support. Although an alliance pledge might not affect the intentions of the allies themselves, it would be useful for deterring opponents and for influencing the behavior of nonallied states. Even when states share common goals, an alliance may well be desirable for coordinating on means for attaining the goals.

The claim of invalidity is also weak because an alliance at least increases the likelihood of assistance, even though the ally does not fully share one's interests. Any increase in the certainty of others' intentions, especially their military intentions, is a plus. An exchange of promises of military assistance is rational when the rise in the probability of aid, combined with the state's need for aid, yields a surplus of benefits over costs.

There are several reasons why this might well be the case, even when the parties' interests are quite divergent. First, the partner's need for aid, along with norms of promise-keeping and reciprocity, may be strong enough to counter the disparity of underlying interests. Second, as discussed more fully below, the act of allying can create common interests that did not previously exist—for example, interests in resisting expansion by the likely opponent(s) of the alliance. Third, states entering an alliance may redefine their "selves" so that they embrace at least some of the partner's interests as their own. Fourth, once having formed the alliance, its members will have a joint interest in keeping it alive; this common interest may very well overcome a divergence of self-regarding interests. Fifth, general reputational considerations may counsel honoring alliance commitments even when the allies have few other specific interests in common. For all these reasons, alliances between states with few shared interests need not be mere "scraps of paper."

Nevertheless, both logical reasoning and empirical observation suggest that alliances are more highly valued, and are more likely to form, when their members have substantial interests in common. In practice, of course, the interests of allies usually are neither fully shared nor unshared, but partially shared. The more fully they are shared, the greater the net value of the alliance, that is, the greater the perceived surplus of benefits over costs. There are two reasons for this: costs are inherently more certain than benefits; and costs are lower when interests are shared. Costs are suffered in carrying out one's own side of the agreement; benefits are enjoyed when the ally carries out its. Each ally will be surer of its own intentions than of the partner's and therefore surer of the costs than the benefits. When the allies' interests are mostly shared, costs are low because neither ally is promising much more than it would do anyway. Benefits are moderate but still significant because, although the ally has an interest in coming to one's defense even without an alliance, one cannot be sure of its intentions; the alliance pledge will reduce the uncertainty. When interests are divergent, on the other hand, the costs of alliance are high because the contract commits the parties to fight for interests not their own. Benefits are relatively low because the ally's pledge must be heavily discounted. Thus alliances between states with common interests are more likely to yield a net gain. States prefer not to ally with others that do not share their interests because, although they will feel quite constrained to honor their promise to support the ally's interests, they are not at all sure the ally will feel likewise.

The two extremes of shared and divergent interests correspond to two different ideal-type motives for entering an alliance. One is the "guarantee" motive: when one already has a strong interest in defending another state, whether or not the other state reciprocates, one may wish to make one's intentions clear in order to deter potential attackers and reassure the ally. Examples are the British guarantee to Poland in 1939 and the U.S. guarantee to the Western European countries through NATO. The other is the "get help" motive: to gain another state's aid in one's own defense, one promises to defend that state, when one would not have been motivated to defend it without the alliance contract. An approximate example is the Franco-Russian alliance of 1894: the two countries' underlying interests in defending each other against Germany were less central than the increased confidence in being defended that was generated by the agreement itself. In the first type, the alliance agreement is an act of communication intended only to clarify one's existing intentions; in the second, the agreement is a true exchange of commitments. Most alliances have some mixture of these two characteristics—in "get help" alliances, for example, the partners will have at least some interest in defending each other apart from the alliance contract.[19]

Especially when the interests of allies are somewhat divergent, or when they are subject to change, expectations arising from an alliance contract will need to be periodically validated. The partner will need to be reassured that one's underlying interests are not so at odds with the contract that the alliance is no more than a "scrap of paper." Means of validation include joint military planning, supporting the ally in a dispute with a third party, or public restatement of the alliance pledge.[20] The vaguer the alliance commitment, the greater the need for validation. Thus Great Britain found it necessary, after negotiating the vague Entente Cordiale with France in 1904, to reassure France repeatedly of its loyalty. The joint military planning that took place from 1906 onward was an important means of reassurance and of transforming the entente into a quasi-alliance. Even formal alliances will gradually weaken unless they are reconfirmed by subsequent behavior. For example, the Franco-Russian alliance of 1935 became a dead letter through the failure of the parties to implement it.

After a general definition, the next step in a scientific enterprise is to identify variations in the object of study and to classify these variations in some logical order. One broad dichotomy is between explicit pledges of mutual assistance and agreements that tacitly raise expectations of mutual support by reducing the amount of conflict between the parties, that is, *ententes*. Alliances differ from ententes in that their force rests on a promise that is superimposed over existing conflicts rather than on a reduction of the conflicts, although of course an alliance agreement may include some explicit conflict reduction.[21] Ententes should in turn be differentiated from agreements between adversaries that do not reduce their conflict enough to change their basic relationship. Thus opponents may achieve a *detente*—a reduction of tension—but remain primarily adversaries. Or they may agree to a designation of spheres of influence or even a partition of third areas where they have been wont to compete. Although such agreements do not themselves create even a quasi-alliance, the perception by other states that the parties have moved closer will affect the parties' alignments with these others somewhat as if they had negotiated an entente. Sometimes the label "entente" is given to a disposition to cooperate based simply on shared interests rather than on a negotiated reduction of conflict. In such cases, the concept of entente merges into tacit alignment, as discussed above.

We can classify formal alliances, first, according to size. The smallest possible membership, obviously, is two. Most historical alliances in fact have had only two members; only a few have been larger than three or four. The large alliances of the post-1945 period, such as NATO with its sixteen members, are exceptions, associated with a brief bipolar structure of world power. The largest alliances in the pre-1945 multipolar system were wartime alliances organized to put down an especially powerful and aggressive state, such as Napoleonic France. Such alliances are often called "coalitions." A large number of states get together for a specific purpose, and when that purpose is accomplished, the group disbands. A contemporary example is the coalition of twenty-eight states organized by the United States to evict Iraqi forces from Kuwait in 1990.

Alliances may be unilateral, bilateral, or multilateral. A unilateral alliance might seem to be a contradiction in terms. The term seems appropriate for *guarantees*, however, in which one state commits itself to defend another but the other undertakes no obligations—as with the British guarantee of Poland and other eastern European countries in 1939. Expectations of support are generated, but only in one direction. A related phenomenon, somewhat less specific and binding, is the broad unilateral declaration or "doctrine" by which a strong state commits itself to defend all other states or all states in a region against a particular threat; examples are the Truman and Eisenhower doctrines. Most alliances are, of course, bilateral or multilateral, the members undertaking reciprocal obligations.

A further differentiation is between equal and unequal alliances. Equal alliances—between states of similar strength—tend to generate reciprocal and symmetrical obligations and expectations. Alliances between strong and weak states are generally characterized by asymmetrical expectations if not obligations—that is, they take on the character of unilateral guarantees, whatever the wording of the alliance contract. Moreover, they tend to be dominated by the stronger member, which uses the alliance as a vehicle for asserting influence or control.

Alliances differ according to purpose. First, there is the obvious distinction between offensive and defensive alliances. This distinction is not as clear-cut as it might seem, first, since an ostensibly defensive agreement may cloak offensive aims, and second, because a state may have to undertake a tactical offensive in order to defend itself, its ally, or its interests effectively. Alliances may also mix offensive and defensive purposes— even aggressors, after all, are interested in security as well as aggrandizement. Purely or primarily offensive alliances are rather rare; an example is the German-Italian "pact of steel" of 1936.

[12]

Within the category of defensive alliances, we can identify several motives. The dominant motive in most cases is that of security against external attack. A second motive is to increase the state's internal security or domestic political stability. Alliance tends to legitimize an existing government and thus to discourage dissidents; it may even promise the ally's aid in suppressing internal disorder. Another possible motive is to control the ally.[22] An alliance can generate leverage over the partner via the implicit or explicit threat to withdraw. Beyond this, the alliance gives one some entrée into the ally's decision making through a norm of consultation. Examples of using an alliance for control purposes are the U.S. employment of NATO to control West Germany, and German control over Austria by means of the alliance of 1879. Alliances may also function as cloaks for imperial domination, as the Soviets used the Warsaw Pact during the cold war.

Several distinct types of alliance fall short of a pledge of active military support. One is the *neutrality* agreement, in which each party agrees not to join in an attack on the partner. Neutrality agreements can take on either an offensive or a defensive cast, depending on the parties' aims. A good example of the defensive type is the German-Russian Reinsurance Treaty of 1887, in which these states agreed to be neutral if either were attacked by a third power but not if Germany or Russia itself took the initiative in attacking. The offensive kind is exemplified by the Franco-Italian agreement of 1935, in which France agreed to be neutral if Italy attacked Ethiopia.

In a *nonaggression* treaty, as the name implies, the signatories agree not to attack each other. The underlying purpose of such an agreement, again, may be defensive or aggressive or possibly both. Typically, a weak country making a nonagression pact with a powerful one will be defensively motivated. A strong country may use such a pact for offensive purposes—to lull a victim into complacency or discourage it from looking for allies. Stalin provides an example of mixed motives. By signing a nonaggression pact with Hitler in 1939, he sought chiefly to avoid war by deflecting German aggressiveness westward, but he also made substantial offensive gains himself in occupying eastern Poland with Hitler's permission.

Treaties of mutual defense (or offense), neutrality agreements, and nonaggression pacts relate to one another in telescopic fashion. A nonaggression promise logically subsumes a pledge of neutrality: if one is not going to attack the partner, one is also not going to join an attack on it. A mutual defense alliance subsumes both the others: in pledging to come to one's aid, the partner logically also promises not to attack, and not to participate in attack on, oneself. One might say that a neutrality agreement or nonaggression treaty yields about half the benefits of a defensive alliance: at least the partner's resources will not be directed against the self even if they are not positively committed on one's behalf. If one has previously deployed forces against the partner, these forces are now released for deployment against the adversary.

It is also possible to mix these different kinds of pledges in one agreement, each becoming operative in a different contingency. Indeed, such mixtures were quite commonplace in nineteenth-century alliances. A particularly popular one was the *holding the ring* agreement, in which the members agreed to be neutral if the partner were attacked by only one other state but to come to its defense if it were attacked by more than one opponent. For instance, this provision in the Anglo-Japanese alliance of 1902 meant England would stay neutral in case of war between Russia and Japan alone but would come to Japan's defense if France joined Russia. The purpose of such an agreement, as in this case, is to deter friends of the ally's adversary from entering the fray, hence to "hold the ring" for the ally while it is defeating its main adversary.

Any alliance will have a preclusive effect, that is, it will block the ally from entering into a contradictory agreement with someone else, in particular an alliance with the opponent. This is obviously the primary effect of a neutrality agreement, but it is sometimes also the chief motive for a mutual defense alliance. Thus Bismarck made his alliance with Austria in 1879 primarily to prevent Austria from allying with France and Russia or with France and England. England made its alliance with Japan in 1902 in part to prevent Japan from making a Far Eastern settlement with Russia to the detriment of British interests.

Another set of variations relates to the scope of the commitment undertaken in a defensive alliance, that is, the *casus foederis*. Who is the opponent? What actions by the opponent call for a response? What response is required? These are the essential components of an alliance commitment. They are treated with varying explicitness in alliance contracts. Opponents are usually identified in nineteenth-century alliances; in twentieth-century, especially post-1945, alliances, they usually are not. When they are not identified, however, it is clear from the context who the adversary is understood to be. The opponent's action that will trigger the *casus foederis* is typically stated as "attack," but this term is subject to qualifiers. Thus an alliance may require action only in defense against an "unprovoked" attack, a term which leaves partners an obvious loophole for reneging but which can be used also to reassure the designated adversary that the alliance is not aggressive. Alternatively, the triggering contingency may be stated simply as being "at war," which is much broader and gives the agreement an offensive cast. It also gives a member the right to claim assistance in defense of its interests outside its own territory. The commitment may be explicitly limited geographically, perhaps to defense of the homeland of the members or to a specific region.

[14]

Thus the NATO commitment is limited to the "North Atlantic area," which is specifically defined.

The type of commitment—what the parties are committed to do if the *casus foederis* is triggered—is also subject to considerable variation. At one extreme, they may be obligated to come to the assistance of an attacked partner immediately, in a specified manner, and with specified amounts of forces. For example, the Franco-Russian alliance of 1894 said that in case any member or members of the Triple Alliance were to mobilize, France and Russia were to "mobilize all their forces immediately and simultaneously." Then, if either power were attacked by Germany, the other would "employ all her available forces to fight Germany." The "available forces" were specifically defined as 1,300,000 men for France and 700,000 to 800,000 men for Russia. Near the other extreme would be agreements requiring the parties merely to "consult" or, as in the Southeast Asia Collective Defense Treaty of 1954, to "act to meet the common danger in accord with its constitutional processes." The North Atlantic Treaty of 1949 strikes a middle ground in requiring a member to take "such action as it deems necessary, including the use of armed force," although this commitment was strengthened by the declaration that an armed attack on any member "shall be considered an attack against them all."

Alliance agreements sometimes go beyond the defense of home territories, by specifying certain interests or goals outside homelands that the parties agree to support or promote by diplomatic means. Often this is the *status quo* itself; sometimes, a change. The Mediterranean Agreements of March and December 1887, among Great Britain, Austria, and Italy, spoke of diplomatic cooperation to maintain the status quo in the area of the Mediterranean, Adriatic, Aegean, and Black Seas. The Reinsurance Treaty of 1887 between Germany and Russia said Germany would lend "moral and diplomatic support" to Russia's efforts to gain control of the straits between the Black Sea and the Mediterranean.

Lying between tacit alignments based on common interests and formal alliances based on treaties is a range of diplomatic vehicles that express some degree of obligation short of that implied by a treaty. These include oral agreements and oral statements (private or public) and demonstrations of various kinds, military or otherwise. Then there is a variety of written instruments—for example, exchanges of notes, joint démarches and communiqués, minutes, memoranda of understanding, and executive agreements. Advantages of these informal vehicles over formal treaties are that they are more flexible and thus more easily adapted to changing circumstances, they are less public and hence less subject to domestic constraints, they can be more quickly arranged or negotiated, and they are less constraining as diplomatic precedents. Their disadvantage is that they are less reliable, since they have less legal and moral force and the parties' reputations are less engaged. They communicate some degree of mutual support and permit some specification of the terms of support but leave the parties a fairly easy "out" if necessary.[23] Informal agreements may supplement formal treaties—for example, by elaborating on the nature of commitments, specifying forms of joint military action, or setting up institutions and procedures for consultation.

Finally, alliances vary in their anticipated duration. Most formal alliances specify a duration. In the multipolar era before 1939 a typical period was five years, although often they were renewed. Alliances in the bipolar period from 1945 to 1990 were expected to last longer; the North Atlantic Treaty, for example, was to be in force for twenty years and was renewed twice for the same interval. Less formal arrangements, such as ententes, typically do not specify duration. In the case of ententes, that is because the conflict settlements that form the basis of the agreement are assumed to be permanent. There is also a class of ad hoc temporary arrangements, formed for a specific purpose, which are presumed to last only until that purpose is accomplished. Examples are the joint British-Russian warning delivered to Germany in 1875, intended to deter Bismarck from his apparent intention to attack France, and the multinational military expedition sent to put down the Boxer Rebellion in China in 1900. On a larger scale are coalitions organized during wartime for the specific purpose of blocking a major aggressor—for example, the shifting coalitions against Napoleonic France. By contrast, "alliances," as defined above, have a contingent rather than an immediate purpose: they are formed to deal with a specified event that may or may not happen at any time during their life, rather than a situation that is already occurring.

THE SYSTEMIC CONTEXT OF ALLIANCES

Alliances cannot be understood apart from their context in the international system. The system provides much of the motive for allying, and the nature of alliances varies with characteristics of the system. Alliance formation and maintenance are basic systemic processes. The systemic context of alliances may be described in terms of four analytic entities: structure, relationships, interaction, and units. Relationships and interaction are aspects of systemic process: system structure and acting units provide "external" and "internal" inputs into the process. The following analysis is based on the "neorealist" theory of international politics,[24] but it expands that theory by introducing elements of process.

The preeminent characteristic of the international system, which differentiates it sharply from domestic systems, is that of anarchy, meaning that it is a system without a government. A principal consequence of anarchy is insecurity. States in an anarchic system must be constantly concerned about security and survival, because they are surrounded by other states that have the capability to attack and perhaps to conquer them. Consequently, they must take protective measures, one of which is to form alliances. Alliances focus and direct the otherwise diffuse fears generated by anarchy. They tend to eliminate anarchic fear as between the allies; on the other hand, they promote fear in others against which they are apparently directed. Alliances thus partake of the *security dilemma*: given the irreducible uncertainty about the intentions of others, security measures taken by one actor are perceived by others as threatening; the others take steps to protect themselves; these steps are then interpreted by the first actor as confirming its initial hypothesis that the others are dangerous, and so on in a spiral of illusory fears and "unnecessary" defenses.[25] In the alliance version of the security dilemma, alliances intended for mutual defense are seen as potentially aggressive by their apparent targets; these states then seek security by forming a counteralliance, which is perceived in turn by members of the first alliance as possibly aggressive. As with the arms race version of the dilemma, the parties gain little or no security while taking on substantial costs. The costs are nevertheless undertaken, because of uncertainty about others' intentions and the much greater costs that would be suffered if no alliance were formed and those intentions turned out to be malign.[26]

A tendency toward balance of power is also deducible from anarchy. Competitive security seeking produces equilibrium, much as, in classical economic theory, competitive profit seeking produces an equilibrium of supply and demand at the lowest possible price. If any state or alliance becomes dangerously powerful or expansionist, others will mobilize countervailing power through arms or alliances. Even when there is no "great disturber," states will ally to improve their security, and the system will tend to divide into two opposing camps.

Anarchy also is responsible for the well-known fact that alliance treaties are ultimately unenforceable. Since there is no central power that can enforce contracts, observance of any agreement will depend largely on the self-interests of the parties. Although there are norms that pose some costs for noncompliance, the norms are weak because the costs are small compared to the value of "interests." Thus the value of any alliance must always be discounted by the likelihood of the partner's defection. On the other hand, paradoxically, the danger of the ally's defection, and the wish to avoid provoking it, is one factor that tends to hold alliances together. Anarchy simultaneously makes the cohesion of alliances problematic and makes holding them together a primary policy task.

The combination of insecurity and the nonenforceability of contracts—both a result of systemic anarchy—generates the central dilemma of alliance politics. The freedom of states to use force against each other, and the fear that this freedom inspires, provides the primary incentive to ally. Yet states cannot fully trust their allies to live up to their agreements. Thus anarchy is at once the basic cause of alliances and their Achilles' heel.

A peculiar characteristic of international anarchy, as compared to "hierarchical" domestic systems, is that gains relative to others tend to increase one's capability to make further gains. Whereas in domestic politics the gains and losses in political encounters are counted mainly in terms of "intrinsic" and absolute values—things valued for their own sakes and not for their instrumental or power content—the payoffs in international security interaction are counted largely in terms of "strategic values," that is, changes in relative capability. This, of course, follows from the lack of a sovereign power, which forces states to rely on self-help for their security and other goals. Gains and losses of capability tend to generate further gains and losses unless the loser takes measures to stop the process or the gainer loses motivation. This tendency is expressed in the familiar "domino theory": any accretion of territory to an aggressor not only increases its ability to take more but also stimulates its contempt for the resolve of potential defenders. The aggressor is thus both strengthened and emboldened to make further attacks, which, if successful, strengthen and embolden it even more, until it eventually dominates the entire system. The alliance analogue to the domino theory is the notion of "bandwagoning": a successful aggressor attracts allies that hope to share in the spoils and/or that are unsuccessful in forming or gaining protection from a defensive alliance.[27]

The second major aspect of system structure is polarity: how power resources are distributed in the system. The "poles" of the system are the great powers, considered as unitary actors; they are not alliances or blocs. A bipolar system contains two great powers; a multipolar system, more than two; a unipolar system, only one. The international system was multipolar from its beginning in the sixteenth century until approximately 1945; it was bipolar from 1945 to 1989; and it appears at present to be unipolar, though incipiently multipolar.

Several propositions can be deduced about differences between alliances in multipolar and bipolar systems.[28] Perhaps the most obvious one concerns the determinacy of alliance partners. In a multipolar system, who allies with whom is structurally indeterminate. Apart from particular, nonstructural conflicts that may block certain pairings, each state is logically eligible to be either friend or enemy of any other state. In a bipolar system, by contrast, alignments are largely, although not entirely, determined by structure. At minimum, the two superpowers will always be rivals, never allies, so long as they are superpowers. The sufficient reason for this is that there is no other state in the system powerful enough to threaten either one and thus to provide an incentive to ally. Since the only conceivable threats to their survival come from each other, their relationship is naturally and logically competitive, although the intensity of the competition may vary through various degrees of detente or "cold war."

Alignment of the lesser states in a bipolar system is only partially determined by structure, however. Some may be coerced into alliance with a superpower, and such coercion may be structurally motivated, as in the case of Soviet coercion of the Eastern European countries during the cold war. Others, such as the Western European states, will be so obviously threatened by one superpower, for geographic or other reasons, that they will turn to the other for protection. Still others will tend to ally with the superpower that is the least threatening, or the most supportive against local rivals, or the most rewarding financially—or they will not ally with either superpower. Nonaligned states, however, will be under the tacit protection of one or the other superpower. Alignments of the lesser states with each other will be affected by the degree of perceived threat from a superpower. Thus the common threat from the Soviet Union ruled out alignments by Western European countries against one another during the cold war, while the Middle Eastern states, feeling less threat from the Soviet Union, were freer to align and realign according to local conflicts and interests.[29]

In a multipolar system there is almost always a degree of uncertainty about who is friend and who is foe. Alliance agreements reduce the uncertainty but can never eliminate it, because they are ultimately unenforceable. A corollary is that of flexibility: states can readily defect and realign if their interests require it. Although flexibility may be inhibited by internal factors such as national or ideological sentiment, the system itself does not foreclose alternatives.

The existence of alternatives and the uncertainty of alignment generate an endemic distrust among allies. All must be concerned about the danger of being abandoned; hence all must take care that the ally does not become disillusioned and restless. As Kenneth Waltz has noted, flexibility of alignment produces rigidity of policy. To discourage the ally from defecting, one is constrained to frame one's own policy, to some extent, to suit the ally's interests. By contrast, in a bipolar system, rigidity of alignment permits flexibility of policy, because even if the ally dislikes one's policy, it has nowhere else to turn.[30]

Rigidity of policy in a multipolar system may lead to entrapment in a war over the ally's interests. Reducing this danger requires avoiding excessively tight commitments, but such avoidance risks abandonment by a dissatisfied ally. This is the "alliance security dilemma," discussed in Chapters 6 and 9.

A pervasive concern in a multipolar system is the fear of being attacked from the rear while one is militarily preoccupied in another direction. Logically, states must keep forces deployed against all possible enemies. If they concentrate against one, they leave themselves vulnerable to others. This anxiety might be stabilizing or destabilizing, depending on whether the state concerned is a potential aggressor or potential defender. Presumably, it would help deter aggressors, thus contributing to stability. But it might also deter nonaggressive states from helping the victim of aggression, thus fostering instability. An important motive for alliance making, for either an offensive or a defensive purpose, is to "cover the rear," that is, neutralize states that might be tempted to attack while one's forces are committed to another front.

Relationships

In the neorealist perspective, causal influences on behavior are found either in system structure or in the internal characteristics of states, although the theoretical focus is on the structural effects.[31] The processes by which these influences make themselves felt are not specified, however, nor is behavior itself, the dependent variable, analyzed in any detail. For Waltz, the leading neorealist, behavior is either "relations" or "interaction," or sometimes both, and indeed, in his writings these two terms often appear to be synonymous.[32] In my view, however, they each mean, or ought to mean, something quite different. Interaction is behavior: actual communication between states, or some physical action, such as armament or war, that impinges on others. Relations or relationships are not behavior itself but the situational context of behavior: the conflicts, common interests, alignments, and power relations that motivate and shape behavioral choice.* Relationships lie between structure and interaction; they are the conduit through which structural effects are transmitted to behavior. Like-

---

*In order to avoid co-opting for a specific purpose the label of our entire discipline, I prefer the term "relationships" to "relations." There does seem to be a subtle difference of meaning between the two terms. "Relationship" seems to connote something more static than "relations," closer to "existing state of affairs" than to activity of some sort, thus closer to what I have in mind. The distinction between relations and interaction is common in other social sciences, particularly sociology, social psychology, and ethology. See, for example, R. A. Hinde, "Interactions, Relationships, and Social Structure," *Man* 11 (March 1976), 1–17.

Figure 1-1. System structure and process

Unit attributes	Structure	Relationships	Interactions
Preferences	Anarchy	Alignment	Preparedness
Perceptions	Polarity	Interests	Diplomacy
Politics		Capability	Action
		Interdependence	

wise, the internal characteristics of states influence interaction largely through their effects on relationships.[33]

The principal components of relationships are familiar enough; they simply have not yet found their logical niche in neorealist theory. They are *alignments and alliances, common and conflicting interests, capabilities,* and *interdependence.* Note first what these things are not. They are not structure, since they are not systemwide concepts, but characteristics of relationships between particular states. Nor are they interaction; they establish the context of interaction but are not action itself. They are the proximate sources of behavioral causation, constrained broadly by more "distant" causes such as system structure but operating to some extent independently. They also complete the causal path from unit attributes to interaction, since it is through their effects on relationships that unit variables such as values, ideologies, and interests make themselves felt on behavior. Figure 1-1 shows the linkages I have in mind.

Alignments and Alliances

Alignment is preeminent among the relational variables because it marks the lines of amity and enmity in the system and thus determines the general kind of relationship—adversarial, allied, or indifferent—each state will have with every other. Consequently, it also determines the focus and significance of other relationship variables: conflicts, capabilities, and interdependence. Alignments, whether or not they have been formalized as alliances, are essentially expectations in the minds of statesmen about whether they will be supported, opposed, or ignored by other states in future interactions. These expectations will, of course, be held with varying degrees of confidence. Their principal sources are conflicts and common interests among states, differences in capability, observation of each other's past behavior, and formal alliances.

Alignments and alliances are plainly not structure, since they affect neither the organizing principle of the system (anarchy) nor the distribution of resources among states (polarity). For Waltz, system structure means "how [units] stand in relation to one another (how they are arranged or positioned).''[34] He clearly excludes alignments from this definition. Alignments are akin to structure, however, since they have to do with how resources and capabilities are aggregated in the system. They supplement structure by specifying in more detail "how units stand in relation to one another." They complete the "arrangement" by including the intentions and expectations of states, along with their capabilities, as determinants of how they "stand." If alliance commitments were absolutely binding and enforceable, every alliance would change system structure by reducing the number of actors.

Since commitments have some force, and since states, once allied, become somewhat dependent on each other, alliances in a multipolar system might be said to have quasi-structural effects. They identify friends and foes more clearly, and they aggregate power among friends. Thus they concentrate power in the system and focus insecurities and dependencies between particular states and groups of states. These effects are not greatly dissimilar to those that follow directly from structure in a bipolar system. The difference, of course, is that in a multipolar system the identifications and power concentrations are considered provisional and temporary; they turn on political declarations between approximate equals, not on unequal distributions of power among states. Since these are large and significant differences, alliances are best considered relationships that are affected by structure and that may have quasi-structural effects but are not constitutive of structure.

It is also a mistake to conflate alignments with the fleeting interactions that may create or change them. In his zeal to show that alliances are not structural, Waltz stresses their ephemerality: structure has nothing to do with "groupings that may now and then form" or "relations that form and dissolve."[35] Yet alliances are often very durable; as relationships they are certainly more durable than the interactions by which they "form and dissolve." Alignment may be affected by interaction, as when an alliance is negotiated. It is not in itself an interaction, however, but a state of mind that influences, or may be influenced by, interaction. In the other direction, alignments may modify the consequences of system structure. For instance, the concern about "relative gain," which is, in general, a consequence of anarchy, is far less among allies than it is between opponents.[36] Alliances, such as NATO today, may outlast a structural change that logically calls for their dissolution.

Conflicting and Common Interests

The relationships of states include their conflicts and common interests. The explicit incorporation of conflicting and common interests enriches neorealist theory by explaining more variation in behavior than is possible by structural reasoning alone. Thus structural logic predicts that balances of power will form in response to threats. But they will be slower to form, or they may not form at all, if the balancers have conflicts with each other. Or consider the Waltzian axiom, mentioned earlier, that the flexibility of alignment in a multipolar system induces rigidity of policy—meaning that the existence of alternatives to a present alliance creates a need to tailor one's own policy to suit the ally, lest it defect.[37] A state's policy toward its allies need not be rigid if its allies have serious conflicts with other states, such that alliance with these others is out of the question. The original hypothesis can stand as a statement of structural logic, but a relational rider can now be added: the degree of rigidity of policy will depend on the compatibility of the ally's interests with those of other states.

It is not as easy as it might seem to distinguish, and establish casual priority between, interests on the one hand and conflict or commonality on the other. Interests may generate conflict, or conflict may generate interests. The following presents first a typology of security interests and then a discussion of interest relationships, whether conflicting or shared.

We should distinguish between interests as concrete goals and the values in terms of which they are valued. Broadly speaking, there are three types of value-currencies in international relations: intrinsic, strategic, and reputational. Intrinsic values are end-values, valued for their own sakes, not for what they might contribute to other values. They include economic values, moral values, and prestige values. Interests that are valued intrinsically vary widely, from the protection of the property of nationals abroad, to stopping the drug trade, to the preservation of national independence. Strategic and reputational values, on the other hand, are instrumental; interests valued in these terms are valued not for themselves but for their contribution to the protection or promotion of other interests in the future. They are "interests defined in terms of power," to recall Morgenthau's memorable phrase.[38] Typical strategic interests are the control of territorial space, energy sources, or particular geographic features, to the extent these things contribute to national power and security. Reputational values include resolve reputation vis-à-vis adversaries and loyalty reputation with allies. Whereas strategic interests are valued for their resource or capability content, reputational interests are interests in projecting an image of intentions. Specific interests are often valued in more than one value-currency, but for convenience I assume they are valued chiefly in one or another and hence refer to strategic, reputational, and intrinsic interests.[39]

Strategic interests are largely derived from the structure of the international system and the alignments that form within it. Thus systemic anarchy generates, for all states, a strategic interest in preventing any potential adversary from gaining resources, especially at one's own expense or the expense of one's ally. Strategic interests are valued not directly but derivatively from the further strategic or intrinsic interests that would be endangered by their loss, especially their loss to an adversary. More precisely, the strategic value of any territory outside the state is a function of how much its loss to an adversary would increase the probability of attack on other territories, and the probability of losing them if attacked, times the strategic and intrinsic value of such other territories and the cost of defending them.* The ultimate "other territory," of course, is that of the state itself; it is largely the value of that ultimate interest that confers strategic value on lesser interests in the state's environment.

Since strategic interests are future-oriented, they vary according to the weight that policymakers impute to the future. A myopic perspective might ignore strategic value entirely and value the consequences of current interaction solely in terms of intrinsic values. An example is the Munich crisis of 1938, when the British and French virtually ignored the Czechoslovakian military capabilities. Strategic interests will also be affected by a state's attitude toward risk: risk-aversion will tend to inflate strategic values; risk-acceptance, to reduce them.

Strategic interests also arise from alliances and alignments. The conventional wisdom says alliances reflect the shared interests of their members and the competing interests of their opponents. Alliances often *create* interests that did not previously exist, however, in three possible ways. First, states may ally simply, or mostly, to ease the general insecurity of anarchy, not because they have any particular interests in common with the ally or because they fear attack by any particular state. In so doing, a state chooses not only its friends but implicitly also its opponents. Those left out will

---

*The calculation of strategic interest may be represented crudely by the formula $V = d(PQV')$, in which V is the strategic and intrinsic value of the immediate interest, V' is the strategic and intrinsic value of the "next" interest, P is the probability of attack on the next interest, Q is the probability of losing a war over that next interest, and d is the anticipated change in the expression PQV' as a result of losing the immediate interest, V. In short, the strategic value of the immediate interest is the reduction of the expected value of the next interest if the immediate one is lost. V' subsumes the strategic and intrinsic values of the whole chain of "next" interests up to and including the value of the homeland itself. The formula ignores war costs.

The distinction between strategic and intrinsic interests parallels to some extent recent writing about relative and absolute gains. Intrinsic values tend to be absolute: one is not much interested in comparing one's own to others' stocks of them, although there are exceptions, such as prestige or status. Strategic values, since they have to do with power, tend to be measured relatively—an opponent's gain is one's own loss and vice versa. For pioneering work on relative gains, see Joseph M. Grieco, *Cooperation among Nations: Europe, America, and Non-tariff Barriers to Trade* (Ithaca: Cornell University Press, 1990), and Duncan Snidal, "Relative Gains and the Pattern of International Cooperation," *American Political Science Review* 85 (September 1991), 701–27. For a different approach, closer to my reasoning here, see Robert Powell, "Absolute and Relative Gains in International Relations Theory," *American Political Science Review* 85 (December 1991), 1303–21, and Robert Powell, "Guns, Butter, and Anarchy," *American Political Science Review* 87 (March 1993), 115–33.

perceive themselves as possible targets of the alliance; they will feel threatened by it and begin to take measures against it, and that will sharpen the allies' initial image of them as potential adversaries. The state thus acquires a strategic interest in defending its chosen ally or allies and in resisting expansion by its apparent opponent(s). Its interests, in other words, are a function of its decision to ally, not the other way around. The alliance focuses and specifies the otherwise diffuse strategic interests that are generated by anarchy itself.

Second, if states do identify specific opponents and interests before they ally, they will acquire each other's interests to some extent as a result of allying. Their interests may have been somewhat divergent in the first place, and the parties will recognize that continuation of the alliance may depend on their being not only tolerant but also supportive of each other's previously unshared interests. Thus, through their common interest in preserving the alliance, the unshared interests become shared. Third, an alliance will tend to cancel or weaken conflicts that may have previously existed between the allies themselves, when they viewed each other as potential adversaries. Having come together in a common enterprise, the allies will tend to downplay their conflicts, so as not to endanger the common goal. Moreover, the conflicts themselves, to the extent they arose originally out of concerns about relative power, will be weaker when the parties begin to think of themselves as friends rather than enemies.

Once interests are thus created or modified by alliance or entente, they will tend to solidify and intensify as tension rises between the alliance and its opponent(s). Thus Britain's interest in supporting France and resisting Germany became steadily stronger after the Entente Cordiale of 1904 as a consequence of the bellicose German reaction to it.

The conventional notion is still valid as a partial explanation: alliances sometimes only reflect prior interests. That is most obvious with informal alignments that are based on shared interests rather than a treaty contract. Usually, as in our cases, the relation between interests and alliances is some mixture of reflection and creation. The initial impetus toward alliance may come from a recognition of existing shared interests; then the formation of the alliance generates additional shared strategic interests as the parties identify each other more firmly as friends and others more clearly as adversaries.

The alliance may create not only an interest in blocking the adversary's expansion but also an interest in fostering power expansion by the ally. Both interests, however, will be limited by the thought that the alliance may be temporary. If the present ally may be a future adversary, the state will be reluctant to encourage its strengthening, even though this might be useful in the short run. Similarly, if the present adversary may be a future friend, the interest in resisting its expansion may be diluted. Thus multipolar structure itself places a ceiling on the extent to which interests are created by alliance choices.

Strategic interests are strongly affected by the polarity of the system. Thus, in a bipolar system, the strategic interests of the superpowers, at least, are largely determined by the power structure itself, whereas in a multipolar system, strategic interests vary with the pattern of alignment. As a consequence, strategic interests are much clearer and more stable in a bipolar than in a multipolar system.

A further distinction worth making is between general and particular interests. General interests are interests in some general state of the system; particular interests are interests in specific objectives and usually with respect to specific other countries. Each type may have either strategic or intrinsic content, or a mixture of both. Thus all states derive from structural anarchy a general strategic interest in resisting any aggressor that appears to be bidding for domination of the system. General intrinsic interests are systemwide, but they are not generated by system structure. An example is a revolutionary state's interest in spreading its ideology worldwide. Particular strategic interests are more specifically defined and are valued mostly for their power content. Examples are the British traditional interest in the independence of the low countries, and the Russian interest in controlling the Straits of the Bosporus and the Dardanelles. Examples of particular interests with primarily intrinsic content might be the Italian interest in the South Tyrol before 1914 or the American interest in Israel after 1945. Cases with both strategic and intrinsic content include the French interest in recovering Alsace-Lorraine after 1871 and the U.S. interest in Western Europe during the cold war.

Conflicts of general interest are more difficult to resolve by negotiation than are conflicts of particular interest, because the former involve fundamental disagreement about the distribution of power and values in the system. Thus the alliance negotiations between Britain and Germany around the turn of the century failed, and later settlements of specific issues failed to produce a real entente, largely because the basic conflict was general, between Germany's aggressive *weltpolitik* and the British determination to maintain both colonial ascendancy and a balance of power on the European continent. In contrast, the 1904 entente between Britain and France was much easier to negotiate and flowered into a quasi-alliance because the several colonial disputes between the two countries did not involve a conflict about the general distribution of power.[40]

When general and particular interests are contradictory, which one takes precedence will usually depend on the perceived seriousness of the general threat. In the case just mentioned, the general interest of Britain in a balance of power gradually superseded particular conflicts with France.

Conversely, in the 1930s, Britain allowed its lack of particular interest in eastern Europe to overcome its general interest in the balance of power, largely through a failure to perceive the seriousness of the German threat to the balance. The priorities were reversed with the British guarantees to Poland and other small European states in 1939.

The difference between general and particular interests underlies the distinction sometimes drawn between occasional and permanent allies.[41] Especially in a multipolar system, the general interest in balancing overweening aggressors fosters temporary alliances, since such major disturbers may arise in any quarter; after one is blocked, another emerges, and the disturber of the past becomes the partner of the present. Alliances based on common particular interests are longer-lasting, since such interests change much less frequently than the identities of general threats to the system. Thus what is perhaps the most durable alliance on record, the British-Portuguese alliance, is based entirely on common particular interests. In sum, the alliance pattern in a multipolar system will reflect two independent tendencies: (1) the balancing of perceived general threats to the system, which is a function of systemic anarchy, and (2) the matching of alliances with particular interests. The two tendencies will wax and wane in their relative importance, but both will always be present in a mixed reality. The vaunted flexibility of a multipolar system is associated with the balancing tendency; the system becomes more sluggish to the extent that alignments are based on particular interests.

Of course, interests, by themselves, are not relationships. There is an interest relationship only when interests (of any type) are in conflict or are shared between states. No relationship exists, obviously, when interests are merely different, that is, compatible but unshared. This distinction is not as clear as it might seem, however. The conventional wisdom says conflict arises out of the incompatibility of interests: interests are primarily unit attributes, determined exogenously by internal values; whether they are in conflict or held in common between states is more or less accidental, a function simply of their content. But as the discussion of strategic interests has suggested, interests are often endogenous to the system and alignments that form within it; they are a result, not a cause, of conflict. Conflict and commonality are generated by the selection of enemies and friends in the process of alliance formation. The relationship forms first; interests consonant with it then follow and amplify it. Here again, reality is a mixture: interests, and conflicts and commonalities among them, are both internally and systemically derived; they are partly independent of, and partly generated by, alignments.

An interest relationship has two dimensions: its direction—whether it is one of conflict or of commonality—and its intensity—the degree of conflict or of sharing. The intensity of shared and conflicting interests is a compound of scope and depth. Between adversaries, the scope of their conflict is the extent to which their interests are incompatible; similarly, between allies, the scope of their common interest is the proportion of their total interests that is shared. Depth refers to amount of value that is attached to conflicting or shared interests. Thus a conflict relationship may be narrow but deep, as in the conflict between France and Germany after 1871 over Alsace-Lorraine, or broad but relatively shallow, as in the many conflicts between Britain and Russia in the Near East and Asia.

Capability

Most writers on international relations employ the term "capability" to mean the amount of military forces and resources transformable into military forces that are controlled by individual states. Thus, for Waltz, capability is a unit attribute, and the distribution of capabilities among states determines systemic polarity, one aspect of system structure. This usage is fine for the purpose of comparing system structures and describing structural constraints. But it leaves unlabeled an important alternative meaning of capability: what a state can accomplish with its military forces against particular other states.[42] This meaning is closer to the dictionary definition of capability than Waltz's; it means what an actor is able to do with its resources, not the aggregate of the resources themselves. Defined in this way, capability is neither a unit nor a structural characteristic but a relationship between states. It is a potential result of using forces rather than an inventory of forces and resources. It denotes the *potential outcome* of a military interaction and thus forms an explicit link between system structure and interaction between units. It becomes a relationship between states rather than a property of separate states. A state's capability is different vis-à-vis each other state or combination of states—for example, it can defeat some states in warfare but not others.

Waltz's meaning should be retained, however, for designations of systemic polarity. Obviously, nothing can be said systemwide about the distribution of capability if each actor's capability depends on which other actor it is confronting. For that purpose, the appropriate measure is simply the size of actual and potential military assets, for which I suggest the label "power resources." The word "resources" implies an endowment or property of something rather than the effect of using that thing in interaction with others. This label is virtually synonymous with Waltz's definition of "capabilities" as "size of population and territory, resource endowment, economic capability, military strength, political stability and competence."[43] It is a better label for the distribution component of system structure because "power resources" can logically be compared among units across the system, whereas "capability," defined as a dyadic relationship, cannot be. The reformulation does not affect our capacity to generalize about structural effects, but it releases the term "capability" for another important meaning that is otherwise without a label and that bears more proximately on the behavior of states.

Several theoretical advantages are gained thereby. For one thing, the redefinition permits the incorporation of the offense-defense balance into neorealist theory.[44] Thomas J. Christensen and Jack Snyder have shown how this concept may be employed to reduce the indeterminacy of structural logic. They ask why the alliance behavior of European states in the decade or so before the First World War was so different from their behavior in the 1930s, despite the fact that the system was multipolar in both cases. In the earlier period, states allowed themselves to be dragged into war by their allies, as if they were in a "chain gang," but in the later period they "passed the buck" to allies in an attempt to stay out of war. Some important variable other than system structure must have been at play. That variable, the authors suggest, was the prevailing belief as to whether offensive or defensive capabilities were superior. The belief in the superiority of offensive power in the pre-1914 years, they argue, increased the urgency of coming to the aid of allies, since allies on the defensive could be quickly overrun. The opposite belief in the superiority of the defense in the interwar years reduced that urgency.[45] Of course, these beliefs turned out to be wrong in both cases; nevertheless, they were beliefs about what forces could accomplish if used, rather than about comparative inventories of forces.

Defining capabilities according to what they can accomplish permits theoretical access to the economic notion of "asset-specificity." Different types of military forces will have different kinds of utility against different opponents, or different values in an alliance, just as the specific assets of firms will affect the kind of relationship they develop with other firms.[46]. Thus the British navy traditionally had great value for defending the home islands and the colonies but had much less value in a continental European war—that "the British Navy does not run on wheels" was a reason often given by Continental statesmen for discounting British power. Nuclear weapons can deter attacks, but they cannot take and hold territory. Nonmilitary assets will have political utility according to the specific vulnerabilities of others; for example, the Gulf states are able to use their oil weapon to greater effect against the European states and Japan than against the United States. Such distinctions are lost sight of when capabilities are defined as an undifferentiated inventory of forces and resources.

Defining capabilities as consequences rather than as tools permits the subsumption of geographic factors within capability. Geographic features such as distance and topography are essentially modifiers of capability. Kenneth Boulding's "loss-of-strength gradient" expresses the distance factor as a discount of capability.[47] Britain's topographical position behind the Channel strengthened its defensive capability but did nothing for its offensive strength. Location may either enhance or detract from capability, as far-flung imperial bases have enhanced British naval capability and various choke points around its periphery have inhibited Russia's.

The revised definition of capability also provides an explicit link between the static resources of a state and the political power that the resources may generate. The latter is typically defined as the ability to affect someone else's behavior by the threat of harm or the promise of reward. The threat or the promise is backed by resources of some sort, but it is the target's anticipation of the consequences of the use of the resources—their capability—that is the proximate source of the power. A threat gives the target a choice between accepting these consequences or giving in to the threatener's demand. If the choice is to give in, power has been successfully exercised; if not, the capabilities may be used to carry out the threat, but power, strictly speaking, is absent, except as the threat's fulfillment serves as a new threat relevant to some future demand. Of course, states may gain power from other bases than military resources; for example, allies have power over each other by virtue of their relative dependence (see the next section). Specifying the capability content of military resources—the amount and kind of deprivation they could inflict on others' values if used—makes them more nearly commensurate with other power bases.

In moving from resources to capabilities to power, we move from the general to the specific. Successive links in the chain establish ever-narrowing constraints on subsequent links. The structure of the system, in the sense of polarity, is a function of the comparative resources of the major actors without regard to their application. The capabilities of states, on the other hand, are specific to task and to target; like power, they have a "scope," a "domain," and a "weight." Power, however, must be even more exactly specified. As David Baldwin has pointed out, power is "policy-contingent":[48] it will vary according to the specific demands one might make of another party.

Alliance Dependence

Typically, "interdependence" is defined in economic terms. But states may depend on others for a variety of values, including political or military security. For the purpose of this book, I wish to consider interdependence, or mutual dependence, between politico-military allies. Dependence is to the alliance relationship as capabilities are to relations between adversaries: each has to do with the comparative ability of the parties to harm each other and with what this implies for their relative influence. As capability refers to the amount of damage adversaries can

[30]

inflict on each other by direct military action, dependence is the amount of harm allies can do to each other by deserting the partnership or failing to live up to expectations of support.* The implicit or explicit threat to inflict such harm can be a source of intra-alliance influence. It is important to note that the relative influence of allies turns not simply on their relative military strength and potential, as is often assumed, but on their comparative dependence on, or need for, each other's aid, which is a more complex notion.

The military dependence of a state on an ally is a function of the degree of threat it faces from its adversary, the extent to which the ally can contribute to deterrence and defense against the threat, and the availability and cost of alternative means of meeting the threat. The threat, in turn, is a function of (1) the degree of conflict of interest with the adversary, (2) the likelihood that the adversary (or the state itself, offensively speaking) intends to resolve the conflict by force, and (3) the relative military capability of the state and its adversary. The greater the ally's potential contribution to meeting any shortfall in capability, the greater the dependence on the ally. But dependence is also a function of the availability and attractiveness of alternatives. The obvious alternative ways of meeting the threat are other allies, increased military preparedness, or appeasement of or perhaps military action against the opponent. In general, the allies will be more dependent on each other's support the greater the threat from the adversary, the greater the reliance on the ally for meeting the threat, and the fewer and less desirable the alternatives. Interdependence may be symmetrical or asymmetrical and high or low. When allies are asymmetrically dependent, the least dependent one, ceteris paribus, will have the most influence. When they are about equally dependent, they may have trouble influencing each other. When mutual dependence is high, the alliance will be cohesive; when it is low, the alliance will be fragile.

The concept of alliance dependence might be broadened to include "political dependence," that is, the benefits the allies expect from each other's diplomatic support on future occasions short of war. Threats to withhold such support could then be a source of intra-alliance influence. In this broadened definition, dependence would include not just one's need for, or expected benefits from, the ally's military aid but also the benefits ex-

---

* Alliance dependence is an instance of what Keohane and Nye, referring primarily to the economic realm, call "vulnerability" interdependence: "an actor's liability to suffer costs imposed by external events even after policies have been altered." The "altering" in the case of alliances would be shifting to another alliance, or perhaps to another security measure such as arms increases, after loss of a current ally. That is, one is dependent on an ally only to the extent the ally provides benefits greater than those of the next-best alternative. See Robert O. Keohane and Joseph S. Nye, Jr., *Power and Interdependence: World Politics in Transition* (Boston: Little, Brown, 1977), pp. 13–19.

pected from the alliance's political halo over an indefinite future. Such expectations will expand or contract as the ally's support or nonsupport is experienced in specific instances over time.

Relationships: Summary

The addition and elaboration of a concept of relationships would considerably enrich the theoretical arsenal of neorealism, at an acceptable cost in reduced parsimony. Deductions from structure point only to broad systemic constraints on the policy choices of states. Within this broad range, choices and outcomes are still quite indeterminate. The range of indeterminacy is narrowed—the scope of the theory is broadened—by introducing several relationship variables, especially interests, capabilities, alignments, and interdependence. Considering these factors permits finer-grained predictions and explanations than are possible from structural reasoning alone. If, as Waltz says, system structures only "shape and shove," relationship patterns give a more decided push.

The internal characteristics of states also work their effects through relationships. Relationships form at the intersection of the attributes of states—where interests become conflicts, forces become capabilities, and vulnerabilities become interdependence. It is the assessment of these intersections—How much conflict exists between my interests and my opponent's interests on this issue? Who would win a war between us at what cost? Do I need the help of my ally and will it help?—that bears directly on a state's decisions and behavior, not its own "unit attributes" in isolation.

In short, the consideration of relationships amounts to specifying several missing links in neorealist theory between structure and unit attributes on the one hand and interaction and behavior on the other. The principal missing link is simply *alignment*. Contrary to the general belief, neorealism does not say much about what causes states in a multipolar system to identify each other as friends or enemies or about the consequences of such identification. If we have a theoretical knowledge of the dynamics of alliance formation and alliance management, and of how these dynamics are related to the logic of structure, we can predict and explain far more than we can from structure alone. The theory is further enriched when we include generalizations about the effects of conflict and common interest; they will determine the intensity of friendships or enmities. The capability relationship adds variation for inequalities of strength among major powers and incorporates the offense-defense balance. Relative capabilities between enemies determine how much they can hurt each other; the interdependence of allies determines how much they need each other's help. Thus these missing links are also closely linked to each other.

Taken together, these four relationships describe the principal ingredients in a bargaining situation. Alignments determine what kind of bargaining it will be, whether directed primarily toward the resolution of conflict, as between adversaries, or toward the realization of common interest, as between allies. Between adversaries, as between allies, interests establish the goals of bargaining and their degree of compatibility, whereas capabilities and dependence make up the leverage available for pursuing the goals. Thus a consideration of relationships enables the analyst to connect two large bodies of theory—structural realism and bargaining—that have been up to now only tenuously and vaguely associated. If relationships comprise the goals and available means in bargaining, the notion of interaction, to which we now turn, subsumes bargaining as a behavioral process.

Interaction

Interaction is any behavior that impinges on or is influenced by some other party. It is, therefore, the principal dependent variable in our theoretical scheme and, along with its outcomes, ultimately what we are trying to explain. It is to be differentiated from relationships by the fact that it is action—policy choice or the implementation of choice—rather than the expectations, values, and power relations that shape action and choice. Interaction is the process by which alignments, interests, capabilities, and dependence are translated into outcomes. Of course, it may take myriad forms, from wars, crises, arms races, and alliance agreements to visits of dignitaries and summit meetings.

Waltz has little to say about interaction per se, not because he considers it unimportant but because it is outside his theoretical purpose, which is to assess the effects of system structure on behavior. For him, it is an unexamined dependent or intervening variable, or an umbrella term for many variables, which lies between structure and outcomes. Implicitly, he identifies it with process and tends to conflate it with "relations."[49] As argued above, relationships and interactions should be treated as separate phenomena, the former closer to structure on the causal chain, the latter closer to outcomes. Of course, we already have a fair amount of theory about interactions—for example, on arms racing, warfare, alliance formation. What follows is an attempt to organize this theory and link it to what has been said earlier about relationships and structure.

Interaction may occur in many different relational contexts, but to simplify, consider two kinds of security relationships: allied and adversarial. In each relationship, we can postulate an interaction "game" that may be played in any of three "arenas"—preparedness, diplomacy, and military action. Diplomacy includes all verbal communication between states, including alliance formation and intra-alliance bargaining, as well as all

Figure 1-2. Interaction arenas

		Preparedness	Diplomacy	Action
Adversary game	conflict	arms race	threats of force	war
	cooperation	arms control	concessions	war limitation or termination
Alliance game	cooperation	burden-sharing/ joint planning	promises of support	chain-ganging
	conflict	free riding	threats of defection	buck-passing

communication and bargaining between adversaries. The two physical arenas, preparedness and action, involve interactions between allies as well as between adversaries. Thus, as shown in Figure 1-2, there are six interlocking interaction arenas. The adversary and alliance relationships discussed above determine interaction payoffs, and the parties' perception of them determine their interaction choices. Of course, the six arenas do not include all conceivable forms of international intercourse, but they constitute the core of security interaction.*

Interaction in each arena may have either a cooperative or a conflictual emphasis, as demarcated by the dotted lines in Figure 1-2. The adversary game is mostly competitive: threatening to fight one's opponents, preparing to fight them, and actually doing so. The alliance game is mostly cooperative: promising to defend or to fight cooperatively with others, sharing the costs of preparedness with others, and actually fighting jointly. The dominant form of interaction in each arena may be leavened by a dash of its opposite, however. Thus the adversary game in the preparedness arena may include arms control as well as arms competition. The alliance game in this arena consists of competitive burden-shifting (free riding) as well as equitable burden-sharing and joint planning. Diplomatic communication between adversaries may involve concessions as well as threats, and allies may balance their promises of support with threats of defection. The principal interaction between adversaries in the action arena is, of course, war-fighting, but it may also involve cooperative efforts, as in war-limiting or war-terminating. Between allies in that arena, joint war-fighting is the cooperative aspect, whereas buck-passing is the competitive side.

Within limits, policies in the three arenas are mutually substitutable. For

---

*There is some overlap between the arenas: for example, diplomacy may involve communication of threats, promises, proposals, and intentions regarding preparedness or action policy, and physical moves in the latter arenas will supplement diplomatic declarations.

example, preparedness measures might substitute for alliance, or military action might be undertaken to avoid future preparedness costs or alliance dependence. The overall national security "problem" might be conceived, theoretically, as that of optimizing across the six arenas. That subject goes far beyond the scope of the present study, however, so the following remarks are limited to alliances and the diplomatic arena.[50]

The distinguishing activity in the diplomatic arena is verbal communication. Between allies and adversaries alike, the prototype of verbal cooperation is the "promise," and of verbal conflict, the "threat." An alliance rests essentially on an exchange of promises; hence Arnold Wolfers's definition: an alliance is "a promise of mutual military assistance between two or more sovereign states."[51] Promises between allies are analogous to threats between adversaries. The credibility of both turns on the perceived interests that underlie them. Perceptions of others' interests translate into expectations about their future behavior; expectations of support or hostility constitute the pattern of alignment discussed above. Both promises and threats are communications that seek to strengthen, weaken, or otherwise change existing expectations. Both do this by making one's own behavior conditional on the behavior of the other and by implicating values that would be lost if the communication is not fulfilled. Both are meant to influence the behavior of another in the direction of cooperation, but promises do this by a prospect of reward, whereas threats do it by the prospect of punishment. Both usually intensify an existing relationship: alliance pledges increase solidarity between partners, and threats increase tension between opponents.

In each relationship, the opposite kind of communication plays an obligato theme. Allies threaten to withhold support in order to restrain each other; enemies may promise concessions in order to compromise their disputes. The primary communication itself implies the other as counterpoint: promises imply a threat to withhold what is promised if the condition of the promise is not fulfilled; threats imply a promise to withhold punishment if the demand is met.

There are, however, some important differences between promises and threats. Promises are supported by the social norm that promises must be kept; the rule *pacta sunt servanda* (treaties must be observed) is its expression in international law. There is no equivalent norm supporting the fulfillment of threats, which must turn entirely on self-interest. In other words, promises create a social obligation that arises from the fact that another actor has been induced to rely on one's word. The obligation attaches a moral cost to nonfulfillment over and beyond the costs to one's reputation and other interests. One question we ask of our case studies in later chapters is how much allies feel constrained by this norm.

Whereas the fulfillment of threats is clearly conditional on the other party's behavior, promises may or may not be so contingent, depending on the timing of the adversary's challenge. If the challenge comes before the allies have had a chance to demonstrate their loyalty, there is no conditionality: they are obliged to do what they have promised. If an ally has already reneged on its own obligation, however, its partners are released from theirs.

This conditionality constitutes the major source of leverage that allies have over each other. Each ally knows it will be denied the benefits of the alliance if it reneges on its own promise. This sanction may be virtually automatic, unlike that in the case of threats, which generally require a special effort to carry out, since fulfillment is usually costly. This automaticity may be qualified, however, in some instances, for at least two reasons. First, alliance commitments, to the extent they are public, are also threats to an adversary. Even when an ally has betrayed one's trust, one may still want to keep one's own commitment in order to preserve one's reputation for resolve in the adversary's eyes. Second, a state may have an interest in defending its ally apart from the formal alliance commitment. Then, to reciprocate the ally's previous disloyalty would be to "cut off one's nose to spite one's face."

An interesting variant on the promise is the "assurance." Assurances are to promises as warnings are to threats. Warnings are statements to an opponent of what one already has an interest in doing, as distinct from threats, which create such an interest or at least express an intention that did not previously exist. Similarly, assurances are statements to friends and allies that one is committed, by one's own interest, to aid them whether or not a formal promise has been given; promises, on the other hand, generally create a commitment by engaging additional values. Unlike threats and promises, which in different ways establish new commitments, warnings and assurances merely convey information about one's prior intentions.[52]

Defining alliances as promises emphasizes their communicative quality. But, of course, they are much more than acts of verbal communication, and that is perhaps a deficiency in Wolfers's definition. It would be more accurate to say they are not the promise itself but the expectations of mutual support that follow from a promise, from supportive behavior, and from the interests that lie behind the promise and the behavior. An alliance *is* thus a relationship, although it is created by interactions. For present-day alliances such as NATO, the relationship would include their organizational structure of committees and commands, their cross-national peacetime deployments, their integrated strategies, and the like.

A prominent kind of interaction in both the adversary and alliance games is that of bargaining. Adversaries may bargain about anything from arms control to crisis resolution to war termination. Allies bargain about

Figure 1-3. Models of strategic interaction

a. Adversary game

A \ B	C	D
C	0, 0 Compromise	-5, 5 A backs down
D	5, -5 B backs down	-10, -10 War

b. Alliance game

A \ B	C	D
C	3, 3 Compromise	1, 5 B's terms accepted
D	5, 1 A's terms accepted	0, 0 No agreement, alliance breakup

the initial terms of the alliance and then about such things as policies toward their common opponent or their respective contributions to the military effort. In either game, the bargaining power of the players will depend on the several dimensions of their relationship and their perception of them. Thus the relative bargaining power of adversaries will depend on their perceptions of their comparative capabilities and the relative intensity of their conflicting interests. Between allies, bargaining power will turn on perceptions of their comparative dependence, commitments, and intensity of interest in whatever they are bargaining about. Since these relationship factors are not easily observable, their perception will be mediated by observance of each other's behavior. The principal function of actual bargaining communications is to modify others' perceptions of these relationships and of one's own behavior, so as to enhance one's own bargaining power.

The connection between relationships and interactions is well captured in a simple two-by-two game matrix, such as those shown in Figure 1-3. Such matrices are often called models of strategic interaction, since the play of the game involves an intersection of two strategies (choice of either column or row), which produces an outcome. They may also be interpreted as bargaining models. Each of the four potential outcomes denotes a dimension of relationships. Thus, in a matrix representing an adversary crisis, as in Figure 1-3a, capabilities are in the DD cell: the numbers reflect the probable result of a clash of forces in terms of each party's estimated cost of fighting and the cost or value of defeat or victory. The interests of the parties in the object of the bargaining are located in the DC and CD cells; the difference in the payoffs to each party in these cells reflects the amount of conflict of interest between them. And, of course, the numbers in the CC cell show the payoffs for compromising the conflict. Similarly, in a matrix representing an alliance negotiation (Fig. 1-3b), the DD cell shows the costs of nonagreement or alliance breakup, a function of the parties' interdependence; the CD and DC cells show the extent of conflict between the allies over the issue at stake—say, over the terms of the alliance contract or the stance to be taken toward an opponent; and the CC cell shows the values for a possible resolution of that conflict.

The outcomes "war" and "alliance breakup" in the DD cells are the extreme possibilities; DD might mean merely a worsening of relations, such as increased tension between adversaries or a reduced expectation of future support between allies. In all four outcomes, the payoffs incorporate potential payoffs in future plays (discounted for their present value) as well as any change in the likelihood that future plays will occur. Thus, for example, the CD payoff in the adversary game might include, besides immediate intrinsic losses, a strategic loss of capability in future plays. Each of the matrices in Figures 1-3a and 1-3b may thus be considered the first round of play in a supergame of many reiterated plays, with each play changing the relationship context of each subsequent play.

A game model provides a concise theoretical nexus among all the systemic elements thus far discussed: structure, unit attributes, relationships, interaction, and outcomes. Only the last three show up in the matrix explicitly, but structural constraints and unit characteristics will have worked their effects via their input into relationships, that is, into the payoffs for each cell. Thus the flexibility of alliances in multipolarity appears as relatively high payoffs in the DD cell of Figure 1-3b, reflecting the existence of alternatives if a present alliance breaks up or an attempt at alliance formation fails. Relatively equal payoffs in the DD cell show the symmetrical dependence typical of multipolarity; the asymmetrical dependence in alliances in a bipolar system would appear as unequal DD payoffs.

The game model makes clear how interaction choices and outcomes are proximately constrained by the relational pattern: relationships establish the payoffs for interaction choices. Relationships are themselves constrained by system structure and unit attributes. The payoff pattern amounts to a "structure of the situation" that both subsumes systemic and unit influences and bounds interaction strategies and outcomes. In this way, a game model can serve as a focus for integrating structural and process effects.

The connection between relationships and interaction clearly runs both ways. Not only do relationships shape interaction choices; interactions may also change relationships. Thus an alliance negotiation changes alignments, an arms race changes capabilities, a crisis may change the level of conflict between adversaries and the degree of interdependence between allies, and a war may change all these things.

The chapters that follow elaborate on and illustrate some of the themes just discussed. Chapter 2 presents a theory of alliance formation. Chapter 3 describes the framework for analyzing historical cases of alliance formation and, with Chapter 4, offers three case studies: the Austro-German alliance of 1879 and its sequel, the Three Emperors' Alliance of 1881, and the Franco-Russian alliance of 1891–94. Chapter 5 relates the theory to the cases, assessing the plausibility of the theory in the light of evidence from the cases and from the history of other alliances in the pre–World War I era. Chapter 6 turns to the topic of the management of alliances once they have formed, that is, to the determinants of influence in intra-alliance bargaining, as the members seek simultaneously to protect their own interests and to preserve the alliance. Chapters 7 and 8 survey the history of the Austro-German and Franco-Russian alliances from the perspective of Chapter 6's theory and present twenty-two case studies of alliance bargaining. Chapter 9 summarizes the evidence from the cases that bears on the "alliance security dilemma" and alliance norms.

PART I

ALLIANCE FORMATION

[2]

Theory: Alliance Formation

This chapter presents a deductive theory of alliance formation in a multipolar system. (Empirical evidence bearing on this subject is reserved for the next two chapters.) The type of alliance implicitly in view is the mutual defensive alliance formed in peacetime. The principal questions considered are, (1) What are the benefits and costs of alliance? (2) What incentives to ally arise from the anarchic and multipolar structure of the system? (3) What incentives derive from nonstructural factors such as inequalities of military strength and conflicting or common interests? (4) What determines who allies with whom? and (5) What determines how the benefits and costs of alliances are allocated among their members?

THE VALUE OF ALLIANCES

States form or join alliances, we may suppose, if the benefits of doing so are greater than the costs. The benefits are counted chiefly in terms of the increased security resulting from the partner's commitment, and the costs largely in terms of the autonomy sacrificed in the commitment to the partner. Both the benefits and the costs are measured from the security and autonomy enjoyed in the prealliance alignment pattern.

The most important security benefits of alliances may be listed as follows:

1. Enhanced deterrence of attack on oneself.
2. Enhanced capability for defense against attack on oneself.

Defense enhancement translates into some combination of the following:
  a. Greater probability of aid from the allied state.
  b. Greater probability of successful defense when the ally's help is forth-coming.
3. Enhanced deterrence of attack on the ally.[1]
4. Preclusion of alliance or alignment between the partner and the oppo-nent. Alliance precludes the partner from allying elsewhere not only be-cause it binds the partner to the self but also because it satisfies the partner's security needs, thus reducing its motivation to look elsewhere.
5. Elimination of the possibility of attack by the allied state.
6. Increased control or influence over the allied state.

Some subsidiary security benefits from alliance are greater ease of joint planning and deployment and possibly reduction of peacetime armaments cost and potential war costs.

The principal costs of alliance are:

1. The risk of having to come to the aid of the ally, when one would have preferred not to do so in the absence of commitment. This risk subsumes not only the simple failure of deterrence but also the possible provocation of an opponent to attack.
2. The risk of entrapment in war by the ally because the ally, more confident of one's support, becomes reckless, intransigent, or aggressive in disputes with its opponent.
3. The risk of a counteralliance.
4. Foreclosure of alternative alliance options. This is the cost side of the preclusive benefit: alliance forecloses alliance alternatives for both (all) members; eliminating the partner's options is a benefit, but eliminating one's own is a cost.
5. General constraints on freedom of action entailed in the need to coordi-nate policy with the ally and perhaps to modify one's preferred policy to suit the ally's preferences.

In addition to these benefits and costs, alliances may involve values not directly related to either security or autonomy. For instance, allies may give each other "side payments" on matters unrelated to their mutual defense commitments, such as a free hand in some colonial venture or a promise to support the partner diplomatically in realizing interests in con-flict with a third party.

States that are ideologically similar will gain satisfaction by allying; ide-ological opponents may suffer psychic costs. There may also be domestic gains or costs, as when a regime strengthens or weakens itself internally by allying.

The list above merely identifies the central benefits and costs of alliance. It says nothing about their magnitude and the determinants of magnitude.

Essentially, the size of the security benefits for each party is determined by three factors: (1) the state's alliance need, (2) the degree to which the prospective partner fulfills that need, and (3) the actual terms of the alliance contract. Alliance need is a function chiefly of the threat posed by the state's adversary: the adversary's capabilities relative to the state's, and the degree of conflict with the adversary. The greater the shortfall between a state's own military strength and that of its opponent, and the deeper the conflict with the adversary, the greater the state's alliance need and the more the state will value any alliance that satisfies that need. Different prospective allies will satisfy the need in different degrees, depending on the capability they can contribute and their perceived reliability. The prospective benefit from the ally's capability must be discounted if there are any doubts about whether the ally will honor its commitment. Such doubts may arise from many sources, but they will be minimized to the extent the ally has a prealliance interest in coming to the state's defense.

The size of the costs and risks of alliance is chiefly a function of similar factors in the ally's relationship with the adversary (which may be a different adversary than one's own). The weaker the ally, the more one will have to contribute to its defense if it is attacked; and the more intense its conflict with its adversary, the more likely it will be attacked or perhaps initiate war. The cost of alliance is also affected by one's own interest in defending the ally even without alliance: the greater this interest, the less onerous the commitment.

Rational alliance building does not mean simply maximizing one's benefits and minimizing costs. Theoretically, the principle of marginal utility applies. That is, a state should add allies and increase alliance commitments up to the point at which the "last" unit of commitment to the last-chosen ally yields a marginal value equal to its marginal cost and risk, assuming that marginal utility is decreasing and marginal cost is increasing. Of course, this rule covers a multitude of complexities, including different estimates of benefits and costs among decision makers or between decision makers and publics.[2]

An important background factor in estimating the costs and benefits of alliance is whether the allies have a strategic interest in coming to each other's defense even without an alliance commitment. Even when they have such an interest, there are still net benefits to be gained by allying. Costs would be low, because the allies would not be promising to do anything they would not do anyway. Benefits could be substantial, however, because of increased certainty about the partner's intentions. A formal alliance would also increase deterrent benefits, since the adversary might not be fully aware of the partners' interests without the alliance commitment.

Another important element in the prealliance situation is the possible existence of conflicts between prospective allies. Such a conflict might figure as a cost or as a discount of alliance benefits. It is a cost if negotiation of the alliance requires its settlement, with costly concessions by both sides. Thus an alliance between France and Germany after 1870 would have required some settlement of the Alsace-Lorraine problem; the cost of such a settlement made a Franco-German alliance highly unlikely. A conflict requires a discount of benefits if the dispute is not settled and the parties consequently have doubts about each other's loyalty. An alliance between ideological opposites must also be discounted by such doubts and by the psychic, political, and moral costs of doing business with Evil.[3]

A fully rational calculation of alliance values must be farsighted; it must take account of consequences in the distant as well as the immediate future. One important future possibility is the formation of a counteralliance. A counteralliance, or increased cohesion in an existing enemy alliance, will reduce the value of the present alliance. Thus the present value of the present alliance must be discounted by the anticipated capability and cohesion of the counteralliance and by the probability that it will form. The present value of the alliance might also be appreciated for its potential to attract additional members in the future. Estimates of its value should take account of its predicted efficacy in foreseeable crisis confrontations and wars with opponents. The value or cost of all such anticipated future events must be discounted by some coefficient that reflects their lower present value.[4]

The alliance value calculus should be wide-angled as well as farsighted. That is, alliance architects should take account of effects on parties other than themselves and their adversaries. Any alliance will have third-party repercussions, perhaps extending throughout the system. The extent of these "externalities" will depend mostly on common interests and conflicts of interest between third parties and alliance members. The estimated cost of alliance should include the risk of alienating any others whose support is deemed valuable and possible. The value of alliance should include the increased likelihood of support from states that have interests in common with the ally.

Thus, when Bismarck made his alliance with Austria in 1879, he acquired Great Britain as a "sleeping partner" owing to the coincidence of British and Austrian interests in the Near East. The Franco-Russian alliance of 1894 illustrates a negative externality. Although formally directed at the Triple Alliance of Germany, Austria, and Italy, it worked against Britain, which moved closer to the Triple Alliance because of colonial conflicts with France and Russia.

It is possible to arrange most of the essential and immediate security benefits and autonomy costs of alliance in a formula. The virtue and intent of the formula is to show the logical relationship of these factors, a quantitative analogue to the kind of calculation a rational statesman might perform qualitatively. (No claim is made for empirical applicability.) Its resultant is the net security-autonomy value of a prospective alliance.[5] Consider the following notation, with respect to a potential attack on one's own state by a given (state) opponent:

S	= security-autonomy level
Pa	= probability of being attacked
1−Pa	= probability of not being attacked
Ph	= probability of being helped by the ally (the ally's "loyalty")
1−Ph	= probability of not being helped by the ally
Pvh	= probability of victory with the ally's help
Pdh	= probability of defeat despite the ally's help
Pv	= probability of victory without the ally's help
Pd	= probability of defeat when the ally does not help
V	= value of victory
D	= value of defeat
Ch	= cost of war with the ally's help
C	= cost of war when the ally does not help
	With respect to potential attack on the prospective ally:
Paa	= probability of attack on the ally
1−Paa	= probability of no attack on the ally
Pha	= probability of oneself aiding the ally
1−Pha	= probability of oneself not aiding the ally
Pvha	= probability of victory when one aids the ally
Pdha	= probability of defeat when one aids the ally
Pva	= probability of the ally's victory without one's help
Pda	= probability of the ally's defeat when one does not help
Va	= one's own value of successful defense of the ally
Da	= loss to oneself when the ally is defeated
Cha	= cost of aiding the ally
Ca	= cost of not aiding the ally

then:

$$S = \{[Pa\ (Ph)(Pvh)\ (V + Ch)] + [Pa\ (Ph)(Pdh)\ (D + Ch)] + [Pa\ (1-Ph)(Pv)(V + C)] + [Pa\ (1-Ph)(Pd)(D + C)] + [(1-Pa)(V)]\}$$

minus

$$\{[Paa\ (Pha)(Pvha)(Va + Cha)] + [Paa\ (Pha)(Pdha)\ (Da + Cha)] + [Paa\ (1-Pha)(Pva)(Va + Ca)] + [Paa\ 1-Pha)(Pda)(Da + Ca)] + [(1-Paa)(Va)]\}.$$

This equation would have to be applied twice, once to find the state's security-autonomy level before alliance (S1) and again to estimate that level after allying (S2). The difference between the two applications is the net gain from alliance, the alliance's security-autonomy value. This quantity is obviously an expected utility, the basic utilities being the values for winning or losing a hypothetical war and the costs of fighting it, and the probabilities referring essentially to "deterrence," "defense," and "alliance loyalty." Most of the alliance benefits listed above are in the first major term of the equation—the set of terms enclosed in the first set of braces {}—and most of the costs are subsumed in the second major term.

The second set of terms measures "autonomy"; the difference in their reading over the two applications might be considered autonomy lost by allying. By a narrow definition, autonomy might seem to be affected only by the probability term Pha, the probability of oneself defending the ally and how much this probability is increased by alliance. A broader definition, however, would include the utility terms Va, Da, Cha, and Ca, which reflect the magnitude of the losses and gains when one aids or does not aid the ally. The term Paa, probability of attack on the ally, normally would be reduced by alliance, reflecting the extended deterrent effect; this effect would reduce autonomy losses, since one is less constrained by alliance obligations if attack on the ally is deterred. Note also that the difference between prealliance and postalliance Pha is lower (and autonomy costs are lower) to the extent one would defend the ally even without an alliance. Finally, the formula does not tap constraints on one's diplomatic freedom in peacetime as a consequence of allying; thus it is an incomplete measure of autonomy costs.

The calculus is incomplete in other ways. In particular, it does not include the preclusive value of alliance. This would be the difference between one's S level with no alliance and one's S if the ally were instead to join another alliance, especially the alliance most threatening to oneself. The formula also omits the possible benefit of controlling or influencing the ally. A thorough calculation would also have to include the probabilities of attack by any great power in the system and any combination of them. The prospective ally would have to be considered a possible adversary in the prealliance calculation but not in the postalliance one. Expanding the prospective alliance to three members would immensely complicate the analysis. To minimize complexity, the formula includes no coefficient for discounting the future. Despite these limitations, the formula has the virtue of identifying the principal components of alliance value and cost and showing how they are linked logically.

Rational alliance formation is a matter of optimizing across security gains and autonomy losses.[6] Presumably, states will seek the maximum surplus of gains over losses. Both security and autonomy will be affected by the alliance commitment, especially its scope and its explicitness. A broad commitment, covering most of the interests of both parties, or operative against more than one conceivable opponent, will yield maximum security gains but also entail maximum sacrifices to autonomy in the ob-

[48]

ligation to the partner. Conversely, a narrow commitment will minimize both gains and losses. An explicit, clear commitment (whether narrow or broad in scope) will enhance both security gains and autonomy costs; an ambiguous one will limit both gains and costs. Since security and autonomy are substitutable, states may choose from a variety of combinations, and allies may value different combinations differently. Actual security-autonomy ratios in an alliance agreement will be determined by a bargaining process, described later in this chapter.

A Systemic Model of Alignment and Alliance

Having established the principal benefits and costs of alliance, we turn now to an analysis of how these incentives and disincentives are affected by (1) the structure of the international system, (2) inequalities of military power resources among the major states, and (3) particular conflicts and common interests among these states. Here we are concerned not so much with how an individual state might assess its alliance incentives under each of these conditions but how the general process of alliance formation, systemwide, is affected by them. We proceed by the method of successive approximations: by sequentially grafting conditions (2) and (3) onto a simple model of (1). The basic model is in the spirit of neorealist theory. Along the way, however, we make some use of certain other theories, among them collective goods, coalition theory, game theory, and bargaining theory. Once the model is developed, we return to a focus on individual states at a somewhat lower level of abstraction and assess the process of negotiating the terms of an alliance contract.

Systemic Incentives to Ally

In order to isolate the effects of anarchic system structure on alliance formation, we begin with a highly unrealistic model that simply assumes out all other factors. Imagine a system of six states. Assume they are equal in actual and potential military strength and that there is no technological advantage for either the defense or the offense. There are no particular conflicts or affinities among them—no territorial disputes, no ideological attractions or repulsions, or the like. The states are interested only in political survival and in maximizing their chances of survival, that is, in "security."* Their information about others is incomplete: none can be

---

*This assumption departs from the real world, where some states occasionally desire to expand for reasons other than security. It rules out offensive alliances and even single-state aggressors with nonsecurity or beyond-security goals. It does not rule out security-motivated aggression, however, nor does it rule out fears of attack and defensive measures

sure that others' interests are limited to survival and security, and none can be confident of its estimates of others' power resources. Finally, assume the states are unitary, rational actors.

The situation thus limned is obviously a condition of Hobbesian anarchy. All states fear attack by others, simply because others have the capability to attack and their intentions are unknown. And indeed, aggressive attack is possible, even though the states are interested only in security, because security can be increased by acquiring resources from others and because fear of attack may precipitate preemptive attack.

Collective Goods and Balance of Power

Before inquiring into what might motivate alliances in such a system, we must first address a preliminary question: What incentives exist for the states to come to each other's defense in the absence of alliances? This is a necessary preliminary, because alliances will be made only if they improve their members' security over the no-alliance condition.

The question appears to precipitate a collision between two theories: balance of power and collective goods. According to the balance of power theory, each actor in our system has an overriding interest in its own survival. From this interest it derives an interest in preventing any other actor from dominating the system—that is, from gaining control of more than half the system's military resources. This ultimate interest in turn generates an interest in preventing any other state from significantly increasing its resources by conquest, since gains in power capabilities facilitate further gains. Thus an aggression by any actor logically will be resisted by all other actors, and an equilibrium restored.

The logic of collective goods[7] undercuts the balance of power theory, however. The collective good, of course, is security. In the idealized situation being contemplated here, security meets the technical requirements of a collective good: if anyone supplies it (by stopping the aggressor), all parties enjoy it whether or not they contributed to its supply, and the consumption of it by any one party does not reduce its availability to others.

Each state will have two powerful incentives not to act against an ag-

---

against attack, including alliances, because a sufficient cause of such fears and measures is incomplete information about others' intentions in an anarchic world. The known presence of revisionist states—those with offensive goals motivated by "greed" rather than security—would drive the logic of the model harder for status quo states but would not affect its basic dynamics. For a model that explicitly includes revisionist as well as status quo states, see Randall L. Schweller, "Tripolarity and the Second World War," *International Studies Quarterly* 37 (March 1993), 73–103. For the distinction between greed and security motivations for expansion, see Charles L. Glaser, "Political Consequences of Military Strategy: Expanding and Refining the Spiral and Deterrence Models," *World Politics* 44 (July 1992), 497–538.

gressor. One is the hope or belief that others can and will do the job; if this is correct, the abstainer can enjoy the collective good without contributing. The other incentive to abstain is the fear that if one acts, others will take a "free ride"; in that event, one gets stuck with the entire cost. These motives to abstain may be supplemented by others, such as the belief that this particular conquest represents the aggressor's "last demand"; the hope that the attacker and victim will "bleed each other to death," leaving others more secure than before; the fear of being attacked "in the rear" while one is aiding the victim; the hope that the victim will be able to defend itself unaided; and the prospect that, even if the attack succeeds, subsequent attacks can be deterred by alliance among the remaining states.

If all abstain, for any of these reasons, the collective good is not provided, or, rather, a collective "bad" is suffered if the aggression succeeds. All but the aggressor are less secure than before because the aggressor has increased its capabilities and one potential resister has been eliminated. If the same attacker attacks again, the incentives to stand aside will still exist and in some respects will have increased. The cost of resisting will have increased, and for that reason the chances of being left alone against the aggressor will also have risen, since other states will have a greater incentive to avoid the costs of resistance. If we reason from these collective goods considerations alone, it seems likely that a single state could eventually dominate the system after a series of successful aggressions.

How are these seemingly contradictory theories to be reconciled? By taking account of the potentially increasing costs of *inaction* over repeated challenges and assuming that these costs increase faster than the costs of action. Although the collective goods logic prevails early in an aggressor's career, the balance of power eventually triumphs. With each successful conquest, the aggressor presents a greater threat to the security of the remaining states because of its increasing capability and increasing confidence that it will be unopposed. Hence the defenders' collective good in blocking further encroachments increases dramatically with each round. It increases faster than the cost of resistance, because the ultimate "bad"—extinction of a state's independence—is almost infinitely bad, whereas the cost of fighting wars is tolerable—at least that was the case in prenuclear times. At some point, the cost of resistance will be assessed as lower than the cost of allowing the aggression to succeed. At that point, cooperative resistance is likely, although not certain, since some states might still be tempted to free ride if they thought their own capabilities were not essential to defeating the aggressor. Fully collective resistance becomes certain only when the attacker would gain control of more than half the power resources in the system with one more successful attack. At that point, all remaining states would be fully motivated to resist, for if they did not, their own conquest later would be certain.[8] This scenario is congruent with much international history, wherein balancing coalitions typically do not take shape until aggressors have made substantial conquests.

Alliances in Pristine, Egalitarian Anarchy

Would there be any incentives to form defensive alliances in peacetime in the system just described? It might seem not, since there are no particular conflicts or common interests among the states. Systemic anarchy alone, however, is enough to generate certain general motives for alliance. Anarchy implies both a *need for help* and a *concern for others*. The need arises basically from the physical possibility of being attacked and the lack of full information about others' intentions. Alliance with at least some others would reduce the pervasive insecurity of anarchy. The very unlikelihood of being defended by others on grounds of specific interest would make it all the more desirable to increase the likelihood by formal commitment. Such commitments would counter the temptation for potential defenders to abstain which arises from the collective goods dilemma. They would also remove the ally from the list of potential attackers and would preclude the ally from allying against oneself. Since alliances are substitutable for armaments, they might permit the reduction of arms burdens.

Concern for others is not an altruistic matter but a self-interested one; it arises from the general strategic interest in preventing a concentration of power in any other state, as discussed above. Although this interest would operate in the absence of alliance, it also generates incentives to ally in peacetime with potential victims of attack, to reduce the latter's vulnerability to threats and to deter attacks. Thus both direct security needs and strategic interests in the security of others provide incentives for alliance in this system, though perhaps only moderate ones in the absence of specific conflicts with other states.

A defensive alliance in this ideal system would perform two functions that are linked yet worth separating analytically: identification of friends and enemies, and aggregation of power resources.*

The most obvious effect of alliance making would be to establish patterns of amity and enmity—to identify, for states outside as well as inside the alliance, their most likely friends and foes. The first alliance would identify clearly only friends; but it would provisionally identify those left out as enemies, at least with greater certainty than before, and these others would feel threatened by it. Some of them might form a counteralliance;

---

*The distinction between the two functions can be seen in the difference between neutrality agreements and defense alliances. Neutrality agreements identify friends but do not aggregate power; defense alliances perform both functions.

members of the two alliances would then more clearly identify each other as opponents.

These identifications, in turn, would create specific strategic interests in defending allies and resisting opponents. Before alliance formation, states would have no particular interest in defending or resisting specific other states; they would have only a general but inchoate interest in not allowing any state to achieve system dominance. Now they would have a clear strategic interest in resisting the acquisition of power resources by any member of the opposing alliance and in defending, and perhaps even promoting expansion by, their own allies. Thus the "identification effect" of alliance formation increases concerns about relative gains in relations between adversaries and reduces such concerns in relations between allies. Indeed, the greater the solidarity of alliances—the firmer the identification of certain others as friends—the more the states involved will seek joint gains rather than gains relative to each other or even absolute gains for themselves. These effects are limited in a multipolar system, however, by the likelihood that relationships will be temporary. Some resource gains by an opponent who may someday be an ally may be acceptable; gains by a present ally whose allegiance is uncertain may have to be restricted.[9]

The second main function of alliance formation is to increase the allies' capabilities against their opponents. Part of this increase is the result of the identification effect just mentioned: military resources previously deployed against the ally can now be redirected against enemies. In addition, of course, the allies pool their resources by an exchange of promises, so that each ally has available against its adversary at least some of the partner's capabilities as well as its own. Alliances, in short, enhance the potentially deployable resources of each ally in two ways: first, by releasing resources from their previous commitment against the ally; second, by an exchange of promises of mutual support.

The exchange of promises also creates new interests for the allies, but different interests from the strategic ones discussed above. Whereas strategic interest is an interest in preventing opponents from increasing their resources, especially at the ally's expense, the interest created by an exchange of promises is the interest in having the ally's help in one's own defense—that is, the interest in encouraging the ally to fulfill its promise. Derivatively, the interest is that of maintaining a reputation for loyalty, since the ally can be expected to keep its promise only if it expects oneself to reciprocate.

Note the difference between the two kinds of interest. Both are created by the alliance contract, but strategic interest is created merely by the choice of ally and identification of the enemy, whereas reputational interest is a function of the reciprocal nature of the alliance bargain. Strategic interest is an interest in preventing a shift in the control of resources from the ally to an opponent, whereas reputational interest is an interest in maintaining the ally's incentives to fulfill its side of the alliance contract— assuming these incentives are at least partly a function of the ally's confidence in one's own intent to fulfill the contract. Whereas strategic interest is an interest in maintaining control of tangible resources, reputational interest is an interest in fostering a certain image of oneself in the mind of the ally.

The reason allies can simultaneously have a strategic interest in each other's defense and a reputational interest in proving their loyalty is the irreducible uncertainty about whether strategic interests will be sufficient to motivate them to come to each other's assistance, along with the structural possibility of defection and realignment.

Alliance formation also weakens or eliminates the systemwide collective goods dilemma concerning whether or not to resist an aggressive state. The temptation to abstain and pass the burden of resistance to others is weakened by the newly generated strategic interest in resisting a clearly recognized opponent and by the reputational interest in supporting allies. Abstention in fear of being left alone on the field with the opponent is also less likely, because, with allies, there is less likelihood of being caught alone. Allies may still attempt to pass the buck or free ride, but the risks of doing so are higher and clearer: possible defeat by an opposing alliance or the defection of an alienated partner.

Nonsystemic Incentives to Ally

Thus far our model has abstracted from inequalities of strength and from particular conflicts and common interests between specific states. The purpose has been to get a clearer view of the purely systemic incentives for and consequences of alliances. We have established that there would be modest incentives to ally in such a hypothetical world of pristine anarchy, that the identity of allies would be completely indeterminate, but that the formation of alliances would tend to create both friendships and enmities, and interests consistent with them. It is time now to reintroduce strength differences and conflicts of interest to see how they change the incentives. Two bodies of theory are available to assist our reasoning: coalition theory and game theory. Coalition theory, as developed largely in the discipline of social psychology, seeks to predict and explain who will align with whom when the weights of the players vary but (usually) when the values of possible winning coalitions are equal. We can take this as a starting model for the international condition wherein the only difference among the state-actors is that they vary in their military power and potential. Game theory, by contrast, generally assumes that the weights of the players are equal (or that variations in weight are unimportant); what varies is the value of each of the possible coalitions. In the following sections, I attempt to combine these two approaches so as to take into account simultaneously the effects of differences in military resources and of common and conflicting interests among states on the formation of alliances. I do this, first, by translating asymmetries in resources into payoff differences for the various possible alliances and then adding to these numbers further payoffs for conflicts and common interests among the players. The result is a set of composite payoffs for each conceivable alliance under various salient combinations of strength and conflict asymmetries.

Coalition Theory and Strength Differences

First, let us relax the assumption of equal strengths and permit moderate differences among the actors in military power and potential. This, of course, introduces more realism into the model; to keep it manageable, however, we must also reduce the number of states to three. Later, when we introduce game theory, we increase the number of players.

Social psychologists and sociologists have developed several theories and models about coalitions in the triad, in order to predict which of three possible coalitions will form when the weights of the players vary and the values of the coalitions are identical. For example, one of these theories, that of William A. Gamson,[10] assumes that the payoffs to members of a winning coalition vary with their shares of the coalition's resources. It predicts that the smallest winning coalition will form, because it maximizes the payoff to each of its members. Thus, when weights are equal among the three players—A = B = C—it is indeterminate which coalition will form. When two players, B and C, are equal and individually weaker than, while jointly stronger than, the third player—A > B = C, A < B + C—the coalition BC will form, since it gives B and C larger payoffs than either could get in alliance with A. If, on the other hand, B and C are each stronger than A and equal to each other—A < B = C—either AB or AC will form, since B's and C's resource shares, and hence their payoffs, are larger in those alliances than in BC. When B and C are individually weaker but jointly stronger than A and unequal between themselves—A > B > C, A < B + C—B and C will ally. Each party seeks to join "that minimal winning coalition with total resources closest to the decision point," that is, with more than, but closest to, 50 percent of the total resources in the triad.[11]

This logic is at least a starting point for the analysis of the effects of unequal military strengths on alliance likelihoods and alliance benefits and costs. The following builds on Gamson by translating strength differences among the players into payoff differences among alliances and among their members. Some of Gamson's assumptions are revised. It is not assumed, for example, that the overall values of the possible coalitions are identical and constant. It is not assumed that the payoff to a given coalition will be divided among its members in proportion to the resources they contribute. Instead, individual payoffs are a function of security gains. Specifically, assume the following:

1. Payoffs are the net security gains from making a defensive alliance.
2. Information is incomplete—in particular, participants are uncertain about each other's interests and intentions in the absence of alliance.
3. Alliances commit their members equally to come immediately to the defense of an ally when its home territory is attacked and to continue fighting until the status quo ante is restored.
4. Alliances increase the probability, but do not ensure the certainty, that the victim of attack will be supported.
5. Although alliances are for defensive purposes only, actors fear that they might be used offensively.
6. There is no military advantage for either the offense or the defense.
7. Force levels are not affected by the formation of alliances.

To simplify, we count alliance payoffs in terms of only three of the alliance benefits listed previously: deterrence, defense, and preclusion. Deterrence is the effect of an alliance in reducing the probability of attack; defense value is an increase in the probability and reduction in the cost of successful defense; preclusion is the value of blocking the ally from allying with one's opponent. Deterrence and defense include the effect of redeployment, against the adversary, of forces the allies had previously deployed against each other. This leaves out of account certain lesser benefits such as controlling the ally.

We consider only one alliance cost, the risk of having to come to the ally's defense immediately when the ally is attacked, when strategic interest would counsel otherwise. States in a tripolar system will have an ultimate strategic interest in preventing each other's conquest. Alliance commitments may be inconsistent with this interest if the ally is perceived to be stronger than or equally as strong as its opponent. Then a state might wish to stand aside or delay its intervention until it became clear that the ally would lose the war unless helped. Practically, the cost then would be the moral and reputational costs of reneging on or delaying the fulfillment of the alliance commitment.

Other costs, such as the reduction of diplomatic flexibility, are omitted. We simply assume that these lesser benefits and costs either will cancel out or will not be large enough to affect outcomes significantly. Finally, assume that increases or reductions in deterrence, defense, and preclusive benefits come in increments of 20 "security units."* Obviously, this is a heroic assumption; it is introduced only to give some precision and clarity to the argument.

The model does not permit predictions of which alliance will form or how intra-alliance payoffs will be divided; its purpose is only to show how alliance incentives are affected by strength differences. As a benchmark, the payoff numbers assume equal treaty commitments in any alliance that forms. Predictions of alliance matchups, terms, and payoffs require a gamelike model that takes account of conflicting and common interests and the bargaining process. The present model may be regarded as a step in the development of such a model.

Figure 2-1 and Table 2-1 compare hypothetical alliance payoffs in four power configurations among three states. We ask first of each configuration, What are the incentives for the states to come to each other's defense when there are no alliances? and then, What are the incentives to ally? Both questions must be asked and answered, because the value of a formal alliance, presumably, is the difference between values enjoyed before and after its negotiation.

In the first configuration, Figure 2-1a and Table 2-1a, where strengths are equal, each state has a 50–50 chance of defending itself against one attacker. Further, each can be fairly sure of being helped if attacked, or at least if it is losing a war, since all three have a strategic interest in preventing the merging of the resources of the other two.[12] Consequently, the deterrent and defense benefits of an explicit alliance in advance of attack would be low. They would not be zero, however, since alliance commitments would increase the perceived likelihood of being supported. An alliance would permit the allies to redeploy against the opponent the forces they had previously deployed against each other. These two defense benefits might be worth 20 security units each; their deterrent consequences might add another 20. An alliance would also yield preclusive value: preventing the ally from allying with the third party against oneself. The cost of the alliance—say 20 negative units—would be the cost of the commitment to defend the ally at the outset of a war, when cold strategic interest would counsel delaying until it was clear the ally would be defeated if not supported. Thus an alliance yields each member 80 units of benefits and 20 units of cost, and each two-party alliance is worth 120 units, as shown in Table 2-1a. This represents the amount of alliance value generated solely by anarchy—that is, by fear and uncertainty about others' intentions that obtains even when the parties' strengths are equal and

---

*Of course, there is no reason why, in reality, these quite different benefits and costs should be equally valuable and valued precisely that much. At this point, we are engaged in constructing a model, not in testing it. The main purpose of the model is not to generate hypotheses for empirical testing but to clarify the basic logic of alliance formation.

Figure 2-1 and Table 2-1. Strength differences and alliance values

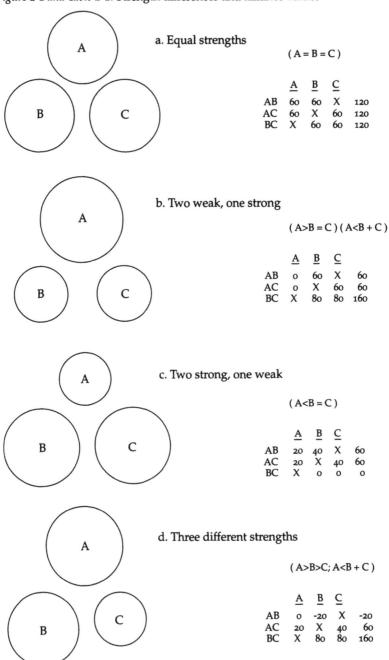

a. Equal strengths

(A = B = C)

	A	B	C	
AB	60	60	X	120
AC	60	X	60	120
BC	X	60	60	120

b. Two weak, one strong

(A>B = C) (A<B + C)

	A	B	C	
AB	0	60	X	60
AC	0	X	60	60
BC	X	80	80	160

c. Two strong, one weak

(A<B = C)

	A	B	C	
AB	20	40	X	60
AC	20	X	40	60
BC	X	0	0	0

d. Three different strengths

(A>B>C; A<B + C)

	A	B	C	
AB	0	-20	X	-20
AC	20	X	40	60
BC	X	80	80	160

there are no particular conflicts among them. It will serve as a benchmark for the calculation of alliance values in the following cases, where strengths are unequal, and later, when conflicts and commonalities of interest are introduced.

The second case, Figure 2-1b and Table 2-1b, shows two weak states and one strong one, with the aggregate capabilities of the weaker states being superior to those of the strong state: $A > B = C$; $A < B + C$. When no alliances exist, B and C, in their own interest, will defend each other, and A will defend either B or C. B or C has no interest in defending A, since A can easily defend itself against a single attacker.

Alliance BC has greater value than in our first configuration, and its components are different. Its deterrence and defense values are greater by reason of the increased threat its members face; on the other hand, due to their clearer strategic interests, the alliance only marginally increases the likelihood, already high, that they will come to each other's defense. Preclusive value is lower than in the previous case, since A, now the stronger party, has less incentive to ally with B or C. The cost of alliance is very low, since B's and C's alliance commitments merely make explicit their strategic interests. Thus, plausibly, BC is valued one security increment higher by each of its members than in the benchmark case, at 80 each: benefits are about the same, though differently composed, but costs are lower. Thus the aggregate value of this alliance is 160.

Alliances AB or AC would yield deterrent and defense benefits to B or C, against each other, by increasing the likelihood and promptness of A's assistance and by eliminating the need to deploy forces against A. B or C would also gain by precluding A from allying with the other. These benefits would be partially offset, however, by the cost of the commitment to A, which contradicts the strategic interests of B or C: each would prefer to side with the other rather than with A in case of war with A. These alliances carry no deterrent of defense benefits for A since A can defend itself without help against either of the others; thus A would value them only for their preclusive effect: preventing a BC combination. Even this modest gain is offset by the cost to A of being committed to fight for one of the others from the beginning, when it would prefer to wait and then intervene on the losing side. In sum, for B or C, an alliance with A yields 80 positive units at a cost of 20, for a net of 60. It is worth nothing to A, for whom its costs cancel out its benefits. In the aggregate, AB and AC are each worth 60, with the entire value going to the weaker members. Of the three possible alliances, BC (alliance between the weaker states) is considerably more valuable than in the benchmark case of equal strengths, while AB and AC (alliance between a strong and a weak state) are substantially less valuable.

The third and fourth configurations may be treated more summarily. In

[59]

the third, Figure 2-1c, the two strong states, B and C, have no incentive to ally. A, the weak state, has only a weak incentive, since, although it needs protection, it can count on being defended by either of the others even without an alliance. B or C would gain moderate security against each other by allying with A, and they would sustain no costs, since they already have strategic interest in defending A. Overall, AB and AC are only half as valuable as the benchmark case, and BC has no value. In the fourth configuration of unequal strengths, Figure 2-1d, an alliance between the two stronger states, A and B, is worth less than nothing because of its negative value for the weaker of the two; alliance between the two weaker, B and C, is worth a great deal; and alliance between the strongest and weakest, AC, has about the same value as in the preceding example.

What may be concluded from this exercise? The following may be suggested, at least as hypotheses:

1. Inequality of strength creates some degree of alignment short of alliance—that is, it generates strategic interests which in turn give rise to expectations of support or nonsupport by others. Thus weaker states will expect that they will come to each other's defense and that they will be defended by stronger states against other strong states.
2. Formal alliances generate both benefits and costs and thus modify alignment expectations. Benefits and costs will vary according to their consistency with prealliance interests and expectations.
3. Alliances that are consistent with strategic interests are worth more than those that are not, primarily because their costs are less.
4. The most valuable alliances are those between weak states threatened by a strong state.
5. The least valuable alliances are those between two strong states against a weak one.
6. When a strong and a weak state ally, most of the value goes to the weak state when the opponent is weak; most goes to the strong state when the opponent is strong.

Conflicts and Common Interests

Now let us increase the realism of the model by introducing the possibility of particular conflicts and common interests among states. The only prealliance interests of states, I have assumed until now, are the rather general ones that arise from the structure of the system and from inequalities of power in the system. That is, states have a general interest in resisting aggrandizement by strong states and, at the extreme, in preventing any state from gaining control of more than half the power resources in the system. But, of course, states have many other more particular interests, both strategic and intrinsic, which bring them into conflict with or which they hold in common with certain other states.[13] I have in mind,

[60]

for example, territorial conflicts such as the Alsace-Lorraine issue between France and Germany between 1871 and 1914 or the conflict over the Balkans between Austria-Hungary and Russia. Common ideological values among the three eastern monarchies—Germany, Russia, and Austria-Hungary—and between the western democracies—Britain and France—also influenced alignments during this period.

Such conflicts and commonalities, along with power differentials, generate a pattern of alignment that exists prior to and independently of formal alliances. That is, states will have some expectation of being supported in war or crises by states with which they share interests and values, and of not being supported, or of being opposed, by states with which they have conflicts. These expectations will in turn generate strategic interests of the kind discussed earlier: states will be motivated to resist expansion by others with which they are in conflict. Obversely, they will have some incentive to prevent losses, or perhaps even to promote expansion, by states with which they share interests, notably, an interest in resisting a common adversary. Alignments will be clearest, of course, when conflicts and common interests on different issues are mutually reinforcing rather than cross-cutting and, likewise, when expectations generated by the configuration of power are similar to those arising from the pattern of interests.

Geographical location and topography will modify either the pattern of conflict or the pattern of power resources, or both. Thus states in close proximity and hence with frequent interaction are likely to find materials for conflict.[14] In addition, proximity maximizes their power vis-à-vis each other, so that they see each other as threatening on power as well as interest grounds. They will tend to perceive each other as enemies rather than as allies. They will see themselves as aligned with states on the opposite side of their enemy, in the well-known "sandwich" pattern of international politics. States that are protected by some geographic feature, such as a body of water or a mountain range, will gain defensive power thereby and are less likely to experience friction with others. They are less likely to develop either strong alignments or strong enmities and may be attracted to policies of "splendid isolation."

Alliance Incentives and the Pattern of Alignment

The pattern of alignment increases incentives to ally and increases the predictability of partners, compared to our initial hypothetical system of pristine anarchy. Obviously, states will have more reason to ally when they have specific conflicts with other states, thus more reason to fear attack, than when their only sense of threat comes from systemic anarchy. Equally obviously, they are more likely to ally with states with which they have common interests than with those with which they have conflicts.

The strength of incentives to ally and the determinacy of partners will depend on the intensity of conflicts and the degree of strength inequalities, and whether these variables are mutually reinforcing or opposed. When conflicts are severe and particularly when the same states are in conflict on several issues, the drive to ally formally will be strong and the likely partners will be quite clear. When conflicts are mild and nonreinforcing and strength differences are small, there may be little more pressure to ally than in our initial model of pure anarchy, or the probable identity of allies will be quite ambiguous.

Note that the systemic incentives to ally persist and underlie the incentives that arise from specific conflicts and strength differences. Structural anarchy continues to generate a substratum of insecurity that is intensified and focused by particular threats and enmities. The plethora of alliance options provided by structural multipolarity is narrowed, but not eliminated, by the pattern of common interests, conflicts, and capabilities. Structure generates pervasive fears and indeterminate options; particular interests and conflicts focus the fears and narrow the options.

When formal alliances are superimposed on a prior pattern of interest and capability, they will modify the expectations and intentions that were inherent in that pattern. If these prior alignments are fairly well defined, alliances may merely formalize and sharpen them, strengthening and codifying preexisting expectations and interests rather than creating new ones. But if prior alignments are ambiguous, formal alliances will to a greater extent independently determine relations of amity or enmity, much as they would have if there had been no specific conflicts and inequalities in the system. Indeed, the exigencies of bargaining may produce alliance lineups that run counter to the preexisting conflict-affinity pattern and largely replace it.*

The alignment pattern may also be modified by the settlement of specific issues in dispute between rivals. Such settlements may shift the balance of conflict and common interest in the parties' relationship, sufficient to create an entente or quasi-alliance. Lesser settlements, such as detentes, may also be seen as alternatives to alliances. The reduction of conflict with an adversary may contribute as much to security as an alliance against it. Conflict reduction, of course, requires concessions, but these may be less onerous than the costs and risks of alliance.

Returning now to our developing model, assume again a tripolar system. Conflicts would change the alliance values presented earlier, along the following lines. A conflict between two states would increase the de-

---

* An example is Britain's ententes with its erstwhile colonial opponents, France and Russia, in 1904 and 1907, after alliance negotiations with its "natural" ally, Germany, had collapsed.

Table 2-2. Alliance values in a tripolar system with varying strengths and varying conflicts between actors

No conflict	Conflict between A and B	Conflict between A and B; A and C	Conflict between B and C
Configuration I: strengths equal: A = B = C			
AB = 120 (60, 60)	AB = 80 (40, 40)	AB = 80 (60, 20)	AB = 120 (40, 80)
AC = 120 (60, 60)	AC = 120 (80, 40)	AC = 80 (60, 20)	AC = 120 (40, 80)
BC = 120 (60, 60)	BC = 120 (80, 40)	BC = 120 (60, 60)	BC = 80 (40, 40)
Configuration II: two weak; one strong: A > B = C; A < B + C			
AB = 60 (0, 60)	AB = 20 (−20, 40)	AB = 20 (0, 20)	AB = 60 (−20, 80)
AC = 60 (0, 60)	AC = 60 (20, 40)	AC = 20 (0, 20)	AC = 60 (−20, 80)
BC = 160 (80, 80)	BC = 160 (100, 60)	BC = 160 (80, 80)	BC = 120 (60, 60)
Configuration III: two strong; one weak: A < B = C			
AB = 60 (20, 40)	AB = 20 (0, 20)	AB = 20 (20, 0)	AB = 60 (0, 60)
AC = 60 (20, 40)	AC = 60 (40, 20)	AC = 20 (20, 0)	AC = 60 (0, 60)
BC = 0 (0, 0)	BC = 0 (20, −20)	BC = 0 (0, 0)	BC = −40 (−20, −20)
Configuration IV: unequal strengths: A > B > C; A < B + C			
AB = −20 (0, −20)	AB = −60 (−20, −40)	AB = −60 (0, −60)	AB = −20 (−20, 0)
AC = 60 (20, 40)	AC = 60 (40, 20)	AC = 20 (20, 0)	AC = 60 (0, 60)
BC = 160 (80, 80)	BC = 160 (100, 60)	BC = 160 (80, 80)	BC = 120 (60, 60)

terrent, defense, and preclusive value each placed on alliance with the third party. It would reduce the incentive for the third party to ally with one of the pair, however, since the third party would not feel threatened by others who were preoccupied with their own dispute. Moreover, if attacked by one of the others, it could feel fairly confident of being assisted by the other, even without an alliance. The conflict would reduce the value of alliance between the conflicted states themselves because it would introduce doubt about each other's reliability, or, alternatively, because the conflict would be costly to resolve. Two states, both in conflict with a third, would place a high value on alliance with each other, although this value would be discounted by the likelihood that they would defend each other in any case. Table 2-2 shows these effects superimposed on the four configurations of military resources presented earlier as Figures 2-1a–d and Tables 2-1a–d. For simplicity and continuity with those models, assume that conflicts result in increments or decrements to alliance value of 20 security units.

Consider Configuration I: equal military strengths and potential. Recall that alliance values were 120 for each of the three conceivable alliances when there were no conflicts within pairs, as in the first column. Suppose there is a conflict between A and B, as shown in the second column. This conflict reduces the value of coalition AB, according to our assumptions, by 20 for each party or 40 overall, to 80. The value of AC is unchanged at 120: although its value for A increases because of the increased threat A faces from B, its value for C decreases by a similar amount because C is less threatened by B when B is preoccupied with its dispute with A. The value of coalition BC is also unchanged at 120, for the same reasons.

If there are conflicts of interest between A and C, as well as between A and B, as in the third column, the values of AB and BC remain the same as in the preceding example while the value of AC declines. AB is unchanged at 80 because, though it is worth more to A owing to A's conflict with C, it is worth less to B because C's conflict with A makes C less threatening to B. Similarly, BC is unchanged at 120 because the A–C conflict increases its value to C while reducing its value to B. AC declines from 120 to 80 because the conflict between these two reduces the value of their alliance by 20 apiece.

The case in which there is conflict between B and C but not in the other pairs is analogous to that of the first example, above, where there was conflict between A and B. Compared to the no-conflict situation, BC loses value for both its members, while the value of the other pairs remains the same because of offsetting considerations.

Moving to Configuration II, the first column in the table shows that an alliance between a strong and a weak state is worth less to the stronger than when strengths are equal, as in Configuration I, but that alliance between the two weaker states is worth more to both. In the second column, the conflict between A and B reduces the value of their alliance. The other two alliance possibilities keep the same total value as in the no-conflict situation but this value is divided differently between the parties, since they are affected differently by the A–B conflict. The reader may (or may not!) wish to check the calculations in the other combinations.

The values in Table 2-2 still do not permit us to predict for all cases which alliance will form or how an alliance's value will be divided among its members. Outcomes are the proximate results of a bargaining process, which is more or less indeterminate. The values in the table, reflecting the distribution of military resources and conflicts in the system, will, however, predispose bargaining outcomes in certain directions, to the advantage of one party and the disadvantage of another, through their effects on the parties' relative bargaining power. Those values may be considered the "inherent" worth of prospective alliances to their members before negotiation about specific contract terms. To give some empirical meaning to the notion of "inherent" alliance values, assume they are the values of a simple mutual and symmetrical commitment to defend the home territories of the allies. Actual alliance negotiations may result in asymmetrical commitments, commitments other than defense, commitments extending beyond home territories, or side payments of various kinds. Rational bargainers will attempt to fashion terms that maximize the total value of the alliance, and this value will be apportioned roughly according to their relative bargaining power. To incorporate the bargaining process, and thus to develop further our alliance formation model, we turn now to game theory.

GAME THEORY AND BARGAINING

N-Person Game Theory: The Bargaining Set

Game theory is useful to illustrate the logic of alliance formation when both the military strengths and the interests of states are different, as is realistically the case. The most useful game model for our present purposes is the bargaining set solution in N-person cooperative theory.[15] This is one of several solution concepts that seek to predict at least a range of probable outcomes in an indeterminate situation. It is useful because of its realistic orientation around a bargaining process. In order to highlight the logic of the model, we start with certain standard assumptions from "cooperative" game theory; then we modify them to bring them closer to international reality and to the models presented earlier.

Assume there are three or more players. They are rational utility maximizers. Communication is allowed; hence alliance agreements are possible. If alliances form, they are completely binding and enforceable. There may be coalitions of any number of players, including all players. Each alliance has a value, which is awarded as the outcome of a competitive game that the alliance plays against excluded players; that value is distributed among its members in proportions previously agreed on. Information is complete—in particular, the players have full knowledge of each other's preferences among possible coalitions and possible contract terms. Utilities are transferable.

Three modifications to these assumptions will bring them closer to the empirical world. First, alliance agreements, no matter how "binding" they may be in international law, are never absolutely or practically so. Thus the real alliance game is somewhere between the "cooperative" and "noncooperative" variants of N-person game theory, the latter being the case where communication and hence coalition formation are entirely ruled out. In other words, alliance agreements may be made, but there is some subjective probability that they will not be honored. Thus the players' payoffs must be discounted by a "disloyalty coefficient" representing the probability of the ally's defection.

Second, the value of alliances, and the payoffs to individual players, are not awarded at a discrete point as the outcome of a single contest with an opposing coalition, as the theory assumes. At least in a defensive alliance, they are experienced in a continuous stream through time, mostly in the form of enhanced security, including reductions in the likelihood and expected costs of future confrontations with adversaries. Theoretically, however, the stream may be concentrated at the moment of alliance formation by reducing anticipated future payoffs to their present values.

Third, the assumption of complete information must, obviously, be modified, to partial information. International actors will not even know very precisely their own values for different alliances, let alone those of others. States will have some information bearing on these values, however, enough to make rough estimates. We may assume that such estimates are made, based on perceptions of one's own and others' situations and past behavior.

Finally, although a "coalition of the whole" corresponds to the notion of "concert" in international relations, I assume that such a coalition is not valuable enough to occur. I further assume that players excluded from a coalition get a payoff of zero.

Alliance possibilities may be classified according to their "feasibility," their "competitiveness," and their "relevance." A feasible alliance is one that is at least as good as the status quo* for all its members; an infeasible one is worth less than the status quo for at least one member. Feasible alliances may be competitive or noncompetitive. A competitive alliance yields at least as much value for all its members as they could get in any other alliance; a noncompetitive one is inferior to a feasible alternative for at least one partner. A relevant alliance is a noncompetitive one that nevertheless influences the bargaining within and among the competitive possibilities.

We now return to our developing model, starting with a three-actor system and moving to a five-actor one.

Three Actors

In bargaining set theory, payoffs to members of each potential coalition are established by a sequence of threats and offers that exploit the alternatives available to each actor.

Consider a case (call it Case 1) in which all three of the possible alliances in a three-actor system have the same aggregate inherent value: AB = 120, AC = 120, and BC = 120.[16] The empirical parallel might be a situation in which the military strengths of the states are equal and there are no specific conflicts or attractions in any pair, as shown in the first example in Table 2-2, Configuration I. All three possibilities improve on the status quo, and there is no reason for any state to value any of its alliance options over the others. All three are both feasible and competitive. Which alliance

---

*The term "status quo" may be defined as what the situation is or is likely to become in the absence of alliance.

will form is indeterminate. The division of the payoff within the alliance that does form is determined, however: each member gets half, or 60. Suppose A offers B a 70, 50 division favoring A. B would reject this proposal and could enforce a 60, 60 split with the following unanswerable argument: "I can negotiate a 60, 60 deal with C. You cannot outbid me for C's allegiance, because to do that you must offer C more than 60, which means you must accept less than the 60 I am offering you. Therefore you must accept my offer." A similar argument would enforce an even division in the other two possible alliances. Thus the payoff division is determined for whatever alliance forms, but which one that will be is indeterminate.

Figure 2-2 illustrates Case 1. The line PQR represents the various possible payoff combinations in alliance AB. The line MQS represents possible payoffs in alliances AC or BC which give C equal payoffs in each one. The payoffs to C increase, and to A or B decrease, with movement on MQS toward the origin. C's payoff is maximized at M, where the payoff to A or B, in alliance with C, is zero. The point S is a hypothetical point where C's payoff is zero and A's or B's is maximized; here C is indifferent between allying with one of the others or remaining alone. Q is the equilibrium point that defines the payoff—60—that each party can expect in each of the alliances available to it.

As a variant of Case 1, assume the potential alliances are valued unequally: AB = 120, AC = 100, BC = 80, as in Figure 2-3. Here again, although it is less obvious, who allies with whom is not predictable, but the division of the value of each alliance is determined. The predicted divisions are AB: 70, 50; AC: 70, 30; and BC: 50, 30. The decline in the values for AC and BC, compared to the previous example, have increased A's payoff, and reduced B's and C's payoffs, in whatever alliance forms.

Consider negotiations between A and B. Suppose B proposes an even split at 60, 60. A could rightly object and insist on 70, 50—asymmetrical commitments, or side payments in its favor. A could argue that B "deserves" no more than 50, since that is all it could expect to get in alliance with C. B is limited to 50 in BC because anything more would reduce C's payoff below 30, which C would not accept because 30 is available to it in alliance with A. A could also point out that it could get 70 from C, so it must have at least that much from B. B cannot counter these arguments, so it must accept A's proposal.

The same logic holds for the other two pairs; any proposal deviating from those listed would be blocked by the disadvantaged party. No party could get more than, or need accept less than, it could get in its alternative alliance. The payoff in the alternative is established by how much the alternative partner could get in *its* alternative, and so on around the triad. In the case of B and C, their payoffs in alliance BC are as large, but no

Alliance Formation Bargaining with Varying Alliance Values

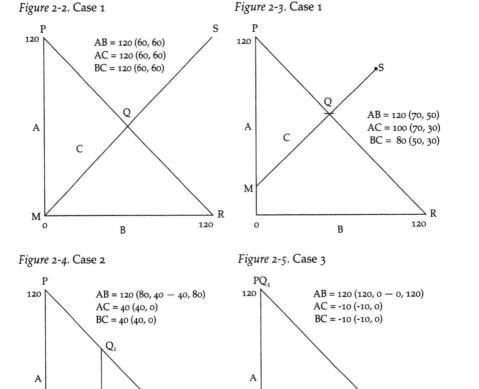

Figure 2-2. Case 1

AB = 120 (60, 60)
AC = 120 (60, 60)
BC = 120 (60, 60)

Figure 2-3. Case 1

AB = 120 (70, 50)
AC = 100 (70, 30)
BC = 80 (50, 30)

Figure 2-4. Case 2

AB = 120 (80, 40 — 40, 80)
AC = 40 (40, 0)
BC = 40 (40, 0)

Figure 2-5. Case 3

AB = 120 (120, 0 — 0, 120)
AC = -10 (-10, 0)
BC = -10 (-10, 0)

larger, than 50 and 30, because these are the amounts available to each of them in their alternative alliance with A. This example also illustrates the counterintuitive result that the most valuable alliance is not necessarily the one that forms: BC is just as likely to form as the other two, even though its aggregate value is least.

The changed position of MQS in Figure 2-3 shows the increased benefit to A and lowered benefit to B in alliances AC or BC, as compared to the preceding example. The shorter distance between S and Q shows the reduced payoff to C in either AC or BC.

In both variants of Case 1, equilibrium occurs at a point that equalizes each party's payoffs across its two alliance options. Bargaining consists of finding this point and perhaps becoming resigned to it after a period of cycling around it. In Case 2, there is no such point but rather a bargaining range wherein the distribution of alliance benefits is indeterminate. Also in contrast to Case 1, which alliance will form is determined.

Consider the following aggregate alliance values, for Case 2, before bargaining: AB = 120; AC = 40; BC = 40. All three alliances are feasible in that they are all better than the no-alliance status quo, but AC and BC are noncompetitive because A and B could each do better in alliance with each other than they could conceivably do in alliance with C. Indeed, even if all the benefits in AC or BC went to B or A, they would prefer AB. The only uncertainty, the only object of bargaining, is the terms that A and B will settle on. Each could get 40 (or almost 40) in alliance with C; because of their superior bargaining power over C, they can drive C's payoff down to zero or close to it. Therefore, A and B will each demand 40, as a minimum, in their bargaining with each other. They will negotiate terms somewhere between 80, 40 and 40, 80.

Figure 2-4 illustrates Case 2. The most obvious difference between this model and Figures 2-2 and 2-3 is that the line MS, representing payoffs in alliances AC or BC, does not intersect line PR, which shows the possible payoff distributions in alliance AB. S, the point at which A or B get all the value in alliance with C, falls short of PR. The lines running vertically and horizontally from S, showing what A and B could get in alliance with C, also demarcate the bargaining range for A and B, between Q_1 and Q_2, that is, between payoff divisions of 80, 40 and 40, 80. Any offer outside this range can be bettered in alliance with C, since C would accept anything greater than zero. Note that although C is "odd man out," that does not take it out of the game; the potential values of the alliances that are noncompetitive (AC and BC) are still influential in setting the range of conceivable terms in the alliance that occurs. In this variant, AC and BC are relevant even though they are noncompetitive.

It is also worth noting that even though the general outcomes in Cases 1 and 2 are different, they are contiguous models in that they simply show different situations on either side of a boundary represented by the placement of S directly on PQR. When S is northeast of PQR, it is uncertain which alliance will occur, but the payoffs are determinate. In moving S southwest, across the boundary into Case 2, we gain determinacy about which alliance forms but lose the unique determination of payoffs.

Case 3 (Fig. 2-5) is the simplest of the three: A and B are negotiating an alliance when neither has any feasible alternative. Empirically, this could be the case, in our three-party situation, when both A and B have severe conflicts with C, so that alliance with C is worth less than zero, that is, less than no alliance at all. This is similar to Case 2 in that only alliance AB can form and the distribution of its value is indeterminate. It differs from Case 2 in that the bargaining range has substantially widened. The minimum acceptable terms for each party are set by the party's valuation of the no-alliance status quo, not of an alternative alliance that improves on the status quo.

Of course, many variants of these cases are possible: for example, a version of Case 2 in which one party's alternative alliance with C is worth more than the other party's. This would shift the position of MS, as in Figure 2-3, but in this case it would change the location of a bargaining range, Q_1–Q_2, not of a specific settlement point Q, to the first party's advantage. A variant of Case 3 would be one in which one party has a feasible alternative and the other does not. In this situation, the first party, of course, has the advantage; it can expect to get anything between the value of its alternative and the total value of the alliance being negotiated.

Table 2-3. Payoffs in three-member alliances in a five-actor system

	Aggregate value	Before bargaining	After bargaining
ABC	80	(50, 10, 20)	(55, 10, 15)[a]
ABD	20	(10, 0, 10)	(0, 0, 0)
ABE	100	(50, 10, 40)	(55, 10, 35)[a]
ACD	70	(40, 20, 10)	(55, 15, 0)[a]
ACE	20	(10, 10, 0)	(0, 0, 0)
ADE	70	(50, 10, 10)	(0, 0, 0)
BCD	10	(5, 5, 0)	(0, 0, 0)
BCE	20	(10, 10, 0)	(0, 0, 0)
BDE	10	(5, 5, 0)	(0, 0, 0)
CDE	50	(30, 10, 10)	(15, 0, 35)[a]

NOTE: A linear programming procedure was used to compute the payoffs after bargaining.
[a]Competitive alliance.

More than Three Actors

When we increase the number of actors beyond three, the logic becomes more complicated but produces the same two classes of outcomes: either several alliances are equally possible (competitive) and it is indeterminate which one will form, but the payoffs to individual members are indeterminate; or only one alliance is possible, and the payoffs to its members are indeterminate within a bargaining range. Suppose that there are five states and that only three-member alliances can be competitive. Table 2-3 shows the ten possibilities. The column furthest left lists the aggregate value of each alliance. The first set of numbers in parentheses is each party's inherent value for each alliance, defined as a hypothetical value for symmetrical commitments, before bargaining about specific contract terms. The second set of numbers in parentheses shows the alliance pay-offs after bargaining.[17] Bargaining does not affect the aggregate value of an alliance but does affect the distribution of that value in alliances that are competitive, that is, for those valuable enough to have some chance of being formed. The competitive alliances are ABC, ABE, ACD, and CDE. Those remaining are not competitive because their aggregate value is not sufficient to give all their members as much as they could get in some alternative. For example, ABD is not competitive because its total value of 20 is not sufficient to pay A and B the 55 and 10 they could get in ABC or ABE. Since they cannot form, the payoffs in the noncompetitive alli-ances after bargaining are shown simply as zero for all parties.

Any one of the four competitive alliances could form. Which one occurs is indeterminate, but the parties' payoffs are determined for whatever al-liance they join: they get the same payoff in each of their available options. This is a five-player version of Case 1 above: several alliances are possible, and all are equally likely.

The alliance that forms, and the payoffs to its members, are arrived at by a process of bargaining that establishes the actual contract terms. Note that the ultimate payoffs are different from what they would have been had a contract been made at symmetrical terms; the outcome of bargaining favors some and disadvantages others. Thus A's payoff in ABC or ABE increases by five units over its payoff under equal commitments, while C's and E's decline by five. This reflects A's more favorable alternatives. In turn, E can extort a substantial advantage in the terms of CDE, and C and D must accept sacrifices, because of the relatively high payoff E gets in ABE. Only B gets an ultimate payoff in ABC and ABE which is equivalent to what it would get under the baseline of symmetrical com-mitments.

We would have Case 2 in the five-party model if we substantially in-creased the value of one of the competitive alliances. Suppose we increase ABE to 200. Each party would get considerably more in this alliance than in any other; hence ABE is now the only competitive alliance. The other formerly competitive ones—ABC, ACD, and CDE—become noncompeti-tive; they cannot form, but they are still relevant: they continue to influ-ence the bargaining process among A, B, and E by establishing the minimum payoffs each will accept. With the increase in the value of ABE, its members now have available a "surplus," over and above their mini-mums,* which they will divide up by a process of bargaining. Just where

---

*The minimums of A, B, and E would not be what they could get in their alternative alliances in the previous example, because these amounts would themselves increase, ow-ing to the increased value for ABE. The better payoffs to A, B, and E in their alliance would allow them to reduce to zero the payoffs to C and D in the alternatives—ABC, ACD, and CDE—with commensurate increases for themselves. Thus the payoffs to A, B, and E in

Table 2-4. Payoffs to two-member alliances in a five-actor system

Aggregate value		Payoffs after bargaining
AB	= 100	(60, 40)
AC	= 80	(60, 20)
BC	= 60	(40, 20)
AD	= 40	(0, 0)
AE	= 40	(0, 0)
BD	= 40	(0, 0)
BE	= 40	(0, 0)
CD	= 40	(20, 20)
CE	= 40	(20, 20)
DE	= 40	(20, 20)

the division will occur is technically indeterminate, but this alliance will be certain to form.

The logic is similar when we consider only two-member alliances. In that case, however, we must drop the standard game theory assumption that only majority coalitions can "win," or, in our present terminology, be competitive. Assume, instead, that two-party alliances generate payoffs in the form of security gains against other players previously identified as adversaries, or likely to become so as a consequence of the alliance. Such an assumption models historical multipolar systems more accurately than the previous model; typically, alliances tend to form initially between two states, against a limited number of others. Other members, of course, may be added subsequently. The negotiators of a two-member alliance may conceive it as a stepping-stone to a larger one—as Bismarck apparently considered his alliance with Austria in 1879 a step toward an agreement with Russia, or as the British government viewed its entente with France in 1904 as a move toward Russia. Then, of course, the expected value of such future additions will enter into present payoffs for the pair.

Assume the alliance values in Table 2-4 for the ten possible pairs in a five-member system. The numbers in parentheses represent how these values would be allocated within each pair at the end of the bargaining process. (The hypothetical "before bargaining" payoffs are omitted.) Noncompetitive alliances, as before, are given a postbargaining value of zero.

In Table 2-4 there are six competitive alliances, any of which might form, with equal likelihood. Payoffs to their members are determinate: each player gets the same payoff in any alliance it joins. If a player offers less

---

these alternatives, and their minimums in bargaining with each other, are 70, 10, and 50, respectively, not 55, 10, and 35. B's minimum does not change when the value of ABE is increased, because 10 is the most B can get in alliance BCD when the payoffs to C and D are zero.

or demands more than is available elsewhere, its bid will be rejected. With two-member alliances, two alliances with separate memberships may form, possibly in confrontation.

As in the previous example, a small change in the value of one of the alliances can have a substantial ripple effect across others, perhaps even eliminating some from competitive status. Suppose we increase the value of CD from 40 to 50, increasing C's payoff in that alliance from 20 to 30. C can now hold out for 30 in AC, BC, or CE, which means that C's partners in those alliances get less: A's payoff in AC is reduced to 50; B's in BC, to 30; and E's in CE, to 10. These three alliance possibilities have become noncompetitive because A, B, and E now can get more elsewhere. These possibilities are still relevant, however, to the bargaining in the remaining competitive alliances—AB, CD, and DE. One of the latter three will form, and the payoffs to their members will be indeterminate within a bargaining range established by the changed amounts that each can expect in alliance with C. Thus a change in the value of one alliance eliminates three from the competitive ranks and renders indeterminate the bargaining situation in the remaining three.

In negotiating an alliance, each player must estimate not only its own relative valuations of the alliances open to it but the values of others' alliance alternatives as well. Theoretically, it considers the value of its prospective partner's best alternative in ascertaining the partner's minimum position, and this value will depend in turn on estimates of the value of the alternatives open to the protopartner's alternative allies. In the real world of incomplete information, such estimates can only be vague and uncertain, with much room for miscalculation and misperception. Overestimating the value of the partner's best alternative will produce a bad bargain; underestimating it may block agreement altogether. Even if the partner's alternatives are estimated accurately, its value for the alliance under negotiation may be misestimated with, again, nonoptimal results.

Implicit in these models is that if the payoffs to individual members of a coalition change through time, thus changing the aggregate value of the coalition, either the coalition will collapse, perhaps to be followed by the formation of a different one, or the payoffs to members of the existing coalition will be tacitly or explicitly renegotiated. Theoretically, there is always a multilateral equilibrium among all players, but it is a shifting one that constantly reflects changes in all parties' interests and situations and consequently the values of their alliance options. An equilibrium exists when no party can better its payoff by joining a different alliance or by going it alone.[18]

Where there are cross-cutting coalitions on different issues, each player may be a member of several coalitions, cooperating with some others on some issues but against them on other issues. The total payoff for each player would then be the sum of what it earns in all coalitions of which it is a member.[19]

What do we learn from this exercise? What specific hypotheses does it suggest regarding the process of alliance formation? I would venture the following:

1. The allocation of payoffs in an alliance will reflect the members' inherent values for the alliance and the value of their available alternatives.
2. The parties, in estimating the value of their own and the protopartner's alternatives, must consider the value, to all their members, of all potential alliances in the system.
3. Consideration of each other's alternatives will reveal either a bargaining range, set by the value of the alternatives of each party, wherein the contract terms will fall, or a determinate point representing the terms at which payoffs to both (all) parties in this alliance are just equal to what they could get elsewhere.
4. There will be a bargaining range when both (all) parties value the alliance under negotiation higher than their best alternative; this alliance will form, but its terms are indeterminate.
5. Payoffs will converge on a point when all feasible alliances are comparably valued by all their parties; in this case, any one of these alliances can form and the payoffs to its members are determinate.
6. The most valuable alliance, overall, need not be the one that forms.
7. Some alliances, which logically cannot form, will nevertheless influence the payoff distributions in those that do form.

The exercise leaves unanswered the critical question, How does one (either the researcher or the statesman) calculate these alliance values empirically? Is there any way such values can be derived from the historical record? If not, what good is the model, since its working is critically dependent on the numbers? As just noted, some hypotheses about the process of alliance formation are derivable from it, and these hypotheses may be testable empirically even without specific alliance values. The model can be viewed modestly as a quantitative analogue of what occurs qualitatively. If it has seemed severely abstract, that is the price to be paid for clearly exposing the underlying logic.

We can take a small step back toward the real world by narrowing our focus from the whole system to the parties actually negotiating an alliance. Alliance bargaining, by and large, takes place as a "two-person game." Other "persons" are present in the background, or on the sidelines, as alternative partners or as enemies or neutrals, but the statesman's attention is mostly focused on the single state with which he is trying to negotiate an alliance. So it is appropriate now to shift our focus to the bilateral process of bargaining.

Bargaining in Alliance Formation

Although the configuration of conflict and capability will predispose the system toward certain alliances, the identity of partners and how they divide up the benefits of alliance will be decided ultimately by a process of bargaining. Bargaining in alliance formation shares certain essential characteristics with other bargaining situations. The protopartners have both common and conflicting interests: a common perception that they can both increase their security by allying, and a conflict over the terms of the alliance contract. Each will offer terms—a proposed set of mutual commitments—that are advantageous to itself. Each tries to get its way on the terms by threatening, implicitly or explicitly, to frustrate realization of the common interest by breaking off negotiations, by allying elsewhere, or by making a deal with the opponent. The ultimate terms will reflect the parties' relative bargaining power. Bargaining power in alliance formation is largely a function of two broad determinants. The first is the parties' inherent valuations of the prospective alliance, which depend chiefly on their need for alliance as measured by the degree of threat they face from an adversary, their ally's capacity and will to satisfy the need, and on how much they value the autonomy that would have to be sacrificed in allying. The second is the comparative availability and attractiveness of other alliance alternatives, valued similarly, and of nonalliance alternatives, such as increased armament or concessions to the opponent.[20] Thus, ceteribus paribus, the party that values the alliance least or has the better alternatives will be able to demand and get terms advantageous to itself. It might, for example, be able to get a stronger and broader commitment from the partner than it has to give, or it might be able to extort side payments extraneous to the mutual security commitments, such as a free hand in some colonial area. But if the party with the lesser value for the alliance also has the less attractive alternatives, the contract terms will be more balanced. In general, we may postulate that a state's bargaining power in alliance formation is a function of the ratio of its inherent value for the alliance to the inherent value of its alternatives, and the more powerful bargainer will be the one for which this ratio is lowest.

Other factors that may sometimes affect bargaining power include time preferences of the bargainers and their attitudes toward risk. Although it is not always possible to separate time preference from intensity of preference, a bargainer who wants an agreement soon will be at a disadvantage in dealing with someone who is in no hurry. And a bargainer who is averse to risk—more so than justified by his preferences—will usually lose out to a party who is more risk-acceptant.[21] Bargainers may also vary, of course, in their bargaining skill, their information-processing abilities, and their domestic constraints. For the moment, we assume bargainers are equally endowed with or hindered by such factors.

Assume the alliance under negotiation promises better payoffs for both parties than they could get elsewhere—that there is a "surplus" to be divided by negotiation. Both can gain within a range, the end-points of which are the values each party could obtain in its best alliance alternative, including the alternative of no alliance. Strictly speaking, it is indeterminate where, within the range, the settlement will fall. John F. Nash, how-

Alliance Formation Bargaining

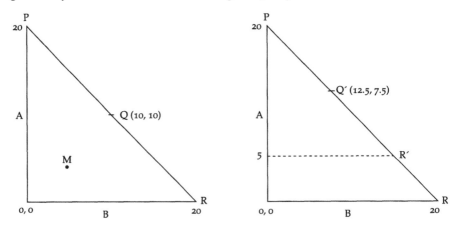

Figure 2-6. Symmetrical alternatives   Figure 2-7. Asymmetrical alternatives

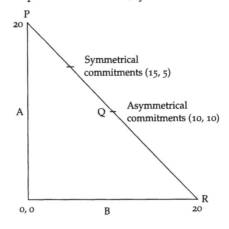

Figure 2-8. Unequal inherent values; symmetrical alternatives

ever, showed that it will fall at the point at which the product of the utilities of the bargainers is maximized, given certain plausible assumptions.[22] Thus in Figure 2-6 the bargaining range runs between P and R, the values of each party's alternatives, and Q is the Nash solution. The line PQR is also the Pareto-optimal line that marks the maximum benefit the parties can achieve jointly. Once the parties are on this line, any improvement of the terms for one bargainer can only be at the other's expense. If they are below this line, say at point M, they can still gain jointly. Moving upward from M, the parties might bargain about the type of alliance to form—nonaggression pact, pact of neutrality, entente, mutual defense alliance, and so on—until they arrive at the type that is mutually most advantageous on the Pareto-optimal line. Then they would move back and forth on that line, each party offering terms favorable to itself, until theoretically they settle at Q, the Nash solution.

The Nash solution gains some support from considerations of bargaining power. One source of bargaining leverage is to have good alternatives. The best alternative available to each party will establish the minimum it will accept in the current negotiation; thus the party with the superior alternatives will find the bargaining range skewed in its favor. In Figure 2-7, for example, the value of A's alternative has increased to 5, while B's remains at zero. This raises A's minimum and truncates the bargaining range to its advantage. A can now demand a settlement in its favor, theoretically at Q', where A gains 12.5 and B gains 7.5, the Nash solution. A second source of bargaining power is the parties' inherent valuation of the alliance. Suppose the parties have equally desirable alternatives, so that the bargaining range runs from 20, 0 to 0, 20, as in Figure 2-8. Then suppose A inherently values the alliance more than B, so that when commitments are symmetrical, A gains 15 and B, 5. B has the greater bargaining power, since it would lose less than A from a bargaining breakdown. Thus B can force A to accept asymmetrical commitments or side payments favoring B, pushing the contract terms toward the Nash solution at 10, 10. Of course, various combinations of asymmetries in alternatives and in inherent valuations may occur, but the ultimate bargain, theoretically, will be at the Nash solution.

The logic of the Nash solution, or of bargaining power, may sometimes be dominated or considerably skewed, however, by normative or empirical factors. For example, a norm of equality may push the bargain toward equal commitments, with only marginal deviations from this norm consequent on the parties' relative bargaining power. Or such a norm may produce equal commitments to mutual defense, with asymmetries in bargaining leverage affecting only the allocation of nondefense side payments. The salience of empirical features such as the identity of the parties' principal opponents or their geographical situations may shift the bargain to one party's advantage.

To summarize the argument of this chapter: Alliance formation in a multipolar system is a product of systemic anarchy, strength inequalities and conflicts and common interests among the states, and a bargaining process. Specific outcomes—who allies with whom and how the net benefits of alliance are divided—are the direct results of bargaining. But they will be strongly influenced by the background context of system structure and relationships, which will determine the values of potential alliances and the relative bargaining power of the actors. This context may absolutely foreclose some combinations; more likely, it will narrow the range of indeterminacy that is usually present in bargaining.

We turn now to the historical record to see whether our models have empirical parallels.

[3]

The Austro-German Alliance of 1879 and the Three Emperors' Alliance of 1881

We turn now to our case studies of alliance formation. The choice of cases was constrained, first, by the obvious requirement that they be taken from a multipolar international system, since my theoretical goal was to work out and illustrate the logic of only such a system, not a bipolar or unipolar one. Within that constraint the limitation of cases to the period before World War 1 has both advantages and disadvantages. On the negative side, the sample is not as diverse as it would have been had the cases been picked from a wider historical span. The positives outweigh the negatives, however. Although greater diversity through time would have, in principle, increased the generalizability of the findings, it would have decreased confidence in the findings themselves by multiplying variables. Case comparison is most fruitful when a maximum number of explanatory factors varies similarly across cases, narrowing the range of potential explanations of different outcomes. Moreover, the incentives and disincentives to form any particular alliance will be strongly influenced by the alliances already in existence; studying alliances over a relatively short span of contiguous time is most likely to capture these influences.

Of course, any attempt to separate "cases" from the seamless span of human history is bound to be somewhat artificial. The artificiality may seem even greater than usual here because of the separation of cases of alliance formation from a continuing process of alliance management. Still, the empirical world offers some justification for this distinction as an analytical tool. When a state, or pair of states, begins to consider allying, it usually considers alternative partners, and these potential partners may also canvass their options. But once having settled on a particular alliance, statesmen tend to concentrate thenceforth on making it work, on realizing its potential, and to stop looking for alternatives, at least for the moment.

During the period under review, although management of existing alliances was a continuing activity, there were episodic outbursts of alliance formation during which the focus of attention was the establishment of new relationships rather than the nurturing of existing ones.

There were three such formation episodes in the 1879–1914 period. The first, 1879–81, had as its principal result the establishment of the Austro-German alliance, but it also produced a connection between these two countries and Russia. *Inter alia*, Germany also sounded out England. This episode may be considered a two-stage affair: Bismarck had in mind a majority coalition between Austria-Germany and either England or Russia, but he made sure of Austria before moving to the ultimate goal. The second episode, 1889–94, featured the formation of the Franco-Russian alliance between 1891 and 1894, but it also included Germany's cancellation of the Russian connection in 1890 and an unsuccessful German overture to Britain in 1889. The third formation period centered on Britain's efforts to escape from isolation in the face of a rising threat from Germany in the early 1900s. These efforts resulted in an alliance with Japan in 1902 and negotiation of the British *ententes* with France and Russia in 1904 and 1907.

Only the first two of the episodes are presented here as full-blown case studies. Thus our two cases of alliance formation are the Austro-German alliance of 1879, combined with the Three Emperors' Alliance of 1881, and (in Chapter 4) the Franco-Russian alliance of 1891–94. The Triple Alliance with Italy and the Anglo-French and Anglo-Russian *ententes* are treated briefly in Chapter 5 for purposes of comparison. Of course, there were other alliances that took shape during the period: Rumania's alliance with Austria and Germany in 1883; the Reinsurance Treaty between Germany and Russia in 1887; the Mediterranean Agreements signed by England, Austria, and Italy in 1887; and various agreements between Austria and Russia concerning the Balkans. These are less central cases; nevertheless, I draw on whatever evidence they generate that is relevant to the theory.

As we consider these cases, three questions will be foremost: Why did this particular alliance, and not some other one, form at this time? Why were the benefits and costs of the alliance divided as they were? and, What was the nature of the bargaining process by which these decisions were made?

The analysis entails estimating numerical values for all alliances that might have formed in each of the formation periods just mentioned—that is, the competitive and relevant possibilities. Such a value is simply the sum of the values placed on an alliance by each of its prospective members.

The most difficult problem for empirical analysis, in terms of the models presented in the previous chapter, is to devise some way of attributing such values plausibly. Plausibility is more important than precision; that is, a calculus that approaches but does not exceed the degree of precision by which statesmen might actually make their evaluations is better than one that tries to attach exact utilities and probabilities to all relevant factors. Thus we simply estimate, on a scale from 1 to 4, the value a state would reasonably place on each major component of alliance benefits and costs and then sum these values to get a total alliance value.

These estimates are obviously of the rough-and-ready variety, yet they can be more than mere hunches. For example, the deterrent and defense value of an alliance to a state is a function of the comparative capabilities and the degree of conflict among the state, its adversary, and its ally. Objective measures of capability are available, and degrees of conflict can be plausibly estimated, at least on the coarse scale suggested here. Minimally, deterrent and defense value is zero if the ally's capabilities are insufficient to fill the deficit between the one's own strength and the adversary's. Beyond this, if the ally can fill this deficit, deterrence and defense value is positive, increasing with higher levels of conflict with the adversary, or higher levels of likelihood that the adversary will attack.

Similarly, estimates of the costs and risks of alliance turn, in part, on a comparison of the ally's capabilities with those of its opponent and the degree of conflict between the two. The weaker the ally, the higher the cost of defending it, and the higher the conflict, the greater the likelihood that one will be called on to do so.

Other benefits and costs, such as the value of precluding the ally from allying elsewhere or of controlling the ally, are more difficult to estimate, but clues can be found in the general context, in the writings and utterances of statesmen, and in the interpretations of diplomatic historians.

Once values have been established in this manner for all competitive and relevant alliances, it is possible to explain why one formed and not another and why the values of the alliance were allocated as they were. An analysis of the bargaining process can also be undertaken. That is the procedure I follow in this chapter and the next. Because of the imprecision of measurements, it can hardly be considered a definitive test of the relevant theory, but it qualifies as a "plausibility probe," defined as a preliminary inquiry as to whether the theory appears plausible enough to warrant more rigorous testing.[1]

THE EUROPEAN SYSTEM, 1879

Resources

The European great powers in 1879 are deemed to be five: Great Britain, Germany, France, Russia, and Austria-Hungary. Italy, of borderline status, is omitted in order to simplify. The United States is omitted because it

Table 3-1. Percentage shares of military resources and potential among European great powers, 1880

	Iron-steel production	Energy consumption	Population	Defense appropriations	Defense personnel	Average
Great Britain	60.7	57.4	14.3	21.0	15.5	33.8
France	13.3	13.3	15.1	26.0	22.9	18.1
Russia	3.7	2.5	38.0	24.8	33.0	20.4
Germany	18.7	21.6	17.6	17.0	18.0	18.6
Austria-Hungary	3.5	5.2	15.1	11.0	10.4	9.0

SOURCE: Calculated from figures in Paul M. Kennedy, "The First World War and the International Power System," *International Security* 9 (Summer 1984), 7–41.
NOTE: Because of rounding, not all columns add to 100.

was not yet a full participant in world politics. Japan is omitted because it was active only in Asia.

An index of the potential military resources of these five states was constructed out of five components: iron and steel production, energy consumption, population, defense appropriations, and defense personnel. The last two are presumably good indicators of immediately available military power; the first three tap a country's longer-range mobilization potential. A composite index of resources was contrived by calculating, for each component, each country's percentage share of the *total for all five countries* (not the world total) and then averaging these shares across the five components. The resulting figure for each country may be taken as that country's share of the total military potential of the European great powers. A more complex index could have been devised, but considering the important nonmeasurables that any index must omit, this one is probably as valid as any.

Table 3-1 shows the composite resource index for 1880. The raw figures and percentage shares for each of the components, at ten-year intervals to 1914, are in Appendix A.

Great Britain was clearly the leading European power in 1880. It controlled about a third of great-power military resources and potential, a function of its substantial lead in industrialization. The shares of France, Russia, and Germany were about even at 18.1 percent, 20.4 percent, and 18.6 percent, respectively, though they were quite different in content. Russia's depended heavily on raw manpower, France's and Germany's more on industrial strength. Of these three, France was the weakest in overall economic resources, having lost the industrially rich provinces of Alsace and Lorraine in the war with Prussia-Germany in 1870–71. It compensated for this loss by maintaining rather large active military forces;

[82]

indeed, the French defense budget was the highest of all and half again as large as Germany's. Russia's defense expenditures were nearly as high as France's, thus offsetting the underdevelopment of its economy. Britain's highly developed economy was offset in the calculation of overall resource share by its low number of men under arms.

Austria-Hungary was obviously the weakest of the five, combining low levels of industrial production with relatively small forces in being. Its weaknesses on these hard indicators were accentuated by further weaknesses in its internal polity. One such weakness was the division of the empire into two parts after its defeat in the Austro-Prussian war of 1866. Another was the ethnic division among Germans, Magyars, and Slavs, with each group embracing different internal and external goals. The potential breakup of the empire was a source of political weakness during the entire period under review.

For our present purpose, what is worth noting is that Germany's resource share was slightly larger than France's and slightly smaller than Russia's. Thus Germany (give or take marginal percentages for error and for intangible factors not included in the index) could reasonably balance France or Russia separately but not together. Alliance with Austria was indispensable for a possible war against a combination of those two powers and would be useful in a war against Russia alone.

Conflicts and Common Interests

The primary axes of conflict in the late 1870s were those between Great Britain and Russia over their clashing imperial interests from Constantinople to China and between Austria and Russia over the Balkans. England and Austria thus had much in common and could usually be found working together, at least when the issue was Russian expansion in the Near East. Britain's direct interest there was maintaining Turkish control of the straits at Constantinople, mainly to inhibit the Russian Black Sea fleet's egress to the Mediterranean. Britain had no direct interest in the Balkans but supported Austria there out of a general strategic interest in blocking any enhancement of Russian power.

Germany was a satiated power, having accomplished national unification as a by-product of successful wars against Austria and France in 1866 and 1870–71. It had a latent though potentially serious conflict with France over the French desire to reclaim the lost provinces; this meant France and Germany could not be allies no matter how much their day-to-day relations might improve. As Bismarck, the great German chancellor, saw them, the primary interests of Germany were to keep France from acquiring allies and to preserve peace among the other powers—especially between Austria and Russia—so that they would have no need to seek an alliance with France. Beyond this, Germany had a strategic interest in preventing the conquest or breakup of Austria-Hungary so as to block a consequent increase in Russian power. For Bismarck, Austria's interests in the Balkans were "not worth the bones of a Pomeranian grenadier," but the maintenance of Austria as a great power was a vital German interest. There were no serious conflicts between Germany and Britain or between Germany and Russia. Since 1873 Germany, Russia, and Austria had been associated in a rather innocuous political grouping known as the Three Emperors' League, which expressed their common attachment to monarchical institutions. The German and Russian royal families were linked by marriage and by close personal relations. Friction between Germany and Russia occurred toward the end of the decade, however.

A complementary interest in resisting Germany and Austria existed between France and Russia as a consequence of the Franco-German enmity, the Austro-Russian conflicts, and the integral relationship between the two Central Powers. This tacit alignment was weak, however, because of mutual ideological distaste and the parties' differing particular interests. Between France and England there was colonial conflict, though it was less intense than that between England and Russia and less serious than it would become in the 1890s. Their rivalry in Africa and Asia was a source of irritation but not of deep conflict, and it was offset by the empathetic effects of similar political institutions and culture. On the whole, French and British relations were good.

This pattern of capabilities and interests in the system implied a loose set of alignments, a set of expectations about who was likely to support whom, to what extent, and in what contingencies. For instance, it was clear that Germany's strategic interest could not permit a serious defeat of Austria by Russia. The coincidence of British and Austrian interests in the Near East made them tacit allies against Russia. It was widely believed that in the event of a Russo-German war, France would enter on Russia's side. Common democratic institutions in France and Britain gave rise to expectations that these two countries would collaborate. But from 1871 to 1879 there were no formal alliances in the system.

THE AUSTRO-GERMAN ALLIANCE OF 1879

Background

The Austro-German alliance of 1879, first in the great system of alliances constructed by the German chancellor Otto von Bismarck, marked a new departure in the style of alliance making. Previously, military alliances had generally formed only during war or when war was imminent and did not outlast their immediate purpose. The Austro-German alliance was the first major alliance concluded in peacetime, and it was intended to be long-lasting. After an initial term of five years, it was renewed several times and did not dissolve until its defeat in World War I.

The traditional Russo-German friendship came under strain during the war scare of 1875, when Russia joined England in a formal warning to Germany intended to deter an attack on France, which was (erroneously) believed to be imminent. This incident impressed on Bismarck that the other European powers were determined to preserve a strong France. It also began a steady deterioration of Russo-German relations, marked by increasing personal hostility between Bismarck and the Russian chancellor, Alexander Gorchakov. *Pari passu*, Bismarck moved closer to Austria. Before the war scare, he had said that if it came to a choice of allies between Russia and Austria, he would prefer Russia; after the scare, the reverse was clearly the case.

German-Russian relations worsened further in the aftermath of the Russo-Turkish war of 1877–88 and the Congress of Berlin, which reduced Russia's gains from the war. It was a humiliating setback for the Russians, and they blamed Bismarck, as president of the congress, for masterminding it and for unfairly supporting the Austrian position on specific issues. They exaggerated Bismarck's bias, but that he was biased there is no doubt.

This crisis wrecked the Three Emperors' League by exacerbating the rivalry between Austria and Russia in the Balkans and by heightening suspicion between Germany and Russia. German-Russian relations continued to deteriorate after the congress. The Czar complained bitterly to the Kaiser that the German members of the various commissions set up to implement the congress's decisions were consistently voting against Russia. Was this how he was to be repaid for the "services" he had rendered in deterring Austrian assistance to France during the Franco-Prussian war? If Germany did not change its ways, it would forfeit the traditional Russian friendship. The consequences, he said, might be "disastrous" for both countries. The Russian press published violent denunciations of Bismarck along the same lines. Bismarck retaliated by orchestrating a press vendetta against Gorchakov, apparently hoping to force his removal. Russian troops began concentrating on the German border. There were rumors of alliance feelers between Russia and France. By March 1979 Bismarck had begun to think seriously about an alliance with Austria.

Alliance Negotiations

The Austrian government had hankered after an alliance with Germany since 1871, when the Germanophile, Count Andrássy, replaced the Germanophobe, Count Beust, as foreign minister. Andrássy was a Magyar, among whom hatred of Russia, the sponsor of Pan-Slavism, was strong. Andrássy had made several alliance overtures during the 1870s, each one politely rebuffed by Bismarck. Bismarck had tempered his rejections, however, with words calculated to sustain Austrian hopes.

Increasing friction between Germany and Russia increased the German sense of dependence on Austria and brought relations between the two countries steadily closer during the first six months of 1879. What finally convinced Bismarck of the need for a formal alliance was news of the impending retirement of Andrássy. The Austrian foreign minister's successor, Bismarck feared, would be less friendly toward Germany and might even negotiate an anti-German alliance with France and Russia. A powerful military-aristocratic clique in Austria still favored such an agreement as a means of reversing the verdict of 1866. In order to head off this possibility, an alliance had to be negotiated with Andrássy before he left office.

Bismarck and Andrássy met at Gastein on August 27–28, 1879. Bismarck suggested a general defensive alliance by which the two states would pledge to defend each other against any and all comers. Andrássy demurred: a general alliance meant Austria would be committed to aid Germany against France; such a commitment would antagonize France and, by extension, France's friend, England. Austria could not afford to jeopardize its friendship with England. Andrássy suggested instead a defensive alliance against Russia only. Having thus staked out their initial positions, the two men agreed to consult their sovereigns, and Andrássy consented to defer his resignation.

Andrássy had little difficulty with Emperor Francis Joseph, but Bismarck found Kaiser Wilhelm vigorously opposed to the alliance. The Kaiser was the uncle of the Russian Czar Alexander, he was personally fond of his nephew, and he placed a high value on the long tradition of friendship between the two monarchies. Consequently, he saw no need for an alliance with Austria against Russia and at first refused to give Bismarck permission to continue the negotiations. After further pressure, he finally agreed to discussions of a general defensive alliance against any or all attackers, that is, not directed against Russia and with no specific mention of Russia.

These instructions were, in effect, an injunction to Bismarck not to make any concessions from his opening proposal, and when he next met Andrássy, on September 22, he loyally defended this position. Andrássy, however, was adamant. Any general treaty, he insisted, would be interpreted as directed against France. This would antagonize England, France's friend and Austria's tacit ally. It would also provoke France to enter into an alliance with Russia. The only treaty acceptable to Austria, he again stated, was one directed only against Russia. He was willing, however, to include a pledge of "benevolent neutrality" in case of attack by some other power.

Bismarck made one last effort. He rose from his couch, moved close to Andrássy, and looking the Hungarian steadily in the eye, said: "All I can say is: consider carefully what you do. For the last time I urge you to give up your opposition." Then, in a threatening tone: "Accept my proposal, else . . . else I shall have to accept yours. But," he added with a laugh, "it will cause me a damned lot of trouble."[2]

The text the two men then agreed to was essentially the same as the draft Andrássy had prepared beforehand. It provided that if either party were attacked by Russia, the other would come to its assistance with all its forces and that neither would make a separate peace. If either were attacked by some other state, the other would observe benevolent neutrality. If such other state were assisted by Russia, however, the partners were obliged to assist each other with all their forces.[3]

Of course, this result directly contradicted the instructions Bismarck had received from his sovereign. There followed a monumental struggle between the two men, with Bismarck deploying all his formidable intellectual powers in support of the treaty and the Kaiser stubbornly maintaining his view that it was a mistake and a betrayal of a friend. Since Bismarck was making a case, he no doubt exaggerated; still, his memos to the Kaiser are remarkable statements of the kinds of considerations he considered relevant.

Russia could no longer be trusted, he warned. The oral reassurances of the Czar counted for little against the hostile tone of the Russian press and the continued threatening military activity. Even though the Czar's personal friendliness might be sincere, Alexander was unable to resist the machination of anti-German influences in Russian officialdom and the influence of "Pan-Slav revolutionaries." Therefore, it was necessary to have a defensive alliance with Austria in order to deter a Russian attack against either Germany or Austria. Such an alliance would not pose a threat to Russia, since it would merely reconstitute the old German Confederation, which Russia had not found threatening. Russia could even become a third party to the alliance, thereby resurrecting the Three Emperors' League of 1873.

The principal advantage of the alliance, however, Bismarck emphasized, was that it would preclude a possible combination of Austria, France, and perhaps Russia against Germany. Rumors of Russian feelers to France had been picked up by German diplomats in Paris. Austria would be tempted to join this combination if it were not assured of security against Russia by an alliance with Germany. Besides blocking this possibility, the alliance would bring England tacitly to Germany's side via the interests it shared with Austria in the Near East. (It would, in other words, not only prevent Germany's diplomatic isolation but create a majority coalition with Germany as its leader.) The alliance with Austria, with England as a silent partner, would even block a Franco-Russian alliance, since Russia could not count on France's help in a war against England.

Bismarck assured his master that alliance with Austria was highly preferable to alliance with Russia. Austria was the more dependable ally because it would be more dependent: "Austria needs us; Russia doesn't." Russia could survive a war without allies; Austria could not. Thus Germany could control Austria but not Russia. Moreover, Austria, as the more democratic state, would be less able than Russia, for internal political reasons, to renege on its commitment or realign. And the instability of Russian domestic politics, with its "revolutionary elements," made for uncertainty about Russian loyalty.

Finally, Bismarck argued that the cost of the alliance to Germany would be small, or nil, because its own interests demanded that Germany defend Austria even without an alliance. Of course, Bismarck also rehearsed Andrássy's reasons why Austria could not accept an alliance directed explicitly or implicitly against France.[4]

Bismarck's arguments failed to convince the eighty-two-year-old emperor, who made essentially three counterarguments, all of them weighty. First, the alliance would surely drive Russia and France together. Second, if there were to be an alliance, equity demanded that Austria promise to defend Germany against attack by France. Third, why couldn't the alliance with Austria be extended to include Russia, thus recreating the Three Emperors' League?[5]

To break the impasse, Bismarck had to resort to the threat of resignation, of the entire cabinet as well as himself. The Kaiser had to yield, because, as he put it, Bismarck was more necessary to the country than he. The treaty was signed on October 7, and ratifications were exchanged on October 17, 1879.

Assessment of the Bargaining Process and Outcome

From a reading of the explicit terms of the alliance, it might appear that Austria had got the best of the bargain. Germany was committed to defend it against its enemy, Russia, but Austria was not obliged to defend Germany against Germany's principal enemy, France. A closer analysis, however, including implicit benefits and costs, shows that the alliance's payoff was more equally divided. Although the terms of the alliance document appeared to favor Austria, Germany placed a greater inherent value on the alliance, whatever its terms.

Table 3-2. Inherent benefits and costs of Austro-German alliance of 1879

Benefits	Germany	Austria
Deterrence and defense against direct attack	2	3
Extended deterrence of attack on ally	1	1
Preclusion	3	1
Control of ally	2	1
Third-party effects	2	0
Offensive benefits	0	1
	10	7
Costs		
Commitment to ally	0	−2
Entrapment by ally	−1	0
Provocation (including counteralliance)	−2	−2
Reduced flexibility	−1	−1
Third-party effects	0	−2
	−4	−7
Net value	6	0

Benefits and Costs

Table 3-2 shows the inherent benefits and costs of the alliance to each party. These are not the values of the agreement the two countries actually negotiated in 1879 but the values of the alliance before bargaining about specific contract terms, operationalized as the values for a hypothetical agreement with exactly symmetrical commitments. In this case, that would have meant commitments to mutual defense against Russia *and* France, which happened to be Germany's initial proposal.

Each item in the table is given a positive or negative value between 1 and 4, and these scores are summed to produce an inherent alliance value for each party. These numbers may be taken to represent increments or decrements of security, or of "S" in the formula given in Chapter 2. This is a very crude procedure, admittedly, but it is about as precise as the ambiguity of the data will permit. At least this much precision is useful for analytical purposes. The numbers should be taken not as confident assertions of actual values but rather as heuristic aids for isolating, clarifying, and comparing incentives and disincentives and for giving them enough precision to fit them into a bargaining model.[6] They serve to illustrate the logic that a rational bargainer might employ in assessing the value of alliance proposals, even though he did not precisely quantify them.

Germany's direct deterrent and defense benefit from the alliance was rather low because there was little objective likelihood of an attack by Russia, and Germany could plausibly defend itself against such an attack without Austrian assistance. Still, there was the possibility of a combined attack by Russia and France, in which case Austrian assistance would be indispensable. Bismarck was sincerely concerned about the threatening behavior of Russia after the Congress of Berlin, even though he exaggerated the significance of these irritants. For him, the combination of Russian military power and threatening behavior gave the alliance with Austria at least some deterrent and defensive value.

With symmetrical commitments, as in Bismarck's opening proposal, the alliance would have also provided deterrence and defense against attack by France. A French attack without Russian help was unlikely and could be easily repulsed; on the other hand, a combined Franco-Russian offensive was a more serious contingency, for which Austrian assistance would be very helpful, even essential. Overall, a score of 2 for deterrence and defense against direct attack seems warranted.

Deterrence of a Russian attack on Austria—"extended deterrence," in today's jargon—was a lesser but still important incentive for Germany. Such an attack was more likely than a Russian attack on Germany, in view of the sharper and more tangible conflicts between Russia and Austria. Russia might well attack if it thought it could count on German inaction. Inaction was not likely, in light of the fairly obvious German strategic interest in defending Austria even without an alliance; nevertheless, an alliance would ensure against miscalculation. This was worth a score of 1 to Germany.

Bismarck's primary motive in negotiating an alliance with Austria was preclusive: to prevent Austria from allying elsewhere. Above all, Austria must be blocked from joining a coalition with France and Russia—his worst nightmare. Not that this was objectively likely: the military-aristocratic clique that still harbored thoughts of a war against Germany was in the minority. Bismarck reasoned, however, that if Austria were unsupported by Germany in a severe crisis with Russia, the internal political balance might shift and Austria might be driven by its weakness to make a deal with Russia about the Balkans, leading to an anti-German alliance with Russia and France. In short, Austria might bandwagon.[7] This would be a disaster for Germany almost comparable to a Russian conquest of Austria. What brought the preclusive motive to the fore and triggered the German decision for alliance was the announcement of Andrássy's pending retirement and his possible replacement with someone from the anti-German faction. Judging from the prominence of the preclusive theme in Bismarck's utterances and writings, it seems to rate a score of at least 3.

Bismarck also hoped to control Austria via the alliance. Austria would be the more dependent partner because of its more serious conflicts with Russia and its relative weakness. This dependence could be exploited. As Bismarck put it, in every alliance there was a horse and a rider; with

Austria he could be the rider.[8] Austria's dependence might be somewhat offset by its knowledge of Germany's strategic interest in its continued existence, which would reduce the credibility of German threats of non-support. Nevertheless, Austrian dependence would still be great enough for Germany to exert some control over Austrian policy and hence to forward one of Bismarck's primary aims: to prevent the outbreak of war between Russia and Austria. Control was a less prominent motive, on the record, than preclusion, but it was important enough to justify a score of 2.

The category of third-party effects is designed to catch alignment effects on states other than the prospective allies and their putative opponents. The most important such effect for Germany may have been to induce Russia to join in rehabilitating the Three Emperors' League. Indeed, some historians claim that this was Bismarck's chief motive in making the alliance with Austria. Russia, seeing that, with German backing, Austria could no longer be coerced, would join the other two in a fallback policy of accommodation. This view gains support from the fact that such an alliance took shape only two years later. A score of 2 seems justified.

Germany had no revisionist goals; therefore, it gained no offensive benefits from the alliance. Adding these scores yields a prospective benefit of the alliance for Germany of 10.

The costs of the alliance for Germany were small and can be dealt with more summarily. The cost of having to fulfill the commitment to Austria is set at zero because strategic interests dictated that Germany defend Austria even without an alliance. There was some entrapment risk entailed in the possibility that Austria, surer of German support, would be less accommodating in confrontations with Russia. The alliance would hardly provoke either France or Russia to attack, but it might well provoke a counteralliance. General policy flexibility for Germany would be reduced, but only slightly, since it would have the dominant voice in alliance policy.

These cost estimates sum to −4 and represent chiefly losses of German autonomy as a consequence of the alliance. Subtracting these losses from estimated benefits yields a net value to Germany of 6. Remember, however, that this is the estimated value of the alliance to Germany assuming symmetrical commitments—our benchmark for inherent value—not its value under the terms actually negotiated, which were less beneficial to Germany.

For Austria, the most important benefit from the alliance was deterrence and defense against a possible attack by Russia. Because of its military inferiority to Russia, it could defend itself only with German aid. Moreover, Austria's conflicts of interest with Russia in the Balkans made a Russian attack appear distinctly possible. The deterrent and defense value of the alliance had to be discounted somewhat by the likelihood that

German aid would be forthcoming even with no alliance; nevertheless, there was still considerable value in a formal commitment: to get the Germans committed morally and legally as well as by strategic interest and to clarify German intentions for the Russians. On a scale of 1 to 4, this deterrent and defense value appears to rate a score of 3.

The preclusive value of the alliance for Austria lay in blocking a possible German-Russian alliance. This possibility could not be ruled out, because of a long-standing tradition of cooperation between those two countries and the ties of blood and sentiment that existed between their ruling houses. Their lack of tangible common interests, however, made a formal alliance unlikely. Thus Austria's preclusive benefit could not have been greater than 1.

Likewise, extended deterrence was only a minor motive for Austria. Of course, an alliance would enhance deterrence of a Russian or French attack on Germany, but only marginally so, since Germany itself was powerful enough to deal with each of these countries separately. Only in the event of a Franco-Russian alliance would the addition of Austrian to German capabilities be critical. Thus extended deterrence value could not have been greater than 1.

The control factor had some value for Austria simply because it would enjoy more influence over German policy in alliance with Germany than not allied. As the weaker and more dependent partner, however, Austria was bound to be more subject to control than controlling. Hence, a score of 1 compared to Germany's 2.

Since Austria had some revisionist goals in the Balkans, it stood to benefit from potential German backing for them. These goals were rather inchoate at this time, however, so the offensive benefit of the alliance to Austria was no greater than 1.

The principal alliance cost for Austria was that of having to come to Germany's assistance in case of attack by Russia or by France. This cost was high, because it was not, as in Germany's case, offset by a prealliance strategic interest in defending the ally. Austria had no interest in defending Germany against Russia or France separately, because Germany was capable of defending itself in those contingencies. A commitment against France, as in Bismarck's initial proposal, would be particularly contrary to Austrian interests. Only in the case of a combined Franco-Russian attack would Austria have a strategic interest in helping Germany, but even then the interest would be problematical, for Austria might see its interest in bandwagoning with the dominant side, as Bismarck feared. Thus the alliance committed Austria, unlike Germany, to actions that might run contrary to its interests. The commitment was a more onerous obligation for Austria than for Germany, rating a cost of −2.

The alliance entailed little entrapment risk for Austria, because Germany was hardly likely to become more reckless or intransigent in dealing with France or Russia as a consequence of having allied with Austria. The provocation factor—the risk of provoking either attack or counteralliance—logically should be weighted about the same for Austria as for Germany: -2. Likewise, Austria probably would lose about the same freedom of action as Germany: -1.

Austria perceived the third-party effects of a symmetrical alliance as negative—the possible alienation of Britain if the alliance were directed against France as well as Russia. These two countries were on friendly terms; hence if France were antagonized, Britain might be as well and might withdraw its support of Austria on issues in the Balkans. This risk might have entailed a cost of -2.

Summing the benefits and costs for Austria yields a value of zero. Benefits of 7 are just offset by costs of -7. Again, bear in mind that this is not the value to Austria of the alliance that actually was negotiated; it is the value of a symmetrical mutual defense commitment, against both France and Russia, as in Germany's initial proposal. The overall joint value of this hypothetical agreement would have been 6, the entire value going to Germany.

After assessing the benefits and costs of the prospective alliance, the next step in the analysis is to establish the alternatives available to the parties. These alternatives included doing nothing, increasing armaments, or allying with someone else. The anticipated value of the best of the alternatives would set the parties' minimum acceptable terms in their negotiations with each other. Logically, the agreement ultimately negotiated would lie on the bargaining range bounded by these minimums. Within this range both parties could improve themselves over the best of their alternatives.

Alliance Alternatives

The bargaining process in making the Austro-German alliance in 1879 and the actual allocation of the costs and benefits of the alliance were affected by the alternative alliances available to the bargainers. The principal alternatives, for both parties, were agreements with England or Russia. Thus the next step in the analysis is to estimate values for these alternatives. To complete the picture, values for all other possible dyadic alliances between great powers are also estimated. This, of course, is no more than educated guesswork, with no claim to empirical accuracy, but it serves to make our model run in terms of the historical record and thus to provide at least a partial explanation of that record.

As before, we assume a five-state great-power system (leaving out Italy) and further assume that only two-party alliances can form. Table 3-3 lists the ten conceivable possibilities, including some negative ones. As in Table

Table 3-3. Values of potential alliance dyads, 1879

	Aggregate value	Inherent allocation	Allocation after bargaining (potential)
Austria-Germany	6	(0, 6)	(2.5, 3.5)
Austria-England	3	(2, 1)	(2, 1)
Germany-England	2	(1, 1)	(1, 1)
Germany-Russia	3	(2, 1)	(3, 0)
Austria-Russia	1	(0.5, 0.5)	(1, 0)
England-France	1	(0.5, 0.5)	(1, 0)
Austria-France	0	(0, 0)	(0, 0)
Russia-France	0	(0, 0)	(0, 0)
Russia-England	−2	(−1, −1)	(−1, −1)
Germany-France	−4	(−2, −2)	(−2, −2)

2-3, the apportionment of alliance values is shown in three columns, the first listing aggregate values, the second, inherent values—operationalized as values for a symmetrical commitment for mutual defense—and the third listing the potential allocation after bargaining.

These potential alliances may now be classified according to the three-fold scheme presented in Chapter 2. Germany-France and Russia-England are infeasible because of the high degree of conflict between their members: any alliance would require settling these conflicts at costs greater than any conceivable gains. The only competitive alliance is Austria-Germany: it dominates all other combinations involving these two states. Two of these others—Austria-England and Germany-Russia—are only marginally noncompetitive and are directly relevant to the bargaining between Austria and Germany: what Germany or Austria could get in these alliances sets the minimums acceptable to them in their own negotiations. The terms of the Austro-German alliance will fall somewhere within a range bounded by what each could expect in alliance with England or Russia, respectively—that is, 2 for Austria and 3 for Germany. Two other possibilities—England-France and Russia-France—are also relevant but only in the second-order sense that the values available to England and Russia in these alliances help establish the maximum terms England or Russia might offer Austria or Germany, respectively. The following discussion attempts to justify these evaluations and classifications for Germany's and Austria's alliance alternatives.

Germany's alliance alternatives. An alliance with Britain would have enhanced German security against Russian and/or French attack. Anglo-Russian hostility made a British commitment against Russia quite credible, and France would hardly dare attack Germany with a hostile Britain at its shoulder. These benefits had to be discounted, however, by the questionable capability of Great Britain in land warfare. Moreover, the costs to Germany of a commitment to Britain were likely to be substantial. Since Britain was relatively secure in its home islands, the principal benefit it would expect from any alliance would be assistance in defense of the empire, especially India, and of approaches to the empire, as at the Straits and Constantinople; but the German strategic interest in defending the British Empire was virtually nil. Further, the coincidence of British and Austrian interests in the Near East meant Britain could be counted on to support Austria against Russia even without an alliance. Finally, an English alliance would widen the breach with Russia and foreclose indefinitely Bismarck's aim of a rapprochement with Russia. These asymmetries in capabilities and interests reduced the value to Germany of alliance with England. Nevertheless, the Germans made several vague alliance overtures during the period under review. The first, in 1876, was answered favorably by Benjamin Disraeli, the British Prime Minister, but not followed up by Bismarck. In the following year Bismarck asked London whether the British would be benevolently neutral in the event of a war between Germany and a Franco-Russian coalition. The disappointing British response was to promise moral support to Germany.

In September 1879, while negotiating the treaty with Austria, Bismarck posed virtually the same question. Count Munster, the German ambassador in London, was instructed to inquire what England's policy would be in the event of a Russo-German war. Disraeli told Munster that, in return for German support of British interests in the Near East, "we will guarantee that France shall not move, in case such a policy were to involve Germany in a conflict with Russia. We will in that case keep France quiet, you may depend upon us."[9] Curiously, this response did not seem to satisfy Bismarck, who noted on Munster's report, "Is that all?" He told Munster the English statement was inadequate; unless tangible English aid were certain, Germany would have to avoid a war with Russia in the Near East. He instructed the ambassador not to raise the matter again.

The motives for the German probe, and the lack of follow-through, have puzzled historians. The consensus is that Bismarck sincerely wanted an agreement with Britain but lost interest when the Russians, the day after the Munster-Disraeli conversation, indicated interest in rehabilitating the Three Emperors' League.[10] Bismarck preferred this to the alliance with Britain, despite the recent friction; consequently, he simply dropped the latter.

It seems that Germany could have had an alliance with Britain on the minimal basis of German support of British interests in the Near East in return for a promise of British deterrence of France in case of a German-Russian war. The principal benefit for Germany would have been insurance against a joint attack by France and Russia, Bismarck's greatest fear.

The chief cost would have been the risk of being pulled into an Anglo-Russian war over Turkey or control of the Straits. Both the benefits and the costs were substantial, and it is hard to say which would have been the greater. Apparently, Bismarck thought the benefits would be greater; otherwise he would not have made the offer. His tacit retraction in favor of a Russian connection is understandable: with that he could get his insurance against a two-front war with no risk of entrapment in a Near Eastern war.

It is not clear whether Bismarck considered the British connection an alternative to the Austrian alliance or a supplement to it. Nevertheless, it would have been an option available to Germany if the Austrian negotiations had broken down. In line with Bismarck's own lack of enthusiasm for it, we give it a value of 1. If it was worth about the same to Britain, its aggregate value would have been 2.

Another plausible German alternative was a defensive alliance with Russia. These two countries had a long tradition of military collaboration, dating back to the Napoleonic Wars. There were no direct territorial conflicts between them. The recent friction was essentially an emotional hostility spiral, fed by the press and personal animosity between the two heads of government, rather than a conflict over substantive issues.

The greatest benefit to be obtained by alliance with Russia was preclusion of the dreaded Franco-Russian combination. On this point, it was clearly superior to the connection with Austria, which positively risked provoking this combination, as the Kaiser had pointed out. But a Russian alliance would risk a different counteralliance, almost as dangerous, among France, Austria, and England. With British support, France and Austria might feel capable of prosecuting a joint revanchist war against Germany. Another risk was that of entrapment in a Russian quarrel with Britain. On the point of control, alliance with Russia was clearly inferior to alliance with Austria: Russia would be less dependent than Austria by virtue of its strength and its French alternative. The alliance with Austria gave Bismarck not one ally but two: England came along informally via its tacit alignment with Austria. Alliance with Russia would give Germany one ally and one formidable new enemy: England. The behavior of Bismarck shows, however, that he placed a considerable value on alliance with Russia, more than on alliance with England, although less than on the connection with Austria. A value of 2 seems plausible, as does a somewhat lesser value of 1 for Russia, and hence an aggregate value of 3.

Austria's alliance alternatives. In principle, Austria could have allied with France, Britain, or Russia or with some combination of these three. An alliance with Britain would have been an anti-Russian combination. It would have contributed to Austrian security and perhaps prospects for expansion, but its value was limited by common interests: Britain was likely to support Austrian interests in the Balkans even without an alliance. It would have provided some deterrence and defense against Russian attack but not as much as the alliance with Germany. It would also have given some security against the remote possibility of attack by Germany, but it would not have been strong enough for offensive action against Germany. It was worth perhaps 2 on our scale from 1 to 4. It would have been less valuable to Britain, perhaps 1, for an aggregate value of 3.

An alliance with France would have been offensive, with both parties aiming to overturn the results of their losing wars with Prussia. The alliance would not have been strong enough for this purpose, however, although it might have served to defend against a German attack. But it would not have sufficed to defend against a German-Russian combination, which might well have taken shape in response. Score: 0.

An alliance or at least rapprochement with Russia was not out of the question for Austria, in spite of their conflicts in eastern Europe. The two states had shown a capacity to negotiate settlements of these conflicts or at least to put them aside temporarily. Bismarck had advocated a grand settlement between the two, involving a partition of the Ottoman Empire-in-Europe. With Russia, indeed, the Austrian option was more precisely accommodation than alliance. An aggregate value of 1—0.5 each for Austria and Russia—seems plausible.

The best Austrian alternative, we conclude, was an alliance with Britain. Thus we may take its value to Austria, 2, as the marker for Austria's minimum acceptable terms in its alliance with Germany.

Bargaining Process

In the estimation of these minimums, the column in Table 3-3 labeled "allocation after bargaining" is more relevant than the "inherent allocation" column. This is because Austrian or German bargainers would estimate the values of their available alternatives in terms of what they could actually negotiate with the alternative partners. This might be more or less than their inherent value of these alliances. In the case of their alternative alliances with England, the inherent and bargained values happen to be identical for both the Anglo-Austrian and Anglo-German alliances. For England, the bargained value for both is 1, because it can get at least this in a hypothetical negotiation with France. England will demand this much in any negotiation with Austria or Germany, leaving values of 2 and 1, respectively, to the latter.

In the case of the Russian alternative, however, Austria and Germany could count on bettering their inherent values in negotiation because of

Russia's weak bargaining position. Its position is weak because it has no good alternatives. The French alternative has not yet become practical politics. Thus, in any bargaining with Russia, Russia's minimum will be the value of the status quo of no alliance, assumed here to be zero. Germany or Austria, therefore, since they have the very good alternative of alliance with each other, should be able to force Russia's payoff down nearly to zero, even though its inherent value of alliance with them is greater than zero. Thus, in the table, Austria and Germany get the entire aggregate value of any alliance with Russia, 1 and 3, respectively.

In particular, the value of 3—what Germany could expect to get in an alliance with Russia—is Germany's theoretical minimum payoff in alliance with Austria. Austria's theoretical minimum is its expected payoff of 2 in its alternative alliance with England, which exceeds what could be expected in alliance with Russia.

The next step in the analysis is to estimate the empirical minimum positions of Germany and Austria in their actual negotiations. This is not easy and of course involves some guesswork. Take the case of Germany. Given Germany's high inherent valuation of the alliance, almost any terms would have been acceptable. For example, merely a German unilateral guarantee of Austria against Russia, with no reciprocal commitment by Austria, might have satisfied Bismarck's aims of preclusion and control. Somewhat more favorable to Germany would have been a bilateral agreement against Russia, but without the Austrian pledge of neutrality in a Franco-German war. We can plausibly take the latter as the closest practical approximation to Germany's theoretical minimum of 3—the expected value of the alternative alliance with Russia.

We have estimated that the best alternative available to Austria was alliance with England. Austria's practical minimum in the negotiations with Germany would have been a set of terms approximately equal to Austria's value for this alternative, set at 2 in Table 3-3. It is clear that the initial German proposal for a general defense alliance against all comers had less value for Austria than the English alternative—indeed, it was no better than, or perhaps worse, than no alliance at all. It was below Austria's minimum and hence outside the bargaining range. What might have been minimally acceptable to Austria was this proposal, plus some form of English accession to it, perhaps along the lines discussed by Disraeli and Munster. This would have erased the Austrian fear of antagonizing England by the tacit commitment against France. We may assume this to be the approximate Austrian minimum, the other end-point of the bargaining range.

Figure 3-1 depicts the salient proposals and possible outcomes. The origin represents the status quo, valued at zero for both parties. Points Ma and Mg are the minimally acceptable terms for Austria and Germany,

Figure 3-1. Austro-German alliance negotiations, 1879

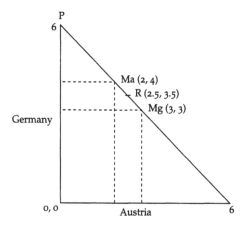

respectively, roughly equivalent to their prospective payoffs in their best alternative alliances. Ma gives Austria a payoff of 2 and Germany one of 4; Mg gives each a payoff of 3. MaMg is the Pareto-optimal line, whereon both parties do better than their minimums and any improvement for one party is necessarily at the other's expense. It delimits the bargaining range whereon any mutually beneficial and efficient agreement must fall. The initial German proposal for a general treaty of mutual defense is at point P. Despite the symmetry of its terms, it is highly favorable to Germany and unfavorable to Austria—perhaps even negatively valued by Austria. Its value for Austria would have been improved, perhaps enough to be just acceptable, if Britain had been persuaded to join. Thus, if Bismarck had carried the British negotiations to a conclusion, a bargain might have been available with Austria just at Ma, Austria's minimum. That Bismarck did not do this, but let the English talks drop, may well be explained by his recognition that he did not have the bargaining power to get an agreement at Austria's minimum.[11]

The Nash theorem predicts that agreement will take place at the midpoint of the bargaining range, which would be 2.5 for Austria and 3.5 for Germany, represented by point R in Figure 3-1.* This is a fair evaluation of the agreement actually reached: a mutual defense agreement against Russia, with Austria promising only benevolent neutrality in case of a French attack on Germany. Although the explicit terms favored Austria, this was more than offset by the greater German inherent value for the alliance.

* The joint utility surplus over the parties' minimums is 1; a division of 0.5, 0.5 maximizes the product of the payoffs.

[99]

The same prediction can be made by reasoning from bargaining power. At points "higher" than R, say, close to the Austrian minimum, Austria gains very little and Germany a great deal. Thus Austria can more credibly threaten to terminate negotiations. Germany makes concessions rather than terminate, because it still has much to gain even when the terms favor Austria. Germany stops conceding at R, because "below" R the terms become so favorable to Austria that Austria's threat to stop negotiating is no longer credible but Germany's threat becomes more so. In other words, the motive for moving toward the midpoint and for stopping at that point, that is, the explanation for the Nash solution, can be located simply in the parties' comparative value for the alliance, which determines their relative bargaining power. In this case, Austria was able to exploit Germany's higher value for the alliance to get terms favorable to its own interests. Not that there was a great deal of struggle; Bismarck simply recognized he was outgunned and capitulated rather easily.

It is worth repeating that the two elements in bargaining power—inherent value and alternatives—have different effects on the bargaining. Alternatives establish the bargaining range, whereas comparative inherent value influences where within the range proposed terms will fall. In this case, Austria's alternatives were somewhat inferior to Germany's, skewing the bargaining range in Germany's favor. But its lesser inherent need for the alliance provided Austria with the leverage to move the final terms closer to Germany's minimum.

One or two other descriptive points about these negotiations are worth making. There was not much conflict or struggle about details. There was no extended series of concessions and counterconcessions. There were simply two general proposals for mutual defense commitments, one drafted by each bargainer, and one of these drafts, Andrássy's, was the final choice. Moreover, there were no explicit threats. Each negotiator might have threatened to break off negotiations and perhaps to choose an alternative ally, but neither did so.

These characteristics of the bargaining may be attributed to two characteristics of the situation: (1) the high salience and moral attraction of formal equality, amounting perhaps to a tacit rule, and (2) the large amount of common interest relative to conflict. The terms were not politically equitable in that only Austria's, not Germany's, principal enemy was to be defended against, but at least they were equal in the formal sense that the same commitments were undertaken vis-à-vis Russia. Equal commitments are "salient" in Schelling's sense: it is difficult to see any other terms around which the parties' expectations can converge to produce a determinate outcome.[12] They are also "fair."

The parties also had a strong common interest in reaching some agreement, regardless of its specific terms. Thus they were not inclined to engage in tough bargaining by making only small concessions or by making threats. Threats to ally elsewhere would have risked destroying the common interest. Moreover, the parties were sufficiently aware of each other's alternatives that they did not have to be flaunted.

Finally, although the parties did not misperceive each other's direct communications in the bargaining, they did somewhat misperceive each other's alternatives. Bismarck, in particular, exaggerated the value to Austria of an alliance with France and Russia and thus overestimated Austria's minimum position. To a lesser extent, Andrássy exaggerated Germany's Russian option. The effect, of course, was to narrow the bargaining range and to shift relative bargaining power somewhat in Austria's favor.

THE THREE EMPERORS' ALLIANCE OF 1881

Background

The second stage in the alliance formation episode of 1879–81 involved the addition of a third party to the Austro-German combination. The two candidates were Great Britain and Russia. Because they were the most attractive alternative allies for Austria and Germany, respectively, during their negotiations with each other, it was only natural that these two should be considered the best candidates for alliance expansion once the core members had reached agreement.

Bismarck had opened tentative negotiations with both governments even before concluding his deal with Andrássy. The overture to England has been described above. Bismarck preferred Russia to Britain, largely for ideological reasons—the instability and unreliability of parliamentary regimes. Possibly, his probe to Britain was intended to ascertain whether a fallback alternative existed there in case his preferred Austro-German-Russian combination failed to work. The British reaction was enough to tell him that such an alternative did exist, without any need for a response on his part. He simply put the information in reserve while he pursued the opportunity with Russia.

Negotiations

The negotiations with Russia were initiated by Russia. The Russian move was apparently precipitated by rumors of an impending Austro-German alliance. The initial Russian objective was an agreement with Germany alone. Its chief motivation was to deter Austrian resistance to a Russian attempt to establish preponderance in Bulgaria and to preclude Britain from having an ally in case of a struggle over the Straits.[13] A secondary motive was to neutralize or weaken the new Austro-German combination, which the Russians suspected was directed against them. By systemic logic, Russia should have turned straightaway to France as a counterpoise. But France was still an ideological pariah in Russian eyes and too unstable to be relied on. Consequently, for Russia it was a case of "if you can't lick them, join them." Lacking the means to balance its Germanic neighbors, Russia had only one option: to conciliate them. Common political values and the traditional friendship with Germany helped make this course palatable.

Peter Saburov, the Russian ambassador in Constantinople, visited Bismarck on September 26, carrying assurances from the Czar of Russia's good and peaceable intentions. Bismarck responded cordially and soon broached the idea of rehabilitating the League of the Three Emperors. He explained that his negotiation with Austria was intended as a first step toward that objective. He had wanted to "dig a ditch" between Austria and the western powers, by reassuring it of German assistance in the event of Russian attack. With Austria thus reassured, it would be possible to move to the second act, the negotiation of a three-party agreement. Saburov said the Czar would not be opposed to this provided it was profitable to Russia.[14]

After this conversation Bismarck wrote out a draft of a new agreement. Its essential provisions were that Germany would remain neutral in the event of an Anglo-Russian war and would prevent any other state from aiding Britain; likewise, Russia would be neutral in a Franco-German war and prevent any other state from aiding France. In addition, Russia would respect the territorial integrity of Austria, provided Austria did not seek to expand in the Near East beyond its rights under the Treaty of Berlin.[15]

Bismarck insisted on including Austria, arguing that if it were left out, it would become distrustful and move toward the western powers. Saburov expressed reluctance but did not flatly reject the idea, apparently sensing that he could make good use of it in further negotiations.

After a three-month recess Saburov reopened negotiations in Berlin on January 20. He brought with him a new demand, which the Czar had insisted on: German support for Russian control of the Straits, or at least for the closure of the Straits. Bismarck admitted that this was a legitimate objective but linked it to the inclusion of Austria: for geographical reasons, Germany could do little by itself to prevent the violation of the Straits by England, but Austria was in a position to threaten Turkey and force it to fulfill its obligation of neutrality.

No doubt the Russians themselves had had such a linkage in mind. Nevertheless, Saburov withheld the quid pro quo: his instructions did not contemplate the inclusion of Austria, he said; therefore, he would have to consult the Czar. Before leaving, however, he gave Bismarck a draft of a preliminary agreement à trois, which included the new Russian demand.[16]

Bismarck approved of these terms and added a provision for resolving disputes between any two members by mediation of the third.

When Saburov returned to Berlin in early March, he was able to convey his government's acquiescence to the inclusion of Austria. The Russians had recognized its value for achieving their aims at the Straits; for the time being, they would soft-pedal their quarrels with Austria in the Balkans. The German and Russian governments were now in accord on the general outlines of the projected agreement. The next task was to persuade Austria. But when Bismarck undertook to do this, it turned out not to be easy. Having just acquired the protection of Germany against Russia, on very favorable terms, the Austrians could see no benefit for them in now admitting the enemy into the club. It could prove costly by alienating England, Austria's informal ally and Russia's enemy. Austria had opted for a policy of confrontation of Russia rather than conciliation; Bismarck was asking now for a virtual reversal of Austrian policy. At least so thought Baron Haymerle, the successor to Andrássy as Austria-Hungary's foreign minister. He rejected Bismarck's overture, saying Austria's policy was "the permanent blocking of Russia."[17] Instead, he proposed bringing England formally into the Austro-German alliance. Bismarck would have none of this; he was no longer interested in an agreement with Britain now that Russia had shown itself amenable. Any agreement with England, Russia's inveterate enemy, would be sure to torpedo the developing rapprochement with Russia.

The situation was transformed by the British election of April 1880, which brought to power the fire-eating Liberal, William Gladstone. Gladstone favored a tough policy toward Turkey, to end the Ottoman government's persecution of its Christian subjects, particularly in the Balkans, a policy that ran parallel to Russia's. Indeed, the English and Russian governments began cooperating in bringing pressure on the Turks, through a joint naval demonstration. Although Gladstone insisted on calling this a manifestation of the "Concert of Europe," it appeared to the Austrians as a veritable reversal of alliances. Indeed, Saburov had warned that continued Austrian intransigence might persuade the Czar to come to terms with England rather than the Central Powers.[18] The political change in England gave a decided boost to Russia's bargaining power in the negotiations, just as it weakened Austria's.

Haymerle immediately saw that he could no longer count on English support in resisting Russian attempts to coerce Turkey. Nor could he depend on German assistance, since Bismarck had said repeatedly that the Austro-German alliance was operative only for an actual Russian attack on Austria. The developing friendly relations of Russia with both Germany and England raised the specter of Austrian isolation. The only viable alternative seemed to be an accommodation with Russia.

Thus Haymerle was more flexible at a meeting with Bismarck on September 4 and 5, 1880. He admitted that, without British support, Austria could no longer resist Russian attempts to unify and control the state of Bulgaria; therefore, he would concede these Russian aims in return for Russian recognition of other Austrian interests in the Balkans. The German chancellor responded enthusiastically, suggesting an agreement that would give Russia security at the Straits and control of a unified Bulgaria,[19] in return for an Austrian free hand to annex Bosnia-Herzegovina. Haymerle agreed with this in principle but advanced a number of additional conditions that amounted to Austrian dominance in Rumania and the western Balkans. He demanded the annexation of the Sanjak of Novipazar as well as Bosnia-Herzegovina and a free hand for military action against Serbia.[20] Moreover, the German-Austrian alliance must not be weakened; indeed, Haymerle wanted it extended to cover an Austro-Russian military clash over Rumania.[21] Bismarck reacted noncommittally to this last proposal. At the Austrian's suggestion, he agreed to sound out the Russians and to prepare a draft agreement.

Bismarck and Saburov, who had now been appointed Russian ambassador to Germany, prepared a new draft in November. Essentially, they put the finishing touches on the agreement they had already reached the previous February. They retained the provision for mutual neutrality in case of war with a fourth power, mediation by the third party in case of disputes between any two signatories, recognition of Austrian interests in Bosnia-Herzegovina, and closure of the Straits to all warships. There was to be no modification of the territorial status quo in Turkey's European possessions without prior agreement, and no troops were to be sent into Turkey, Rumania, Serbia, or Montenegro without such agreement.

Bismarck sent the new draft to Haymerle and Emperor Franz Joseph in January 1881, along with a covering letter from Kaiser Wilhelm emphasizing Austrian benefits and deemphasizing Russia's. But Haymerle had misgivings. The mediation provision, he felt, might be used by Bismarck to escape his obligations under the alliance with Austria. It seemed to codify the underlying political effect of the agreement—the loss of Austria's position as the sole friend of Germany. On Bosnia, Russia was promising only to respect the status quo, Austrian occupation, withholding approval of annexation. So Haymerle rejected these two points and maintained his previous demand to annex the Sanjak. He also renewed his demand to extend the German commitment under the Austro-German alliance to cover Rumania. Bismarck refused any alteration of the alliance treaty but agreed to sign a declaration that the new treaty did not supersede it.[22]

Subsequent negotiations were marked by a steady Austrian retreat, under brutal pressure from Bismarck. In April, for example, he threatened to conclude a treaty with Russia without Austria.[23] Haymerle gradually gave way on all points except his demand for the right to annex Bosnia-Herzegovina and the Sanjak. He tried to make a last stand on this issue, but Russia held firm. Haymerle had to be satisfied with a separate protocol in which Austria reserved the right to annex these territories. The treaty was signed in Vienna on June 18, 1881.

Assessment of the Bargaining Process and Outcome

The Three Emperors' Alliance was a different kind of agreement from the Austro-German alliance. Thus it is somewhat misleading to say it was an expansion of the membership of the latter. The Austro-German treaty was a pact of mutual defense assistance; the Three Emperors' treaty was essentially a pact of neutrality: each member promised to remain neutral if any of their number went to war with a fourth great power; they would also attempt to localize the conflict.[24] Note also that the pact was potentially an aggressive as well as a defensive instrument. There were no limiting conditions concerning the circumstances of the outbreak of war: the *casus foederis* would come into force whenever a party "should find itself at war with a fourth Great Power."

The framers of the document repeatedly referred to this core commitment as a "guarantee against coalitions": it guaranteed each of its signers against an adversary coalition led by its principal opponent: for Germany, France; for Russia, England; for Austria, Italy. At Russia's insistence, the neutrality and localization commitments applied also to a war against Turkey, even though Turkey was not considered a great power. This gave Russia a free hand against Turkey, although it applied only if the three parties had reached a previous agreement regarding the results of the war.

Beyond these core commitments, the remainder of the document had to do mostly with side payments to Russia and Austria in the Near East, with Russia getting the lion's share. The most important of these was German and Austrian recognition of the principle of the closure of the Straits to all warships and their agreement to coerce Turkey to enforce this principle. Germany and Austria also agreed to the eventual unification of Bulgaria and Eastern Rumelia, which were thought to be potential Russian clients.

Technically, there was no contradiction between the Austro-German alliance and the new Three Emperors' agreement, since the former was entirely defensive and the latter's obligation of neutrality applied to relations with states outside the three. By and large, the two treaties spoke to different sets of interests. There was plenty of room, however, for contradiction and tension between the political implications of the two agreements. The Three Emperors' treaty was bound to increase Russian expectations

Table 3-4. Benefits and costs of Three Emperors' Alliance, 1881

Benefits	Austria	Germany	Russia
Preclusion	0.5	2	1
Reduced conflict (between partners)	0.5	1	0.5
Control of ally	0	1	0
Offensive effects	0	0	1
Ideology	0.5	0.5	0.5
Side payments received	0.5	0	1
Total benefits	2	4.5	4
Costs			
Effects on previous alignments	−1	0	1
Side payments paid	−0.5	−1	0
Lost flexibility	−0.5	−0.5	−1
Total costs	−2	−1.5	0
Net value	0	3	4

of German political support in the Balkans and on the Straits issue, expectations that would certainly clash with Austrian expectations. There was no escaping that the Austro-German alliance, considered in its political as well as its military implications, had been weakened by the weakening of the German commitment.

Benefits and Costs

Table 3-4 shows how the various benefits and costs of the Three Emperors' Alliance might have been valued at the time of its signing in 1881. This accounting is intended only to illustrate that the agreement yielded substantial security value to both Russia and Germany and hardly any to Austria. It also shows roughly the constituents of each party's value. Since it was in essence a neutrality agreement, its primary value and significance was in precluding each party from allying with the other parties' principal adversaries. Germany gained the most on this dimension, because a Russian alliance with France would be a more serious setback for it than an Anglo-German or Anglo-Austrian alliance would be for Russia, or a Russian-Italian one for Austria. The Russians gained more in blocking England from acquiring allies, however, than Austria did in isolating Italy. The agreement also reduced conflict among the parties themselves, somewhat more to the benefit of Germany than to the others because of the high German stake in the maintenance of peace. But Russia and Austria also gained from the general reduction in their hostility level. Russia, especially, could feel that it had greatly eased the threat of an aggressive Austro-German combination against it.

Germany was also the principal gainer on the dimension of control of allies; the formal addition of Russia as a contender for its support gave

Germany a powerful means of coercing Austria. The agreement had some offensive value for Russia, because the article about the Straits clearly contemplated a possible Russian war against Turkey. All three parties presumably shared equally in the psychopolitical value of monarchical solidarity. The Russians got the best of the side payments in the promise of support on the Straits and on the unification of Bulgaria. The side payments to Austria on Bosnia and the Sanjak were (generously) worth no more than half of Russia's. Germany got no side payments.

On the cost side of the ledger, the agreement had a serious negative effect for Austria in its alliance with Germany: no longer was Austria assured of support from Germany in political disputes with Russia. The political halo of the alliance had contracted; more clearly than before, the German commitment was restricted to the military *casus foederis*—a direct Russian attack on Austria. To a lesser degree the agreement would weaken Austria's relations with Britain, although this damage might be temporarily in remission during Gladstone's ministry. The effects on the Austro-German alliance were positive for Germany in enhancing its capacity to control Austria. Russia also gained substantially through the increased dominance of Germany in the Austro-German relationship.

Germany and Austria shared the costs of the side payments to Russia, but Germany bore the brunt in the dangerous commitment to support Russia on the Straits issue. All three of the partners lost diplomatic flexibility: Germany and Austria gave up their English option, and Russia sacrificed its French one—a more significant cost for Russia than for the others.

Alliance Alternatives

In order to explain this outcome, it is necessary to glance at the alternatives available to the parties. The following list includes the potential three-and two-member alliances that are estimated to have been competitive or at least relevant to the bargaining.*

Austria-Germany-Russia	7	(0, 3, 4)
Austria-Germany; Germany-Russia	5	(−2, 2, 5)
Austria-Germany-England	0	(0, 0, 0)
France-Russia	0	(0, 0)

*To simplify, the values are estimated as they were or might have been after bargaining, omitting their inherent prebargaining values. The latter, for the Three Emperors' Alliance, would have been slightly less favorable to Russia and more so to Germany, and about the same for Austria. In other words, Russia gained and Germany lost marginally in the bargaining process, chiefly via the side payment on the Straits issue. Note also that the estimates are after Gladstone's accession. The election of the British Liberals in 1880 increased the value of the alliance for Austria and Germany and reduced it for Russia.

The only competitive alternative to the Austria-Germany-Russia combination was a separate deal between Germany and Russia, which would have severely disadvantaged Austria and advantaged Russia, and was less attractive to Germany, compared to the tripartite deal that was actually negotiated. France-Russia was noncompetitive but relevant to the bargaining since it established the minimum terms acceptable to Russia. It was still blocked by ideological prejudice, despite its obvious systemic merit; hence its low valuation for both parties. With Gladstone in power, Austria-Germany-England had depreciated in value since 1879, yet it was relevant because it established Germany's minimum in bargaining with Russia. These alternatives established minimums of zero for Russia and Germany and −2 for Austria in their negotiations with one another.

Bargaining Process

The outcome of the bargaining, so lopsided to Austria's disadvantage, may be explained by Austria's dependence on Germany on all three of the dimensions of alliance dependence: military weakness compared to the adversary (Russia), conflict with the adversary, and alliance alternatives. The most desirable alternative for Austria was simply a return to the status quo of the Austro-German alliance, dropping the project of a deal with Russia. But if Austria had held out for this, Germany and Russia probably would have made a bilateral agreement, which would have been very costly to Austria via a weakening of its ties to Germany. Bismarck, who did all the negotiating with Austria, including pressing Russia's demands, explicitly threatened such a separate bargain.[25] Even though he preferred to include Austria, the bilateral deal with Russia had a substantial positive value for him which served as his minimum payoff in negotiating with Austria. In the illustration, this value of 2, compared to Austria's minimum of −2, enabled Bismarck to push the Austrian payoff to zero and raise his own to 3.

The stance of Great Britain was a crucial determinant of Austria's bargaining power vis-à-vis Germany and Russia. With the Tories in power under Disraeli, Austria could count on unflinching British support against Russia on almost any issue in the Balkans. Hence, before the British election of April 1880, Haymerle was able to resist the German-Russian pressures. But it turned out that the British role as "sleeping partner" in the Austro-German combination was a function of party politics. After Gladstone and the Liberals came to power in 1880, the partnership dissolved (if only temporarily), dramatically increasing Austria's dependence on Germany. Haymerle was then forced to accept virtually all the German-Russian program.

[4]

The Franco-Russian Alliance
of 1891–1894

According to strict systemic logic, the Franco-Russian alliance should have followed directly after the Austro-German alliance in 1879. France had a serious conflict with Germany, and Russia likewise with Austria, and the alliance of the Central Powers was directed explicitly against Russia and implicitly against France. The theory of the balance of power says alliances breed counteralliances. Yet it took fifteen years for this counteralliance to form. Part of the reason, no doubt, was the diplomatic virtuosity of Bismarck. Bismarck "beat the system" by taking one his opponents into his own "system" and isolating the other. Only when his successors "cut the wire to St. Petersburg" in 1890 did the Franco-Russian alliance become practical politics.

Other factors also contributed to the delay. There was strong ideological repugnance between the French republic and the Russian autocracy, as well as ideological and dynastic kinship between Russia and the two Central Powers. The Russian leaders, especially the Czar, had little confidence in the reliability of French policy, given the frequent cabinet changes. The particular interests of the two countries were quite different: France had little interest in the Balkans or the Straits, and Russia could not care less about Alsace-Lorraine. These differences gave rise to apprehensions about being entrapped in a war over the other party's interests. France also feared that an alliance would provoke the hostility of Britain, Russia's archenemy, and drive Britain and Germany together. French military leaders brooded about the slow Russian mobilization, which might permit the Germans to fight the two countries in sequence—first France, then Russia. Both parties worried that Germany might even be provoked to attack. Finally, during the first half of the 1880s, both countries were so absorbed in colonial affairs, where their principal antagonist was England, that they

Table 4-1. Percentage shares of military resources and potential among European great powers, 1890

	Iron-steel production	Energy consumption	Population	Defense appropriations	Defense personnel	Average
Great Britain	50.2	51.3	13.8	22.6	16.9	31.0
France	11.9	12.7	13.8	26.7	21.8	17.4
Russia	6.0	3.9	39.9	20.8	27.2	19.5
Germany	25.8	25.1	17.8	20.7	20.2	21.9
Austria-Hungary	6.1	7.0	14.9	9.2	13.9	10.2

SOURCE: Calculated from figures in Paul M. Kennedy, "The First World War and the International Power System," *International Security* 9 (Summer 1984), 7–41.
NOTE: Because of rounding, not all columns add to 100.

were little conscious of the German-Austrian threat. Indeed, throughout the 1880s Russia was formally associated with Germany and Austria in the Three Emperors' Alliance and its replacement, the Reinsurance Treaty of 1887 with Germany.

THE EUROPEAN SYSTEM, 1890

In 1890 Great Britain was again the leader among the five major European powers, although its industrial superiority was beginning its long secular decline (Table 4-1). Since 1880 Germany's resource share had increased rather markedly, largely owing to its burgeoning economic development. France's and Russia's shares had declined slightly. Germany had passed Russia in aggregate resources, and France had begun its long relative economic decline. France maintained its position among the great powers primarily by means of large defense appropriations. Russia's relative economic backwardness was offset by its lead in men-under-arms. Aggregating for comparative alliance strengths, the French-Russian combined index still exceeded the Austro-German, 36.9 percent to 32.1 percent, but this margin was 6 percent smaller than in 1880.

NEGOTIATING THE FRANCO-RUSSIAN ALLIANCE

Overtures

The first moves toward alliance were made by military figures. Military men on both sides, ignorant of the formal political ties between Russia and Germany, were confident that neither Russia nor France could avoid participation in a war between the other and Germany. General N. N. Obruchev, chief of the Russian general staff, made contact with French officers in the early 1880s, in particular with Colonel (later General) Raoul le Mouton de Boisdeffre, who would become chief of the French general staff. These two men were to play leading roles throughout the negotiations. In November 1888 the Grandduke Vladimir, while visiting Paris, asked to have a specimen of the new Lebel rifle. The request was granted and led to a Russian order for the rifles. Delegations of Russian generals and military engineers came to study the new rifle and observe French processes for manufacturing gunpowder. In return for these favors, the French defense minister, Charles Freycinet, asked for, and received from the Russian ambassador, assurance that the rifles would never be used against Frenchmen.[1]

These beginnings of military collaboration were soon followed by the development of financial ties, including several large loans by French banks to the Russian government. French investments in Russia increased sharply after Bismarck, in 1887, in one of his most serious mistakes, banned the deposit of Russian securities as collateral for loans on the Berlin money market, in retaliation for Russian measures against German landowners in Poland. This forced the Russians to turn to Paris to satisfy their insatiable need for funds, a need the French were only too glad to satisfy.[2]

Various political events in the latter 1880s, some deliberate, some accidental, served to move the two countries closer. The Mediterranean Agreements of 1887, engineered by Bismarck, created a formal tie between Russia's principal opponents, Austria and Britain. These agreements also hardened the deadlock between France and Britain over Egypt.[3] The death of the old German Kaiser in 1888 and, soon after, the ascension of young Wilhelm, whom the Czar regarded as a "pipsqueak,"[4] virtually ended the sentimental tie between the Russian and German royal houses. The eclipse of the charismatic General Georges Boulanger introduced a more moderate tone into French domestic politics, reducing the Russian ideological distaste. The Pan-Slav nationalist movement in Russia agitated for a French connection. German coolness toward Russia after the fall of Bismarck in 1890 also increased the attractiveness of France as an ally.[5] The augmented strength of French military forces following reforms carried out in the late 1880s, along with an improvement in the speed of Russian mobilization, virtually eliminated the possibility that Germany would be able to defeat the two countries seriatim.[6]

The turning point on the road to alliance was the German refusal to renew the Reinsurance Treaty with Russia in June 1890, after the forced resignation of Bismarck. This treaty had called for neutrality in case of an attack on either party and German diplomatic support of Russia's aims in Bulgaria and at the Straits. Allowing it to lapse was the first and most serious policy error of the new German leadership, especially since they could have renewed the treaty at a bargain price. For Nikolai Giers, the

Russian foreign minister, even a tenuous German connection was better than a French one. He was willing to accept a substantial modification of the agreement, in both substance and form, in order to retain some sort of formal tie. But the Germans refused to put anything in writing, although they insisted their policy would remain unchanged. The puzzled Russians naturally interpreted this refusal as a sign of German hostility.[7]

With their foreign policy thus simplified, the German government embarked on a "new course," the main goal of which was better relations, even an alliance, with England. Almost automatically, this involved a further cooling of relations with Russia. Russian leaders and press became increasingly sensitive to evidence of German hostility. The first sign came with the conclusion of a colonial agreement between England and Germany by which the Germans traded Zanzibar and some other east African territories for the North Sea island of Heligoland, which they valued for strategic reasons. The Russian government interpreted this as a move toward a German-English alliance. The hearty welcome given the German Kaiser when he visited England in August was seen as confirming evidence.[8] The Russians, feeling isolated, now began thinking more seriously about teaming up with that other lonely state on Germany's westward side.

A change of government in France in March 1890 brought to power Freycinet, as premier and minister of war, and Alexandre Ribot as foreign minister. Both men were enthusiastic supporters of the idea of a Russian alliance and were to contribute much to its realization. Freycinet, in a previous stint as minister of war, had brought some order out of the disorder created by his predecessor, Boulanger. He had significantly strengthened and reorganized the French armed forces. Freycinet shared with Ribot the belief that this increase in military capability, to a level of rough equality with Germany's, enabled France to pursue a more ambitious foreign policy than had been possible in the previous two decades.[9] Like the Russians, the French were also alarmed at the increasing evidence of Anglo-German cooperation.

Early Military Negotiations

The first explicit move toward alliance, though still unofficial and even covert, took place at the Russian military maneuvers at Narva in August 1890. The Kaiser and several German military officers had been invited to observe the maneuvers, but the Czar also invited General Boisdeffre, assistant chief of the French general staff, who was well acquainted with Russian military figures through an earlier stint as military attaché in St. Petersburg. Boisdeffre was treated with marked courtesy by the Czar and had several talks with General Peter Vannovsky, the minister of war, and

General Obruchev, the chief of staff. Virtually under the noses of the German military leaders, the three men exchanged ideas and preferences about how they might jointly wage war against Germany. Their conversations revealed two major areas of disagreement, one about military strategy, the other about the form of a possible agreement.

General Obruchev presented two strategic scenarios. If the initial German offensive came principally against Russia, the Russian armies would first retreat to a triangle south of Warsaw and from this position launch an attack against Austria, while going on the defensive against Germany. If the major German thrust were directed against France, Russia would undertake an offensive, but again, against Austria, not Germany. In that case, the French should go on the defensive, fall back on their new fortifications, and let the Germans tire themselves out attacking them. The Germans thus having weakened themselves, and the Russians having in the meantime defeated the Austrians, the two armies would then jointly go on the offensive against Germany. It was a Russian "Schlieffen Plan": the ally was to hold off its enemy while the Russians dealt with theirs; only later would the Russian forces be thrown fully against the ally's enemy.

This, naturally, was not exactly what Boisdeffre wanted to hear. He took issue with the Russian concentration against Austria rather than Germany, but Obruchev held his ground. Boisdeffre nevertheless declared himself satisfied with this preliminary exchange in his report back to Paris: "It is perhaps regrettable that he would take the offensive against Austria and not against Germany; but what is important is that Russia would go to war in the face of an attack on us; and this, I believe, is what she would do."[10]

A second point of dispute concerned whether an agreement should be formal and explicit, as the French insisted, or informal, as preferred by the Russians. The conflict hinged largely on relative preferences for deterrence or defense. The Russians were primarily interested in deterring German intervention in an Austro-Russian war; a vague agreement would accomplish that without provoking Germany and without completely foreclosing the possibility of restoring the traditional tie with Germany. It had the bonus of reducing the risk of entrapment in a French initiative to recover Alsace-Lorraine. The French, on the other hand, were interested in warfighting as well as deterrence; they wanted explicit assurance of Russian assistance in an actual Franco-German war. In particular, they wanted a pledge of simultaneous mobilization, which would force the Germans to wage a two-front war from the start. The French worried about Russian buck-passing: without a binding agreement, the Russians, in the event of war, might decide to concentrate their efforts on Austria and let France deal with Germany alone.

First Round: The Franco-Russian Entente

Serious negotiations at the political level got under way in the spring of 1891. The French were the more desirous for an alliance but at first hung back, trying to hide their eagerness.[11] Thus they forced the Russians to make the first moves. Giers wrote Ribot: "The *entente cordiale* that has happily been established between Russia and France represents a factor essential at this moment not only from the standpoint of the mutual interests of the two parties but also ... for the creation of a certain counterweight to the influence of the Triplice."[12] He also hinted to the French ambassador, Antoine Laboulaye, that the time had come to make more precise this unwritten entente.[13] The Russian ambassador, Baron Mohrenheim, announced that the Czar intended to confer Russia's highest decoration, the Order of St. Andrew, on the French president, Sadi Carnot.

The decisive impetus toward serious negotiations came from the premature renewal of the Triple Alliance in May 1891 and a flood of rumors that Great Britain had joined it. The rumors were given credibility by British naval visits to Fiume and Venice in June and July, at which King Umberto of Italy and Emperor Franz Joseph were present. On July 4 the German Kaiser made a formal state visit to London, where he was given an enthusiastic reception.[14]

Russian government figures seem to have taken as fact that some new diplomatic tie had occurred between Britain and Germany. Their lingering hopes of repairing the wire to Berlin now apparently dashed, they began to feel that sense of isolation that had depressed French spirits for so long. On July 12 Laboulaye was summoned to see Giers at the latter's Finnish dacha. The foreign minister asked whether, in view of England's "more or less direct" adherence to the Triple Alliance, "we should not take one more step along the path of the entente." The ambassador suggested a military convention between the two general staffs. Giers replied, "Why not an agreement between the two governments?"[15] The Russians were coming around, not so much because of French entreaties but because of their fears of being left alone facing a hostile Anglo-German combination.

Meanwhile, significant exchanges were taking place in the military channel, some two thousand miles away. General Obruchev was vacationing in France with his wife. General Boisdeffre sought him out, and arrangements were made for talks at Obruchev's wife's chateau in the Dordogne. At their meeting on July 15 and 16, the two men communicated their quite different preferences about the focus and scope of an alliance, war aims, and military strategies. Boisdeffre began by returning to his Narva proposal for simultaneous mobilization if either country were attacked by Germany. Obruchev replied that this was not sufficient: any agreement should take account of the parties' interests outside their own territories, such as the "East" (i.e., the Balkans), where Russia might become involved with Austria. Boisdeffre objected that their mutual goal of early defeat of the main enemy would not be served if the Russians were to concentrate initially against Austria, any more than if the French were to concentrate against Italy. Obruchev professed to see no difference between attacking Germany or Austria; it was all the same enemy, and the enemy should simply be attacked where it was weakest.

Obruchev went on to outline Russia's war objectives: conquest of the Austrian province of Galicia and control of the straits at Constantinople so as to prevent British entry into the Black Sea. France's principal aim, Boisdeffre said, would be the recovery of Alsace-Lorraine.

Obruchev continued to resist the Frenchman's urging for an explicit military agreement "that would put an end to the uncertainties, the equivocations, and the insecurity." This was unnecessary, Obruchev said, because the interest of Russia in the European equilibrium ensured that it would come to the defense of France. Boisdeffre replied that he did not doubt these words but that they fell short of an official commitment.[16]

Exactly one week after the Obruchev-Boisdeffre and Giers-Laboulaye exchanges, on July 23, a French naval squadron arrived, by prearrangement, at the Russian naval base at Kronstadt, near St. Petersburg. There followed two weeks of extravagant festivities during which the French officers were entertained nonstop and wildly cheered by huge and enthusiastic crowds. The Czar stood bareheaded during a playing of the French revolutionary anthem, although he did stop the orchestra halfway through with an impatient "Enough, enough."[17]

Most observers interpreted the Kronstadt visit as evidence of, or constitutive of, an implicit alliance between the two countries, requiring no documentary codification. This interpretation suited Giers and the Czar very well, but the French were determined to get something in writing. Ribot and Freycinet, seizing the moment, fired off to Laboulaye on July 24 a draft of a proposed agreement. It provided that the two countries would (1) concert their efforts in any situation that threatened the peace of Europe, and (2) mobilize immediately and simultaneously should any member of the Triple Alliance mobilize. Laboulaye saw Giers on August 5 and 6. Giers thought the geographical scope of the alliance should be broadened beyond Europe. Since England had now associated itself with the Triple Alliance, it was not enough to limit the agreement to actions initiated by the three original members. He had in mind, no doubt, that an Anglo-Russian conflict was most likely to arise outside Europe, notably over the Turkish straits and Constantinople. Giers also took issue with the second clause of the French draft; he proposed to omit any reference to mobilization and to remove any obligation for the parties to agree in advance on military measures. The French accepted the first change but resisted the second, arguing that the consultation on measures to be taken in case of a threat of aggression must be compulsory, not optional. Giers, assisted by Laboulaye, drew up a counterdraft that was a compromise between the French and Russian views: it made no provision for mobilization but called for "agreement on measures" for "immediate and simultaneous adoption" in case either party were threatened with aggression. It dropped the reference to the Triple Alliance in the French draft, again implicitly broadening the target of the agreement to include England.[18]

The French government accepted this draft immediately, and by an exchange of letters between Ribot and Giers on August 27, it entered history as the Franco-Russian "entente" of 1891. It was not a treaty and not yet an alliance, but it was an important first step toward an alliance. It followed Russian preferences more than French ones. Ribot, however, in his letter of ratification, made clear the French desire that the agreement be followed up soon with a military convention specifying in detail how the two countries would cooperate in case of war or crisis.[19]

Incidentally, the British gave a boost to the French negotiators by inviting the French squadron, on its way home from Kronstadt, to stop off at Portsmouth. The French accepted with alacrity, for the visit, by hinting that they had an alternative, would strengthen their bargaining power with Russia and hedge against the possible failure of further negotiations. On the other hand, the visit may have shown the Russians that the British connection with the Triple Alliance was not as tight as they had thought and thus reduced the urgency of an alliance with France. It might then explain Giers's stickiness in the final round of negotiations and the outcome favorable to Russia.[20]

The Russians were well satisfied with the agreement; indeed, they would have preferred to stop there. The knowledge that it existed would be sufficient to deter German intervention should they get involved in war with Britain or Austria: at the same time, it was vague enough to enable them to avoid entrapment in a Franco-German war. The Russians were primarily concerned with the British threat to their interests, not the German.[21]

The French were not satisfied. The agreement did not commit the Russians to mobilize as soon as Germany mobilized or to come to France's aid in case of a war with Germany. Russia might pass the buck to France for dealing with the German attack, concentrating its own efforts entirely against Austria. This first agreement failed to come to grips with the parties' divergent interests: France's principal enemy was Germany; Russia's were two others, Austria and Britain. As William L. Langer says, "the two powers shook hands in passing, but did not set out on a promenade arm-in-arm."[22] The French made clear that they considered the agreement only a first step, to be followed by a more specific understanding on military implementation.

Among the first moves of the Russian and French governments after the agreement was to reassure their opponents. Giers, traveling through Europe, assured German leaders of the two countries' peaceful intentions. French representatives in Egypt were instructed to tone down their anti-British activities.[23]

Second Round: The Military Convention

The French kept pressing for a military convention during the fall and winter of 1891–92. The reluctant Czar finally agreed that, if they wished, the French could send a high-ranking officer to Petersburg to negotiate whatever they had in mind. Giers, in extending this invitation to the new French ambassador, Gustave-Louis Montebello, added that there was no reason for haste.[24] The French were in no mood for delay, however. General Marie-Joseph Miribel, the French chief of staff, immediately set to work drafting a statement of principles as a basis for a military convention. The paper called for mutual assistance in case of attack on either country by the forces of the Triple Alliance, and immediate and simultaneous mobilization at the first sign of mobilization by the Triple Alliance. It then explained the necessity for concentrating on the principal opponent, Germany. The French would direct 1,300,000 ground troops (five-sixths of their active army) against Germany, and Russia would use 700,000 to 800,000 for this purpose out of a total force of 1,600,000. These forces should be concentrated as fast as possible on the German frontier "in order to deprive [the Germans] from the outset of all possibility of shuttling their forces between east and west."[25]

Giers and Vladimir Lamsdorff, Giers's assistant, after reading this document, agreed that it would be unacceptable to Russian military leaders. Furthermore, as Lamsdorff confided to his diary: "The commitment they are demanding of us would give the French a carte blanche for adventures and for the provocation of conflicts in which it would be hard to distinguish who had really started the affair; and then we would be obliged to support them with an army of 800,000 men! . . . We, presumably, would destroy Germany for the benefit of the French, and they then, even in the best of circumstances, would leave us to finish things off with the Austrians and with the other Eastern powers as best we might, giving us no help at all."[26] Thus Lamsdorff saw in the French document first a danger of entrapment and then a prospect of abandonment.

The Russian military reaction to the French proposal was expressed in a long memorandum prepared by General Obruchev in April or May 1892. Its main point was a call for simultaneous mobilization of French and

Russian forces in case either were attacked by any member of the Triple Alliance, not just by Germany or the whole alliance, as the French desired. This stipulation was necessary to foreclose French abandonment in the event of an Austro-Russian conflict. The French must be required to mobilize even if Austria alone attacked Russia; otherwise, Germany might persuade France to stand aside. Then Russia would be compelled to fight not only Austria but also the bulk of the German forces. Of course, putting this obligation on France would place a corresponding obligation on Russia to mobilize and go to war in case of a conflict between Italy and France, but the gain was worth the cost. Since Obruchev stated unequivocally that mobilization itself was an act of war, he was saying, in effect, that both allies must not only mobilize but proceed to war whenever any member of the Triple Alliance initiated mobilization.

Obruchev also objected to the French proposal's precise specification of forces to be committed by each party against Germany. Russia must retain "full freedom" to deploy its forces in a way best calculated to deliver a "decisive blow" at the armies of the Triple Alliance. This might mean concentrating against Germany, but it might also mean concentrating against Austria first, depending on circumstances.[27]

When Giers saw this memo, he wrote to the defense minister, General Vannovsky, and to the Czar, expressing strong opposition to the French proposal. It would unacceptably limit the Czar's freedom of decision and would require that Russia immediately attack Austria and Germany as soon as the Italians mobilized on the French border. Therefore, Russia should not bind itself by any formal convention; the earlier exchange of notes had created a sufficiently "firm foundation" for any common military action with France. The Czar's response (from his vacation home in Denmark) was, "I entirely share your opinion, and fully approve all that you said to the Minister of War."[28]

Ribot became so exasperated with the Russian procrastination that he fixed a time limit. If the negotiations produced no result by the end of August, he warned, he would be obliged to bring the matter before the cabinet. Ribot was aware of the Czar's desire to keep the discussions absolutely secret, so this move was an attempt to coerce him by the threat of publicity. Ribot also advised the Russians that when General Boisdeffre went to Russia to attend the annual maneuvers in August, he would expect to resume negotiations about the treaty.[29]

Boisdeffre arrived in Petersburg on August 1 bearing a draft of a military convention that gave formal effect to the principles earlier stated in the Miribel draft. It said, inter alia, that if the forces "of the Triple Alliance or of Germany alone" should mobilize, France and Russia would immediately mobilize, and similarly if the Triple Alliance or "Germany alone" should attack, France and Russia would commit all their forces against Germany except those "absolutely indispensable on other fronts."[30]

Boisdeffre's principal interlocutors, as usual, were Generals Vannovsky and Obruchev. Vannovsky was opposed to any specific military obligations. There was no need for a formal agreement, the minister said; a gentleman's agreement would suffice. Vannovsky pointed to the instability of French governments and the requirement for approval by the French assembly, which collided with the Czar's insistence on absolute secrecy. Vannovsky also expressed the fear that Germany might be provoked to declare war once it knew of the agreement.

Obruchev was somewhat more forthcoming in that he did not oppose any military agreement as such. He refused to fix a definite figure for the number of troops to be deployed against Germany, however, and he emphasized the need for a commitment to joint mobilization whenever any single member of the Triple Alliance—notably Austria—should mobilize.[31]

The deadlock on this last point was broken by a telegram from Ribot authorizing Boisdeffre to yield. After all, the French consoled themselves, an Austrian mobilization would be sure to provoke a Russian mobilization, which in turn would provoke a German one. (All concerned assumed mobilization would inevitably be followed by war.) The two critical clauses of the final draft (actually a modification of the French draft) read as follows:

1. If France is attacked by Germany or by Italy supported by Germany, Russia will employ all her available forces to attack Germany. If Russia is attacked by Germany or by Austria supported by Germany, France will employ all her available forces to combat Germany.
2. In case the forces of the Triple Alliance, or of one of the Powers composing it, should mobilize, France and Russia, at the first news of the event and without the necessity of any previous concert, shall mobilize immediately and simultaneously all their forces and transport them as near to the frontiers as possible.[32]

Another provision repeated the troop figures suggested by the earlier Miribel proposal and stated that "these forces shall engage to the full with all speed, so that Germany will have to fight on the East and West at the same time."[33] The Russians, rather surprisingly, accepted the figure of 700,000 to 800,000 men which they were to deploy against Germany. Other clauses provided for exchanges of information, no separate peace, and duration: the alliance would last as long as the Triple Alliance. There were two anomalies in the document. First, the first and second clauses of the French draft were simply reversed, with the mobilization clause now coming after the clause calling for action. Second, there was an apparent contradiction between the clauses: the mobilization clause called for mobilization in case any member—for example, Austria or Italy—should alone mobilize, but action was required only if one of these secondary powers was supported by Germany. Historians have puzzled over this, in view of the assumption by both sides that mobilization meant war. Thus the French, for instance, could find themselves actually going to war against Austria before Germany had committed itself. The French did not like the mobilization clause but swallowed it to get an agreement. The most plausible explanation why the Russians insisted on it is the one given by Obruchev at an earlier stage of the negotiations: if France did not mobilize immediately in response to an Austrian mobilization, Germany, by astute crisis diplomacy, might be able to deter France from mobilizing at all. The agreement could be interpreted as a compromise: the action clause protected France against entrapment in an Austro-Russian war, and the mobilization clause assured Russia of some support in an Austro-Russian crisis.[34]

Boisdeffre and Obruchev signed the document on August 14 and Vannovsky took it to the Czar. The latter indicated his approval "in principle" but wanted Giers to be consulted. Giers's response was that such an exchange between chiefs of staff was acceptable only if it contained no binding obligations. Thus the document should be considered only a draft, and if the Czar wished to express approval to Boisdeffre, that approval should be only in principle.[35]

From this point on, and for the next year and a half, the Franco-Russian alliance project went into a kind of limbo. So far, there was a vague statement of consultative principles—the entente agreement of 1891—and a military convention that had been negotiated and signed by the two chiefs of staff. The latter, of course, had no legal standing. It might have been considered merely a technical agreement for implementation of a decision for war, should such a decision be reached by the political authorities. This is the interpretation that the Russian side, with the possible exception of Obruchev, would have preferred. But its content belied this interpretation. It specified the contingencies in which the two countries *would* go to war, not just what they would do *if* such a decision were taken. It was, in fact, itself an alliance treaty, an elaboration and specification of the much vaguer agreement of 1891. Thus, by implication, it required the formal approval of the highest authorities in each country. The Russians did not care for this implication at all because of their concern for secrecy. Indeed, it was they who had insisted on calling it a "military convention" so as to avoid having to communicate it to the French parliament. In his final audience with Boisdeffre, Czar Alexander insisted that the convention not be disclosed to the French cabinet. Russia needed at least two years of peace because of internal problems, he said, whereas if the convention became known to the Germans, they might launch a preventive attack.[36]

Third Round: Ratification

During the fall of 1892 and the spring of 1893 further movement toward a full-fledged alliance was blocked by domestic instability in France. Behind this was the famous Panama scandal, which implicated many French politicians, and the Russian ambassador, in a corrupt scheme to build a Panama canal. This led to three drastic cabinet changes, much to the disgust of the Russian Czar. His distaste was overcome, however, by developments exterior to French-Russian relations. One was a crisis between France and Great Britain over the boundary between French Indo-China and the independent state of Siam. The French appeared to have won the crisis by forcing a withdrawal of British ships by an ultimatum. That turned out to be mistaken, entirely due to a misunderstanding, but in the world's eyes (including Russian eyes) the impression lingered that somehow the French had faced down the British. This made them a more attractive ally.[37]

Further impetus was provided by a deterioration in Russo-German relations. Negotiations for a commercial treaty broke down in the spring of 1893, and a tariff war ensued. By contrast, a Franco-Russian tariff treaty was concluded in June. A German military bill was introduced in November 1892 and finally passed, amid noisy debate, in July 1893. The bill increased the German armed forces by 80,000 men, not a huge figure but enough to raise Russian fears of German aggressiveness. The Czar's response was to concentrate more troops in Russian Poland. The French seized the opportunity to press for a definite confirmation of the draft convention. General Miribel wrote to the Czar, drawing attention to the German increase, informing him of a strengthening of French forces, and expressing confidence that Russia would do the same.[38]

On October 13, 1893, a Russian naval squadron dropped anchor in the French port of Toulon, in reciprocation for the earlier French visit. There followed a series of celebrations and demonstrations of popular enthusiasm even more extravagant than that which had greeted the French fleet at Kronstadt and St. Petersburg. The French people were overjoyed at finally having found a friend. The Russian foreign office was less pleased, fearing that such emotional abandon might provoke the Germans. In any case, in the eyes of the European publics, a Franco-Russian alliance now definitely existed.[39]

After Toulon, the denouement moved swiftly. The Czar returned from his vacation in Denmark late in October, having just received the Miribel letter and a letter from Vannovsky agreeing with Miribel's view that the German army bill indicated aggressive intentions. If he needed any more persuading, he got it from Obruchev at a meeting early in December; after this meeting Obruchev wrote to his friend, Boisdeffre, that an exchange of notes could now take place. Giers capitulated on December 18. On December 27, after an audience with the Czar, he signed and sent to the French ambassador a note averring that the "draft military convention . . . may be considered from now on as having been definitely adopted in its present form." The ambassador replied, on January 4, 1894, with a note repeating Giers's language and confirming that the French government also regarded the convention as having entered into force.[40] The long road to a Franco-Russian alliance had finally reached its end.

ASSESSMENT OF THE BARGAINING PROCESS AND OUTCOME

If the 1891 entente and the military convention are taken as a unit, the alliance terms favored the French, though only marginally. The Russians would have liked to stop with the entente, which gave them all they wanted: enough French commitment to deter Germany from attacking Russia, yet enough vagueness to enable them to avoid entrapment in a Franco-German war. They were persuaded to accept the much more specific military convention because of unrelenting French pressure, continued German coolness, and the activity and persuasiveness of one Russian official—Obruchev, the chief of staff. Obruchev not only did the drafting on the Russian side in collaboration with the French but was apparently responsible for convincing the vacillating Czar. The two other actors on the Russian side, the foreign minister and the defense minister, remained personally opposed until the end, although, of course, they formally acceded to the Czar's wishes.

Because of its greater specificity and detail, the convention was the dominant of the two agreements. Its terms favored French preferences. Unlike the entente agreement, it specified Germany as the principal enemy and called explicitly for "immediate and simultaneous" mobilization in response to mobilization by the Triple Alliance or any one of its members. It required the deployment and immediate commitment of roughly half the Russian army to battle against Germany, whereas the Russians had initially proposed sending most of their forces against Austria. The French made only one concession, agreeing to mobilize in case Austria alone mobilized, thus taking some risk of provoking an avoidable war with Germany, but it was not a large risk since it was highly unlikely that Austria would mobilize without German support. This French "victory" is puzzling, at first glance, because it is inconsistent with the fact that the French were the more anxious to have the military convention and played the role of petitioner throughout its negotiation. The following more detailed analysis may help clear up the puzzle.

Benefits and Costs

Both countries gained deterrent value: Germany was now ensured of having to fight a two-front war if it attacked either one. The deterrent effect increased both allies' freedom of action against England outside Europe, since Germany would be less likely to take advantage of their preoccupation; as noted, this effect was especially important for Russia. Defense value against Germany was greater for France than for Russia, because of France's greater vulnerability to German attack and its greater degree of conflict with Germany. Russia's enormous manpower reserves were especially valuable to France in view of its own demographic weakness. These combined effects thus marginally favored France.

Consideration of the parties' security levels before the alliance, however, indicates an even greater deterrent-defense gain for France. An important determinant of prealliance security is the parties' expectation of being assisted in war as a consequence of the other's strategic interest. It was more likely that France would aid Russia against Germany even without an alliance commitment than that Russia would aid France. One reason was that France had a greater particular interest in conflict with Germany— Alsace-Lorraine—than Russia did and was quite likely to take the opportunity of a Russo-German war to recover the provinces. In addition, Russia had less defensive strategic interest in defending France than vice versa, because Russia could more likely survive a German onslaught after a German conquest of France than the other way around. Because of these situational differences, France gained more deterrent and defense value than Russia did by formalizing the alignment—that is, the alliance contract increased the probability of Russia helping France more than vice versa.

Both countries also benefited from the extended deterrence that their own commitment provided the ally: reduction of the probability of attack on the ally minimized the likelihood of having to come to the ally's aid. France gained somewhat more preclusive benefit than Russia did because a rehabilitation of the Three Emperors' League or the Reinsurance Treaty was more plausible than a French deal with Germany.

The control factor—how much the agreement enhanced the parties' ability to influence or restrain each other—probably favored France slightly. Before the alliance France was more dependent on Russia than vice versa and thus more vulnerable to threats of nonsupport; the formalization reduced the credibility of such threats. At the same time, the joint planning process that the alliance inaugurated increased the parties' mutual influence.

The third party most affected by the alliance was Great Britain. England could now expect to meet more resistance in its colonial struggles with either party. For the alliance partners, this additional deterrent benefit was more important to Russia than to France because of Russia's greater conflicts with Britain. Beyond this, the combined Russian and French fleets in the Mediterranean might be able to challenge British dominance there. If so, it might serve to detach Italy from the Triple Alliance, since Italy, for geographical reasons, was dependent on the dominant naval power.

Another potential benefit to both parties, although rarely discussed, was the prospect that the alliance provided for realizing their revisionist aims. Even if they had no plans to use the alliance deliberately for offensive purposes, such purposes could easily be grafted onto an initially defensive war. Revisionist aims probably were more important to France; regaining Alsace-Lorraine probably was worth more to it than controlling the Straits was to Russia.

Against these benefits must be counted four kinds of costs: commitment to defend the other, risk of entrapment, risk of provoking the opponent, and loss of diplomatic freedom of action. Commitment cost was marginally greater for Russia than for France, because Russia was less motivated than France to intervene in the other's war with Germany in the absence of an alliance. France's risk of entrapment was somewhat greater, because Russia was more likely to take advantage of the alliance to challenge Austria in the Balkans than France was to challenge Germany over Alsace-Lorraine. Both parties worried that the alliance might provoke Germany to attack. Both countries lost some diplomatic autonomy—France to ally with Britain, Russia to ally with Austria or Germany. Both also sacrificed military autonomy.

Table 4-2 shows an estimated value for each of these benefit and cost items on a scale from 1 to 4. The result is a net gain of 5 for France and 3 for Russia. As in the German-Austrian case, these are inherent values— the parties' valuation of the alliance before the negotiation of specific contract terms. These valuations were not terribly asymmetrical, less so than in the German-Austrian case. They became more symmetrical during the negotiations, because of minor French concessions, which perhaps changed the payoff division to 4.5, 3.5.

What explains this apparent French victory? At first glance it seems that the French gained more than they should have. The French clearly wanted the alliance more than the Russians did. The Russians ought to have been able to persuade the French to make more concessions, on the ground that they had less to lose than the French by a breakdown of the negotiations.

Table 4-2. Benefits and costs in the Franco-Russian alliance

	France	Russia
Benefits		
Deterrence and defense against direct attack	4	3
Extended deterrence	1	1
Preclusion	2	1
Control	2	2
Third-party effects	1	2
Offensive aims	2	1
	12	10
Costs		
Commitment to defend ally	−2	−3
Entrapment by ally	−2	−1
Provocation of opponent	−1	−1
Reduced flexibility	−2	−2
	−7	−7
Net values	5	3

At least, they might have been able to force an equal division of the total payoff. Can their failure to do so be ascribed to a French advantage in available alternatives?

Alliance Alternatives

Of the fifteen pair-wise alliance possibilities in 1890, several were already in existence. Austria and Germany were allied by their pact of 1879 and had added Italy to their combination in 1882. Britain, Italy, and Austria were allied rather vaguely by the Mediterranean Agreements of 1887. Of the remaining possibilities, only two—Russia-France and Germany-England—were competitive in the sense that they improved on the status quo and dominated all other nonextant possibilities for both their members. All the others were simply infeasible because of the existence of unbridgeable conflicts between their putative members, or, as in the case of Austria-France, between one partner and an ally of the other. This meant that in the bargaining toward formation of one of the competitive possibilities, the minimum acceptable terms for each party were those equivalent to the value of no alliance, not the value of some other potential alliance.

The two competitive possibilities did not compete with each other, of course, since their memberships were different. Britain and Germany were following parallel foreign policies at this time, and as we have seen, Britain was generally thought to have become at least a de facto member of the Triple Alliance. Bismarck had sought to formalize the relationship with an alliance proposal to Lord Salisbury in 1889, but the prime minister, although sympathetic, considered the moment inopportune. The post-Bismarckian German government, although friendly toward Britain at first, eventually destroyed its British option by its erratic and overbearing behavior.

The Franco-Russian was by far the most attractive unrealized alliance in the early 1890s. France had quietly suffered its isolation at Bismarck's hands for twenty years; now Bismarck's successors had succeeded in isolating Russia as well. It was only natural that the two outcasts should seek security in each other's company. Both faced serious external threats, and moreover, both had revisionist goals. Neither had alliance alternatives that were remotely as attractive as each other.

For France, England was a possible alternative for a distant future, but few Frenchmen perceived this future in the context of the colonial squabbles of the 1890s. Conflicting colonial aims with Italy in North Africa temporarily blocked any serious attempt to wean it away from the Triplice. Russia had few options either, although somewhat more than France. England, of course, was not one of them. Nor was Germany, for the present, given recent changes in German policy; yet there were no outstanding conflicts between Russia and Germany, and it was quite possible that German policy might revert to its pro-Russian tradition. Giers and other pro-German officials in Russia kept hoping for this, although the Czar had apparently given up on the German option. Austria was a further possibility. It would not have taken a herculean diplomatic effort for Russia to settle its major differences with Austria—indeed, it did exactly that only four years later. The Russians were apparently blind to this possibility in 1892–93, however.[41] Thus, in terms of subjective perceptions and preferences, neither party had any good immediate alternative to alliance with the other. If anything, the Russians had better potential alternatives than the French. Thus the apparent French advantage in the bargaining outcome cannot be explained by superior alternatives.

Bargaining Process

In further quest of explanation, we might have recourse to certain ad hoc hypotheses exterior to formal bargaining theory. For example, Samuel Bacharach and Edward Lawler hypothesize that when a bargainer wants a goal badly enough, he may be able to reach it or approximate it simply by the magnitude of the "effort" he is willing to put forth, which may be sufficient to overcome the bargaining weakness that otherwise usually stems from wanting something badly.[42] The French certainly put a great deal of effort into the alliance project; perhaps they simply wore down the Russians by their sheer persistence. The explanation might also be sought in the locus of power within the Russian decision-making unit. Within the

Figure 4-1. Hypothetical payoffs in Franco-Russian alliance formation

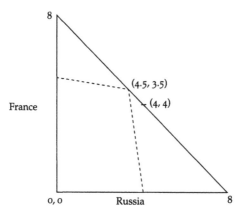

four-man group, Giers and Vannovsky were opposed to any military convention at all; Obruchev favored it and ultimately convinced the Czar. Since the Czar was all-powerful, the Russian payoff may have reflected only his preferences, which would have given a higher value to the alliance than an average across the group. Finally, the explanation may reside in the salience and normative force of equity. The terms of the alliance were equitable. If Russia was to mobilize when France's enemy mobilized, then France would have to mobilize when Russia's enemy mobilized. It was reasonable that France should throw its entire army against Germany while Russia sent half its against Austria and half against Germany. But equity in the contractual terms of the alliance gave an advantage to France, because of its greater inherent value for the alliance. It seems quite likely, in other words, that the equity principle was strong enough to overcome the Russians' superior bargaining power on other grounds.

The bargaining situation may be pictured on a two-dimensional diagram, similar to what was done for the Austro-German alliance. The diagram, Figure 4-1, is less useful in this case because of the difficulty in finding plausible alternatives to the actual outcome. In the valuations estimated above, there were eight security-autonomy units to be divided up. At the extremes, either France or Russia gets all eight, although it is difficult to imagine what these extremes would be empirically. The outcome is at 4.5, 3.5 favoring France, a deviation from the Nash solution, which is 4, 4. The latter outcome, which the Russians might have reached, had they been aware of or used their potentially superior bargaining power, might have included a greater Russian force deployment against Austria and a smaller one against Germany or perhaps a side payment such as a French pledge of diplomatic support to Russian aims in the Near East.

A possible reason the Russians did not press for a more favorable outcome may be that there was far more common interest than conflict in the bargaining situation. A straight-line contract curve represents a high degree of conflict—what one party gains, the other loses—for any movement on the curve. The convex dashed-line curve shown in Figure 4-1 may be a more realistic portrayal of this case, and perhaps most cases of alliance formation. This curve reflects a higher ratio of common to conflicting interest. The inherent payoffs—the payoffs before bargaining about specific terms—are at the "bulge" of the convex curve. Any movement on the curve to the right of this point disadvantages France substantially at little gain to Russia; any move to the left of this point hurts Russia considerably at little gain to France. Consequently, the parties have little incentive to bargain hard in order to squeeze the last drop of gain out of their bargaining power, and every incentive simply to go directly to the point that maximizes their joint interests, even though at this point one party is benefited more than the other. This may well be the most equitable solution in terms of the language of the treaty. The 4.5, 3.5 outcome may have been acceptable to Russia because any move to improve Russia's payoff would have cost more in common values than it was worth in self-interested Russian values.

Finally, it is possible, although speculative, that the Russian leaders held back from tough bargaining with France because of the prospect of financial aid. Between 1888 and 1891 the Russian government received six loans from French banks, totaling more than three billion francs. Much more was to be lent during the life of the alliance; nevertheless, there is no evidence that its anticipation affected the negotiation of the alliance.

[5]

Conclusions: Alliance Formation

The task of this chapter is to bring together the theory of Chapter 2 and the evidence from the case studies in order to explain the formation of major alliances in the pre-World War I period. I try to answer chiefly the following questions: Why did alliances occur at all? When they occurred, what determined who allied with whom? When an alliance formed, what determined how its benefits and costs were allocated? What was the nature of the bargaining process through which the terms of the alliance were decided?

Although there is some overlap, the theories presented earlier tend to emphasize different aspects of alliance formation. Thus neorealist theory tends to center on the first two of our questions: Why ally? And with whom? The first and major part of this chapter marshals evidence from the cases bearing on these questions, organized around four clusters of variables: (1) the anarchic and multipolar structure of the system, (2) the differing military capabilities and potential of the great powers, (3) the conflicting and common interests of those powers, and (4) their domestic politics, including their ideological and ethnic makeup.

The third and fourth of our questions—how alliance payoffs are divided, and by what process—are emphasized in N-person game theory and two-party bargaining theory. Thus the latter part of the chapter draws out from the cases evidence bearing on these theories. The case material is not limited to the three case studies already presented but includes material from other alliances of the period, especially the British ententes with France and Russia. The analysis, however, is limited to the formation phase of the alliances studied; their subsequent "management" is taken up in Part II.

Alliance Motives

The relative causal weight of our four variables can best be assessed through evidence bearing on statesmen's motives and interests. Here the fourfold classification of state interests presented in Chapter 1 is helpful. Strategic interests are interests valued for their instrumental power content; intrinsic interests are valued in nonpower currencies. Cutting across the strategic-intrinsic dichotomy is the contrast between general and particular interests. General interests are interests in a general state of the international system, such as a balance of power or the global spread of democracy. Particular interests are interests in specific, local states of affairs. General strategic interests arise from the nature of the international system, notably its anarchic structure and the distribution of resources within it. General intrinsic interests, such as spreading an ideology globally, are generated internally. Taking or holding a strategic strong point is a particular strategic interest; the desire to incorporate an ethnic irredentum is a particular intrinsic interest. Particular interests may, of course, be valued both strategically and intrinsically. The particular interests that are most germane for our purposes are those that are in conflict between states or perhaps that are shared in varying degree.* Obvious examples are the Franco-German conflict over Alsace-Lorraine or the Anglo-Austrian common interest in resisting Russia at the Straits.

Of course, such distinctions are not entirely satisfactory; the world does not sort itself out so neatly. Nevertheless, they are of some use for classifying systematically the various motives that our cases reveal to be operating in alliance formation. Thus we can say, without much distortion, that if a statesman says he is allying in order to preclude the ally from lining up with anyone else, he is acting according to a general interest, that is, responding to systemic pressures. He is acting to prevent the general distribution of power in the system from shifting against him. The same could be said of the decision maker who is motivated simply to fashion a majority coalition, without reference to any particular opponent or threat. But if the alliance is sought for protection against a state with which one has a specific dispute, it is primarily motivated by particular interest. Something similar could be said when a state is chosen as an ally because it shares one's own particular interests. But note, in these two latter examples, that their context is still that of systemic anarchy, to which must be attributed part of the motivation, even if it is not primary. In

---

*The third item in our theoretical pantheon—conflicting and common interests—refers to such particular interests.

many, if not in most, cases, in other words, both general and particular interests are at play.

I have excluded domestic politics from the theory, largely on grounds of parsimony: no theory of international relations can possibly include all relevant variables, and it can legitimately be claimed that a theory based on systemic reasoning alone captures enough of the sources of causation to be useful. Our cases, however, show that domestic factors sometimes make a difference. This is not the place to attempt to develop a full-blown theory of domestic politics and international relations, if such a thing were possible.* What follows is merely a typology, intended as a framework for a later survey of domestic variables in the cases. It attempts to sort out these variables by kind and according to how they might affect the process of alliance formation.

Domestic Politics and Alliance Formation

Speaking most broadly, all the variables in our theory—system structure, strength inequalities, and particular conflicts and common interests, as well as bargaining strategies and tactics—must pass through a domestic politics prism consisting of the perceptions and values of decision makers and the domestic constraints that bear on them. Systemic constraints make themselves felt only through people who make decisions, even if, sometimes, those people are not fully aware of them. Particular conflicts and common interests between states are a function, first, of the interests and values that people in office hold on behalf of their state, and second, of their perceptions of the interests and intentions of other states. Likewise, strength inequalities and ideological differences must be domestically perceived and evaluated. Occasionally, the domestic prism may be strong enough to breach or bend systemic constraints. More often it operates to point outcomes in more specific directions than could have been predicted on grounds of system structure or strategic interests but still within the bounds of systemic constraints.

Domestic factors may be said to establish a set of constraints that are

---

*The most promising basis for such a theory is Robert D. Putnam's "two-level bargaining," wherein possible outcomes in international bargaining are determined by the overlap of "win-sets"—agreements ratifiable at home—between the bargainers. It seemed especially appropriate for my study because of its focus on bargaining. It turned out, however, not to be applicable because of empirical limitations: alliances were often negotiated in secret, and domestic influences were far more general and diffuse than those posited in Putnam's theory. See his "Diplomacy and Domestic Politics: The Logic of Two-Level Games," *International Organization* 42 (Summer 1988), 427–60. See also Peter B. Evans, Harold K. Jacobson, and Robert D. Putnam, *Double-Edged Diplomacy: International Bargaining and Domestic Politics* (Berkeley: University of California Press, 1993).

supplementary to systemic constraints. Usually, domestic politics limits decisional choices within narrower bounds than do systemic constraints, but that may not always be true. The broadest domestic constraints, such as ideological predilections and repulsions, or types of regime, may leave the statesman more freedom of maneuver than systemic ones. Decision makers may be constrained more narrowly, and perhaps more temporarily, by their party or factional allegiances or by their need to form and maintain governing coalitions. In any country, whether a democracy or autocracy, parties or factions hold different "philias" and "phobias"—different preferences for alliance with particular other states. Such preferences toward actual or potential allies tend to complement hard and soft attitudes toward adversaries: "hawks" are ultraphobic toward present opponents and ultraphiliac toward present allies; "doves" tend to be soft on adversaries and suspicious of allies. Whose preferences are actualized in governmental policy will, of course, be affected by the relative domestic influence of the groups. In some cases, policy will simply reflect the preferences and beliefs of the party in power; in others, policy will be a bargained product of the preferences of several groups. The groups involved may divide on bureaucratic rather than party lines; for example, military leaders might favor one alignment, foreign office people another. Various coalitions across parties and bureaucracies are possible and, indeed, common.

The preferences and beliefs of domestic groups will help establish values for the state's alternative alliances and thus determine which ones are "feasible" and "competitive," as these terms were defined in Chapter 2.* Briefly, feasible alliances are those that are considered no worse than the no-alliance status quo by the dominant domestic groups in both (all) their members; competitive ones are those that are at least as or more attractive than other feasible alliance options to such groups—again, within both or all the states involved.

Since the relative influence of parties and factions is subject to change, a state's alliance preferences may also change as groups move up or down the domestic political ladder. Policy changes that occur in one state, in a kind of ripple effect, may stimulate changes in other states as they reevaluate their alternatives. The values that states place on their alternative alliance options will fluctuate not only with the changing balance of influence among their own factions but also with their decision makers' observation of such changes in other states.

Individuals are sometimes crucial determinants. In some cases, only one

---

*In terms of Putnam's theory, a feasible alliance is one for which the domestic "win-sets" of its members overlap; a competitive one is one in which at least some of the payoffs available in the area of overlap are for both parties as good as or better than those attainable in any alternative.

or two persons may have virtually complete control of foreign policy. Their alignment biases may be so clear that when they assume power they immediately trigger a reappraisal of alignments throughout the system. Some leaders may be so skilled in manipulating the system that they can loosen or evade systemic constraints at least temporarily.

Domestic and international bargaining may interact in various ways. In one obvious way, the statesman may find domestic constraints useful in establishing a credible minimum position in an alliance negotiation. Conversely, a politician may use an alliance offer from another state to buttress his domestic position. An individual decision maker in one country may appeal to allied decision makers to bring pressure on his home government. One government may tailor its alliance policy deliberately to raise or lower the influence of a faction in another government.

We turn now to an assessment of how each of these broad factors—system structure, strength differences and particular conflicts between states, and internal politics—affected the formation of alliances between 1879 and 1907.

THE AUSTRO-GERMAN ALLIANCE, 1879

At least part of the motivation for the Austro-German alliance can be traced simply to anarchy and multipolarity. Bismarck wanted to ally with *somebody* in a threatening world. There were three possible partners: Russia, Austria, Britain. Russia was temporarily ineligible because of its threatening behavior, yet Bismarck kept it in view as a possibility. He toyed with Britain but chose Austria. Bismarck heavily stressed preclusive reasons—blocking Austria from allying with France and Russia—an eminently systemic rationale.

Austria, too, was motivated partly by systemic position. Sandwiched between two powerful opponents, it needed to be allied with one, even if it had no particular conflicts with either. Andrassy, like Bismarck, also had preclusive motives: he feared an eventual coalition between Germany and Russia which would divide up the Hapsburg dominions; attaching Germany to Austria would reduce this danger.[1]

The alliance was also a natural consequence of the pattern of relationships, of particular interests and strength inequalities. Austria had longstanding differences with Russia in the Balkans. There were no direct conflicts between Austria and Germany, and the two had a positive common interest in preserving the Hapsburg monarchy. Otherwise, however, their interests only partly converged. Germany did not fully share Austria's interests in the Balkans and the Near East. Bismarck saw Germany's interest in partition: the eastern Balkans to Russia, the western portion to

[133]

Austria. Thus he did not endorse Austria's desire to keep Russia out of the Balkans entirely. Austria had no interest in Germany's conflict with France. The alliance was largely built on Austria's need for German help against Russia, and Germany's strategic interest in preserving the Austro-Hungarian state, especially to keep Austrian power out of Russian hands.

Strength inequality also contributed to Bismarck's choice of ally. He felt he could control Austria, but not Russia or presumably Britain. As a powerful country itself, Germany did not need a powerful ally; it was more important that it be able to control the ally it selected. Intrinsic, specifically ethnic and ideological, values also contributed: Bismarck emphasized the "organic" nature of the connection between the two Germanic states. His rejection of Britain is also explainable mostly by the nonstrategic factor of ideology: Bismarck was always skeptical of the reliability of Britain as a parliamentary democracy.

Domestic political factors had discernible yet relatively minor effects on the formation of the Austro-German alliance. One such factor was Bismarck's feud, partly personal and partly political, with the Russian chancellor, Gorchakov, and his campaign to have the latter replaced by Paul Shuvalov, the Russian ambassador in London, whom Bismarck considered a better friend of Germany. The failure of this campaign, along with various manifestations of Russian hostility, apparently decided Bismarck to make his alliance with Austria. The timing of the move toward Austria was influenced by another domestic development: the impending resignation of the pro-German Austrian foreign minister, Andrássy. Bismarck feared that Andrássy's replacement might be someone from the anti-German camp who would take Austria into alliance with Russia and France. Austrian domestic policies had lately been moving in an anti-German, pro-Slav direction. In Germany, alliance with Austria had strong popular support, but Bismarck was not one to be influenced much by public opinion.[2]

Thus the Austro-German alliance reflected all the motivations just listed. General systemic motives were perhaps dominant for Germany; motives of particular interest, for Austria. Power inequality and ethnic-ideological affinities motivated both parties to a lesser extent. The effects of domestic political variables appear to be minor but, admittedly, are difficult to assess because they turn on counterfactuals.* If Bismarck had succeeded in getting rid of Gorchakov, would he have considered an Austrian alliance unnecessary? Would Andrássy's replacement have blocked an alliance with Germany? The answers are most likely no: Bismarck's systemic in-

---

*Domestic pressures apparently became more compelling in Germany in later years. Thus Fritz Fischer argues that Wilhelmine Germany adopted expansionist policies, and even welcomed war, partly in order to control left-wing forces. Fischer, *War of Illusions: German Policies from 1911 to 1914*, trans. Marian Jackson (New York: Norton, 1975).

centive to ally with Austria probably was strong enough to prevail, whatever the makeup of the Russian government, and Austria's national interests in conflict with Russia would have dominated any anti-German tendencies in Andrássy's successor.

Another factor that contributed to the German motivation was the temporary hostility spiral between Germany and Russia that developed in the wake of the Congress of Berlin. Charges and countercharges in the press, military activities on both sides, Russian resentment over German policy on several minor issues, and especially the Bismarck-Gorchakov quarrel led to exaggerated fears on both sides.[3] Hostility spirals are generally explainable in systemic terms as a consequence of the security dilemma: in a world of incomplete information, when two parties begin to identify each other as opponents, defensive measures on one side are bound to look threatening to the other, and the latter's own countermeasures, likewise, appear as a threat to the first party, thus producing an illusory spiral of tension. In this case, domestic and systemic factors reinforced each other: once the internal factors had stimulated a sufficient initial degree of mutual suspicion, the system took over and escalated it. And with every upward ratchet, Germany moved a step closer to Austria.

THE THREE EMPERORS' ALLIANCE, 1881

The Three Emperor's Alliance was largely preclusive in Bismarck's perspective: it blocked the Franco-Russian combination that was the logical counter to the German-Austrian one. This was a systemic motive in that it served the general German interest in frustrating the formation of a balancing alliance. Russia was also driven partly by preclusive motives: blocking a German or Austrian alliance with Britain. The Russo-British conflicts themselves, however, were largely conflicts of particular interests in the Near East and Asia. Another systemic motive for Bismarck, as he explained to the Russian ambassador, was the desirability of being in a majority coalition. The recruitment of Russia also eased a potential two-front war problem, which was mostly a function of system structure and geography, although it was exacerbated by Germany's particular dispute with France. Similarly, the alliance protected Austria's rear in the event of a war with Italy.

These systemic motives were intertwined with particular conflicts and common interests. A strong motive, at least for Bismarck, was to moderate the Austro-Russian conflict, and this incentive was shared to some degree by the other parties. Side payments to Russia, especially concerning the closure of the Straits, satisfied its particular interests.

The principal effect of power inequality in the alliance's negotiation was to weaken the bargaining power of Austria. Once Austria had lost its British option, its military weakness meant it had virtually no choice but to accept what Germany and Russia had agreed on.

Nonstrategic (intrinsic) affinities were underlined by the title given to the alliance. Monarchical solidarity was an important motive, especially for Russia, overriding the anomaly of being allied to two states that were themselves allied against it. Austrian leaders, too, could feel that their institutions were strengthened by alliance with like-minded states.

Aside from this mutual ideological attraction, the domestic development that bore most strongly on the alliance negotiations occurred in an external party, Great Britain. The shift from a Tory government under Disraeli to a Liberal one under Gladstone reinforced Bismarck's belief that Britain was too unreliable for an ally and that it was therefore necessary to revive the *Dreikaiserbund*.[4] The change in Britain also grievously weakened Austria's bargaining power by removing its most plausible alliance alternative; and it strengthened Russia's leverage by reducing its external threat and hence its need for the alliance.

The agreement was concluded in the face of strong contradictory domestic currents in both Austria-Hungary and Russia—from the anti-Russian Magyars in Hungary and the anti-Austrian Pan-Slavs in Russia—although these pressures were not felt directly on the negotiations, which were conducted secretly.

FRANCO-RUSSIAN ALLIANCE, 1891–1894

The Franco-Russian alliance had basically a systemic cause: it was a belated response to the Austro-German (and later Triple) alliance that threatened both countries. Its immediate precipitant, however, was the need to counter an even larger agglomeration of power that the two governments perceived to be taking shape: the apparent adhesion of Britain to the Triple Alliance. This was preeminently a systemic motive: a potentially dominant coalition was being formed. If Russia and France came together, they stood a chance of blocking it; otherwise, they might be defeated individually. Here again the preclusive motive was operating, though not as strongly as in the German-Austrian case: France, in particular, was concerned to discourage Russia from bandwagoning to the dominant group.

The interests of both members were partly systemic and strategic, partly particular and intrinsic. On systemic grounds, as modified by geography, both felt threatened by Germany and the Triple Alliance. Each had a general strategic interest in preventing the other's power resources from falling into German hands. Beyond this, their particular interests diverged.

France focused almost entirely on the German threat; Russia only partly. For Russia, Austria and England were enemies as important as Germany, although not so much as threats as obstacles to Russia's expansionist aims. France, too, had expansionist objectives, but again, solely at German expense. France had colonial aims that conflicted with Britain's, but not as severely as Russia's did. France did not share Russia's particular revisionist aims in the Near and Far East, and Russia did not share the French goal of retaking Alsace-Lorraine. In short, they had strong general interests in common, but their particular interests were divergent, although not contradictory. The common interest in a balance of power against Germany proved a sufficient basis for alliance. The Russians, however, maintained mental reservations about who was the primary enemy—Germany, Britain, or Austria—that would complicate the allies' subsequent relations.

Among domestic factors, ideological differences helped delay completion of the alliance. French distaste for the Russian autocracy inhibited moves toward alliance during the 1880s but had little effect once the decision was taken to go ahead. Russia's worries about French indiscretions and governmental instability contributed to its procrastination in completing the negotiations.

As in the Three Emperors' Alliance, an important domestic element was in a country external to the alliance—in this case, Germany, specifically the genius of Bismarck. By systemic logic, the Franco-Russian alliance should have taken shape soon after the German-Austrian one. That it did not is largely due to Bismarck's diplomatic skills. Bismarck "beat the system" by binding every other power in the system, except France, to Germany in one way or another and thus isolating France. In particular, he kept Russia tied to Germany for nine years, through the Three Emperors' Alliance and then through the Reinsurance Treaty. He succeeded in overriding general systemic forces by appealing to the particular strategic and intrinsic interests of others. Thus he appealed to Russia's intrinsic interest in monarchical solidarity and its strategic interests in the Near East. He tied England to Austria and Italy by emphasizing the commonalities of those three in resisting Russia and France in the Mediterranean. He massaged Italy's colonial aspirations, appeased France on colonial matters, and supported left-wing parties in France to reduce the attractiveness of France to Russia.

Despite his diplomatic virtuosity, Bismarck was less skilled, and/or less influential, at the level of domestic political economy. His economic bullying of Russia, in response to pressures from the "iron-and-rye" coalition in German domestic politics, helped move Russia toward French finance and thence toward a military alliance.[5]

The forced resignation of Bismarck in 1890 was a factor in finally bringing about the alliance. Bismarck's successors thought his alliance system too complex to manage; that is, they lacked confidence in their own ability to keep systemic forces at bay as he had done. Thus, when the Russian connection was cut, these forces immediately reasserted themselves and produced the Franco-Russian alliance.

Domestic politics in Russia and France had some, though only marginal, effect on the outcome. French leadership and public opinion was split, as usual, among pro-British, pro-Russian, and pro-German tendencies. An upsurge of nationalistic fervor in the late 1880s, associated with the name of General Boulanger, stimulated popular and press enthusiasm for alliance with Russia. The parties of the left, on the other hand, opposed the alliance. In Russia, domestic politics had little influence on foreign policy, which was controlled by the Czar and a small circle of advisers. Alexander III himself tended to be pro-French, although he was ideologically repelled by the constant turnover of French governments and especially by the Boulanger episode.[6] He was anti-German and anti-Austrian and consequently was much less disturbed by the collapse of the Reinsurance Treaty than was his foreign minister, Giers.[7] Giers preferred a German alliance to a French one and acted as a brake on the Czar during the negotiations with France, although he did not openly oppose the alliance. His assistant, Lamsdorff, wavered between his ideological distaste for France and fear of entrapment in a Franco-German war, and his belief that a balance of power must be established against the Triple Alliance.[8] The negative influence of Giers may have been offset by the positive influence of the journalist Mikhail Katkov, an extreme Pan-Slav nationalist who agitated ceaselessly for the French connection and had the ear of the Czar.[9] The personal relationship established between Generals Boisdeffre and Obruchev, and especially the latter's energy in overriding the inertia at the Russian court, helped bring the negotiations to closure.

THE BRITISH ENTENTES

The British move out of "splendid isolation" at the turn of the century may be attributed partly to systemic and partly to domestic causes. The systemic causes were the rise in military and industrial strength of other powers, especially Germany and Russia, and the formation of the Franco-Russian alliance, which stalemated politics in Europe. These two factors increased the interest of all European powers in imperial expansion, bringing them, inevitably, into conflict with Britain. The British were faced with more enemies and more conflicts than they could handle with their available military and naval resources. Increasing these resources was precluded by domestic constraints against increasing taxation or reducing social welfare expenditures. The British government dealt with the problem by negotiating away some of the conflicts and by substituting alliances for arms.

Having too many enemies, like having many alternative allies, is, of course, a persistent possibility in a multipolar system. But Britain's turn-of-the-century enemies, France and Russia, had shown by their behavior that they were real enemies, not just potential ones. That is, there were particular conflicts between Britain and these two states, based on internally generated values and interests, which exacerbated systemic rivalry. The existence of these conflicts, chiefly colonial, not only supplied a motive for the ententes but also was helpful in negotiating them, since they provided tangible materials out of which amicable compromises could be fashioned. The absence of particular disputes between Britain and Germany, by contrast, may have contributed to the failure of their negotiations in 1898 and 1901; they could focus only on the far more forbidding task of creating a formal alliance.[10]

Britain's entente partners also were burdened with too many enemies. France learned at Fashoda that it was not capable of simultaneously opposing both Britain and Germany; for it, the entente was also a matter of transforming at least one enemy into a friend. Russia, too, weakened by the war with Japan, had at least one enemy too many. Note that in all three cases, it took a defeat or shock in the colonial arena (in Britain's case, the costly Boer War) to dramatize the parties' overcommitment and shift their attention back to Europe.

Of course, the enemy that made too many for all three states was Germany. Thus the general motive of all three to pare down their commitments and end their rivalry was colored by the newly arisen threat from Germany. This was a classic balance-of-power dynamic: the rise of a new threat submerges differences among the threatened.

Preclusive motives were also at play, especially for Britain. It was not at all clear, at the turn of the century, that France and Russia might not be seduced by Germany into a "continental league." In Russia's case, especially, the pull toward Germany was strong, and it was part of Britain's motivation in 1907 to block that tendency. Similarly, a prominent motive for Britain in allying with Japan in 1902 was to prevent an understanding between Japan and Russia.

The ideological factor worked positively for the Anglo-French entente, negatively for the Anglo-Russian one. The basic ideological kinship between the French and British people, so long smothered by colonial disputes, burst again into full flower and significantly eased the negotiations. Mutual ideological distaste between Britain and Russia inhibited and delayed the 1907 agreement and hampered its implementation.

The most significant domestic political factor in forming the ententes, on the British side, was the political constraint against tax increases or reductions in welfare expenditures. The collision between these constraints and the rising budgetary demands of imperial and foreign policy commitments provided a major impetus for negotiation of the ententes.[11] This was especially so in the case of the agreement with Russia, which promised substantial savings in army expenditures. A further motivation was the growing anti-German sentiment in the press and public opinion, which was reciprocated in Germany.

There were only minor differences in alliance preferences between the major parties—Conservatives and Liberals—and these differences tended to be narrowed by the behavior of other states. The Conservatives were traditionally empire-oriented, anti-French, anti-Russian, and pro-German. They had sponsored the abortive move toward alliance with Germany, against opposition from the Liberals, who favored an agreement with Russia. The pro-German sentiment of the Conservatives began to decline after 1901, however, especially after they awakened to the Germans' naval ambitions.[12] The Tories had themselves worked for an understanding with Russia; Salisbury had tried in 1898, and Lord Lansdowne had initiated negotiations in 1903 only to have them interrupted by the Russo-Japanese war.[13] The Conservatives negotiated the entente with France, as a stepping-stone toward an agreement with Russia; they were supported by the Imperial wing of the Liberals, whereas the Radical wing was skeptical. After the elections of December 1905, the Liberals under Sir Edward Grey strengthened the entente and gave it an anti-German, balance-of-power cast, but this probably would have occurred also under a Conservative government: the security dilemma or hostility spiral that the entente generated in Anglo-German relations eventually would have prevailed.

In France, foreign policy had for many years been an arena of political and bureaucratic conflict—among pro-Russian, pro-British, and pro-German sentiment in the Assembly and public opinion, and between the anti-British colonial ministry and the anti-German foreign ministry. The Fashoda crisis of 1898 temporarily strengthened anti-British, pro-German tendencies, but its longer-term result was to discredit the colonials and shift the balance of internal power in Britain's favor. But again, it is a moot point whether this internal shift was independently causative or merely epiphenomenal; that is, whether any French government would have learned Fashoda's lesson and decided to conciliate Britain in order to balance Germany. Similarly, it is hard to say whether some French foreign minister who was less anti-German than the incumbent, Théophile Delcassé, might have included Germany in the Morocco settlement, thus removing the rationale for the German challenge in 1905, which helped transform the entente into a quasi-alliance. The cashiering of Delcassé during the Morocco crisis testifies to the strength of pro-German forces in the cabinet, but the return to Delcassé's policies after his replacement by Pierre

Rouvier suggests the capacity of systemic forces to override personal views.

There was no significant party conflict in Britain over the entente with Russia in 1907. Differences concerned only motive and rationale, not the end itself. The Tories viewed it chiefly as a settlement of colonial conflicts with a major adversary. The Liberal Imperialists who negotiated it shared that motive but were also driven by the desire to construct a balance of power against Germany. The only significant political opposition came from the more extreme Radicals in the Liberal party, who viewed with distaste any dealings with the Czarist regime.[14] Their ideological repugnance, however, was diluted by the expected welfare benefits of military retrenchment.[15] Their further distaste for power politics was neutralized by advertising the agreement as a settlement of conflicts with an opponent rather than as balancing against another opponent.[16]

Professionals in the Foreign Office tended to be anti-German and so, in the main, gave enthusiastic support to both ententes. They were supported by the navy, which was beginning to be concerned about the growing German fleet. The army, on the other hand, was slow to perceive France and Russia as anything but enemies and initially opposed agreements with both countries. Colonial bureaucrats in Egypt supported the agreement with France, but the government of India resisted the settlement with Russia.[17]

In Russia the domestic politics of foreign policy meant hardly more than the relations between the Czar and his governmental advisers. Czar Nicholas's German sympathies were expressed in his two abortive alliance negotiations with Kaiser Wilhelm in 1904 and 1905. Among his advisers, there were pro-French and pro-German officials but hardly any pro-British. Virtually all were anti-Austrian. These "phobias" and "philias" mirrored Russia's traditional alignments and enmities. A traumatic external event—defeat in the war with Japan—along with its consequences—revolution and military weakness—trumped all these internal currents and produced the move toward Britain in 1906–7. Frustration in the Far East shifted Russia's attention back again to the Balkans and Near East, where its natural opponents were Austria and Germany. Revolution and its offspring, the Duma, strengthened pro-French and pro-British sentiment, on ideological grounds, in the public and press.[18] Pro-German sentiment remained strong in the Russian government and court, however, where the idea of rehabilitating the *Dreikaiserbund* was more popular than a connection with Britain. Nevertheless, Lamsdorff, the foreign minister, recognized the need for a Franco-British orientation to escape "the German yoke."[19] Lamsdorff's replacement by Alexander Izvolsky in 1906 was thought in Britain to presage a pro-German shift,[20] but it was Izvolsky who carried through the negotiation of the entente, against diehard opposition from the military.[21] In doing so, he merely reflected the systemic pressures on his country. Likewise, his care not to antagonize Germany in the process reflected his country's weakness more than pro-German sentiment. Such sentiment did not die, but it was eclipsed in this case by systemic necessities.

SUMMARY: ALLIANCE MOTIVES

It would be quixotic to attempt to estimate, in any exact way, the relative influence of these factors on alliance formation during the period. Not only is the evidence sketchy, but the factors themselves overlap considerably, so that it is not possible to gauge with any precision how much any given decision or outcome was influenced by one factor or another. Nevertheless, what stands out in this brief survey is the pervasive influence of systemic, or structural, factors. Thirty years of alliance making produced the outcome that systemic logic predicts: a balance of power. Most of the interests that motivated states along the way were general and strategic, that is, interests that flowed inescapably from the structure of the system and were valued chiefly for their power content.[22] Statesmen's explicit rationales for their behavior emphasized systemic motives, such as balancing a threat, precluding the partner from allying elsewhere, and countering an alliance already formed. Even when the systemic rationale was overtly lacking, as in the absence of the balancing motive as an explicit or even conscious rationale during negotiation of the Anglo-French entente, it was latently present and asserted itself after the fact. As the foregoing summaries show, there were several instances in which systemic logic triumphed over "unit attributes" that ran the other way—for example, the Franco-Russian alliance and the Russian acceptance of the entente with Britain.

As Robert Jervis has noted, a peculiar feature of the pre-1914 alliance lineups was that several countries appeared to be on the wrong side. Their alignments did not reflect their most obvious particular conflicts or common interests with others.[23] Neither Britain nor Russia had any specific disputes with Germany, but they had some with each other. Neither Britain nor France had any quarrel with Austria; in fact, they shared substantial interests with it in shoring up the Ottoman Empire. Austria and Italy were sharply in conflict over the Trentino and the Balkans; Germany and Austria were economic rivals in the Balkans and Near East. These anomalies are explained by noting that the "right side" was determined primarily by systemic forces and alliance dynamics, and the strategic interests they generated, rather than by particular interests and disputes.[24]

Intrinsic repulsions and affinities—chiefly ideological and ethnic—were

[142]

not unimportant, however. The Franco-Russian alliance no doubt would have formed earlier had it not been for mutual ideological repugnance. The Austro-German alliance was grounded in ethnic and ideological attraction, and it is unlikely that Russia would have joined it had it not been for ideological kinship. One reason the Germans could never bring themselves to ally with Britain, except on terms outrageously favorable to them, was their belief that its democratic system made Britain an unreliable partner.[25]

Our survey shows that although specific situations or individuals in domestic politics sometimes had major effects on alliance formation, more often they were dominated by, or reflected, systemic effects. The outstanding deviation from this picture is Bismarck's delaying of the formation of the Franco-Russian alliance for fifteen years. Thus it is possible for a single individual, if endowed with sufficient will and skill, to overcome systemic forces. But the fact that those who followed Bismarck capitulated to these forces suggests that such individuals are rare.

The Bismarck example is one of an internal factor that actually overcame systemic constraints. Much more common are cases in which the systemic constraints leave considerable room for choice, and domestic constraints then determine actual choices, or at least narrow the range of choice. In such cases, it is often hard to say whether external or internal causation is predominant. For example, the British ententes were responses to both increasing external demands on resources and domestic economic-political limits on available resources. Since constraints, either external or internal, are rarely absolute, Britain faced a choice between satisfying external constraints at some domestic cost—that is, increasing or maintaining armaments—or sacrificing some external goals to meet domestic constraints. Its actual choice was a combination of the two.

There was comparatively little disagreement among British governmental elites about the nature and stringency of the external constraints. All agreed that retrenchment was necessary and that it meant either alliances or settlements with others; they disagreed only about which others, but even this difference evaporated when Germany took itself out as a candidate. In other countries, the "phobias" and "philias" regarding preferable alliance partners were more sharply defined, so that policy choices turned more on who was in charge or on the balance of influence between factions. Thus it made a difference, to Bismarck at least, whether a Hungarian or an Austrian was in charge of the Ballhausplatz in Vienna; he felt he could get an alliance with the former but not the latter.

Systemic stimuli may set up a narrow rather than a broad range of choice, or they may point urgently to a particular option. In such cases, the systemic option may collide with, but will usually overcome, the dominant domestic tendency. For example, in Russia in the early 1890s, the systemic imperative to ally with France overcame a strong pro-German tide in the Russian government and court, as did the need to settle with Britain in 1907. In that case, the defeated element hung on and continued to confuse Russian policy up to about 1912. In others, as in France after Fashoda, the defeated party was drastically weakened or eliminated, and the domestic lineup shifted to match the logic of the system.

As this last example suggests, domestic change that appears to be causal may be merely epiphenomenal, simply reflecting stimuli from the system rather than exerting independent effect. Thus the transformation of the Anglo-French entente from a colonial arrangement to a quasi-alliance is sometimes attributed to the anti-German bias of the Liberal Imperialists or the Foreign Office, but this construal seriously underplays both systems dynamics and the role of German behavior and German power in producing this bias.

ALLIANCE PRECIPITANTS

By looking only at cases where alliances formed, we have avoided the question, Why did alliances take shape when they did and not before or after? The answer suggested by game theory is that alliances form only when all participants believe they can do better in an alliance than they could do by themselves. An alliance possibility does not materialize until at least two states perceive that they are better off acting jointly than separately. This happens, of course, when they both feel sufficiently threatened by some third state or alliance. Such a threat need not be objectively real; an imagined threat is sufficient to precipitate alliance, as an illusory Russian threat triggered Bismarck's alliance with Austria in 1879.

Alliances are often precipitated by specific threatening events. One such event is the news or rumor that a hostile alliance is about to form. Thus rumors that a Franco-Russian alliance was in the making helped motivate Bismarck to conclude both the alliance with Austria and the subsequent one with Russia. Rumors that England had virtually joined the Triple Alliance provided a similar spur to conclusion of the Franco-Russian alliance. Also, a crisis or war can easily catalyze incentives to ally that had previously been only latent. Thus the Fashoda crisis ultimately convinced Delcassé that it was necessary for France to come to terms with Britain. Or a crisis may precipitate alliance simply by exacerbating hostility between two states, thus increasing their perceived need for assistance. The Bulgarian crisis of the mid-1880s triggered both Russia's decision to break with Austria and the desire to renew its connection with Germany. In the case of the British move out of "splendid isolation" after 1900, the specific precipitant was the Boer War, which dramatized both the limitations of England's resources and its surfeit of potential enemies.

An alliance may be precipitated by the failure of negotiations for an alternate alliance. Thus Russia turned to France immediately after the German refusal to renew the Reinsurance Treaty. Britain initiated discussions with Japan soon after the collapse of negotiations with Germany in 1901. After the failure of the Bjorko negotiations with Germany in 1905, Russia became more amenable to British overtures.

INHIBITIONS ON ALLIANCE FORMATION

Fear of Provocation

With surprising frequency, statesmen indicated fears that formation of an alliance would provoke an opponent to attack. Apparently, such fears are an important inhibiting factor on alliance formation. One variant is the fear that the opponent will be tempted to attack one of the new alliance's members before the alliance has had time to solidify or to realize its capabilities. Perhaps the most important reason France did not seek an alliance with Russia until 1890 was the fear that any move in that direction would precipitate a German preventive attack.[26] This also helps explain the urgency with which the French pressed for a precise military convention following their vague agreement of 1891. They worried that the agreement might provoke a German attack without fully committing the Russians or effectively coordinating French and Russian military forces.

Another variant is the fear that the new alliance will be taken as a pretext for an attack that is otherwise motivated. Grey seemed to have this in mind when he declared in September 1906: "The difficulty of making an alliance with France now is that Germany might attack France at once, while Russia is helpless, fearing lest when Russia recovered she (Germany) should be crushed by a new Triple Alliance against her. She might make an alliance between us and France a pretext for doing this as her only chance of securing the future."[27]

A more moderate form of the fear of provocation is the worry that an alliance will antagonize states against which it is, or appears to be, directed, although short of provoking them to attack. Sir Arthur Nicolson, in 1912, reacted coolly to the French ambassador's suggestion to turn the Anglo-French entente into an alliance, saying that "British public opinion would [not] be disposed to welcome such proposals, which would be regarded by many as offering umbrage and a challenge to Germany."[28]

The fear of provocation, however far-fetched it may seem in particular instances, has its roots in the structure of a multipolar international system. First, in systemic anarchy, it is difficult to be sure whether the security moves of others are intended for defense or aggrandizement. A defensive alliance may appear to an opponent as potentially aggressive and thus activate thoughts of preemption or prevention. Second, alliance making involves deliberate choice of one potential ally over others, and the others may interpret that choice as an act of hostility, since they are the logical targets of the new combination. In a bipolar system, by contrast, alliances (and enmities), at least those in the central arena of Europe, are largely ordained by the logic of the system. Since their members have little choice in the matter, their formation can hardly be interpreted as an affectively hostile act. Conversely, and for the same reason, alliance formation in a multipolar system has stronger affective overtones of friendship than in a bipolar system. The near-hysterical outpouring of public emotion at crucial points in the formation of the Franco-Russian alliance dramatically illustrates this phenomenon. The emotional discomfort of isolation, experienced first by France, then by Russia, and finally by Germany, stems largely from a system structure that permits "not being chosen".

To dampen the overtones of hostility in alliance formation, allying states are often at pains to assure others that the new alliance is not directed against them, or that it is only defensive. Thus, after the Anglo-Japanese alliance of 1902, Britain assured Russia that the alliance would operate only in the case of an unprovoked attack on one of the allies.[29]

Worsening relations with the apparent target is only one of the externalities of alliance formation. The effects, positive or negative, may ramify to states other than the alliance members and their designated opponent(s). The choice of one partner, for example, may depreciate the value of alternatives, as Britain's choice of Japan over Germany in 1902 reduced the attraction of Germany and made it easier for Britain to think of Germany as a potential enemy. The Franco-Russian alliance, although formally directed at the Triple Alliance, aroused disquiet in Britain by apparently releasing Russian military resources for use in Central Asia. Lord Salisbury greeted the Austro-German alliance as "good tidings of great joy,"[30] since it seemed to array Germany behind Austria in support of British interests in the Near East. Such externalities are a natural consequence of superimposing a formal alliance over a preexisting network of interests.

Keeping Options Open

Another inhibition on alliance making in a multipolar world is the desire to keep alliance options open as long as possible. To make an alliance with one party is to close off one's options of allying with others, or at least to inhibit them. Foreclosure of options is one of the costs of alliance making, to be weighed against the value of increased security and other benefits. Given the normal uncertainty in a multipolar system about who is friend and who is foe, statesmen may prefer to maintain the uncertainty rather than to end it prematurely or unnecessarily. Keeping options open also minimizes dependence, husbands bargaining power, and avoids antagonizing the states not chosen as allies. With no allies, one can be neither abandoned nor entrapped by them, although against this, of course, must be counted the risks of isolation.

Options to be preserved also include options of conciliating or settling with enemy states. For example, during negotiations with England about the entente of 1907, Izvolsky went out of his way to placate Germany and assure it that the agreement had no anti-German purpose.[31] When Germany began moving closer to England in the early 1890s, Salisbury reacted coolly. Paul Kennedy notes, "A firm and public commitment to the Triple Alliance, in addition to causing a political furor at home and making Britain dependent on such unstable characters as Wilhelm and Crispi, would also render impossible Salisbury's hope of settling Anglo-French and Anglo-Russian differences."[32] One reason for the failure of the Anglo-German alliance negotiations at the turn of the century was that both governments wanted to preserve their options vis-à-vis France and Russia.

An important aspect of the virtuosity of Bismarck was his ability to retain a maximum number of options for himself and close off alternatives for his opponents. Thus he checked Austria by retaining the option of alignment with Russia, an option he exercised between 1881 and 1890. The sacrifice of this option by his successors was one reason Germany finally lost control of Austria. Bismarck also kept Britain in play in order to use it as support for Austria when he was unwilling to commit Germany fully to that purpose. And an obvious hallmark of his system was the closure of options to his main adversary, France, by keeping everyone else tied, one way or another, to Germany.

GAME THEORY AND BARGAINING THEORY

N-Person Game Theory

The dynamics of the N-person game can be seen in outline in the cases but not in detail. The system eventually divided into two coalitions, as the theory predicts. In allocating the costs and benefits of their alliances, the states engaged in a bargaining process crudely similar to that specified in bargaining set theory. Apparently, no state joined an alliance when it could have done better by itself or in some other alliance.[33]

Beyond these very general similarities, there was considerable divergence from the theory. For instance, when alliances were made, the states involved did not have the plethora of alternatives that is suggested in some presentations of the theory. There were no competitive alternatives to the Austro-German alliance or the Franco-Russian alliance, and perhaps one to the Three Emperors' Alliance. In other words, at the time of negotiation, the statesmen involved were not seriously interested in any alliance other than the one they were negotiating. (It might be argued that Bismarck considered a Russian connection while he was negotiating the alliance with Austria; if so, it was not as an alternative to Austria but as a possible later addition.) Other possibilities were relevant in that they affected a party's bargaining position in negotiating its preferred alliance but without promising enough benefit to be competitive.

The only operational alternatives, of course, are those that are perceived. There were a few cases of alternatives that might have existed objectively but were not perceived or were undervalued by one party or the other. One was a possible renewal of the German-Russian Reinsurance Treaty in 1890, which, had the Germans not undervalued it and misestimated the danger of a Franco-Russian alliance, would have been a competitive alternative to the latter. Later the Germans similarly underestimated the danger of England's lining up with France and Russia. Even if they had judged Britain's alternatives correctly, however, it is doubtful that this would have made an Anglo-German alliance possible when it was attempted in 1898 and 1901. The two parties' interests were so different that no bargain beneficial to both was feasible.

The lack of competitive alternatives meant that in all three of the cases that were examined in detail, there was no indeterminacy about which alliance, if any, would form; the only indeterminacy lay in how the benefits and costs of a single alliance would be divided. One does not find in history any analogue to the well-known "dividing the dollar" game in which it is completely uncertain which two of three players will reach agreement, but an agreement, when made, is usually a fifty-fifty split or close to it. It is as if the third player in such a game had simply opted out, leaving the other two with the far more indeterminate task of dividing the dollar between themselves. To use another image, alliance making in a multipolar system is not like perfect competition in an economic system, where many buyers and sellers are present but the market sets the price, nor is it like bilateral monopoly, where the price is set by bargaining between a single buyer and single seller, analogous to a bipolar system. Structurally, it is like oligopoly, with a few sellers (or buyers) collaborating to set the price, but behaviorally, it tends toward duopoly, that is, the few are often only two.

The scarcity of alternatives throws into question the conventional notion of the flexibility of alliances in a multipolar system. There is a considerable difference between the number of alternatives that are physically there and the number that are politically available. Apparent flexibility derives from the plethora of physical alternatives—that is, from system structure. But this flexibility is considerably reduced, as we have seen, by the particular interests and affinities of states, which enhance the attractiveness of some alliances and diminish that of others. For example, alliance with France was not an attractive option for any European state for some years after 1871 because of the risk of being entrapped in a revanchist war with Germany.

The structural flexibility of a multipolar system is also constricted by the tendency of alliances, once made, to generate new interests that are consistent with them. The alliance more clearly identifies friends and foes; the dynamics of the system then generate interests in defending the ally's interests and resources and in resisting the adversary's expansion.[34] The new interests raise the value of the alliance from its value when initially negotiated and diminish the value of possible alternatives. In turn, this improves the cohesion and durability of the alliance. It does not seem, however, to alleviate statesmen's fears that their alliance might collapse; such fears paradoxically contribute to the longevity of the alliance by causing statesmen to cling more tightly to their allies. In both the pre-1914 alliance systems, their members first developed new or stronger interests in defending each other, then were led to tighten their ties still further out of illusory worries about their partners' defection.

If the notion of "alternative" is redefined to include settlement of disputes with an adversary, more alternatives appear. Thus Japanese leaders thought they had the alternative of settling with Russia when they negotiated their alliance with Britain in 1902. The alternative turned out not to be available because the Russians asked exorbitant terms, but the British belief that it was available helped Japan get better terms from Britain.

The threat to turn elsewhere is often used as a source of leverage in alliance negotiations. The uncertainty about whether alternatives are available can lend credence to such a threat. In 1902 the Japanese were aware that however unsuccessful they might be in their approach to Russia, it could only benefit them in their bargaining with Britain. Germany threatened a continental league during the abortive negotiations with Britain in 1898 and 1901. The visit of the French fleet to Portsmouth in 1891 helped the Russians decide to go ahead with the French alliance.

A striking difference between game theory and the pre-1914 alliance history is that coalitions took shape one member at a time, not in a single grand negotiation, as the theory would have it. This may be explained, in general, by the difference between the abstract notion of a dominant coalition's winning a discrete contest, as in the theory, and the reality that states ally for security to be experienced over time. Two states find sufficient security, at least for the time being, in allying with each other. Then, if a counteralliance forms, they find they need more help, so they add a third. If there is no counteralliance, they remain a pair. One value of proceeding one member at a time is that the size of the alliance can be calibrated to the degree of threat it faces. A further benefit is to reduce the complexity and cost of negotiations. Ultimately, of course, the pre-1914 system embraced all the European great powers, as the theory predicts, but the process by which they arrived at that condition is obscured by the theoretical assumption that a single negotiation results in the creation of a majority coalition. It obscures, for example, possible differences between existing members as to which new member is to be added—as Austria and Germany differed about whether to add Britain or Russia in 1880–81 and about adding Italy in 1882. Adding a member may also shift the balance of dependence or bargaining power between existing members and thus cause friction, as the addition of Russia to the Austro-German alliance in 1881 increased the leverage of Germany over Austria.

The pre-1914 history gives some support to Riker's "size principle." According to Riker, coalitions should be just large enough to win, since anything larger would both reduce total winnings (by reducing the number of players in the opposing coalition from which the winnings are to be extracted) and reduce the share of each member (by unnecessarily increasing the number of members among which the winnings must be divided). The parties proceed by forming "protocoalitions" that are enlarged as needed. The ultimate division of the pre–World War I system into two coalitions of about equal strength, and the stepwise process of arriving at that situation, is quite consistent with this theory.[35]

In sum, there is a considerable distance between the absolute freedom of maneuver and clarity of payoffs of the N-person game and the constraints, complexities, and ambiguities of actual alliance formation. Nevertheless, this model is useful for highlighting the core logic of a multipolar world, a logic that operates in subterranean fashion even though it is hard to see in the day-to-day historical record. It is valuable as an aid to theory building, if not as an empirical research tool.

Bargaining Theory

A notable characteristic of the negotiation of the pre-1914 alliances was the width of the bargaining range. Usually, it was much broader than the distance between the parties' initial demands and offers; that is, what the parties offered each other was considerably better than the minimums they would have accepted. Simply getting an agreement was more important than besting the other side in negotiating the terms of the agreement.

This was a consequence of two general factors: the preponderance of common interests over conflict in the parties' relationship and the relative scarcity and unattractiveness of alternatives to the alliance under consideration. The preponderance of common interests meant there was much to be gained for both (all) parties in negotiating an alliance; with a few exceptions (e.g., Austria in 1881), the alliance was considered a substantial improvement on the status quo. The scarcity of alternatives meant the parties' minimum positions in the bargaining approximated the value of the status quo rather than the value of some alternative alliance. Both these factors together tended to generate a broad range of terms that would have been acceptable to the parties in preference to breaking off negotiations. This is in contrast to bargaining between adversaries in a crisis, when, typically, the higher incidence of conflict relative to common interest tends to narrow the bargaining range or perhaps to eliminate it.

Because some element of conflict is present, however, alliance formation usually requires bargaining, not simply the discovery of common interests. Each of the protopartners will want an agreement that maximizes its own benefits and minimizes its costs. Concretely, each will seek to maximize the partner's commitment to its own interests and minimize its own obligations to the partner. If there are side payments to be distributed in addition to the exchange of commitments, each partner will try to maximize its own share. How successful it is will depend chiefly on its perceptions of the situation, its relative bargaining power, and considerations of equity and salience.

Perceptions

Perceptions and misperceptions are crucial in the estimate of alliance alternatives—both one's own and the partner's. Observable in our cases was a general tendency among statesmen to overestimate the prospective partner's options. One effect of this was to raise estimates of the partner's minimum position in the negotiations. Another effect was to exaggerate the preclusive value of the alliance. Both effects tended to weaken the estimating state's bargaining power.

Thus Bismarck exaggerated the alternatives available to Austria in 1879 and those open to Russia in 1881. Austrian leaders had not seriously considered allying with France or Russia as he feared, nor was a Franco-Russian alliance yet a matter of practical politics. In both cases, Bismarck's bargaining leverage was weakened by his illusory fears, resulting in treaty terms more favorable to his partners than to Germany. In 1890 and 1891 the French gave more credence to the Russians' German option than it deserved. Britain probably conceded more to Russia than it needed to in 1907 because it exaggerated the significance of the stillborn Bjorko treaty of 1905. The most likely explanation of this type of misperception seems to be the well-known tendency of decision makers to think in worst-case terms.

Germany after 1890 appears to be an exception to this pattern, however. The German leaders saw little danger of a Franco-Russian alliance when they broke their tie with Russia in 1890. They also badly underestimated the likelihood of British alignment with France or Russia when they demanded a high price for a British alliance in 1898 and 1901. Their error in both cases seems to have been caused by wishful thinking, or "motivated bias":[36] they believed what they wanted to believe.

Implicitly, alliance bargainers must estimate not only their own alternatives and those of their partner; they must also judge how badly each wants an alliance. Bargaining power is a function of alliance need as well as the alternatives available. Here there is less evidence of misperception. Andrássy apparently sensed that Bismarck wanted an alliance badly in 1879, as evidenced by his cool rejection of the chancellor's first proposal for an even exchange of commitments. The Russians from 1890 to 1894 correctly judged—the obvious French impatience made it an easy call—that France wanted the alliance more than Russia did.

In general, the more information the parties have about each other's preferences and alternatives, the more likely an alliance negotiation will succeed. Information about alternatives permits accurate estimates of the bargaining range; knowledge of each other's preferences provides a sense of the "natural" agreement within the range. A paucity of information, on the other hand, may lead wishfully thinking bargainers to entertain overly optimistic expectations about what their opposite number will accept. Thus the German-English negotiations around the turn of the century were a mirage from the beginning, first, because the Germans exaggerated the width of the bargaining range by underestimating England's French and Russian options, and second, because both parties grossly overestimated the commonality of their interests.

Bargaining Power

In two of the three cases of alliance formation that were examined in detail, the terms of the treaty reflected fairly well the estimated bargaining power of the participants. Austria's bargaining power was superior to Germany's in 1879, by reason of its lesser immediate need for the alliance; consequently, the ultimate terms of the alliance favored Austria. Conversely, Austria's bargaining weakness in 1881, due largely to the evaporation of its British alternative, forced it to concede the lion's share of the benefits of the Three Emperors' Alliance to Germany and Russia.

In the other case, however, the Franco-Russian alliance, the outcome did not match the apparent relative bargaining power of the parties. France was the weaker bargainer by virtue of both its greater desire for the alliance and its lack of alternatives; yet it profited more from the terms of the alliance than Russia did. I advanced two ad hoc explanations for this anomaly: (1) that France got most of what it wanted simply by the greater energy and effort of its negotiators, and (2) that although Russia needed the alliance less than France did on military or security grounds, it badly needed the financial help that was potentially available, even though this did not enter explicitly into the negotiations.

Italy and the negotiation of the Triple Alliance illustrates the special advantage of being in the pivot position in bargaining. The pivotal role falls naturally to a state which is weaker than two others that are rivals for its allegiance and which also has moderate conflicts with those two. Thus it may provide enough capability to make whatever coalition it joins predominant but not enough to threaten leadership or control of the coalition. At the same time, it has enough conflict with both the others to be able to make attractive offers. Italy qualified on both counts, being weak and in conflict with France in North Africa and with Austria in the Trentino and the Balkans. By threatening to settle its disputes with one side or the other, it was able to extort benefits from both. Its gains in the Triple Alliance negotiations of 1882 were substantially greater than those of Austria and Germany, and they improved still more in the subsequent renewals.

Equity and Salience

In most of the negotiations studied, norms of equity and considerations of salience were at least as important as relative bargaining power in determining outcomes. This, of course, is what one would expect in a bargaining context characterized by a high degree of common interest and a wide bargaining range. Relative power is a less potent determinant in such a context, so the participants need some exogenous criterion to guide them to one of many possible points of agreement. In most cases, the criterion was equity; when equity was too much at odds with relative bargaining strength, some other salient feature sufficed or side payments were brought into play.

Thus the Franco-Russian alliance treaty of 1894 called for both members to mobilize simultaneously if the Triple Alliance or any of its members should mobilize. This was, on the surface, an equitable commitment, but it favored Russia because it committed France to mobilize in the event that only Russia's enemy, Austria, mobilized. The French did not like it, but the Russians dug in their heels on the equity principle, and the French were forced to accept it. (They eventually got it changed during later military conversations.) A kind of equity, or at least salience, was also evident in the specified troop contributions: compared to France's 1,350,000, Russia was to send only 700,000 to 800,000 against Germany. This happened to be about half the Russian army; having two enemies, the Russians would have to divide their forces equally against them, or so the Russians argued.

Equity lost out to Austrian bargaining power in the Austro-German negotiations in 1879; Andrássy refused to accept a commitment against France to balance the German commitment against Russia. The eventual agreement, for equal commitments against Russia alone, was pseudo-equal, however, and the Austrian promise of neutrality in case of a German-French war took a step back toward real equality.

The equity principle underlay the mutual promise of neutrality in the Three Emperors' Alliance of 1881, but because this promise alone did not accurately reflect Russia's superior bargaining power, Austria and Germany were forced to give side payments to Russia. They promised to support Russia's aims at the Straits and Constantinople and to support the union of Russia's prospective clients, Bulgaria and Eastern Roumelia. Equity was apparently served by a small side payment to Austria (allowing it to "reserve" its right to annex Bosnia-Herzegovina), but this was only a pittance compared to what Russia received.

The equity principle was occasionally so potent that it preempted careful consideration of a country's interests. One such occasion was the revision of the Anglo-Japanese alliance in 1905. The British government felt that the original treaty was inequitable in Japan's favor and proposed to rectify this by getting a Japanese commitment to the defense of India. Japan agreed but insisted, in return, on a protectorate over Korea. After the treaty was signed, the general staff decided it really did not want Japanese troops in India, because of the difficulty of supplying them and because it "would not be consistent with either our dignity or self-respect."[37] Japan, of course, went ahead with the protectorate in Korea. The British made a similar error a year later. Near the end of the entente negotiations with France, Lansdowne asked that France promise diplomatic support for British control of Egypt should this be challenged by other countries—in particular, by Germany. Delcassé accepted on the condition of a quid pro quo: British diplomatic support of France in Morocco. Lansdowne accepted at once, without any discussion and without submitting the proposal to the cabinet.[38] Apparently, it was so obviously a "fair" exchange that a full exploration of its implications was not considered necessary. In this offhand way, Britain undertook a treaty obligation that was to have enormous effects not only in creating a quasi-alliance but also in setting in motion the spiral of hostility and alliance tightening that was to culminate in the war.

Preliminaries

In most of the alliances studied, the substantive negotiations were preceded by a period of overtures and probes, apparently intended both to ascertain whether an agreement was possible and to accustom governments and public opinion to its prospect. The Franco-Russian alliance provides a good example. For about a decade before the serious start of negotiations, there occurred events and acts of little import in themselves which prepared the way for the alliance. These included the award of a Russian medal to the French president, exchanges of officers' visits to annual maneuvers, naval visits, French arrest of a group of Russian revolutionaries, sharing of French military technology, and (not least) French financial loans. Such preliminaries were less prominent in the prelude to the Austro-German alliance and the Three Emperors' Alliance, perhaps because of the community of sentiment that already existed between the governments of those countries. In 1903 a visit of King Edward to Paris, and a return visit of the French president, Emile Loubet, to London created a propitious atmosphere for negotiating the Anglo-French entente. In that case, apparently, such preliminaries were needed to ease the relationship out of its usual tone of acerbic rivalry.

Preliminary negotiations may serve to "de-compose" a major alliance commitment into a series of smaller pieces, each of which is easier for the parties to accept than an all-at-once promise.[39] The best example of such de-composition in our cases is the stage-by-stage negotiation of the Franco-Russian alliance. Several minor military and financial agreements preceded the negotiation of the political entente in 1891. And the prior negotiation of the entente made it easier to move to the full alliance, which was mislabeled a "military convention."

Once alliance negotiations have actually gotten under way, they acquire a momentum of their own.[40] At that point, the parties become sure that both want to ally and that an alliance is possible. Thenceforth, the force of this wish and this belief is sufficient to overcome obstacles and doubts. The Anglo-Japanese negotiations in 1901–2 are a case in point. Neither party entered the discussions with the goal of a full-fledged defensive alliance. Lansdowne wanted only an "understanding," and he kept open the German option; the Japanese carefully probed both the Russian and the British positions to find out what kind of a deal was to be had from each. Gradually, both sides learned that a deal with Russia was unavailable, that Germany would not join them in opposing Russia, and that therefore a bilateral mutual defensive alliance was the only real option available. Negotiations then proceeded *tout de suite*.[41]

Balancing and Bandwagoning

Balance of Power

The formation of alliances, especially in a multipolar system, has long been associated with the idea of balance of power. These two subjects are far from identical, however. The balance of power is a systemic tendency linked to anarchy; alliance formation is an instrument of statecraft. Alliance making is purposive; balancing may be unintended. The two phenomena intersect and run parallel through a certain range of behavior, but beyond that range they diverge.

For example, alliance patterns are determined in part by a systemic tendency toward equilibrium of power regardless of the particular interests of states and in part by particular conflicts and common interests and strength inequalities. The latter factors may suggest several lines of amity and enmity; the systemic constraint toward equilibrium strongly affects which of these potential alignments actually occurs. A balancing coalition will form against a major aggressor, but the particular interests of states will affect the membership of the coalition. In this manner, the balance of power is a systemic cause of alignment, the particular interests and strengths of states are unit-level causes, and alignments and alliances themselves are relationships that are generated by the simultaneous impact of both sets of causal influences.[42]

When balance of power is interpreted not as an automatic systemic tendency but as deliberate balancing, other comparisons emerge. Alliance making is both broader and narrower than balancing. It is broader, for example, in that alliances may be offensive in purpose, whereas balancing is a defensive notion. States may ally not so much to counter an existing threat as to preclude the partner from allying against oneself in the future. Alliances may aim to neutralize a threat rather than to balance it. They may serve primarily a domestic purpose. And as Walt has shown, states may ally with rather than against an aggressive and powerful state, jumping on its bandwagon rather than balancing it.[43]

Alliance formation is also narrower than balancing, for the simple reason that balancing may be accomplished by other means. One obvious method is by military preparedness. Another, less often mentioned, is fighting. Still a third is conciliation of an adversary. These options correspond to the three basic arenas of security policy described in Chapter 1. In a multipolar system, alliances are often preferred over unilateral armament, because no single state is able to defend itself alone against the full array of enemies that might confront it.*

---

* A distinctive feature of a bipolar system, by contrast, is that superpowers can defend

An issue in the debate about the balance of power is whether equilibrium is intended or unintended—whether it requires deliberate policies of balancing by the participating states or is the automatic result of states pursuing their particular interests by whatever means.[44] The pre–World War I experience tends to support the latter view. An approximately even balance between two alliance structures ultimately formed, but it cannot be said that the participating states planned it that way. They aimed for preponderance, or they sought to preclude a future imbalance against themselves, or they conciliated their opponents, or they used alliance negotiations to obtain support for specific diplomatic goals. Their strategies were many and various, and not all of them could accurately be described as balancing in the usual simple sense of accumulating power against a threat. But whatever their immediate motives, the system constrained their efforts in the ultimate direction of equilibrium.

Bismarck's alliances, for example, were intended to create not a balance of power but a preponderance favoring Germany. Bismarck was able to frustrate the systemic tendency toward balance by tying all others, except France, to Germany. The fact that the balance reasserted itself once the German-Russian connection was broken testifies to the underlying strength of systemic forces. But the fact that the Russian tie lasted as long as it did indicates the strength of particular intrinsic interests and their capacity to overcome temporarily the general strategic interest in balancing.

The Franco-Russian alliance was more clearly a balancing arrangement, but it balanced against different opponents, a feature that threatened its cohesion from start to finish. Each partner wanted to concentrate the alliance's resources against its own rival, a conflict that was never fully resolved and that also bedeviled the Austro-German combination. Such divergence adds complexity to the balance-of-power theory, which assumes agreement about the identity of the opponent. In time, of course, the Russian tendency to see Britain rather than Germany as the main opponent was washed out by the rising threat from Germany and the creation of the Triple Entente.

The British ententes with France and Russia illustrate how balancing may be accomplished by easing conflicts with one set of adversaries in order to free up resources for use against another. They also show how balancing may be "unconscious": in making the agreements with France and Russia, Britain had little or no intention of balancing against Germany—it was saving more than redirecting resources—but the agreements

---

themselves without allies, although they make alliances to codify their strategic interest in the space between them.

[157]

set in motion forces that transformed Germany clearly into an enemy that had to be balanced.

On the whole, the pre-1914 experience supports Waltz's theory that the balance of power is an unintended, automatic consequence of systemic constraints.[45] In spite of the great variety of purposes, some of them quite contrary to balancing, that motivated the European powers in their alliance making over thirty-five years, the ultimate result was the creation of an equilibrium between two opposed coalitions.

Bandwagoning

An alternative to balancing is bandwagoning. To bandwagon is to join the stronger side; thus it is the exact opposite of balancing. According to Walt, states may "jump on the bandwagon" of the apparently winning side for one of two purposes: offensive or defensive. The motive for offensive bandwagoning is to share in the spoils of victory. The motive for defensive bandwagoning, by contrast, is fear, not greed; one ingratiates oneself with the winner so as to deflect it from attacking oneself. Bandwagoning of either kind, Walt shows, is rare compared to balancing; it is generally practiced by small or weak states that cannot find reliable defensive allies.[46]

Our cases support Walt's conclusion that bandwagoning is rare. There was only one possible example of offensive bandwagoning: the Balkan League's jumping on Italy's bandwagon in 1912 by attacking Turkey. Even this is not a crystal-clear example, however, since the Balkan states did not actually ally with Italy.

Italy is perhaps another case of quasi-offensive bandwagoning. Italy had offensive aspirations and sought support from stronger states—first Germany, then France—for those goals. These more powerful allies were not themselves clearly expansionist, however, nor could Italy have confidently predicted that either would be victorious in a war. Italy used the security and alliance needs of stronger states to extort their political support for its colonial aims. It did not seek to share in the spoils that might be reaped by stronger expansionist states, as the bandwagoning model would have it. Thus this is a questionable example of bandwagoning; it illustrates how the rich variety of the empirical world fails to conform to ideal types.

In another deviation from the theory, the small states that allied with great powers chose as partners, not those they believed most likely to win or most threatening to them, but those most likely to advance their interests *if* they won. Thus Rumania defected from the Triple Alliance and eventually lined up with the Entente powers because its own primary interest, in Transylvania, could be satisfied only at Austria-Hungary's expense. Similarly, Bulgaria allied with the Triple Alliance because it had interests in conflict with Rumania, Serbia, and Greece, which were linked to the Entente.

The only good example of defensive bandwagoning in the pre–World War I period is Russia's joining the Three Emperors' Alliance in 1881. Russia was not able to balance the Austro-German combination that was forming against it, because it had no available allies. France was still ideologically unpalatable, and Britain, Russia's main enemy, was friendly toward the Central Powers. So Russia joined the Austro-German combination instead. Here again, the case does not quite fit the theory, which says that usually it is small powers which are so weak that they need to bandwagon; Russia was a great power. Russia had other motives besides fear of Germany, including getting German support for its expansionist aims in the Near East. It is interesting to note the parallel between the Russian policy here and the Soviet bandwagoning with Hitler's Germany in 1939: Stalin, too, had both defensive and expansionist aims.

Although actual bandwagoning was rare in the pre-1914 period, statesmen often seemed to believe it was quite frequent and normal. Generally, this belief took the form of the notion that strength attracts: states will tend to gravitate toward other states that are strong, because a strong state brings more value to an alliance than a weak one. Therefore, if one's own state weakens, either materially or in demonstrated resolve, its allies and friends will desert it and move to the stronger side.

Such bandwagoning beliefs were expressed most frequently by German leaders and spokesmen, and German policy often followed the beliefs. Thus the Kaiser thought, when he signed his alliance treaty with the Czar at Bjorko, that France would be irresistibly attracted by the overwhelming power of the new combination. Then, as he said, "the moment the news of the new 'groupement' will have become known in the world, the smaller nations, Holland, Belgium, Denmark, Sweden, Norway, will all be attracted to this new great center of gravity, by quite natural laws of the attraction of smaller bodies by the larger and compacter ones."[47] A constant theme in German colonial diplomacy was that Britain (or France) would agree to German demands when it realized it could make no headway toward its own aspirations without German support. The Germans failed to see that coercion might stimulate resistance rather than acquiescence. Their angling for an alliance with Britain during the 1890s and early 1900s was always colored by the notion that England would eventually come around once it began to appreciate the value of German power. This, of course, turned out to be a self-denying proposition, for the German attempts to demonstrate and advertise their power only frightened and alienated the British.

The belief that strength attracts was sometimes expressed in other countries, too, although not as frequently as in Germany. Sir Edward Grey's

enthusiasm for the ententes with France and Russia brought him into disagreement with his former chief, Lord Rosebery, who warned, "You are
leaning on an aspen and the German emperor has four million soldiers
and the second best navy in the world."[48] Later, in the aftermath of the
Bosnian crisis, Sir Arthur Nicolson, the British ambassador to Russia,
opined, "I should not be surprised if we were to find both France and
Russia gravitating rapidly towards the central powers."[49]

The belief that others will be attracted to one's own strength is incompatible with a belief that others generally balance against power. But a
belief or fear that others will climb on the bandwagon of an opponent that
is permitted to make overweening gains is quite consistent with a belief
in the balance of power. The statesman who entertains such fears may
simply argue that the opponent's bandwagon will roll unless it is
stopped—that is, balanced. Thus the director of military operations of the
British army wrote in 1906: "If our expeditionary force is cut down [i.e.,
out of the budget] then 'goodbye' to the entente cordiale with France. . . .
The only alternative is a selfish isolation which would lead to the combination of all Europe against us under the dictatorship of Germany."[50]
Here the balance of power is seen as the remedy or preventative for bandwagoning.[51]

An analytical problem with the notion of bandwagoning is that it
merges into other concepts that represent different dynamics. Consider
Walt's statement that defensive bandwagoning is "a form of appeasement."[52] Appeasement, in the standard usage, generally means giving in
cravenly to the demands of an aggressor in order to avoid being attacked.
But bandwagoning does not necessarily mean conceding to the powerful
state's demands; it means simply allying with that state. This distinction
may be difficult to apply in practice, because alliance formation is sometimes accompanied by concessions on substantive issues, and settlements
of such issues may establish a quasi-alliance or entente. But if this distinction is not carefully drawn—specifying that defensive bandwagoning
requires a formal alliance—one is in danger of erroneously describing, say,
the Munich agreement as a case of bandwagoning with Hitler on the part
of the western allies.

Another concept that merges with defensive bandwagoning is that of
"abandonment," meaning simply leaving an alliance and perhaps joining
another. Many of the examples cited in discussions of bandwagoning
could just as easily serve as cases of abandonment or fear of it. They
involve the fear that one's own ally will defect and go over to the adversary's side if it begins to doubt one's capacity or will to defend it. Nicolson's warning, cited above, could be interpreted as a fear of abandonment.
What distinguishes abandonment from bandwagoning is that the former
involves leaving an alliance but not necessarily joining another, whereas

[160]

the latter means joining an alliance but not necessarily leaving one. Abandonment may be something that major powers do, and bandwagoning may be limited to small states. But these are formal distinctions that may not be easily observable or even very significant in practice. Whether one's concern is that one's present allies may defect, or that they may join the opponent, or that currently unaligned states will line up with the opponent, the fear is the same—that one will lose power relative to one's adversary. There does not seem to be any good solution to these ambiguities. The concept of defensive bandwagoning should be retained but defined and used with care.[53]

PART II

ALLIANCE MANAGEMENT

[6]

Theory: Alliance Management

Once an alliance forms, its members face the task of managing it. Whether the relationship rests on a formal treaty or merely on recognized common interests, the parties will want to shape and control it so that it maximizes their net benefits. Management may be collaborative and intended to promote joint benefits, as when the allies coordinate their policies toward the adversary or engage in joint military planning. Management may also be unilateral, as when a party seeks to minimize its own costs and risks without sacrificing benefits, for example, by withholding support from the ally in a crisis or by economizing on arms expenditures in the expectation that the ally will take up the slack.

ALLIANCE BARGAINING

Management involves pursuing both common interests and competitive interests and thus is essentially a process of bargaining, either tacit or explicit. The most fundamental common interest is to preserve the alliance; having made the alliance in anticipation of benefits, the partners have a stake in keeping those benefits flowing. The primary competitive interest is to control or influence the ally in order to minimize one's own costs and risks. What gives rise to both these management tasks is the likelihood that allies will have at least some divergent interests or even conflicting interests. Although their common interests will have been sufficient to induce them to ally in the first place, their divergent and conflicting interests will constantly threaten to pull them apart. The job of alliance management, in a nutshell, is to counter these centrifugal tendencies, by either joint or unilateral action, in such a way as to maximize joint benefits and minimize costs to one's independent interests.

Among the most prominent issues in intra-alliance bargaining are the coordination of military plans, the stance to be adopted toward the opponent in a diplomatic crisis, and the sharing of preparedness burdens in peacetime. Some issues involve, implicitly or explicitly, a renegotiation of the original alliance agreement. Thus the scope of the agreement may be extended to additional interests of the parties, to additional geographic areas, or to additional enemies. New members may be added. Generalities in the original agreement may be filled out in detail, as in specifying how soon after the war's outbreak the parties are to have troops at the front and how many troops at which front. The members may also negotiate to settle issues directly in conflict between themselves, issues other than those connected with implementation of the alliance agreement. Some alignments, notably ententes, are based on the settlement of such issues.

Determinants of Intra-Alliance Bargaining Power

The outcomes of bargaining episodes between allies will turn on the parties' relative bargaining power. Bargaining power is a function of three general factors: the allies' dependence on the alliance, their commitment to the alliance, and their comparative interest in the object of bargaining. In general, a state's bargaining power will be greater, the lower its dependence, the looser its commitment, and the greater its interests at stake. These terms are umbrella concepts that subsume several others.

Dependence

A state's dependence on an alliance, in the broadest sense, is a function of the net benefit it is receiving from it, compared to the benefits available from alternative sources. In these terms, states may be dependent on their allies for a wide range of values in addition to military security—for example, prestige, domestic stability, support for imperial ventures. Benefits are *net* because an alliance is an exchange: the values provided by the ally are partially offset by the cost of one's own commitment to the ally. A state is less dependent to the extent it has attractive alternative sources of these values, which may be either its own resources or what is available to it by diplomatic means such as alternative alliances or settlements with opponents. Dependence, of course, runs both ways; allies are mutually dependent for their alliance benefits, over and above what might be available to them elsewhere. Dependence in an alliance, as in any relationship, may be defined concisely and comprehensively as the opportunity cost of terminating it.[1]

In ordinary usage, however, dependence does not comprise all benefits from a relationship. It means reliance on someone else only for core values—that is, for essential needs, not for inessential luxuries. Thus it is useful to reduce the definition of alliance dependence to its military core. Military dependence is a compound of three elements:[2] (1) a state's need for military assistance, (2) the degree to which the ally fills that need, and (3) alternative ways of meeting the need.* Need, in turn, is a function of the extent to which the state's actual and potential military resources fall short of the resources of its potential adversary and the probability of war with the adversary. This probability, for a status quo power, turns on the amount of conflict and tension it is experiencing with its adversary.†

The second factor, the partner's capacity to satisfy one's security needs, is, of course, a function of the ally's military resources and potential. If that falls short of filling one's own resource deficit, one is dependent on the ally only for the amount it supplies. If the ally provides more than enough capability to fill the gap, the surplus does not create more dependency. The ally's contribution may vary also according to its commitment in the alliance treaty: it may promise assistance in certain contingencies but not in others, and only with a portion of its resources.

A state's dependence on its ally also varies with the availability of alternative ways of meeting its security needs. One obvious alternative is alliance with someone else.‡ Other options are increasing one's military preparedness, acquiring additional resources by military action, and conciliating the adversary.

The factors in dependence are subject to constant and perhaps frequent change. Conflict with an opponent will wax and wane; relations with alternative allies will fluctuate. The factors may change in opposite directions, one canceling the other. For example, by 1914 the increased military strength of Germany, relative to France and Russia, tended to reduce its dependence on Austria, compared to seven or eight years earlier, but this reduction was offset by its increased conflict with those opponents.

The mutual dependence of any pair (or group) of allies is affected not just by their relations with each other and with their opponent(s) but also by dependence and conflict relationships throughout the system. For ex-

---

*It should be clear that I am rejecting the standard view that the relative bargaining power of allies is a simple function of their comparative military resources. Military strengths enter the calculus, of course, but only in conjunction with several other variables.

† "Conflict" and "tension" are analytically separable. Conflict is incompatibility of interest; tension may be defined as the felt likelihood that the conflict will produce war in the near future. A high degree of conflict may be accompanied by low tension; the opposite is also possible, though less likely. The two are linked here because of their similar effect on alliance dependence.

‡ The "someone else" may be another member of the current alliance. Thus, if one has two allies, and the ties with one of them weaken, one becomes more dependent on the other. For example, the growing unreliability of Italy in the early 1900s was one reason Germany felt increasingly dependent on Austria.

ample, reduced threat from an opponent may be the result of an increased threat to the opponent from some fourth or fifth party, which leads the opponent to conciliate oneself or one's ally. And the increased threat to the opponent may be the result of the fourth and fifth parties' having settled a dispute between each other or having allied. Conversely, the formation of one's own alliance will have ripple effects far beyond the alliance itself.[3]

Dependence, like power, varies in scope.[4] States may be dependent on their allies for some goals but not for others. Dependence will be greater than the military core values if the alliance agreement provides for side payments going beyond defense of home territories—for example, maintenance of the status quo in a particular region or a "free hand" for some colonial acquisition. Military dependence may be limited to the defense of only some portion of the allies' territories or interests, or to something less than all-out military assistance. The ally's assistance may be needed for defense against two opponents but not a single opponent. Neutrality agreements make the allies dependent, not for military assistance but only for the partner's nonassistance of an adversary. Total alliance dependence, therefore, is the sum of a state's dependence across all its goals and conceivable threats, weighted by the value of the goals and the severity of the threats.

Bargaining power varies obversely with dependence. The more dependent one's partner, the greater one's power over it; the greater one's own dependence, the less power one has.[5] Dependence implies vulnerability: the more dependent the partner, the greater one's ability to inflict harm by withholding values, and the greater one's power to induce a change in the ally's behavior by threatening such deprivation. Thus a threat to break up the alliance or to reduce one's support can be employed to change the alliance's terms in one's favor or to persuade the ally to make concessions in a crisis. The credibility and effectiveness of such threats, however, is always limited by the degree of one's own dependence, as perceived, of course, by the ally. In short, what counts for bargaining power is not absolute, but relative, dependence; generally, the bargaining edge will go to the least dependent party.

Commitment

Another major component in the relative bargaining power of allies is their degree of commitment to the alliance. Like dependence, commitment weakens bargaining power. The more firmly one is committed to the alliance, the less credible, and therefore the less effective, are threats to withdraw support from the ally or abandon the alliance. Such threats, even if mostly implicit or existential, are perhaps the most important tactical source of alliance bargaining power.

[168]

Commitment, however, is even more difficult to define than dependence. Existing analyses define it, alternatively or simultaneously, as a physical act or move that forecloses all options but one, or as an arrangement of values that favors one option over others, or as an obligation to fulfill a promise. I choose to define it in the second sense, as an arrangement of values that disposes one to act in a certain way. Thus commitment is a matter of degree rather than absolutely either-or: although sometimes states will feel themselves to be either committed or not, more often they will be somewhat uncertain about how they will act when the time comes for the commitment to be honored; estimates of a partner's commitment will be even more uncertain and probabilistic.

In alliances, commitment arises from two possible sources, separately or in varying mixtures: (1) the verbal promise in the alliance contract and subsequent elaborations of it, and (2) interests in aiding the ally that would exist apart from the promise.[6*] The contract itself creates a sense of obligation in some degree, that is, it engages moral and legal values that were previously absent or weak in the relationship. It also engages political values, such as prestige and reputation for honoring agreements. All these are values that would be sacrificed if the agreement is not honored.

The degree of verbal commitment varies with the wording of the alliance treaty: for example, regarding the scope of the partner's interests that are covered, the amount of aid pledged to the defense of those interests, and the degree of explicitness and precision in the pledge. A moderate commitment thus covers some but not all of the partner's interests, and/or with something short of absolute precision in the *casus foederis*. The more explicit and precise the verbal commitment, the greater the cost in nonfulfillment and the lower the credibility of the threat of nonfulfillment.

The second component of commitment is commitment-by-interest: a state's underlying interest in defending the partner, apart from the verbal alliance pledge. Often such interests are "strategic"—interests in preventing the ally's resources from coming into the hands of an opponent. If a state has an interest, either strategic or intrinsic, in coming to its ally's aid even before making the alliance, it is more likely to honor its pledge than

---

* Note that these two sources of commitment—indeed, the notion of commitment itself— do not exhaust the incentives for a state to fulfill its alliance obligations. Another important incentive is the desire to preserve the alliance and the benefits accruing to the state from it. This, however, is the state's "dependence," which ought to be kept distinct from its commitment. Dependence stems from the benefits provided by the partner; commitment, from promises made *to* the partner.

The role of commitment is somewhat different in bargaining after an alliance has formed than in its initial formation. In the formation phase, the object of bargaining is the commitment itself—that is, each party's "interest" is to get the most advantageous terms for itself in the alliance contract. After the alliance has formed, the allies' degree of commitment usually is a given that enters into their relative bargaining power over some issue other than their contractual pledges.

if its incentive to do so rests entirely on the moral and legal obligation of the written contract or on the expectation of the partner's reciprocation. Thus, if a state has such a prior interest, it will find it more difficult to make a credible threat to withhold its support; the ally, even if it is dependent, will be able to resist pressure if it knows its own resources are essential to the security of its partner.

When the underlying interest is strategic, there is a difference in how it affects the bargaining power of relatively strong and relatively weak states. A strong state will have a clear interest not only in the existence and independence of a weak partner but also in acting to protect the partner, since the partner cannot defend itself. But a weak state, although it has an interest in the continued existence of its stronger partner, may have no interest in acting to preserve it, if the ally is strong enough to defend itself. Therefore, the strong state cannot credibly threaten to withhold support, whereas the weak state can do so. As Jervis has pointed out, the weaker ally enjoys some bargaining power because of its greater vulnerability.[7] Paradoxically, a weak ally may lack influence because of its dependence but gain influence by reason of its vulnerability and essentiality.

A good example of this paradox is the Austro-German alliance. On grounds of dependence, Germany's bargaining power was clearly superior. Yet Austria was able to exert considerable autonomy and even, at times, to capture the leadership of the alliance, because it was so clear that Germany would have to support it in a serious crisis. Austria's bargaining power was further enhanced by its ability to make a credible threat of nonsupport, in view of Germany's relative self-sufficiency.

Interests

The third major determinant of alliance bargaining power is the parties' interest in the specific issue about which they are bargaining. This factor is sometimes lost sight of in claims that power is a function of dependence.[8] "Dependence" refers only to the degree of harm the partners could inflict on each other by terminating the relationship, just as "capability" means the damage that adversaries could inflict in war. In both cases, "power" in a particular bargaining situation is not such punishment itself but what the parties could persuade each other to concede by the threat of punishment. But this is affected also by the cost of the concession that is demanded. The higher a bargainer values what it is being asked to give up, and the lower it values what the partner would give in return, the more it will resist a particular proposal. Such valuations are independent of the values that would be lost if the threat of punishment were carried out, but they are just as central to bargaining power.

In other words, there are often two value dimensions involved in bargaining. One is the dimension where the common interests are located, where the parties are mutually dependent. The other is the dimension where they are in conflict, the issue they are bargaining about, on which they are making demands and offers. Thus adversaries in an international crisis typically have conflicting interests that are the focus of the crisis, and a common interest in the avoidance of war. The protagonists threaten to harm each other on the dimension of common interest in order to get their way on the dimension of conflict. Their relative bargaining power is a resultant not just of their comparative disutility for war but also of the comparative valuation of their interests in conflict.

Analogously, in intra-alliance bargaining, the parties threaten to extinguish or frustrate the realization of their common interest—ultimately, their shared interest in preserving the alliance—in order to prevail on some other issue on which they are in conflict. Their mutual dependence is a measure of how much hurt they could inflict on each other by breaking off the relationship. The credibility of their threat to do that is affected not only by their degree of dependence and the firmness of their commitments but also by the comparative intensity of their interest in the issue that is the object of the bargaining. Their willingness to risk being hurt— the degree of their determination to stand firm in the face of the other's threat—also turns on some combination of their dependence, commitment, and interest in the issue in conflict. Even if A is the more powerful party because of low dependence and low commitment, this power may be offset by B's higher value on its interests at stake. An ally that is more dependent and more committed than its partner might nevertheless have superior bargaining power if it can convince the partner that it places the greater value on whatever they are negotiating about.

The interests at stake in intra-alliance bargaining typically are conflicting interests in how to implement the allies' common interests vis-à-vis an adversary. The allies have a joint interest in resisting the adversary, but they disagree about how to share the benefits and costs of doing that. These disagreements may occur in any of the three main security arenas: preparedness, diplomacy, or military action. Thus the allies may have conflicts about their relative military contributions, their diplomatic stance toward the adversary in a crisis, or their joint strategy in war. They may also disagree about where to concentrate their efforts. Thus during the 1920s the French and the British disagreed and negotiated about whether the German threat should be controlled by deterrence—that is, by accumulating capabilities—or by moderating German intentions through conciliation.

Intra-alliance bargaining sometimes involves issues other than dealing jointly with the adversary. Allies may disagree, for example, about whether to admit new members, or which ones. Thus before World War I Germany and Austria bargained about whether to ally with Bulgaria or

Serbia. Allies may also have a conflict about which of two adversaries to concentrate against, as France and Russia argued about the proportion of Russian forces to be deployed against Austria and Germany. Allies may have conflicts between themselves that have nothing to do with their adversary, as, for example, Russia and Britain continued to disagree about Persia after negotiating their entente in 1907.

The Bargaining Range

In bargaining between allies, as in all bargaining, agreement may occur anywhere within a range of possible agreements that make both parties better off than if they continued to disagree. If continued disagreement means the collapse of the alliance, then the end-points of this range are the values the parties impute to their best alternative to the present alliance. At this maximum width, the bargaining range is equivalent to their common interest in keeping the alliance alive.

In practice, the range usually is narrower than this, since "no agreement" need not mean the end of the alliance but merely indicates a deterioration of its value or a failure to increase its value. The parties may simply reduce their expectations of having each other's political support in the future. In that case, they will be more willing to stand firm at the risk of no agreement than if they anticipated alliance collapse as the result of failure to agree. But the costs of no agreement and the width of the bargaining range will be affected by the allies' overall dependence on the alliance even when alliance collapse is not the immediate consequence of nonagreement, since any weakening of the alliance in the present will increase the probability of its breakup in the future.

If the bargaining range is narrow, the element of common interest is low relative to the conflict between the parties. The bargaining then will be "hard bargaining," and agreement will be difficult. What is minimally acceptable to each party will also be close to the other's minimum, so that there is little "give" in each party's position. When the range is broad, common interest predominates over conflict, many potential bargains are profitable to both parties, and the bargaining will be "soft." The latter case approaches a "game of pure coordination," wherein there is no conflict and the only problem is to maximize the efficiency of joint action. Much intra-alliance bargaining, presumably, approaches this ideal type: the alliance would not have formed in the first place if common interests had not been preponderant over conflicts. As mutual dependence declines, however, perhaps as the external threat decreases, the bargaining range will narrow and bargaining behavior will become tougher. This is another way of saying that as the threat (or any component of dependence) declines, alliance cohesion will also decline.

As mutual dependence declines, the allies will be more attentive to rel-

Figure 6-1. Alliance interests, dependence and commitment

R, R 0, 0	S, T -5, 5
T, S 5, -5	P, P -20, -20

Interests = T - S = 10
Dependence and commitment = -P = 20

ative gains in their intramural bargaining. While they face a severe threat from an adversary, they will be mostly concerned to maximize their joint gains relative to the opponent and unconcerned about their gains relative to each other; but if the threat declines, they will become less dependent and may eventually begin to think of each other as potential enemies. In that case, they will have to begin thinking about limiting rather than fostering each other's power gains. They will become tougher in bargaining with each other, and agreements will be harder to reach.

Two additional factors may be important in alliance bargaining power: time preferences and attitudes toward risk. The state that is the more impatient for agreement will be weakened thereby. Thus, as described in Chapter 4, France was disadvantaged in the negotiation of the Franco-Russian alliance by its desire for early agreement, compared to the dilatory Russian attitude. Impatience may be partly an artifact of high interests, or it may be generated by situational factors such as the imminence of crisis with an opponent or an impending domestic change. Likewise, risk aversion contributes to bargaining weakness, since bargaining power turns substantially on willingness to risk a breakdown.[9]

A game model may help clarify the relationship among dependence, commitments, interests, and bargaining power. We adopt the standard labels for the payoffs in a two-by-two matrix, as in Figure 6-1: T is the satisfaction of one's own demand, S is the cost of accepting the partner's demand, R is a compromise, and P is no agreement or, at the extreme, collapse of the alliance.

Assume an alliance has formed and a policy issue has arisen about which the allies have conflicting preferences. The situation is as shown in Figure 6-1. Each ally demands its preference (T) and threatens to break up the alliance if the demand is not accepted. If one of the demands is accepted, the payoffs are 5 and −5: one ally gains, the other loses. If there is a compromise, the payoffs will be somewhere between 5 and −5 for each party; we arbitrarily set their value at zero for both parties. If they fail to agree and the alliance breaks up, they move to their P payoffs of −20. This is their loss in moving to their best available alternatives, whether these are alternative alliances or no alliance. P is therefore the measure of the parties' dependence on and commitment to the current alliance. It is the extent that each would hurt each other and itself by simply leaving the alliance. The P payoff need not be the cost of immediate and complete alliance collapse, however, but simply a reduction in the alliance's expected future value.

The effects of commitment are included in the P payoffs as costs that would be suffered if the commitment is violated. Thus, if an ally carries out a threat of defection, it suffers not only the cost of alliance dissolution but also the moral and reputational cost of having violated a promise. It suffers similar but lesser costs if it merely fails to support its ally in a dispute with an adversary, especially if the ally had expected support.

The parties' interests at stake may be conceived as the difference between their T and S payoffs. That is, the interest of each player is 10, the difference between the value of its demand and the value (cost) of acceding to the other player's demand. In the example given, the parties' interests are symmetrical, as is their dependence and commitment, but of course this need not be the case.

The Bargaining Power Index

Relative bargaining power is a resultant of asymmetries in interests, commitments, or dependence, or all three. Ideally, one would like to have exact quantitative empirical measures of these relationships and some method for amalgamating them into a single numerical estimate of bargaining power. Then it would be possible to test how closely their variation correlated with bargaining outcomes. Since such exact measures are not available, we must be satisfied with the closest possible approximation.

Such an approximation can be fashioned by establishing a three-point scale—high, moderate, and low—for each of the three components of bargaining power—dependence, interests, and commitment—and giving each of these ranks a numerical equivalent. Suppose a high degree of dependence is scored as 1; a moderate degree, 2; and low dependence, 3. (The numbers increase as dependence declines, because bargaining power varies inversely with dependence.) Likewise, high commitment is scored as 1, because commitment logically detracts from bargaining power; moderate commitment, then, is scored as 2, and low commitment as 3. Interests at stake in the bargaining are scored as 3 when they are of high intensity, 2 when they are of moderate strength, and 1 when they are low. The interests of the parties may be related in three possible ways: they are opposed, they are shared, or they are indifferent. Since all of the case studies in the next two chapters involve bargaining, and bargaining always involves some degree of conflict, we assume henceforth that the parties' interests are at least partly opposed. Table 6-1 summarizes the scoring code.

Table 6-1. Scoring for elements of alliance bargaining power

	Interests	Dependence	Commitment
High	3	1	1
Moderate	2	2	2
Low	1	3	3

If our assumption is correct that interests, dependence, and commitment are the principal components in an ally's bargaining power, it is reasonable simply to add the scores for each bargainer to arrive at a composite indicator of its bargaining power. Thus, hypothetically, a state with high interests at stake in the bargaining, low dependence on the alliance, and low commitment would have a bargaining power score of 9. Its strong interest would provide an incentive to stand firm in the bargaining, and its low dependence and low commitment would make it willing to stand firm even at a considerable risk of breakdown. The same factors would enable it to threaten credibly to cause a breakdown if it did not get its way. Now suppose the other ally's interests are opposed, but only moderately so, and that it is highly dependent on the alliance and firmly committed. Its bargaining power score would be 4. Its moderate interests are not strong enough to warrant taking a firm stand, especially when, owing to its high dependence, disruption of the alliance would be a disaster and the partner is threatening very credibly to disrupt it. That the second ally cannot itself threaten credibly to leave the alliance further undermines its bargaining power. Comparing these scores, we could plausibly predict that the first ally would prevail. We might also predict, when the composite scores are equal or only one digit apart, that the outcome of the bargaining would be a compromise.

In summary, the interest component of the index reflects what a party stands to gain by standing firm, and the dependence and commitment factors represent what it stands to lose. Together, but working in opposite directions, they make up a party's tolerance for risk, that is, its willingness to stand firm on its own demands at the risk of no agreement and possibly alliance collapse. The actual risk it runs in standing firm will turn on the partner's interests, dependence, and commitment, that is, on the partner's risk tolerance. Its estimate of these three factors in the partner's situation, plus its observation of the partner's behavior, will produce a sense of the likelihood that the partner will stand firm and disrupt the alliance if it does not get its way. Our three-dimensional index captures alliance bargainers' comparative willingness to accept risks as well as their capacity to generate risk. Risk-tolerance and risk-generation capacity together amount to bargaining power.* Thus our index provides a handy, if crude, means of comparing bargaining power between allies.

Perceptions are crucial, however. Relative bargaining power is determined not by some "objective" comparison of interests, dependence, and commitment but by the parties' estimates and perceptions of these things. Their subjective assessments may differ both from those of each other and from objective reality. Hence bargainers may take firmer or weaker positions than some omniscient observer would advise. Presumably, policymakers will have a better idea of the interests and dependence of their own state than those of the allied state. Thus they will have a better basis for judging the bargaining risks they are able to tolerate than the risks they are actually running, which are a function of the partner's risk calculus. In practice, states are likely to estimate the ally's future bargaining behavior from their observation of its behavior in the recent past, or at least use such observation to supplement the chancier estimates of the partner's interests, dependence, and commitment. But, of course, even the observation of concrete behavior is vulnerable to all the well-known pitfalls of cognitive psychology.[10]

Since estimates of the factors in each other's risk calculi are inherently uncertain, all bargainers will have incentives to deceive. As our cases in the following chapters show, deception often takes the form of "putting on a brave face"—carefully not revealing the degree of dependence that is actually felt. Deception may also involve exaggeration of one's alliance alternatives.

The model is applied in Chapters 7 and 8. For now, one example may help clarify its possible application. In the Bulgarian crisis of 1885–87 Austria's interest in frustrating Russia's designs on Bulgaria was high, its dependence on Germany was high, and its commitment to the alliance with Germany was moderate, giving Austria a bargaining power score of 6.

---

* The concept of risk tolerance is logically equivalent to Daniel Ellsberg's "critical risk." The formula for both is $T - S/T - P$, when T is a party's gain from satisfying its own interest, S is its loss from satisfaction of the partner's (opposed) interest, and P is the loss incurred in bargaining breakdown—in our scheme, dependence plus commitment. Thus, in Figure 6-1, both parties have a risk tolerance of .40: each is willing to stand firm on its demand so long as it believes the probability of the partner's also standing firm is less than .40; if it thinks the probability of the partner's firmness is higher than .40, it will concede. Cf. Daniel Ellsberg, "The Theory and Practice of Blackmail," in Oran R. Young, ed., *Bargaining: Formal Theories of Negotiation* (Urbana: University of Illinois Press, 1974), pp. 343–64; for a similar formulation, see Frederik Zeuthen, *Problems of Monopoly and Economic Warfare* (London: Routledge and Kegan Paul, 1930, 1968). See also Snyder and Diesing, *Conflict among Nations*, pp. 48–52.

Germany's interest in restraining Austria was low, its dependence on the alliance was low, and its commitment was high, for a score of 5. The outcome was consistent with these scores. Germany attempted to restrain Austria, but Austria resisted German pressure, encouraged Serbia to attack Bulgaria, and issued a threat to Bulgaria that caused it to back down.[11] Although Germany's bargaining power was strong on grounds of dependence, it was weak on grounds of interest and commitment. Conversely, Austria was weak from the point of view of dependence but strong from the perspective of interests, and its commitment to the alliance was not so solidly based on strategic interests as Germany's.

Our most general hypothesis, to be tested in the following two chapters, is that, when allies' interests are at least partially opposed, resolution of the conflict will favor the party with the highest bargaining power score, that is, the highest-scoring combination of interests, dependence, and commitment. A corollary is that, when the bargaining power scores are about equal (no more than one unit apart), the outcome will be a compromise. It is also possible to make certain informal generalizations about which of the components in these scores—interests, dependence, or commitment— are the most influential.

Types of Alliance Bargaining

Alliance bargaining episodes can be grouped into several distinct types, following the general typology of interactions presented in Chapter 1: preparedness, action, and diplomacy. Allies bargain about their respective contributions to military preparedness, about burden-sharing. They may also negotiate about action, about the joint strategy they will follow in case of war. Compared to latter-day alliances such as NATO, in the pre-1914 era preparedness and action bargaining were less salient, occurring mostly in military staff conversations, which were sporadic and of widely differing intensity.

The most important type of alliance bargaining in the two or three decades before World War I was the diplomatic. Here four subtypes can be identified: renegotiation of alliance terms, addition of members, bargaining about the diplomatic stance to be taken toward an adversary, and bargaining about conflicts between the allies not involving an adversary.

The focus of the bargaining in the first category is on a redistribution of long-term alliance payoffs. The scope and firmness of the allies' commitments is the central object of the bargaining. Typically, the bargainers seek to increase the total value of the alliance while also trying to increase their own particular shares. In pursuit of the latter goal, they may exploit their partners' dependence by threatening, implicitly or explicitly, to leave the alliance.

[177]

Addition of members may also involve a redistribution of payoffs among the original members. It is typically accomplished not by a revision of the original agreement but through a new agreement negotiated between the new member and the original members. Thus the Triple Alliance of 1882, among Austria, Germany, and Italy, was not a revision of the earlier treaty between Austria and Germany but a separate treaty. Like renegotiation bargaining, bargaining over the addition of members tends to center on the distribution of long-term benefits and costs rather than on some particular short-term issue.

A third subtype is the international crisis. In these cases, typically, one ally (the "target") has a deep conflict with its adversary and wants to take a firm position; another ally (the "supporter") supports the target ally in varying degree, from full support of a firm position, to support of a softer position after concessions, to no support, to outright opposition or restraint. The allies bargain, in effect, over the stance to be taken toward their common opponent on some specific issue over which tension is high and war is possible.

A related fourth type of alliance bargaining encounter is negotiation about policy toward an adversary in noncrisis situations. The relatively low degree of tension means the allies do not have to assess the probabilities of war resulting from alternative stances. Also, their interests at stake tend to be less important, so they find it easier than in a crisis to reach compromises. Although they have conflicting preferences over the issue, they are not about to disrupt the alliance over it.

Allies may also bargain about issues directly in conflict between themselves, not involving an adversary. Here an example is negotiations between Austria and Germany about whether to attempt revision of the Treaty of Bucharest, which settled the Balkan Wars in 1913.

All these different types of alliance bargaining can be handled with our bargaining power model. Thus, in the cases of alliance revision, the dependence of the allies is the continuing long-term value they are realizing from the alliance less the value of their alliance alternatives. Their commitment is the degree to which they are currently obligated to defend the partner's interests and the degree to which their own strategic interest dictates aiding the partner. Their interest in a particular episode of alliance revision is to increase their own net value for the alliance by some change in its terms.

What triggers an alliance revision, typically, is some change in the political context that alters the degree and perhaps the locus of threat to the alliance. For example, the Franco-Russian alliance was revised in 1899 because of French fears that the Austro-Hungarian Empire was about to collapse and that Germany would pick up most of the pieces. As in this case, the contextual change may affect the allies about equally, and the

[178]

alliance revision will benefit both. If only one member experiences an increase of threat from its adversary, the balance of dependence in the alliance will change and the more threatened party will suffer a reduction in alliance bargaining power. Its partner may be able to exploit this reduction to get a revision of the alliance's terms to its advantage. The Franco-Russian alliance, for example, was revised again in 1901 and 1902, now at Russian behest, to make it applicable to the Far East and possible war with Britain. One reason Russia was able to get these revisions was the increased dependence of France following the Fashoda crisis in 1898. Later, after Russia's dependence had increased owing to its defeat in the war with Japan, France was able to get the point against Britain rescinded. Thus a series of alliance revisions followed changes in the security environment that shifted the balance of dependence between the allies, first one way and then the other. In each case, the more threatened and more dependent ally had to accept a redistribution of alliance payoffs to the advantage of its partner.

In a crisis with an adversary, the allies' bargaining situation is different and more complex, not only because the adversary is involved but also because more value-dimensions are implicated. The allies are now engaged in implementing their agreement rather than revising it. Their interest at stake in the bargaining, what they are bargaining about, is their interest in a particular stance to be assumed toward the adversary on a specific issue in dispute. Their bargaining leverage over each other will depend heavily, as in noncrisis bargaining, on their long-term dependence on the alliance and their degree of commitment. But it will also turn on their relative interest in the issue in dispute and whether their interests are shared or opposed.

Thus the focus of the allies' bargaining in a crisis is the bargaining demand or concession that one or both allies will make to the adversary. The values they each impute to their preferred stances will include the value they place on the political issue in dispute with the adversary, but it must also include their expected costs of war: the disutility of war times its probability. For each ally, the values attached to these two broad items will determine the amount of risk it is willing to accept in the dispute with the adversary, hence its preferred posture toward the adversary, hence its "interest" in the alliance bargaining.

In short, in alliance bargaining during a crisis, there are two broad value-dimensions involved: the long-term expected value of the alliance and the values engaged in the immediate conflict with the opponent. The ally's long-term expected value for the alliance, its dependence, can be exploited as leverage to get one's way on the choice of strategy toward the adversary. There will be long-term alliance consequences, however, whatever policies the allies adopt and whatever the crisis outcome. A joint firm position that results in victory presumably will strengthen the alliance, just as failure to agree, followed by defeat, will weaken it. The aggregate payoffs the allies impute to various outcomes will include not only the values realized in the short-run conflict with the opponent but also the long-term values added to or subtracted from the alliance relationship, such as their confidence in each other's future support.

THE ALLIANCE SECURITY DILEMMA

So far in this chapter we have been discussing bargaining between allies in specific episodes. We have assumed that the parties seek the best possible outcome for themselves in each encounter, given their interests at stake, their dependence, and their commitment. We now adopt a different focus: how the allies attempt to manage their long-term relationship so as both to preserve the alliance and to maximize their net benefit from it. In the short-term conflicts, we might say, the allies seek to maximize satisfaction of their interests, given their respective degrees of dependence and commitment. Over the long term, attention centers less on particular interests and conflicts with an adversary and more on the manipulation of apparent commitment to the alliance to offset shifts in dependence relations between the allies themselves. The two foci are not mutually exclusive, since short-term tactics and outcomes are bound to affect the long-term relationship and may be chosen in part with the long term in mind. Conversely, changes in the long-term factors, such as relative dependence, affect short-term outcomes.

This dichotomy is the analogue of the distinction, made by Patrick Morgan, between "immediate" and "general" deterrence.[12] Adversaries practice immediate deterrence in specific crisis confrontations; they also seek optimum levels and mixtures of capability and threats to maintain deterrence over the long pull at minimal cost to other values. Similarly, allies bargain with each other to settle immediate disagreements, often about how to deal with an opponent, but they also seek to preserve the long-term health of their relationship, and their own interests within it, apart from specific conflicts with an adversary.

The latter, more general focus in the alliance game may be conceived broadly as the management of the security-autonomy trade-off. The original alliance negotiation, we may assume, will have established an optimum security-autonomy mix for both (all) members of the alliance, given their respective bargaining power. Inevitably, however, changes in the alliance's environment, or in the interests, capabilities, or domestic situations of the members themselves, will disrupt that initial optimum. The outcomes of specific conflict episodes, of the kind just discussed, will shift

[180]

the optimum or change perceptions of it. When such changes occur, an ally will attempt to restore the optimum mix by sacrificing something of one in order to get more of the other. For example, if a state's opponent becomes more threatening, the state may try to tighten the mutual alliance commitment, thus increasing its security, though at some cost to its autonomy. Conversely, if the adversary threat declines, thus producing an "excess" of security, the state may opt to trade some of the excess for more autonomy, by loosening the alliance bonds or by reducing support to the ally on some issues, at some risk of losing the ally's support.[13] The logic here is the familiar logic of diminishing marginal utility: the more one has of something, the less it is worth at the margin; hence there will be incentives to trade items of low marginal utility for items of higher utility, thus maximizing total return. This at least is the theoretical ideal; it is only more or less approximated in actuality.[14]

The security-autonomy trade-off takes on a sharper and somewhat narrower focus in the tension between what Michael Mandelbaum has called the fear of abandonment and the fear of entrapment.[15] This tension may be labeled the "alliance security dilemma." A pervasive aspect of alliances in a multipolar world is the constant worry about being deserted by one's ally. The worry arises from the simple fact that the ally has alternative partners and may opt for one of them if it becomes dissatisfied with present company. There are two components in this fear of abandonment: the subjective probability that the partner will defect and the cost to oneself if it does. The probability will be significant, both because of the existence of alliance alternatives and because of the natural tendency of statesmen to think in worst-case terms. The cost will usually be high, because, in a multipolar system, states tend to be heavily dependent on allies for their security.

The obverse of the fear of abandonment is the fear of entrapment. Entrapment means being dragged by one's commitment into a war over interests of the ally that one does not share. The ally behaves recklessly or takes a firmer position toward its opponent than one would like because it is confident of one's support. As the cost of abandonment is a serious loss of security, the cost of entrapment is an extreme form of lost autonomy.

The risks of abandonment and entrapment tend to vary inversely—hence the dilemma. A possible remedy for abandonment anxiety is to increase one's commitment to or support of the partner, thus increasing its security and reducing its temptation to defect. But this increases the chances that one will be entrapped by the ally—that it, now more firmly counting on one's support, will push a conflict with its adversary over the brink and drag one along with it. Worries about possible entrapment may be reduced by watering down the commitment to the ally or by withholding support in specific crises or disputes with the adversary, but this course risks devaluing the alliance for the ally and causing its defection. Thus, acting to reduce one of the worries tends to increase the other. The dilemma is not immobilizing, however; it merely requires a trade-off: acting to reduce the greater fear by increasing the lesser one.

Abandonment may take one of several forms. One is the formal abrogation of the alliance, the declaratory cancellation of alliance commitments. An ally that defects in this sense may remain unaligned or may realign with another state, possibly its former adversary. Another form is the failure to fulfill alliance commitments, simply to renege when the *casus foederis* clearly arises. More common than either of these is the failure to support the ally diplomatically in a dispute with its adversary, when support was expected. A series of such failures may so devalue the alliance for the partner that, although the alliance remains formally intact, it becomes an empty shell, because the expectations of support that underlay it have been dashed.*

Entrapment is a bit more complicated, involving an interplay of five variables: the ally's interests in conflict with its adversary, the ally's degree of confidence in one's own support, the ally's degree of recklessness, the extent of one's own commitment to and dependence on the alliance, and the degree to which one shares the ally's interests. The first three provide the motive for the ally to push a crisis to the brink; the last two determine whether one will go to the brink, and perhaps over it, with the ally. The greater the ally's interests at stake, the greater its confidence in one's support, and the greater its tolerance for risk, the more likely the ally will challenge and stand firm against its adversary. The firmer one's commitment to the ally, the more likely one will be forced to support it. But this would be truly entrapment only if one does not share the ally's interests.

The risk of entrapment is highly sensitive to the degree of commonality or disjunction between allies' interests. Thus during the 1920s and early 1930s Britain perceived France's eastern European alliances as dangerous nuisances that could only entrap Britain in war outside its interests. For France, of course, the alliances merely symbolized its strategic interests: France would be gravely threatened by German expansion in the east. But after the revolution in the British conception of their interests in the spring

---

* The difference between "commitment" and "support" might be formalized as "supergame" versus "subgame." Alliance commitments are made in a supergame wherein the choices are whether and with whom to ally, and the outcome of which is a mutual promise of support over a series of generally defined contingencies. "Support" or "nonsupport" are plays in specific subgames with an adversary which may or may not bring into effect the contingencies and promises in the general contract. Outcomes in the subgames will affect anticipated payoffs in the supergame. A decline in these anticipated payoffs may precipitate a new play of the supergame that produces a new set of commitments, such as a realignment.

of 1939, by which these interests were revised to match France's, Britain lost its fear of entrapment by French commitments.[16] Of course, when a state would serve its own interests in helping the ally, there is no question of entrapment. For Japan in World War I, it was more a matter of "liberation." By liberally interpreting the text of the Anglo-Japanese alliance, Japan was able to legitimize its overrunning of the German colonial territories in the Pacific.[17]

Entrapment comes in many forms, ranging from the ally's outright and unexpected attack on the opponent, to its directly provoking the opponent to attack, to its holding to a firm position in crisis bargaining which results in the outbreak of war. The dangers of entrapment by attack or direct provocation were sometimes moderated in pre–World War I alliance treaties by the provision that their obligations did not apply to a war "provoked" by the ally. Such clauses came into some disrepute, however, because they made it easier for supporting allies to evade their obligations, that is, to abandon their partners.[18]

The risks of abandonment and entrapment have both a cost and a probability dimension. The cost of being abandoned is largely a function of one's own dependence on the alliance; it is the difference between the security experienced with the alliance and the security that could be obtained in an alternative alliance or no alliance. The probability of abandonment turns mostly on the ally's dependence and degree of commitment, as best these things can be estimated by observing the ally's security situation and recent behavior. The risk of abandonment is the prospective cost times the probability that the ally will defect. The cost of being entrapped is the cost of fighting a war in defense of the ally's interests, discounted by the extent to which one shares those interests. The risk of entrapment is this discounted cost times the probability of having to fight. This probability, in turn, is a function of the probability of the ally's being attacked by, or itself attacking, its opponent, and one's degree of commitment to the ally. Entrapment might mean being dragged into a war started by the ally, but it could also result from a war started by the adversary after the ally has taken an unyielding diplomatic position.

Avoiding Abandonment

Avoiding abandonment is a negative way of stating the primary goal of alliance management: holding the alliance together. The standard response to fear of abandonment, as noted above, is to move closer to the ally in some way so as to increase its perception of one's loyalty. This increases its expected benefit from the alliance and reduces its incentive to defect. There are many ways of moving toward an ally in order to discourage it from abandoning the alliance. One is to renegotiate the alliance contract in the ally's favor. Another is to strengthen one's general commitment by diplomatic communications and public statements. Still another is to support the ally in specific conflicts with its adversary. Such backing provides behavioral evidence that one will support the ally on future occasions, thus increasing its expected value for the alliance.

Allies that are concerned about abandonment will wish to establish a reputation for loyalty so as to maintain the attractiveness of the alliance for the partner. Loyalty reputation is the alliance analogue to the much-analyzed idea of "resolve reputation" between adversaries. Just as adversaries may feel they must stand firm in all disputes with the opponent, to avoid developing a reputation for weakness, so allies may be under some compulsion to support each other repeatedly lest they acquire a reputation for faithlessness. In either case, the underlying assumption is that commitments are interdependent—in the one case, commitments vis-à-vis an adversary; in the other, vis-à-vis allies. In both cases, a "never again" syndrome may operate: if an ally is let down once, the pressure to support it next time is all the greater, just as adversaries may feel that if they show weakness once, they must absolutely stand firm in the next crisis in order to correct that image. The concern for loyalty reputation may work against restraining the ally in order to avoid entrapment, or against maximizing bargaining leverage by fostering uncertainty about one's own intentions.[19] It is also a constraint on buck-passing, free riding, and other collective action problems in a multipolar system, more so than in a bipolar system, where the absence of alliance alternatives makes loyalty virtually irrelevant.

An alternative response to the fear of abandonment is to threaten to defect oneself unless the ally becomes more supportive. Then, if the ally has no intention of defecting, it may tighten its alliance commitment or increase its support in order to head off one's defection. In 1912, for example, after French president Raymond Poincaré learned of a German proposal to Britain for a treaty of neutrality, he instructed his ambassador in London to tell the British foreign minister that "any paper of such a kind, however guarded it may be, will be interpreted in France as the voluntary abandonment of the whole policy pursued since 1904."[20]

But this tactic is clearly risky, since if the ally is considering defection, one's threat may precipitate it. Such a threat may cause the ally to look elsewhere for two reasons: (1) it fears one's abandonment, and (2) the present alliance becomes less valuable to it because of the cost of complying with one's threat.[21] There will be a certain threshold or break-even point at which the ally's expected value from cooperating and remaining in the alliance is just equal to the ally's expected value in defecting and realigning. One's own threat will be effective in inducing the ally to cooperate only if it is on the "stay" side of this threshold after receiving the threat. If the ally is on the other side, the threat will precipitate its defection.

The threshold notion implies a concept of alliance stability. The closer the partners are to their respective thresholds, the more likely the alliance will be pulled apart by the external attractions acting on its members. The system as a whole is alliance-stable when these attractions are weak. That is most likely to be the case when existing allies are tightly bound by common interests and have high levels of conflict with their adversaries.

Discouraging the ally's defection does not necessarily require taking a firmer stand against the ally's opponent. It requires simply taking the stance the ally prefers. Thus during the 1930s the French feared abandonment by the British, who were keeping themselves at arm's length because they feared entrapment.[22] The French responded by supporting and aping the British policy of appeasing Hitler. In this case, the response of standing up firmly to the opponent would very likely have caused Britain to abandon France.

Avoiding Entrapment

The standard response to the fear of entrapment is to move away from the ally, to reduce one's commitment or threaten to withhold support. Less sure of being supported, the ally becomes more circumspect in dealing with its opponent, more inclined to make concessions in order to avoid a fight, more willing to follow one's advice. Moreover, one is less bound to join in if a fight occurs.

Sometimes, however, giving the ally a firm commitment may be a better safeguard against entrapment than distancing oneself. If the ally is deemed unrestrainable, taking a firm position behind it may yet avoid war by causing the opponent to back down; entrapment is avoided through deterrence. Or supporting the ally might improve its sense of security enough that it could feel safer in conciliating its opponent. Thus in the 1920s Britain withheld a commitment to France for fear of stimulating it to take an even more uncompromising stance toward Germany. In retrospect, a more supportive British policy might have allowed France to be more relaxed and accommodating toward Germany, which might have strengthened German democratic forces against the rise of Nazism.

One might also insist on being consulted about or included in exchanges between the ally and its opponent in order better to restrain the ally. If the ally must be given a firm commitment to maintain its confidence in the alliance, it may yet be restrained, and entrapment avoided, by energetic verbal remonstrances.

Entrapment is more likely when the state has a strategic interest in defending its partner than when it faces only the legal-moral injunction of the alliance contract. The latter commitment is easier to escape, on the ground that the circumstances of the war's outbreak do not match the *casus foederis*; knowing this, the ally will be less inclined to risk war. A commitment by interest will be fulfilled regardless of circumstances or treaty language; the greater certainty of support in this case will encourage the ally to stand more firmly against its adversary and accept a higher risk of war.

A state may not mind being entrapped if war is believed to be imminent or inevitable in any case and the state has some doubts about its ally's loyalty. It might have such doubts, for example, when the allies have different opponents and different interests. If the ally precipitates war with its adversary, that at least gets it engaged, which is better than seeing the ally stand aside when one is attacked. Thus the French government before 1914 encouraged Russia to take firm stands in the Balkans, because it feared Russia would abstain from a war that began on the Franco-German frontier. Similarly, Germany, believing war was inevitable, favored its outbreak in the Balkans because it would ensure the commitment of Austrian forces.

The obverse worry, a kind of abandonment fear, is that the ally's forces may get tied down in a subsidiary theater if the ally prematurely undertakes war against its own adversary. This was the case in 1914 when German leaders feared Austrian forces would not be available against Russia if they became committed against Serbia.

The most obvious general antidote to the danger of entrapment is to restrain the ally, through the exercise of bargaining power, from taking undue risks in dealing with its adversary. There are also less coercive methods, however, such as persuasion through consultation. Further discussion of the rather complex subject of restraining allies, which is analogous to deterrence of adversaries, is deferred until Chapter 9.

Determinants of Choice

The severity of the alliance security dilemma, and the intensity of fears of abandonment and entrapment, is largely determined by the same three factors that are the central components of alliance bargaining power: interests, dependence, and commitment. Thus the dilemma will be mild when the allies have a high proportion of common interest, relative to conflict, in their relationship. Then they will obviously have little fear of abandonment, and they cannot entrap each other, by definition, if whenever they fight an adversary it can only be on behalf of shared interests. Since the threat of abandonment has little credibility, they will have little bargaining leverage over each other, and since they have relatively little conflict, they will have little use for such leverage.

Hypothetically, this condition would be approached when the parties confront the same opponent and have similar interests in conflict with that opponent. With a common enemy, the risk of abandonment is low on probability grounds; the ally is not likely to leave one in the lurch, because it is equally interested in resisting this opponent. The risk of entrapment is low not because its probability is low but because its cost is low: even if the ally does drag one into war, one will be fighting for one's own interests as well as the ally's.

In contrast, the alliance security dilemma will be most severe if the allies are threatened by different opponents or when they face the same enemy but have different conflicts with that enemy. Then both the likelihood of abandonment and the cost of entrapment will be high. The allies will simultaneously be skeptical about each other's loyalty and anxious lest they be trapped into "pulling the other's chestnuts out of the fire." An approximate example is the Franco-Russian alliance before World War I. France did not share Russia's interests in conflict with Austria in the Balkans, and Russia had no interest in France's conflict with Germany over Alsace-Lorraine. France and Russia were highly committed via their general strategic interests in each other's survival, but their particular interests had little in common.*

When states' interests change, their relative worries about abandonment or entrapment change accordingly. Thus Great Britain's conception of its own interests shifted radically after Hitler occupied rump Czechoslovakia in 1939. Germany was seen to be congenitally aggressive, with ambitions going beyond bringing ethnic Germans into the Reich. Consequently, British interests expanded to include the defense of all possible German targets: the guarantees to Poland and Rumania followed. The British were no longer worried about being entrapped by the intransigent French in eastern Europe, and the French were no longer concerned about being abandoned by Britain.

When mutual dependence between allies is high and symmetrical, the alliance security dilemma will be severe. This is the case, for example, when the balance of power between two alliances is about even and tension between them is high. Then both the fear of abandonment and the fear of entrapment will be high. The fear of abandonment will be strong simply because of the allies' need for each other's help, although it will be tempered somewhat by the knowledge that the need is mutual and therefore that the partner is unlikely to defect. Entrapment will be feared

---

* The ratio of common to conflicting interests affects primarily the probability of abandonment and the cost of entrapment. In contrast, dependence affects mostly the cost of abandonment and the probability of entrapment. A high degree of mutual dependence implies a high cost of abandonment and a high probability of entrapment—vice versa when mutual dependence is low.

because each ally knows it can hardly refuse support to the partner in a crisis lest the partner defect. By contrast, when mutual dependence is low, abandonment by the ally is of little consequence and for that reason entrapment can be avoided at little potential cost. When the balance of dependence is asymmetrical, perhaps because one ally is more directly threatened by an opponent, the more dependent ally will fear abandonment more than entrapment, while the less dependent partner will worry more about entrapment.[23]

The alliance security dilemma is also affected by the firmness of alliance commitments. The more firmly allies are committed, the less they need fear abandonment but the more they will fear entrapment. Conversely, a vague or ambiguous alliance agreement, such as an entente, tends to maximize fears of abandonment, but it minimizes fears of entrapment. These generalizations need to be qualified, however. Although states that are explicitly allied may be entrapped over the partner's interests that are covered in the agreement, they may find it quite easy to abstain in contingencies not explicitly mentioned; the ally is willing to believe that nonsupport in a particular contingency outside the *casus foederis* does not mean general abandonment. But when the agreement itself is vague, allies may find it necessary to stand by each other in all situations to prove their loyalty; hence the danger of entrapment may not be significantly lower than under a formal alliance.

The degree of commitment between allies will rise or fall during the life of the agreement. The initial agreement may be explicitly renegotiated, increasing (or decreasing) its explicitness, scope, or firmness. Leaders and diplomats may supplement the formal agreement by what they say to each other on particular occasions, such as during a confrontation with an opponent. They may increase their level of commitment by engaging in joint military planning.

As previously argued, the commitment of allies is a function not only of their alliance contract but also of their interests in aiding each other apart from the contract. If the contract is reinforced by underlying strategic interests, clearly the chances of abandonment are lower than if the allies are held together only by their promises. The danger of entrapment is higher, however, because they will find it difficult to stand aside from each other's initiatives in a crisis or credibly to threaten nonsupport when their own interests require defending the ally whatever its policy. The alliance security dilemma will be less severe to the extent the allies are committed by known strategic interests in addition to their verbal agreement, because only one of its two horns—entrapment—is significantly present.

Thus the basic underlying determinants of allies' incentives in their security dilemma are their relative dependence, their interests, and their degree of commitment, as these things are mutually perceived. These factors, however, especially those of other states, are not very observable, since they require estimates of relationships rather than observation of actions. Although they are fairly good indicators of the costs of abandonment or entrapment for the self, they yield only uncertain judgments about likelihood, which turns on the ally's dependence and interests. For more solid estimates of the ally's future behavior, statesmen are likely to rely heavily on observation of past behavior. Behavioral evidence supplements the relational elements to yield more specific and confident expectations. Thus Britain and France were generally concerned about Russian defection throughout the pre-1914 decade because of their knowledge of Russia's rather low dependence on the Triple Entente—its traditional option of alignment with Germany was available until late in the period. They became more specifically and intensely concerned when Russia negotiated a settlement of certain disputes with Germany in 1910.

Whether any particular behavior of the ally stimulates abandonment or entrapment fears sufficiently to require remedial action depends partly on which of these anxieties is already the strongest. The ally's behavior will reinforce either the dominant or the lesser worry. If it increases the fear that is already strong, countervailing moves to reduce that fear probably will be called for. No action will be necessary if the ally's action reduces the greater fear more than it increases the lesser one. Thus, if a state is already mainly concerned about abandonment, an allied action that increases the risk of entrapment, if it also reduces the chances of abandonment, may not be worrisome. For example, a state might welcome a stiffening of its ally's position vis-à-vis a common opponent if the ally's loyalty had previously been in question. Conversely, when it appeared in 1902 that Japan and Russia were about to reach a settlement of their dispute in Manchuria, Lansdowne was not alarmed but relieved that the alliance with Britain had not encouraged Japanese intransigence.[24] Lansdowne applauded the Japanese move because it eased his dominant worry, that of entrapment, more than it heightened his lesser fear, that of abandonment.

Theoretically, a state seeks an optimum mix between the risks of abandonment and entrapment. The optimum turns mostly on its degree of dependence on and commitment to the alliance and its estimate of the ally's dependence and commitment. The relative dependence of allies may change as a consequence of changes in their security environment. As a state becomes less dependent on its ally, it will worry less about abandonment and relatively more about entrapment; in order to ease the latter danger, it may reduce its commitment or support, accepting a somewhat greater risk of abandonment. If the ally's apparent commitment declines, the state will become more concerned about abandonment and may move

Figure 6-2. Adjustment of alliance commitments in response to changing dependence

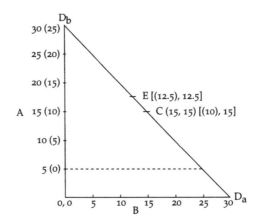

closer to the ally to discourage its defection. Thus shifts in relative dependence and apparent commitment tend to induce offsetting moves that restore an optimum balance between the risks of abandonment and entrapment.

Figure 6-2 may help clarify the process. It shows a bargaining space between two allies, A and B. Anywhere in this space, both are better off allied with each other than with their best alternative, either a different alliance or no alliance. Within the space, both parties enjoy a net benefit from the alliance—their benefit exceeds their cost. Any point within the space represents a degree of commitment by each party. Benefits come from the partner's commitment; costs arise from one's own commitment to the partner. The joint net benefits are maximized anywhere on line Da-Db: any movement along this line benefits one party but only at the expense of the other. Movement from within the space up to this Pareto-optimal line either benefits both parties or benefits one party more than it hurts the other. Points Da and Db are points where, for each party, the net value of the alliance just equals the value of its best alternative. The latter is arbitrarily set at zero.

Suppose that when the alliance is initially negotiated, the partners are committed equally and moderately at point C, which nets them each a value of 15.* These initial payoffs of 15, 15 are the Nash solution, where the product of the parties' payoffs is maximized. These numbers (and

---

*Of course, equivalent verbal commitments do not necessarily yield equal benefits. That assumption is made here only for ease of exposition. I am also assuming incomplete information: the parties do not know each other's payoffs, although they know their own.

other numbers in the diagram) represent net security gains from the alliance.

The allies will be motivated to change their commitments to or actual support of the partner by changes in their relative dependence on the alliance, usually the result of changes in the security environment, particularly in the degree of threat from their adversary or in the availability and attractiveness of alternative alliances. Suppose A's dependence declines, because its adversary's capabilities decline or an important dispute between them is settled, or because A's alliance alternatives become more attractive. A's net payoff from the alliance terms previously negotiated drops to 10, while B's payoff remains at 15, as at point C. In Figure 6-2 this is shown by an upward shift in the horizontal axis, raising A's zero point from which its payoff is measured. By reducing its commitment and hence reducing its risk of entrapment, A can increase its overall payoff. A is not much concerned about being abandoned by B, since B's support is no longer so necessary. So A reduces its commitment to point E, say, by negotiating a revision of the alliance terms, by unilateral declaration, or by weakening its support of B on specific issues. Thereby, it accepts slightly less security in order to have substantially more autonomy; as a result, its aggregate payoff increases to 12.5, while B's payoff declines to 12.5 because of A's reduced support. This, incidentally, is a new Nash solution, where the combined payoffs will theoretically settle after a period of jockeying. It is exactly at the midpoint of the adjusted bargaining range, where the product of the payoffs to the parties is maximized. (A's new payoffs are shown in parentheses, and the new payoff distributions at C and E are shown in brackets.)

An obverse logic applies when A's dependence rises, due either to an increased threat or a deterioration in the value of its alternatives. A will then be motivated to strengthen its support of B in order to reduce the risk of abandonment, which now has become more onerous than the risk of entrapment. This, of course, raises the alliance's value for B, increasing its dependence on the alliance. Thus a change in one ally's dependence leads to a similar change in the dependence of the other.

In general, when an alliance's value for one party changes as a consequence of a change in its security environment, ultimately the value of the alliance will change for both (all) partners. This occurs because the change in value for one partner shifts the distribution of dependence and bargaining power between the allies. That in turn triggers a redistribution of alliance value toward an equality of benefits, hence of dependence. Thus we may hypothesize a constant tendency toward a "balance of dependence" in multipolar system alliances.

The possibility or threat of abandonment is relevant to a much wider range of bargaining goals than reducing the risk of entrapment. Indeed, this possibility is the primary source of bargaining power between allies in a multipolar system. Thus, in deciding how to modulate threats of abandonment and how closely to commit itself to its ally, a state must consider the whole range of issues on which it wishes to maintain influence over the ally. This consideration—the need to maintain general influence in the alliance—probably encourages states to limit their commitments or keep them rather loose or ambiguous. There is a tension, however, between maximizing influence in the alliance and maximizing the alliance's effectiveness against its adversaries. Looseness or ambiguity in alliance commitments may yield influence over alliance partners, but it may also reduce influence and deterrent efficacy vis-à-vis the alliance's opponent(s). To such tensions and cross-effects between alliance and adversarial relations we now turn.

The Interplay between Adversarial and Allied Relations

Up to now, we have considered only relations between allies, independent of their adversaries. But allies deal with their adversaries at the same time they deal with each other—indeed, alliances have no meaning apart from the adversary threat to which they are a response. The alliance and adversary games are virtually opposite sides of a coin, and they interact closely. Strategies and tactics directed toward the ally will have side effects in relations with the adversary and vice versa. Strategy choices in either game must therefore take account of both the direct effects and the side effects.

In particular, the alliance security dilemma interacts closely with the security dilemma between opponents. The latter is well known in the literature as *the* security dilemma, but for present purposes it requires some clarification. Typically, the adversary security dilemma is presented as a model of security competition in the context of systemic anarchy. Even when no state actually has aggressive intent, all are driven to acquire and maintain power, since they cannot be sure of others' present and future intentions and, given this uncertainty, must prepare for the worst. The upshot is a perpetual competition for security which is self-defeating, simply because the players cannot read the others' minds yet know that others have the capacity to harm them grievously.

According to *Webster's Unabridged*, a "dilemma" is a "situation involving choice between equally unsatisfactory alternatives." The security dilemma presents two unsatisfactory alternatives—not surviving or engaging in a costly security competition—but they are not equally unsatisfactory; not surviving is much the worse of the two. In principle, there is choice, but one of the options, the clearly preferable one, will always be chosen. The same is the case with the game theory model of the prisoner's dilemma, which may be interpreted as a formalization of the security dilemma. The "defect" strategy dominates "cooperate" for both players; consequently, in a one-shot game, both defect, producing, as in the security dilemma, a nonoptimal outcome. Thus the term "dilemma" is somewhat strained when applied to these models.

The label fits more comfortably on the dichotomy, described by Jervis, between the "deterrence theory" and the "spiral theory."[25] The two theories (or models) point to a choice between two strategies toward an opponent: toughness or accommodation. The deterrence theory says that if one is tough, the opponent will concede (back down, refrain from attacking), whereas if one is conciliatory, the opponent, interpreting this as weakness, will only push harder. The spiral theory says the opposite: toughness will scare or provoke the opponent into tougher policies, whereas accommodation will persuade it of one's own good intentions and induce reciprocal accommodation. The spiral model is virtually equivalent to the security dilemma model, except that it is not necessarily derived from the logic of system structure and thus is not driven inexorably to an outcome of mutual toughness.

Thus the two theories point to different policy preferences: in deterrence, toughness; in the spiral model, accommodation. Jervis points out that the choice between them logically turns on one's estimate of the type of opponent one is dealing with, whether it is congenitally aggressive or not. If it is aggressive, firm deterrence is required to hold it in check. If not—if, for example, it is interested only in securing the status quo or in adjusting a minor grievance—it should be conciliated. Since it is not easy to know just how aggressive an opponent is, the policy choice is often difficult. Hence the label "dilemma" is apropos in that there is a real choice, not a logical compulsion toward one alternative, and in the sense that a wrong choice in either direction would be unsatisfactory if not disastrous. Jervis's dichotomy is useful also in that it links two contrasting foreign policy philosophies. "Hawks" tend to prefer the assumptions and conclusions of deterrence theory; "doves" prefer the spiral model. For present purposes, therefore, we label it the "adversary security dilemma," with apologies to John Herz and other theorists of the security dilemma in its original sense.[26]

The alliance security dilemma and the adversary security dilemma are directly analogous. Restraint of the ally and deterrence of the adversary are the "tough" strategies, respectively, in each case. Restraint, like deterrence, may, if pushed too hard, trigger a spiral—a spiral of abandonment between allies that is analogous to a spiral of hostility and insecurity between adversaries. On the other hand, if the ally is supported, it may

Table 6-2. The composite security dilemma

	Possible consequences	
Strategies	Alliance game	Adversary game
I Alliance C: Support; strengthen commitment Adversary D: Stand firm	"Goods" 1. Reassure ally; reduce risk of abandonment 2. Enhance reputation for loyalty "Bads" 1. Increase risk of entrapment 2. Reduce bargaining power over ally 3. Foreclose realignment option 4. Solidify adversary alliance	"Goods" 1. Deter or prevail over adversary 2. Enhance reputation for resolve "Bads" 1. Provoke adversary; increase tension; trigger insecurity spiral
II Alliance D: Withhold support; weaken commitment Adversary C: Conciliate	"Goods" 1. Restrain ally; reduce risk of entrapment 2. Increase bargaining power over ally 3. Preserve realignment option 4. Divide adversary alliance "Bads" 1. Increase risk of abandonment 2. Reduce reputation for loyalty	"Goods" 1. Resolve conflict; reduce tension "Bads" 1. Encourage adversary to stand firmer 2. Reduce reputation for resolve

exploit one's support to advance its own interest and entrap oneself in the process—just as an adversary that is appeased might exploit one's apparent weakness to make further gains.

The Composite Security Dilemma

Table 6-2 shows a composite security dilemma that combines the alliance and adversary versions. Each of the strategy pairs, I and II, shows an alliance strategy, together with its complementary strategy in adversary interaction. (The cooperative "C" strategies and the defecting "D" strategies are shorthand for a range of empirical variations discussed presently.) The two columns show the possible direct consequences of alliance and adversary strategies in their respective games.

The column labeled "Alliance game" simply summarizes the earlier discussion of the alliance security dilemma. The column labeled "Adversary game" summarizes the adversary security dilemma: it shows the possible "good" and "bad" effects of conciliation or firmness when one is interested only in maintaining the general status quo. In making choices in either game, states must estimate not only the direct effects in that game but also the side effects in the other game. Consider, first, some side effects in the alliance game of strategies in the adversary game. A "D" strategy of firmness, resistance, or coercion toward an adversary will tend to reassure an ally that doubts one's loyalty and to reduce the risk of the ally's defection or realignment. Opposed to this "good" are several "bads." Firmness toward the adversary may increase the risk of entrapment by the ally, as the ally becomes intransigent through its confidence in one's support. A tough stance also tends to close off one's own option of realignment with the adversary. In addition, toughness may frighten the opponent into moving closer to its own allies, thus solidifying its alliance.

A "C" strategy of conciliating the adversary will have the desirable effect of restraining the ally, thus reducing the risk of entrapment. The ally, observing one's improving relations with the opponent, will have less confidence that one will stand four-square behind it in a crisis; consequently, it will be more cautious in its own dealings with its opponent. The ally may become more amenable in intra-alliance disputes, out of fear that one is considering realignment. Conciliating the opponent keeps open one's option of realignment with it, which is desirable for its own sake as well as for influencing the present partner. Actual reduction of conflict with the opponent will reduce one's dependence on the ally and consequently increase one's bargaining leverage over it. Conciliatory negotiations with the adversary may also weaken its alliance, as its partners begin to doubt its loyalty and seek alternative partners.

The most undesirable side effect of accommodating the adversary is the risk of abandonment by the ally. Its fear that one is contemplating realignment may induce it, not to try to discourage this by strengthening its own alliance commitment, as suggested above, but to realign preemptively or move closer to the opponent. Short of this, the ally will at least become less confident of one's loyalty and therefore perhaps less inclined to fulfill its alliance commitments and more inclined to make deals with its adversary.

Turning now to side effects in the adversary game of moves in the alliance game, we see that full support of one's ally will help deter or coerce a common opponent. A possible bad effect will be to increase tension between oneself and the adversary, as predicted by the spiral model. Conversely, withholding support from the ally, in order to restrain it, is consistent with settling a conflict with a common opponent. It may damage one's own resolve reputation, however, and thus tempt the opponent to be more intransigent and aggressive, as predicted by deterrence theory.

Tension between effects across the two games creates several subdilemmas or trade-offs. One is the "deter versus restrain" dilemma. A state may wish to maintain an image of firmness in order to deter the adversary, but at the same time keep the ally in some doubt about its loyalty in order to hold the ally in check. This would maximize the chances of peace but require sending different signals to each of the other actors. In principle, it is not impossible to send different messages to ally and opponent, but in practice it may be difficult, given the normal porousness of communication channels.[27] Information conditions aside, just where the balance is struck between deterring and restraining will depend partly on the balance of dependence between the state and its ally and partly on the balance of interests between the state and the adversary. If the ally is not very dependent and the state itself has much at stake, restraining the ally will be difficult and may encourage the opponent, so the policy emphasis will be on deterrence. Conversely, restraint will be favored over deterrence if the ally is dependent and the state's own interest in the dispute with the adversary is minor.

The obverse subdilemma is "support versus conciliate." The state may want very badly to hold its alliance together, and thus to support its ally, but also to reach a settlement with the alliance's adversary. There is tension between these two goals, obviously, especially if the ally does not want a settlement. In that case, too much accommodation of the adversary may alienate the ally. Conversely, too much alliance solidarity might ruin a possible accord with the opponent, provoke the opponent to form a counteralliance, or even provoke it to attack. Again, the best that can be hoped for is an uneasy balance between the risk of alliance breakup and the risk of continued conflict with the opponent, paid for with some combination of lukewarm assurances to the ally and stingy concessions to the opponent. The background conditions of alliance dependence, capabilities, and degree of conflict between adversaries largely determine, in practice, the degrees of warmth and stinginess.

The support-versus-conciliate dilemma points to a general characteristic of a multipolar system: the need to retain the allegiance of allies tends to inhibit the resolution of conflict between adversaries. This effect is relatively absent in a bipolar system because the allegiance of allies is hardly in question. It is more prominent in multipolarity after alliances form than before, and still more so as tension rises between alliances. The other side of the coin, however, although less prominent, deserves mention: the fear of provoking an opponent, or the desire to keep open the option of appeasing it, may inhibit closeness between allies. The French reluctance to implement their alliance with the Soviet Union in the 1930s serves as an example.

Such dilemmas are most severe during crises and less so during periods of low tension between adversaries. Thus, in noncrisis periods, contacts across alliances are quite compatible with alliance solidarity, but as tension rises, they become less so. Then any dealings with the opponent are viewed with suspicion by allies, and expressions of solidarity between allies tend to exacerbate tension between opponents.

Sometimes a state's goals in the adversary game and the alliance game are so far apart that a trade-off is impossible or risks the worst outcome of falling between two stools. Then the only reasonable course is to choose the best strategy in one, accepting the inevitable costs in the other. In the 1930s, for example, Great Britain and France might have split the Axis and gained an alliance with Italy if they had appeased Mussolini; or they might have saved the League of Nations and/or deterred Hitler by standing up to the Italian dictator. By their halfhearted economic sanctions they cemented the Axis, ruined the League, and encouraged Hitler.

Since a state's intra-alliance influence increases with the ally's degree of conflict with its opponent (a component of the ally's dependence), the state may benefit from the existence of such conflict and may even try to foster it. Too much conflict, however, runs against the state's interest in avoiding entrapment. Complete absence of conflict between the ally and its adversary would be ideal for escaping entrapment, but then the risk of abandonment would be high. Here again there is a trade-off across the alliance and adversary games: depending on relative dependence and other background conditions, some moderate degree of conflict between the ally and its adversary, but well short of war, would be optimum.

It may sometimes be desirable to combine strategies in the alliance and adversary games so as to produce counterbalancing effects—that is, side effects from one game that run counter to the direct effects in the other game. The side effects provide a useful antidote to undesirable aspects of the direct effects. For example, firmness toward the adversary might be combined with restraint of the ally, the former serving as reassurance to the ally to soften its resentment at being restrained. As our cases show, such mixed strategies are quite common and may yield the optimum combination of security and autonomy. But they risk causing confusion and misperception among other actors.

The alliance and adversary games are closely intertwined; obviously, it is no easy matter for a state to juggle the various cross-effects so as to optimize between security and autonomy. We see in the case studies how allies go about juggling them. One question to be asked of the cases is, When states face these dilemmas, do they tend to grasp either one horn or the other, plumping wholeheartedly, say, for deterrence over restraint or vice versa, or do they try to strike a compromise? And which kind of strategy, the pure or the mixed, is most effective?

In summary, the composite security dilemma creates a grand four-way trade-off between desirable and undesirable consequences in two interlocking games. An optimum mix of abandonment risk and entrapment risk in the alliance game might turn out not to be optimum at all when indirect effects in adversary relations are considered. And resolving the Jervis dichotomy optimally for interaction with the adversary might be quite unsatisfactory in the light of its alliance consequences. Each situation will present its own mix of interdependence, capabilities, and interests which will point toward an optimum for that situation. Finally, to complicate matters further, what a state seeks as an optimum will depend overwhelmingly on its *perceptions* of these underlying conditions, which may be quite different from the ally's and opponent's perceptions. The case studies in the following chapters demonstrate some of these complexities.

Analogies between Adversary Bargaining and Alliance Bargaining

Several analogies can be drawn between alliance bargaining and bargaining between adversaries. The value of doing so is to lay the groundwork for borrowing and applying to intra-allied relations some concepts from the well-developed field of bargaining between adversaries.

Some of the analogies have been briefly mentioned already. For example, the restraint of an ally by the threat of abandonment is analogous to deterrence of an adversary by the threat of war. Loyalty reputation is the alliance analogue to resolve reputation in adversary relations. Bandwagoning in the alliance game is equivalent to falling dominoes in the adversary game. Rising tension may generate an "integrative spiral" between allies that is parallel to an "insecurity spiral" between adversaries. Chain-ganging is the alliance equivalent of arms racing in the preparedness arena and of war escalation in the action arena.

Just as restraint of an ally parallels deterrence of an opponent, both being negative forms of coercive power, so goading of allies parallels compellence of adversaries as positive forms of coercion. An example of goading is Germany's pressure on Austria in 1914 to carry out a quick fait accompli against Serbia. Just as deterrence may be undermined by contradictions between the deterrent threat and one's real interests, so an attempt to restrain an ally may be frustrated by its knowledge of one's strategic interest in defending it. Supporting an ally out of fear of its defection is roughly parallel to appeasing an opponent out of fear of its attacking.

Further parallels are easily found. The point is that the underlying dynamics of intra-alliance relations are in many ways similar to interactions between adversaries. Of course, there are many differences, too, but the amount of similarity suggests that the theory already developed about strategic interaction between adversaries, by Thomas Schelling, Robert Jervis, and others, could be, with some adaptation, a rich source of theoretical ideas for intra-allied relations.

The following two chapters investigate the historical evidence bearing on the theory of alliance bargaining presented earlier in this chapter. The procedure is to trace the comparative dependence of the members of our two alliances from their inception until the outbreak of war in 1914, and to relate such dependence, and the parties' interests and commitments, to the outcomes of intra-alliance bargaining episodes along the way. Twenty-two such episodes are considered: twelve in the Austro-German alliance and ten in the Franco-Russian alliance. In addition, four cases of bargaining between Great Britain and either France or Russia are examined briefly. The object is to assess whether the outcomes of the bargaining encounters are consistent or inconsistent with the existing pattern of dependence, interests, and commitment, when these independent variables are scored as suggested earlier in this chapter.

The following hypotheses, in which the ceteris paribus clause is crucial, are tested, where possible.

Hypothesis A: When the interests of allies are in conflict, resolution of the conflict will favor the ally with the highest bargaining power score on the interest-dependence-commitment index. When the scores are approximately equal, the result will be a compromise.

Hypothesis 1: Ceteris paribus, in alliance bargaining, the least dependent partner will enjoy the most influence, and vice versa.

Hypothesis 2: Ceteris paribus, allies with the most interest at stake in bargaining encounters will have the most influence in such encounters.

Hypothesis 3: Ceteris paribus, the more firmly a state is committed to defend its ally, the less influence it will have in intra-alliance bargaining.

Testing Hypothesis A requires calculating, for each participant in each case, a bargaining power score from estimates of the state's dependence on the alliance, interests at stake, and degree of commitment. Numerical estimates for each of these components, on a scale from 1 to 3, as indicated in Table 6-1, are simply added to produce an amalgamated score for each participant.

The three latter hypotheses involve cross-country comparisons for each of the components separately. The ceteris paribus clause is required because two or three of these variables may vary simultaneously, in which case it is difficult to isolate the effects of one of them. This obviously poses problems for empirical testing, but they are not insurmountable. Even though the causal variables cannot be completely disentangled, it makes sense to inquire which seems to be delivering the most impact, in a reasonable interpretation of the evidence available.

It will be recalled that the three components of bargaining power are weighted equally in our 1-2-3 scoring system. This equal weighting may be taken as a crude null hypothesis. In asking, first, whether the three components combined predict accurately to bargaining outcomes and, second, which of the three components is most influential, we are implicitly attempting to disprove the null hypothesis and substitute for it a weighting that is more accurate empirically.

Chapter 7 considers the Austro-German alliance, with lesser reference to the Three Emperors' Alliance and the Triple Alliance, from 1880 to 1914. Chapter 8 centers on the Franco-Russian alliance from 1894 to 1914, with some attention to the Anglo-French and Anglo-Russian ententes. Chapter 9 draws out from these cases material bearing on the alliance security dilemma and its subdilemmas and on other aspects of alliance management, such as norms and the tensions between concerts and alliances.

[7]

The Austro-German Alliance,
1880–1914

This chapter presents twelve case studies of bargaining between Austria and Germany during the life of their alliance. The cases are embedded in contextual material that attempts to highlight shifts in the allies' relative dependence and commitments and hence, along with their interests at stake in each of the cases, their relative bargaining power.

Figure 7-1 summarizes changes in these factors and related bargaining outcomes between 1880 and 1914. The top graph depicts changes in relative dependence. The X and O lines show dependence as measured solely by military forces and resources relative to a state's primary opponent(s). Austria's primary opponent is assumed to be Russia during the whole period; Germany's is France until 1890 and France-Russia after 1894, with a transition period between those dates when the Franco-Russian alliance was being negotiated. Austria was the more dependent party in terms of military resources until about 1894. Germany was slightly more dependent for six years after that date, largely because the Franco-Russian alliance made it clear that Germany faced two great-power enemies rather than one, whereas Austria could reasonably count on having to fight only one, Russia. From 1900 to 1913 German military dependence slowly declined while Austria's remained about the same.

Table 7-1 summarizes the resource data from which the resource dependency lines in the figure are derived. It shows that in 1880 Austria held 9 percent of total European great-power military resources, as measured by the average of its shares of iron and steel production, energy consumption, population, defense appropriations, and personnel under arms. Its primary opponent, Russia, held 20.4 percent, more than twice Austria's share. Germany's aggregate resources, 18.6 percent of the total, were slightly greater than France's 18.1 percent. Near the end of the pe-

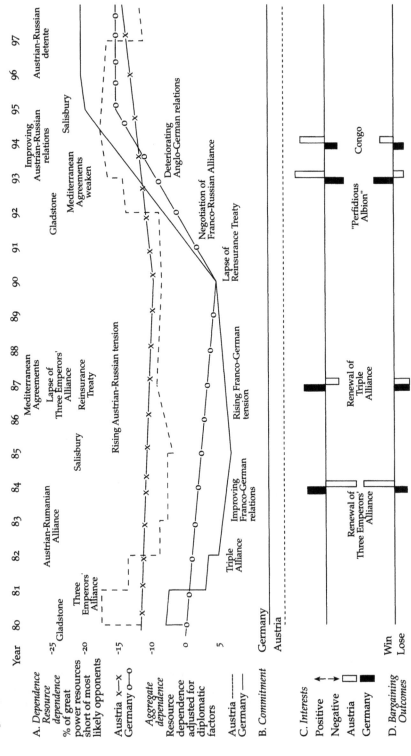

Figure 7.1. Austro-German relations and bargaining outcomes, 1880–1914

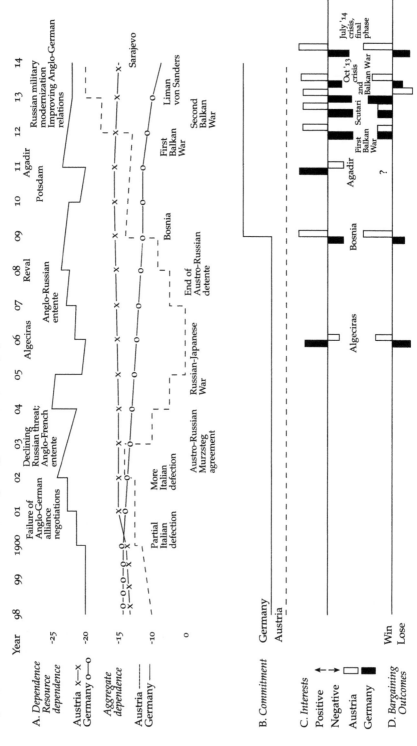

Figure 7.1. Austro-German relations and bargaining outcomes, 1880–1914 (Continued)

Table 7-1. Percentage shares of European great-power military resources and potential, 1880–1913

	1880	1890	1900	1910	1913
Great Britain	33.8	31.0	26.7	23.0	20.4
France	18.1	17.4	15.5	14.9	14.4
Russia	20.4	19.5	23.7	24.6	24.9
Germany	18.6	21.9	24.6	27.9	30.1
Austria-Hungary	9.0	10.2	9.4	9.5	10.2

SOURCE: Calculated from figures in Paul M. Kennedy, "The First World War and the International Power System," *International Security* 9 (Summer 1984), 7–41. Because of rounding, not all columns sum to 100.

NOTE: Percentages of total great-power military resources and potential are defined as the average of percentage shares of iron and steel production, energy consumption, population, military appropriations, and military personnel.

riod, in 1913, Germany's share of total great-power resources had risen to 30.1 percent, and Austria's had increased slightly to 10.2 percent. The 40.3 percent share for both allies together was slightly larger than the Franco-Russian share of 39.3 percent. Shares in the component parts of this index, by ten-year intervals, are given in Appendix A.[1]

The jagged (solid and dashed) lines that bracket the two resource lines in the figure reflect modifications of alliance dependence resulting from the degree of conflict with opponents and the availability of alternate allies. These lines, that is, represent the overall degree of dependence of the parties resulting from the combination of military and diplomatic factors. The direction of movement is more significant than the amount, since it is impossible accurately to measure intensity of conflict between adversaries or the attractiveness of potential alliance partners. These lines represent relative dependence in an ordinal sense. Thus, overall, Austria was the more dependent party from 1880 to about 1894, when the dependency lines cross. After that date Germany was the more dependent, although only moderately so, until 1904, then more so until about 1909, when Austrian dependence increased markedly owing to increased conflict with Russia.

The lines below the dependence graph, part B of Figure 7-1, show the commitment of the parties to the alliance. They reflect two factors: (1) the firmness of verbal commitments as they appear in the original text of the alliance and as they were modified later by more or less formal declarations, and (2) the extent to which the partners are committed to each other's defense by their interests, other than their interests in fulfilling their formal obligations.

The bar graph in the center, part C of the figure, shows the comparative interests of the parties in each bargaining or influence episode. These are different interests than those mentioned above as determinants of commitment, which are interests in directly defending the territory of an ally, usually a strategic interest in preventing the ally's resources from coming under the control of the adversary. The interests in the bar graph are interests in particular bargaining situations in which there is some degree of conflict between the allies. These interests contribute directly to alliance bargaining power in that a strong negative interest in whatever the ally is demanding, or a strong positive interest in one's own demands, tends to strengthen one's incentives to stand firm in the bargaining.[2]

Finally, the bottom bar graph, part D of Figure 7-1, shows the outcomes of influence interactions between the allies, in terms of whose policy preferences prevailed and approximately by how much. The size of wins or losses reflects how much a state's interests were advanced or harmed by the outcome. For crisis episodes, these estimates are measures not of gains and losses vis-à-vis an opponent but of the extent to which the joint policy of the alliance, or the policy of the directly involved ally, diverged from the preferences of the supporting/restraining ally.

It is possible to read from the four displays in Figure 7-1 whether outcomes match predictions that might be derived from the parties' relative dependence, commitment, and interests at stake. For example, Austria's lower dependence, lower commitment, and greater interest involvement (than Germany's) in the Bosnian crisis of 1908–9 would predict an Austrian win with strong German support, which is a fair description of the actual outcome, as shown in the lower bar graph (part D). Of course, the diagram makes no claim to exact measurement; necessarily, it states only general tendencies and gross comparisons, and even then, it must be admitted, with a considerable margin for error.

The components of Figure 7-1 are discussed case by case in the material that follows. For convenience of exposition, we assess the relative dependence, commitments, interests, bargaining power, and bargaining outcomes in the Austro-German alliance over ten-year periods. The procedure is to trace changes in dependence and commitment chronologically, pausing to analyze cases of alliance bargaining as they appear in the historical narrative.

1880–1890

There were two salient bargaining episodes between Austria and Germany during this period: renewal of the Three Emperors' Alliance in 1884 and renewal of the Triple Alliance in 1887. Both were renegotiations of existing agreements.

Austria was the more dependent partner throughout the decade 1880–

90, especially on the indicator of capabilities. On one of the diplomatic dimensions of dependence, degree of conflict with or threat from the most likely opponent, the allies were about equally dependent. Austria's conflicts with Russia in the Balkans were severe enough to suggest a definite possibility of war, although the formation of the Three Emperors' Alliance in 1881 would reduce its likelihood somewhat. Germany's conflict with France over Alsace-Lorraine was more basic and intractable but also more latent.

The other diplomatic dimension—prospects for alternative allies—tended to favor Austria. Although the English option had been dimmed by the advent of the liberal Gladstone government in 1880, it remained alive over the long pull, owing to the convergence of British and Austrian interests in opposing Russia in the Near East and the Balkans. France was a lesser possibility but still plausible. Germany, on the other hand, had no good alternatives. France, of course, was out of the question. Britain had signified interest in 1879, but Bismarck's abrupt withdrawal of his overture had cooled off this possibility and the move toward Russia in 1881 would virtually foreclose it for the present.

We may conclude that Austria was the more dependent ally: its greater military dependence more than offset its slight advantage over Germany on the diplomatic aspects. Thus, on grounds of relative dependence alone, Germany's potential bargaining power in the alliance was somewhat greater than Austria's.

Germany's predominance was reduced somewhat by the element of commitment, however. Although the allies were committed equally by the verbal terms of the alliance treaty, Germany was the more strongly committed in terms of underlying interests. Germany's strategic interest in keeping Austrian resources out of Russian hands, together with Austrian weakness, meant that Germany could not avoid coming to Austria's defense. In turn, this meant that in any bargaining episode or crisis, the German threat to defect or to withhold military aid would not be very credible. Austria also had a strategic interest in blocking Russian conquest of Germany, but it could more plausibly threaten to withhold support since it could expect Germany to be able to defend itself without aid. Thus, curiously, Austria's relative weakness tended to strengthen its intra-alliance bargaining power. Austria was less committed to the alliance than was Germany, because Austria's commitment rested almost entirely on the legal and moral obligation of the alliance treaty, whereas for Germany, this obligation was strongly complemented by strategic interest. Alliance bargaining power tends to vary inversely with degree of commitment; Germany's influence was weakened by its greater commitment.

The first major change in dependence relations occurred with the advent of the Gladstone regime in Great Britain in 1880. This event increased mutual dependence, since both alliance partners felt threatened by the improvement in British-Russian relations that resulted. Austria felt threatened more, however, since Russia was primarily its enemy; hence its dependence increased somewhat more than Germany's. Not only was Russia now freer to press against Austrian interests in the Balkans; Austria had also been deprived of its best alternative to the German alliance.

The Three Emperors' Alliance in turn reduced the mutual dependence of Austria and Germany, but for diverging reasons. They both benefited from the diminished Russian threat, Austria somewhat more so since it was principally its direct conflicts with Russia that were reduced by the agreement. Germany benefited in addition, however, by the foreclosure of the dreaded Franco-Russian alliance. For both reasons, the two Germanic allies became less dependent on each other.

The negotiation of the Triple Alliance with Italy in 1882 redounded more to Austria's benefit than to Germany's. By reducing, if not eliminating, the Italian threat to Austria that arose from their territorial dispute over the Trentino, the alliance decreased Austrian dependence on Germany. Austria's dependence was also reduced marginally by its treaties with Serbia and Rumania in 1881 and 1883, respectively. Both treaties reduced nationalist and irredentist threats to the monarchy and released Austrian capabilities for use against Russia, while perhaps tying down some Russian forces. Germany adhered to the Rumanian alliance, Bismarck thus granting, in effect, the extension of the Austro-German alliance which he had denied during the negotiations two years earlier over the Three Emperors' Alliance.

Alliance Bargaining: Renewal of the Three Emperors' Alliance

The Three Emperors' Alliance was due to expire in 1884, so the parties began negotiations for its renewal in 1883. The talks featured four amendments proposed by Russia and Germany, most of which would have worked to Austria's disadvantage. Austria successfully resisted all but one of them.

Gustav Kálnoky, the Austro-Hungarian foreign minister, first rejected a Russian proposal, backed by Bismarck, to modify the alliance to take account of the eventual collapse of the Turkish empire, granting, in that event, Russian designs on Constantinople. Kálnoky also turned aside Bismarck's perennial suggestion that Austria and Russia divide the Balkans into spheres of influence. With Austrian security increasing, Kálnoky saw no reason to conciliate Russia; with his dependence on the German alliance decreasing, he felt less vulnerable to Bismarck's pressure. Besides, a sphere-of-influence deal would consign Bulgaria to Russia's control, whereas Kálnoky was not ready to give up Austria's aspirations in that direction. He also rejected Bismarck's suggestion to bring Italy into the alliance: this would only confuse things, since Italy's role was to help block Russian aggression if the Three Emperors' Alliance should collapse. He made only one concession: to expand the area wherein unilateral changes in the Balkan status quo were prohibited without prior agreement, from Turkey and Bulgaria, to the whole of the peninsula, including Austria's turf in Serbia and Bosnia.[3] Otherwise, the treaty was renewed for three years on March 27, 1884, without significant change.

Was this outcome consistent with the underlying bargaining power of the parties, that is, with the aggregate of the parties' relative dependence, commitments, and interests at stake? Each of the issues in the bargaining must be considered separately, since the parties' interests were different for each issue, even though their alliance dependence and commitments were the same.

Dependence in this case is dependence on the Three Emperors' Alliance rather than the Austro-German alliance. The Russian dependence throughout the negotiations is coded as high. Austrian dependence is estimated to be low, and the German dependence, high. The Three Emperors' Alliance had always been primarily a Russo-German enterprise, with the Austrians reluctantly dragged along by the Germans. The German dependence (net benefit) lay primarily in precluding a Russo-French alliance; Russia's dependence consisted chiefly in German support of its aspirations in the Near East. Austrian benefits were very small by comparison.

The commitments of all three parties are coded as moderate throughout. Recall that bargaining power is assumed to vary positively with interests at stake, negatively with dependence, and negatively with clarity and degree of commitment. Also recall that it is each party's perceptions of the magnitudes of these items in the other parties' value scheme, along with estimates of its own, that are significant for bargaining. Since the historical record does not provide much data on perceptions, however, we simply assume that the parties' perception of each other's values was accurate.

Two of the issues, the Russian proposal for a contingent partition of the Ottoman Empire and Bismarck's suggestion of an agreement on spheres of influence, may be considered together because of their similarity. The interest of the Russians in either proposal was moderately positive: it would give them control over the eastern Balkans and the Straits, though it would bar them from extending their influence into the western Balkans. The Austrian interest was strongly negative: Kálnoky did not trust the Russians to observe the agreement in Serbia and Montenegro after they had established themselves in Bulgaria;[4] in any case, the Magyar veto prevented Austria from actually incorporating any of the Balkan Slav states. The German interest was positive but low: Germany had no direct interests in the Balkans and the rest of the Ottoman Empire and pushed partition schemes only to dampen conflict between Austria and Russia. In our three-point scoring system (see Table 6–1), these codings, combined with those mentioned above for dependence and commitment, translate to bargaining power scores of 5 for Russia, 8 for Austria, and 4 for Germany. These scores are consistent with the Austrian ability to resist the partition and sphere-of-influence proposals. Hypothesis A in Chapter 6—that the outcome of bargaining will favor the party with the highest composite score on interests, dependence, and commitment (the greatest bargaining power)—is supported.

Bismarck's motive in suggesting that Italy be brought into the alliance is unclear; therefore, we arbitrarily rate the positive German interest as moderate. Austria's interest was moderately negative: Austria had no desire to bring Italy formally into the Balkans, since Italy's interests there ran somewhat counter to its own. Russia's interest was positive and low: Italy might be marginally useful in disputes with Austria. These codings, along with those for dependence and commitment previously mentioned, yield scores of 7 for Austria, 5 for Germany, and 4 for Russia. The scores predict, accurately, that the Austrian position prevails.

The third issue—whether to extend the prohibition on unilateral changes in the status quo to the western Balkans—held a high positive value for Russia and conversely a high negative interest for Austria, because it would tie Austria's hands against Serbia. Germany's interest was moderately positive, since the measure would offer some protection against entrapment in Austrian initiatives. Combining these estimates with the dependence and commitment estimates yields scores of 6 for Russia, 8 for Austria, and 5 for Germany. These scores predict an Austrian success, not the Russian gain that actually occurred. On this issue, Hypothesis A is therefore not supported.

We may attempt to explain this anomaly by reference to factors outside our model that might have affected the bargaining. First, there might have been logrolling or linkage tactics. That is, Austria might have had to pay for its success on the other two issues by granting Russian and German desires on the issue of unilateral change. The record does not reveal any such bargain, however.

Second, the German influence on the negotiations may have been greater than suggested by our numerical model. Such influence could have come from at least two possible sources. Most obviously, the personal influence of Bismarck, with his fabled argumentative powers, could well have been effective apart from any German interest in the issue; and on this isssue the German direct interest was not insignificant. The other source of German influence could have been leverage drawn from the separate Austro-German alliance. German bargaining power in this alliance was slightly superior to Austria's, and, combined with the appreciable German interest in the no-unilateral-change issue in the Three Emperors' Alliance, it might have been sufficient, in tandem with Russian leverage, to overcome Austrian resistance on this point. It might not have been sufficient on the other two points, because the sources of Austrian resistance were stronger there and the bases of German pressure weaker.

Third, norms of equity and the sanctity of the status quo probably worked against Austria on the third issue and in Austria's favor on the other two. It has been well established that in bargaining, the status quo is privileged—that is, the party defending the status quo enjoys an inherent advantage. On the issues of partition and Italian adhesion, the Russians and the Germans were demanding a change in the status quo whereas the Austrians were defending it. This, added to Austria's superior leverage for the reasons cited above, ensured an Austrian success on these issues. But the proposal to prohibit change without consultation was itself based on the sanctity of the status quo; thus the principle weakened Austria's bargaining power on that issue. Austria's leverage on that issue was also weakened by the norm of equity: Russia was demanding only that Austria be subject to the same obligations in its sphere of interest that already constrained Russia in its sphere.

On the whole, our Hypothesis A is modestly but not unequivocally supported by this case. Likewise, the outcome gives only equivocal support to our specific hypotheses, which alternatively postulate a dominant causal effect from each of the three dimensions of bargaining power. Thus Hypothesis 1 says the least dependent party in an alliance will prevail in intra-alliance bargaining. Austria was less dependent on the alliance than were either Russia or Germany. This might explain the Austrian ability to resist German and Russian pressures on the first two issues discussed above, but it is inconsistent with Austria's rather substantial concession on the consultation issue.

There is clearer support for Hypothesis 2: that the ally with the greatest interest in an issue will prevail. Austria's negative interest in the partition issue was greater than Russia's positive interest, and Austria prevailed. Austria also prevailed on the issue of Italian membership, where the opposite interests of Austria and Germany were about evenly balanced. Austria conceded on the issue of no unilateral change, where its high negative interest was balanced by a high Russian positive interest. Thus Hypothesis 2 is weakly supported, in the sense that none of the three outcomes was inconsistent with the distribution of interests.

Hypothesis 3, relating outcomes to the comparative commitments of the allies, is modestly supported. Although there was no difference in the parties' verbal commitments to the Three Emperors' Alliance, the greater German strategic commitment to the Austro-German alliance was consistent with the overall Austrian bargaining success.

German dependence on Austria had been reduced by improving relations with France during the early 1880s. Bismarck encouraged colonial expansion by France in order to divert it from thoughts of revanche, discourage it from alliance with Russia, and bring it into conflict with Britain and Italy. The French government of Jules Ferry, strongly colonialist in orientation, welcomed and exploited the German support.

This period of detente ended with the fall of the Ferry ministry in 1885 and, in particular, with the appointment, as defense minister in the new French cabinet, of the charismatic General Boulanger, an advocate of revanche and a Franco-Russian alliance. Boulanger began a program of military reform and revival and appeared to be moving toward a coup d'etat. A Franco-German arms race got under way, and Russian arms increases were a further worry. These developments significantly increased the German sense of dependence on Austria. They were partially offset, however, by another regime change in England, which substituted the pro-German and pro-Austrian Tories under Salisbury for the moderately pro-Russian Liberals under Gladstone. The change in Britain also marginally reduced Austria's dependence on Germany.

Austrian dependence on the alliance increased sharply, however, as a result of the long crisis with Russia over Bulgaria between 1885 and 1887. The Russians believed they had been granted predominance in Bulgaria by the Three Emperors' Alliance, but the Bulgarians stubbornly refused to be dominated. Austria supported the Bulgarians, in spite of Bismarck's warnings that this violated Austria's treaty obligations to Russia. The Russians failed to establish control of the new state and blamed Austria, somewhat unfairly, since the responsibility lay mostly with the Bulgarians themselves. They also blamed Germany, which they believed, incorrectly, had supported Austria. As a result, a wave of anti-Austrian and anti-German sentiment swept the Czarist empire, and Russia made clear that it would not renew the treaty. Combined with the rise of similar sentiments in France, the danger of a Franco-Russian alliance took on fresh vividness.[5] Thus by 1887 both Austria and Germany were feeling more dependent on each other than they had four or five years earlier.

The great flaw in the Bismarckian system so far—some might call it a blatant contradiction—was that Germany was committed, by the Three Emperors' Alliance, to support Russian aspirations in the Near East but also to defend Austria-Hungary in a war with Russia, which was most likely to break out in precisely that area. To deal with this dilemma, Bismarck hit on the idea of mobilizing others in the defense of Austria's Balkan interests, thus taking Germany off the hook. The principal "other" was England, whose interests in the Near East closely paralleled Austria's.

By a happy coincidence, England's interests in the western Mediterranean were similar to Italy's. Thus a British-Austrian-Italian alliance might not only resolve the contradiction in the Balkans but also relieve some of Germany's burden of supporting Italian aspirations against France in North Africa.

With Bismarck cheering from the sidelines, the First Mediterranean Agreement, among Great Britain, Italy, and Austria, was consummated on February 12 and March 24, 1887, by exchanges of notes. It provided that any change in the political status quo in the Mediterranean, including the Adriatic, Aegean, and Black Seas, could be made only by previous agreement. In addition, Italy promised to support Britain in Egypt, and Britain promised to support Italian aspirations in North Africa.[6] Salisbury commented to Queen Victoria that it was "as close to an alliance as the parliamentary character of our institutions will permit."[7]

The Second Mediterranean Agreement, in December, made more explicit the English and Italian commitments to Austria in the Near East. Its provisions were specifically dedicated to preventing Russian moves against Bulgaria and Russian pressure on Turkey that might give Russia a dominant position at the Straits.[8]

The Mediterranean Agreements had two offsetting effects on bargaining power among the members of the Triple Alliance. On the one hand, Austria and Italy became less dependent on Germany, since they now had the support of England. On the other hand, German hints or threats of nonsupport became more credible, because Germany could point to England's more immediate responsibility on Mediterranean and Near Eastern issues. In effect, Bismarck had passed the buck to England. This move enabled him to avoid entrapment by Austria at very little risk of abandonment. He thus eased the strain on his system caused by the contradictory obligations to Russia and to Austria, and he did so at little or no cost. The contradiction between his support of Russian aspirations in the eastern Balkans and at the Straits and his sponsorship of the Mediterranean triplice was less blatant and hence easier to finesse. The arrangement also served Bismarck's objective of maintaining a certain moderate amount of tension between Russia and Britain, short of war but enough to make each one dependent on German support. Finally, it created an obstacle to an alliance between France and Britain, and this also reduced German dependence on Austria and increased its leverage in the alliance.

Alliance Bargaining: Renewal of the Triple Alliance

It was in this context that the Triple Alliance came up for renewal in early 1887. The Italians sensed that the Bulgarian crisis and the Boulanger threat had increased their alliance value, and they exploited it with great skill. They proposed two amendments to the original treaty: that Austria and Germany pledge their support to Italy in a war with France over Tripoli, and that Italy receive compensation for any change in the status quo in the Balkans favoring Austria. They hinted they would realign with France if the demands were not met. Kálnoky reacted with reserve—he saw entrapment in the first demand and irredentism in the second—but he came under stiff pressure from Bismarck to accept both. Bismarck now placed a much greater value on the Italian connection than he had five years earlier, owing to the increasing threat from France and the heightened conflict with Russia in the Near East, along with news he had lately received about Russian soundings in Paris. Italy was his only ally for the contingency of a French attack, so he wanted to conciliate it. He bombarded Kálnoky with various arguments: that the mention of Tripoli was not really an extension of the original commitment, since the Central Powers would be forced by their interests to defend Italy in any war with France, regardless of how it came about; that Italy would defect to France or Russia if its demands were not met; and that Italian neutrality would be very valuable to Austria in a conflict with Russia over the Balkans, since, in that event, Austria could not count on Germany.[9]

Kálnoky remained obdurate, arguing that Italy's price was too high. He began retreating, however, after Bismarck threatened to make a separate alliance with Italy. Kálnoky tried to get an Italian pledge to assist Austria actively in a war with Russia, rather than merely remain neutral, but this was rejected out of hand by the Italians. Finally, after Bismarck stated that Germany would not allow Austria to "embroil us in difficulties with Russia," Kálnoky could not contain his resentment. He rejected the Italian demands, retracted all concessions he had previously made, and declared he would accept only a simple extension of the 1882 agreement. He explained that if Germany were going to abandon Austria in the Balkans (as implied in Bismarck's speech), Austria would need all its forces there and consequently must avoid possible entrapment by Italy in North Africa.[10]

This outburst precipitated a compromise solution, ingeniously drafted by Bismarck: the Italian demands would be split in half and divided between Austria and Germany. Austria would promise compensation to Italy for Austrian gains in the Balkans (although Austria was able to exempt the annexation of Bosnia-Herzegovina from this proviso); Germany would pledge aid to Italy in a war with France over Tripoli or Morocco. This solution was acceptable to Kálnoky, since it removed the risk of Austrian entrapment in North Africa. It was also acceptable to Italy, since German aid against France was far more valuable than Austrian. The new treaty, consisting of the 1882 treaty and two supplementary agreements, was signed on February 20, 1887.

It was clearly a great victory for Italy, achieved through skillful exploitation of its partners' increased need for its allegiance and its own strong pivot position between France and the Germanic powers. Austria had granted it equal rights in the Balkans, without insisting on active Italian aid in a war with Russia. Germany was now obliged to assist Italy should it undertake an offensive war against France over colonial issues, and Italy gave no quid pro quo beyond its pledge in the original treaty to assist Germany if it were attacked by France. Germany's cost in making this commitment was reduced, however, by the near-simultaneous commitment of Britain on Italy's behalf in the First Mediterranean Agreement. The bargaining power of Italy was enhanced by the fact that it had a plausible alternative (agreement with France), whereas the Central Powers for the present had none, and by the latter's increased sense of threat from France and Russia.

Austria, forced to grant Italy a voice in Balkan affairs, was a net loser. This Austrian concession required heavy pressure from Bismarck, however, and a German willingness to take on the larger share of new commitments to Italy. Kálnoky knew how to exploit the German fears and heightened dependence, thus demonstrating that German dominance of the alliance had its limits.

In terms of Hypothesis A, Italy's dependence on the alliance may be rated as low; Austria's and Germany's, both moderate. The commitments of all three parties may be rather arbitrarily coded as moderate. In the first round of the bargaining, when the two Italian demands were being considered as a package, the Italian interest in having them granted was positive and high, the Austrian negative interest was high, and the German negative interest was only moderate (since Germany would not have suffered in granting Italy contingent compensation in the Balkans). These estimates translate to bargaining power scores of 8 for Italy, 7 for Austria, and 6 for Germany. In other words, Italy's overall bargaining power was strong, Austria's was moderate, and Germany's was somewhat weaker. Germany preferred to give in to the Italian demands rather than risk collapse of the alliance, but Austria appeared willing to take that risk.

Bismarck's idea of dividing the cost of satisfying the Italian demands made agreement possible by lowering the Austrian cost of acceptance (negative interest), from high to low. This maneuver reduced Austria's overall bargaining power score from 7 to 5. Since Austria now had less to lose by accepting the Italian demands, it was less willing to risk the alliance by holding out against them. Thus the significant effect of Bismarck's stratagem was to make Austria more willing to concede, and that was enough to bring about an agreement.

On the whole, Hypothesis A is supported: the party with the highest bargaining power gained the most. As for our specific hypotheses, this case gives fairly strong support to Hypothesis 1, that outcomes reflect relative dependence. Italy was the biggest gainer and was also the least dependent. On the other hand, Austria sacrificed slightly more than Germany even though it was less dependent than Germany on the Italian connection. But this small anomaly could be explained by Austria's greater dependence of the two on the underlying Austro-German alliance.

From the perspective of comparative interests, Italy had a strong interest in having its demands granted, and Austria had a strong interest in not granting them. Germany had a moderate interest in refusing them. Thus, on grounds of interest alone, the combined bargaining power of Austria and Germany was superior and the Italian demands should have been rejected; Hypothesis 2 is not supported. This does not necessarily imply the general unimportance of interests, however; only that in this case dependence relations were more potent than interests.

The case gives stronger support to the dependence hypothesis than to the interest hypothesis—that is, the outcome clearly turned more on dependence relations than on comparative interests at stake. The commitment hypothesis is not supported: all three states were about equally committed to the alliance, but the outcome strongly favored one over the other two. But, of course, this may mean no more than that the ceteris paribus condition was not satisfied: Italy's superiority on the dependence factor simply overwhelmed the symmetry of commitment.

Alliance Dependence: The Reinsurance Treaty, 1887

The Three Emperors' Alliance was also due for renewal during this very busy diplomatic year. But it could not be renewed in its original form, since the Bulgarian crisis had destroyed any further prospect of Austro-Russian collaboration. The Czar insisted that Austria be excluded from any renewal. Hence Bismarck and the Russian ambassador, Shuvalov, drafted a bilateral alternative. The result of their craftsmanship, which became known as the Reinsurance Treaty, was signed on June 18, 1887.

The heart of the treaty was a neutrality clause that required either party to be neutral in case the partner were attacked by a third party. Neutrality was explicitly not required in the event of a German attack on France or a Russian attack on Austria. These exemptions kept the treaty consistent with the German-Austrian alliance and left Russia free to support France against Germany. In addition, there were several side payments, mostly favoring Russia. Germany recognized Russia's "preponderant and decisive influence" in Bulgaria[11] and promised moral and diplomatic support for Russian efforts to control the Straits and Constantinople. Russia was clearly the primary gainer: besides German support for its aims in the Near East, it could now count on German neutrality in any war with Russia's primary enemy, England, and in a war with Austria initiated by

Austria. Germany's principal gain lay in the preclusion of an aggressive Franco-Russian alliance directed against Germany. Although the agreement did not explicitly forbid a defensive Franco-Russian alliance, Bismarck no doubt calculated that Russia would be inhibited politically from exercising that option. The reduced likelihood of a Franco-Russian alliance, and the general dampening of Russian hostility, also reduced German dependence on Austria.

The principal loser was the absent party, Austria. It was now odd man out and in some danger of losing its primacy in Germany's political affections. If it could ever have expected German support for its ambitions in the Balkans, it could hardly expect it any longer. The German-Russian treaty now placed clear limits on the political benefit of Austria's alliance with Germany. At the same time, the threat to Austria from Russia had increased. Counting on German support, Russia would now press harder in its conflicts with Austria, which were no longer papered over with cooperative treaty language. Austrian dependence on Germany, which had been eased by the Mediterranean Agreements, now rose to previous levels.

Despite the Reinsurance Treaty, German-Russian relations deteriorated during the latter part of 1887 and the year 1888. The Bulgarian crisis was still unresolved, the Russian press kept up its attacks on Germany, and Russian troops were concentrated in Poland. Bismarck's attempts to reassure the Russians were undermined by the persistent bellicosity of German military figures, who had managed to influence the new Kaiser, Wilhelm II, in an anti-Russian direction. German-Russian trade relations worsened. Ostensibly in retaliation for Russian discrimination against German landowners in Poland, the Reichsbank was forbidden to accept Russian securities as collateral for loans.

German anxieties were stimulated further by developments in France, where a Boulangist coup or civil war appeared imminent in January 1889. Further disquieting were rumors of a budding military collaboration between France and Russia and the flotation of large new Russian loans on the French money market. Perhaps in response to these developments, Bismarck proposed to England a formal defense alliance against France. Lord Salisbury turned the overture aside, saying the time was not yet right.[12]

The latter years of the 1880s were a time of steadily rising external threat for both Germany and Austria, increasing their sense of mutual dependence. German dependence grew somewhat more than Austrian, since the threat to Germany came from France as well as Russia. Consequently, Germany became markedly more supportive of Austria during 1889. When Emperor Franz Joseph visited the Kaiser in August, the Kaiser assured him that "whatever reason you may have for mobilizing, whether

Bulgaria or anything else, the day of your mobilization will be the day of mobilization for my army."[13]

1890–1900

The clearest trend in the Austro-German alliance between 1890 and 1900, as shown in Figure 7-1, is a rise in the relative dependence of Germany due to the consummation of the alliance between Russia and France. The rising curve for German resource dependence simply reflects the increasing probability of a two-front war during these years. Of course, the Franco-Russian alliance increased Austria's dependence as well, but less so than Germany's, since there was little likelihood of a combined Franco-Russian attack on Austria alone.

The curves for resource dependence are based on the figures in Table 7-1. Germany was stronger than its principal enemy, France, in 1890 but was considerably weaker than France and Russia combined in 1900, by about 14.6 percent of total great-power resources. This may be taken as a crude indicator of Germany's resource dependence on Austria. Austria's resource dependence also increased: its share of great-power resources declined from 10.2 percent in 1890 to 9.4 percent in 1900, while Russia's climbed from 19.5 percent to 23.7 percent. Although Germany became the more dependent ally on resource grounds about 1894, owing to the Franco-Russian alliance, the steadily increasing gap between Austrian and Russian capabilities made Austria about equally dependent by 1900. When the diplomatic context is factored in (producing the solid and dashed lines for overall dependence), Austria was more dependent than Germany in the early 1890s but less dependent after 1895 (when the overall dependence curves cross) because of improving Austro-Russian relations.

Alliance Dependence: Cutting the Wire to St. Petersburg

German dependence increased on diplomatic grounds when it was decided in 1890 not to renew the Reinsurance Treaty. The decision was precipitated by the resignation of Bismarck, who had found himself increasingly at odds with the new Kaiser over both domestic issues and foreign policy, particularly policy toward Russia. The new German leadership, under Georg Leo von Caprivi as chancellor and strongly influenced by Fritz Holstein at the Foreign Office, decided that the treaty was incompatible, at least in spirit, with the Austrian alliance, that it benefited Russia far more than Germany, and that, if it were renewed, the Russians might reveal its terms, which might estrange Austria and England. There was also a hope that taking an unambiguous confrontational stance toward

Russia would persuade England to give a formal guarantee to Austria and Italy and eventually to join the Triple Alliance.[14] Above all, the new government wished to simplify Germany's alliance system; this meant a fundamental shift in foreign policy in which alignments would straightforwardly reflect common interests and England would replace Russia as ally. Thus the Russians were informed that the treaty would not be renewed, and it lapsed on June 18, 1890.

It was a major blunder on Germany's part. Although the treaty did not expressly bar a Franco-Russian alliance, as long as it existed the Russians could reasonably look on Germany as a friend and have no incentive to ally against it. But without it, Germany could be seen as either friend or enemy, and considering the recent troubles in the relationship, it was more natural to take the latter view. Moreover, the very act of nonrenewal could be interpreted as a moderately hostile act, especially in light of recent German moves toward England. Germany threw away an alliance option and thus markedly increased its dependence on its remaining allies.

It was not a careless, unthinking error, but one made after due deliberation. Indeed, it inaugurated a departure in German foreign policy that became known as the "new course." This policy aimed for closer relations with England, even an alliance, and stronger support for Austria against Russia. Germany began to abandon its policy of abstention on the Bulgarian question, moving toward frank support of Austria. The German chancellor, Prince Hohenloe, told the Reichstag: "We stick to the program that if our Austrian friends fall into mortal danger, even by virtue of an undertaking of which we disapprove, we shall swiftly come to their aid."[15] The new approach amounted to a reversal of Bismarck's policy of even-handedness between Austria and Russia and cool reserve toward England. It reflected the greater German dependence on allies which had resulted from cutting the wire to St. Petersburg.

The dramatic French naval visit to Kronstadt in July 1891 alerted the German government to the imminent danger of a Franco-Russian alliance. It sought to discourage these negotiations by friendly moves toward Russia. Russian-German relations began to improve, and the German intimacy with Britain, keystone of the new course, began to fade.[16] The trend became more marked after British elections in August, 1892, which brought Gladstone again to power. With the British Liberals in charge, Germany could not count on British support against Russia ; therefore, accommodating Russia became more attractive as an alternative. On the Russian side, a desire for a commercial treaty and access to the Berlin money market counseled a friendly attitude toward Germany.

The German shift was not 180 degrees, from anti-Russian to anti-British, but a return to the Bismarckian policy of two irons in the fire, striving to be on good terms with both the Russians and the British. The Germans did not give up their hope of some sort of understanding with Britain, but it was the end of the interlude during which Germany had staked everything on resistance to Russia and alliance with England.[17] The new policy, known as "the free hand," emphasized keeping all options open. Germany now began to play off France and Russia against Great Britain in the colonial realm, hoping to extract concessions from both sides and perhaps to embarrass the British enough to persuade them that alliance with Germany was, after all, the prudent course.[18] On Bulgaria and Constantinople, Germany returned to a policy of supporting Russia and restraining Austria.[19] Naturally, the Austrians became apprehensive. In September 1893 Vienna directed a query to Berlin: What will Germany do if Russia occupies Constantinople? The Kaiser replied that this would not be a casus belli for Germany; Austria should not resist but take Salonika as compensation. This was a clear return to Bismarck's preferred policy of defusing Austro-Russian conflict by partitioning the European part of the Ottoman Empire between the two.[20]

The visit of a Russian naval squadron to Toulon in October 1893 further indicated the existence of a Franco-Russian alliance of some sort. Along with news of the permanent stationing of a Russian squadron in the Mediterranean, it triggered a crisis of confidence in the Triple Alliance and the Mediterranean entente. Austria began to fear that Britain, feeling overmatched by the combined Russian and French fleets, would abandon the Mediterranean. In that case, Italy, no longer enjoying British naval protection, would have to defect to France. Germany was subject to similar fears and to the further worry that Austria might defect.[21] Both Germany and Austria-Hungary began feeling more dependent on their alliance and consequently more fearful of abandonment.

Germany's response was to move closer not to its ally, Austria, but rather to its enemy, Russia. If Russia had not yet definitely signed up with France, perhaps it could still be deflected. A German-Russian tariff treaty was concluded in January 1894. During the winter of 1893–94 Germany and Russia were on closer terms than at any time since Bismarck's resignation. French-German relations also improved. These efforts were fruitless, however, for the Franco-Russian alliance was finally ratified by the Czar on January 4, 1894.

Joint Military Planning

The Austrian and German military staffs had engaged in sporadic talks since 1882, becoming somewhat more intimate after Alfred von Waldersee succeeded Helmuth von Moltke as German chief of staff in 1888. Relations began to deteriorate with the appointment of Alfred von Schlieffen as German chief of staff in 1891. Schlieffen decided to reverse the Moltke-

Waldersee plan for a concentration of German forces against Russia in the event of war with both France and Russia. This plan had been the basis of the Austro-German military collaboration for a decade. The military leaders had agreed on a plan for the "double envelopment" of Russian forces in Poland, through a strong German offensive in the north and an Austrian attack in the south. Germany would meanwhile fight a defensive war against France in the west. The German military felt the Austrians had to be assured of strong German support in the east, lest they refuse to take the offensive.

Schlieffen now decided, however, that in a two-front war, Germany had to defeat its opponents seriatim and that this meant concentrating initially against France, with only a weak holding force deployed against the slower-mobilizing Russians. France would be defeated in three to four weeks, and then the western German forces would be shuttled to the eastern front to help the Austrians deal with the Russians. Schlieffen did not worry about the Austrians' failing to play their assigned role, since he had a low opinion of their capabilities anyway.[22]

Naturally, this plan did not appeal to the Austrians, who were informed of it piecemeal between 1892 and 1896. It saddled Austria with the main burden of fighting Russia initially and perhaps also ultimately, in case the expectation of only a brief war against France proved too optimistic. When Friedrich Beck, the Austrian chief of staff, refused to accept this role, Schlieffen called off the exchanges, assuring the Austrian generals not to worry, for the fate of Austria "will be decided not on the Bug but on the Seine."[23] The talks were not resumed until 1909; in the interim the two militaries made their plans with only the most cursory reference to those of the other.

The Schlieffen Plan made Germany more dependent on Austria, since it delegated to Austria the crucial task of holding off Russia during the early stages of a war. In turn, as we shall see, this led to an increased German strategic interest in, and verbal commitment to, Austrian independence and Austrian interests.

Alliance Bargaining: Steering Clear of Perfidious Albion

The German hopes for an understanding with Britain were persistently undermined by mistrust of British motives and reliability. The Germans were obsessed with the suspicion that Britain secretly wanted to foment war among the continental states: first, it would make an alliance with a continental partner; then, after the partner had gotten involved in war, Britain would step aside and let the protagonists weaken each other while it scooped up more colonial prizes. A variant on this theme held that

Britain would make an alliance and then hang back and let its ally get entrapped into defending British interests.

An incident in December 1893 illustrates the baneful effect this attitude had not only on German-British relations but also on Germany's relations with its own allies. Austria, worried about the improvement in German-Russian relations, decided to make a bid for British support. Kálnoky, the foreign minister, in conversation with Lord Rosebery, the British foreign minister, stated that Austria could not defend Constantinople without British help; failing such assistance, it would have to limit itself to defending its interests in the Balkans. Rosebery replied that Britain was determined to defend Constantinople, but to do so, it required the deterrent assistance of the Triple Alliance, to "hold France in check."[24]

Kálnoky recognized that keeping France in check required a pledge by Germany, so he asked Berlin its reaction to Rosebery's proposal. Here was the opportunity the Germans had been waiting for; the British, usually so reticent, were themselves proposing an alliance. Yet the Germans rejected the overture summarily. The reason given was that the proposed agreement was one-sided: Germany would commit itself to threaten France, and ultimately to fight the dreaded two-front war, in defense of an area where there were no German interests, with no guarantee that the British would not withdraw from the fight when it suited their convenience. There could be no advance commitments, the Austrians were told; Britain must first show its seriousness by striking the first blow; if Germany committed first, the British would simply leave the Triple Alliance in the lurch.[25] Another reason for rejecting the proposal was that it conflicted with Germany's current policy toward Russia.[26] Thus Germany threw away the best opportunity that would arise for an alliance with Britain and gravely damaged its relations with Austria. In present-day terminology, the Germans interpreted the British proposal as an attempt to pass the buck, and they simply refused to accept the buck. If England wanted Germany to perform services for it, it would have to join the Triple Alliance and assume definite obligations. "We should then be able to prevent England concluding an isolated peace prematurely," said Baron Marschall, the German foreign minister.[27]

This case is hard to relate to our Hypothesis A, because the Germans appear to have acted contrary to their own interests—that is, they acted irrationally. Even if we interpret rationality very liberally, however, and say that Germany had a high interest in blocking the Austro-British scheme, the hypothesis is still contradicted. Such an interest, combined with moderate dependence and a high commitment to the alliance, gives Germany a bargaining power rating of 6. Austria, with a high positive interest, moderate dependence, and moderate commitment, rates a score of 7. Thus Austria should have prevailed over the German resistance. Nevertheless, the ratings are close, well within the margin for error of our gross estimates.

Nor can the outcome be explained well by our specific hypotheses based on the separate components of bargaining power. Although the dependence of the allies is rated as equal, Germany's was rising (the Franco-Russian alliance was near final consummation), so a more favorable response to the Austro-British initiative might have been expected. An explanation in terms of comparative interest or commitment is not any more plausible. The real reason for the German rejection, it seems, was unreasoning suspicion of British intentions, a factor that throughout this period in German diplomacy is in remarkable tension with the desire to ally with Britain. Whenever that desire seemed to be on the point of realization, as in this case, the old image of "perfidious Albion" got in the way, leading to either a German negative or a German demand for impossible British guarantees.

Alliance Bargaining: The Congo, 1894

Largely because of colonial conflicts, Anglo-German relations continued cooling during 1893 and 1894, despite the formal conclusion of the Franco-Russian alliance. The Germans believed this alliance was aimed at England as much as themselves. The English would eventually realize this and come begging to join the Triple Alliance. Meanwhile, it would not do to appear too eager or permit "perfidious Albion" to push them forward against France and Russia.[28] Colonial concessions were insistently demanded; the English had to be treated brusquely so that they would recognize the necessity for alliance with Germany.[29] Austria and Italy, being far more dependent than Germany on British goodwill, tried to moderate the German policy, with little success.

They succeeded on one issue, however. The Germans, as part of their policy of harassing Britain, were supporting France in a French-British dispute about the boundary of the Congo Free State. Rosebery complained to Austria and threatened to break off the Mediterranean Agreement with Austria if the German attitude continued. In great alarm, Austria, supported by Italy, brought pressure on Germany to soften its policy on the Congo issue. Germany immediately made concessions to Britain, which resolved the problem.

Austria's moderate interest, moderate dependence, and moderate commitment give it a bargaining power score of 6, compared with a German score of 5, based on low interest, moderate dependence, and moderate commitment. Austria is predicted to stand firm on this issue and Germany to concede, which is what happened. Some sort of compromise favoring Austria would also have been consistent with these scores, but the situation did not allow it. Thus our general hypothesis, Hypothesis A, is supported.

The specific components of bargaining power that best explain this outcome are the comparative interests at stake. The interest Austria had in maintaining British support was more important to it than any particular colonial victory over Britain was to Germany. The Germans apparently were motivated to offer their concession because of the much stronger Austrian interest—the friendship of Britain—which, indeed, they shared to some extent. Comparative dependence and commitment apparently did not contribute to the outcome, since the allies were about equal on these indices.

Alliance Dependence

The general pattern of German harassment of Britain and conciliation of Russia continued during the later 1890s. The Austrians, who preferred confrontation with Russia and cooperation with England, were immensely irritated by their ally's following of the opposite policy. They saw the German hostility toward England as weakening the whole Triple Alliance. The traditional Austrian alignment with England in the Near East was being damaged by the Anglo-German antagonism. Italian loyalty to the Triple Alliance, such as it was, could not survive a real break with Britain. Count Goluchowski, who had succeeded Kálnoky as Austrian foreign minister in May 1895, kept pressing for a firmer commitment from Germany, especially to resist a Russian attempt to seize the Straits. The request was rejected, the German chancellor averring that "we shall not allow [the alliance] to be used for vague plans of Austria's in the East."[30] Hohenloe also declined Austria's request for a joint conference of chiefs of staff to discuss the circumstances in which the terms of the treaty would be operative, lest Germany be ensnared in aggressive Austrian plans.

Goluchowski had no more luck with Britain. In 1896 and again in 1897 he proposed a new treaty with more explicit defense commitments, including a commitment to defend Constantinople against Russian attack, to replace the vague Mediterranean Agreements of 1887. Salisbury refused even to renew the 1887 agreement. An unspoken reason for his refusal was the Franco-Russian alliance: the Admiralty had informed Salisbury that the British navy could not defend Constantinople against the combined strength of the Russian and French fleets.[31] The Austrians, however, blamed his refusal on German policy, which had alienated Britain from the Central Powers.[32] The lapse of the Mediterranean Agreement terminated the formal British link to the Triple Alliance and made Austria more dependent on Germany.

The Austro-Russian Detente

Seeing his formal ally and his tacit ally increasingly at odds (Anglo-German relations reached a particularly low ebb in 1896), and failing to get more than equivocal support from each, Goluchowski decided the time had come to settle matters with his opponent. Late in April 1897 he and the Emperor traveled to Russia and reached agreement with the Russian government on four principles: (1) maintenance of the status quo in the Near East, (2) noninterference with the independent development of the Balkan states, (3) cooperation between representatives of the two powers in the Balkans, and (4) mutual agreement about the future territorial configuration in the Balkans if it became impossible to maintain the status quo.[33] If territorial revision should become unavoidable, a new state, Albania, would be established on the Adriatic, and the rest of European Turkey, except for Constantinople and the Straits, would be divided among the Balkan states.

This understanding inaugurated a ten-year detente between these erstwhile enemies. The Russians were willing because their imperial aspirations had now shifted to the Far East, so that they were quite happy to place the Balkans "on ice" for a while. For Austria, the move reflected a devaluation of the alliance with Germany and Italy, an attempt to preserve security by reducing the threat rather than confronting it.[34] It was also a substitute for the weakening British connection. It reduced Austrian dependence on Germany and consequently increased Austrian bargaining power in the alliance. It was undertaken without consulting Germany, to the irritation of Berlin.

Anglo-German Alliance Negotiations

Imperial competition tended to preoccupy all the European powers during the late 1890s. In this struggle it was usually England, as top dog, that was challenged by some combination of the others. Germany collaborated with Russia and France to limit Japanese gains after a war with China, joined with France in blocking British acquisition of a strip of the Congo, fulminated against British policy in South Africa, and briefly conspired with Russia to merge the Triple and Dual Alliances in a grand continental league against England. Germany's new Baghdad Railway project and increased economic assertiveness in the Near East were disquieting to both Britain and Russia. Beginning about 1897, agitation in Germany for a large navy to support a policy of *weltpolitik* presaged the policy that would sink all remaining prospects of an Anglo-German alliance, although neither country realized it for several years.

England felt increasingly overstretched by the need to defend its possessions and perquisites against the pressures of others. Jettisoning its traditional policy of "splendid isolation," it turned to alliances and agreements as a means of relieving the pressure on its military and naval budgets.[35] First it tried Russia, offering a settlement on all outstanding points of friction. The Russians showing no interest, Joseph Chamberlain, the colonial secretary, was authorized to try Germany. Chamberlain made two approaches to Germany, in 1898 and 1901, and was unsuccessful both times. Probably the negotiations were doomed from the start because of the lack of common interests between the two countries. The British were interested only in a narrow and clearly defined agreement for defense against Russian encroachments in the Far East. The Germans were little interested in the Far East but wanted some help in Europe. Consequently, they demanded that Britain join the Triple Alliance and thus bind itself to defend Austria and Italy as well as Germany. Such a British commitment was necessary to compensate the Germans for the alienation of Russia that would be entailed in an alliance with Britain. And because of their deep mistrust of Britain, the Germans demanded that any agreement be signed, sealed, and delivered in the most ironclad way—by ratification by the British parliament, thus binding future parliaments. They realized the price was high but believed the British would eventually have to pay it, since the alternatives of alliance with France and Russia were absolutely foreclosed by severe colonial disputes. Meanwhile, Germany could wait, remaining uncommitted to either side, exploiting the bargaining leverage that this stance provided, and all the while educating the British, by firm pressures, as to the value of alliance with Germany.

The price *was* too high, "too high a fence to ride at," as the British foreign minister, Lansdowne, put it.[36] The British obligation to defend Germany, Austria, and Italy against France and Russia would be far more onerous than the German commitment to defend the British Isles against a French invasion—a task that could be handled by the navy in any case—and would not have been sufficiently compensated by help in defending the empire. Such a treaty would have overturned the balance of power by, in effect, granting European hegemony to Germany. It would have strained if not violated the logic of the system by uniting the two most powerful states in it. So the talks collapsed, as they were destined to from the beginning.

1900–1910

The allies' relative dependence, in terms of military resources, shifted marginally in Germany's favor between 1900 and 1910, as shown in Figure 7-1 and Table 7-1. Germany's share of total great-power resources climbed from 24.6 percent in 1900 to 27.9 percent in 1910, while the combined shares of France and Russia increased only slightly, from 39.2 percent to

39.5 percent. Austria's share increased from 9.4 percent to 9.5 percent, while Russia's was rising from 23.7 percent to 24.6 percent. Note, however, that these gross figures do not fully capture the falloff in Russian military and naval capabilities after 1905 because of the war with Japan. This Russian weakening is suggested on the graph by the sharp drop in German and Austrian overall dependence in 1905, followed by a gradual increase to 1910 as Russian military strength partially recovered.

In the less tangible components of dependence—conflict with opponents and alliance alternatives—the trend for the decade was one of increasing dependence for Germany and not much net change for Austria. Thus Germany's overall dependence increased more than Austria's in the first half of the decade, mainly because of the rise of antagonism with Britain, negotiation of the British entente with France, and the creeping defection of Italy. In the latter part of the period, however, Austria's aggregate dependence increased commensurately owing to the sharply increased Russian hostility after the Bosnian crisis. In combined political and military terms, Germany was the more dependent party throughout the decade even though it was the less dependent on the narrower basis of military resources.

Ties among the Triple Alliance partners continued to deteriorate, largely as a result of the growing Anglo-German antagonism. Italy began its steady drift into the orbit of France by agreements in 1900 and 1902 defining zones of expansion in North Africa and guaranteeing reciprocal neutrality. The neutrality provision directly contradicted the Triple Alliance treaty, which had just been renewed. The Franco-Italian agreements left Germany more dependent on Austria; the reverse less so, since many in Austria already regarded Italy as more enemy than ally.

Austria, bereft of both British and German support, continued and deepened its detente with Russia. Domestic conflict and confusion, along with economic weakness, tended to weaken Austrian military potential around the turn of the century. In 1903, for example, the Hungarian parliament refused to supply recruits for the monarchy's army. These developments, along with the lack of support from Germany, led to further agreements with Russia. The Murzsteg agreement, in 1903, provided for joint Austro-Russian supervision of Turkish reforms in Macedonia. A neutrality agreement soon followed: each would be neutral in case the other were attacked by a third power. Russia was thus protected against Austrian attack in the event it became involved in war with Great Britain; similarly, Austria was protected against Russian intervention in an Austro-Italian war. These moves implied an Austrian devaluation of the German alliance and the Mediterranean entente. They also reduced Austrian dependence on Germany. Austrian dependence declined further between 1903 and 1905, as Russian military resources became almost totally committed against Japan in the Far East.

The Germans' attitude toward their allies during these years might be described as absentminded condescension. In pursuit of their new vision of a German-dominated *Mitteleuropa*, the Germans stepped up their commercial activity in Turkey and the Balkans, paying scant attention to the resentment this policy aroused in Austria. They installed a high protective tariff in 1902 that hit Austrian agricultural exports especially hard. They kept up their appeasement of Russia, encouraging its involvement in East Asia in order to divert it from the Near East and the Balkans. They continued waiting for the English to realize their need for a German alliance, all the while stoking British antagonism and suspicion by their colonial bullying and new plans for a large navy. Thus it came as a surprise to Germany when Britain, in 1904, reached a settlement with France of virtually all colonial issues between them, most notably those concerning Egypt and Morocco. The Germans recognized that they had suffered a major diplomatic defeat, although they put on a complacent public face.[37]

Alliance Bargaining: The First Morocco Crisis

The Entente Cordiale of 1904 was followed almost immediately by a crisis over its provisions regarding Morocco. The Germans, with some justice, believed they should have been consulted and thus demanded that a conference be held to consider the Anglo-French agreement. Their aim went beyond frustrating the French in Morocco and asserting their "rights" as a great power; they also hoped to break up the Franco-British connection by demonstrating British lack of support for France. They seemed to succeed at first, when they bullied the French government into firing their foreign minister, Delcassé, who advocated resisting the German demand. In the end they were completely frustrated, however, since Britain and all the other countries represented at the Algeciras conference, except Austria, unequivocally supported France and secured for it the control of the police and finances of Morocco. The entente emerged stronger than before.

For the present chapter, what is of greatest interest is the Austrian role at the conference. Goluchowski had been of considerable help to Germany in persuading the French premier, Rouvier, to accept a conference. At first Goluchowski declared his support of Germany "through thick and thin."[38] But both he and the Emperor were above all concerned that the conference not lead to a confrontation. When it became clear that the German demand for complete internationalization of the police was unacceptable to France and all the other participants, Goluchowski advised Germany to compromise, since "Morocco was not worth a war."[39] The Emperor, Franz Joseph, implored the German ambassador to avoid isolation in case of a vote, since that might result in a realignment of powers, associating Russia with Britain and France.[40]

The main sticking point at the conference concerned who would control the Moroccan police in the major coastal towns. France demanded control by itself and Spain. Germany proposed allocating one port each to the major European powers or giving the whole task to one or several small states. On March 5, in a preliminary vote, it became clear that Germany was isolated, except for pro forma support by Austria. The Austrian delegate, Count Welersheimb, then suggested a compromise: the police would be French and Spanish in all towns except Casablanca, where they would be commanded by a Swiss or Dutch officer with powers of inspection over all the police. This proposal was reluctantly accepted by the Germans, who needed an escape route. Although it was a substantial concession, it was rejected by the French, who knew they had the power to win it all if they stood firm. The Austrians then undertook intensive mediation. The upshot was agreement on virtually the French terms, except that the police (all French and Spanish) would be subject to inspection by a Swiss officer with no command powers.

The Austrian role did not correspond to the unqualified support that Germany had expected. Nevertheless, Kaiser Wilhelm tried to put a good face on it by congratulating Goluchowski for playing the "brilliant second" and by promising him a "similar service" in the future.[41] The "brilliant second" remark was received in Austria with great annoyance, not only because of its condescending tone but also because of its inaccuracy. Austria had not meekly followed Germany's lead, a lead that could have ended in disaster, but had taken the lead itself in preventing the conference's collapse and salvaging for Germany everything it could realistically have hoped to obtain. Nevertheless, as Theobald von Bethmann-Hollweg later put it, the Germans had "discovered the boundary line beyond which the diplomatic support of Austria refused to go."[42]

It is hard to treat this crisis as an alliance bargaining episode between Germany and Austria because it is impossible to say exactly how much Germany was influenced by its ally and how much by the other participants. Moreover, to the degree that Austria was influential, it was influence exercised not by a threat of defection but by persuasive argumentation and by assuming the role of mediator. In this role, Austria was able to provide, for Germany, a means of disengagement from its initial position with minimum loss of face. Austria could do that, of course, because it was Germany's ally: it was easier for Germany to accept a proposal made by a supportive friend than one made by an adversary.

These caveats stated, and turning to our bargaining power index, we can plausibly say that Germany had a moderate positive interest in frustrating French aims in Morocco, while Austria had no interest, indeed a negative interest, in this goal. Germany was more dependent on the alliance than was Austria, after negotiation of the Anglo-French entente and the weakening of Russia. Both parties were moderately committed to the alliance. These estimates yield bargaining power scores of 6 for Germany and 6 for Austria, scores that predict a compromise on the bargaining stance to be assumed toward France and its friends. This is a fair description of the Austrian proposal and the German acceptance of it. It fell well short of what Germany had been demanding; on the other hand, it would have given Germany more than Austria actually wished it to concede— that is, everything. In the end, of course, Germany had to concede everything, but that was the result of the superior bargaining power of its adversaries rather than that of its ally.

Alliance Dependence

The humiliating and shocking experience of the Morocco crisis triggered a new sense of isolation and encirclement in Germany. The Anglo-French entente had been consolidated, Russia had moved closer to both France and England, and Italy's unreliability had been made quite clear. These results generated a greater feeling of dependence on Austria and a desire to make sure of Austria's loyalty. On May 31, 1906, Chancellor Bernhard von Bülow wrote a long letter to the Kaiser in which he noted that relations with Austria had grown more important than ever, since the monarchy was Germany's only reliable ally; but, he said, Austria should be prevented, so far as possible, from noticing Germany's isolation: "We must therefore not allow Vienna to perceive either that we have too great a need of support from Austria or that we feel ourselves in any way isolated. The Austrians must have the impression that in any event we have full confidence in ourselves. Therefore we must represent our relations with Russia, Italy and England as better than they actually are."[43]

The new Austrian foreign minister, Alois Aehrenthal, who replaced Goluchowski in October 1906, was not to be fooled, however. Fully recognizing the increased German dependence, he sought to exploit it to reduce Austrian dependence on Germany and perhaps even to take the lead in the alliance. To this end, he began improving relations with Austria's potential enemies.[44] His expressions of friendliness toward Italy (a potential enemy even though a nominal ally) were soon reciprocated. He continued cooperating with Russia to persuade the Ottoman sultan to institute reforms in Macedonia and even suggested a restoration of the Three Emperors' League, a thought to which the Czar responded warmly. Because of the increased German dependence, such moves toward opponents could be undertaken with little risk of German abandonment. As Aehrenthal stated, Austria's role henceforth was "to mediate between Germany and Europe."[45]

Germany's dependence on Austria had increased by virtue of the coming together of its opponents, which increased its need for Austrian assistance. Germany was also more committed to Austria in the sense that it was more than ever imperative that Germany prevent the breakup or conquest of the monarchy by Russia. The rise of Pan-Slavism and its attraction to Slavs within Austria-Hungary made internal collapse a real possibility and argued for supporting the monarchy in an active Balkans policy.[46] Austria was still the junior partner, but its capacity to commit Germany in the Balkans and resist German restraint had substantially increased. The two unfortunate facts that Austria was Germany's only sure ally and was weak caused the Germans to be extraordinarily sensitive to any aspersions on Austria's status as a "great power" and to seek to prop up that status at every diplomatic opportunity.[47]

The mutual dependence of the Central Powers was further heightened the following year by the conclusion of an Anglo-Russian entente. The surprising defeat of Russia in the war with Japan in 1904–5 had weakened it and brought home the fact that it was overextended in Asia. Hence the Russians decided to cut their losses in disputes with England, negotiating a settlement in Persia, Afghanistan, and Tibet. Although this move was, on its face, like the Anglo-French agreement, merely a settlement of colonial issues, it implicitly carried an anti-German and anti-Austrian point and signified that Russia was going to refocus its expansionist energies on the Near East and the Balkans. A rapprochement with Japan underlined the change. The German reaction was to move closer to Austria. In a circular letter to German embassies on July 25, Bülow stated, "If it is permissible to embody in a formula our attitude towards the present phase of Eastern politics, it would run as follows: the needs, wishes and interests of Austria-Hungary must be decisive for our attitude in all Balkan questions."[48]

Alliance Bargaining: The Bosnia Crisis, 1908–9

The German determination to back Austria and thus to preserve Austria's status as a great power was dramatically illustrated during the Bosnia crisis of 1908–9. By authority of the Berlin Congress of 1878, Austria had occupied the Turkish province of Bosnia and Herzegovina for thirty years. A democratic revolution in Turkey raised the possibility that Turkey might try to reassert control. Aehrenthal, the Austrian foreign minister, decided the time had come to annex the provinces formally. He and Alexander Izvolsky, the new Russian foreign minister, hatched a plan whereby Russia would support the annexation in return for Austrian support of Russian control of the Black Sea–Mediterranean Straits. Aehrenthal was anxious to assert his independence of Germany, so he did not inform his ally of the plan. He felt sure of German support nevertheless, "since this power is now absolutely dependent on Austria-Hungary."[49]

Izvolsky thought he had got Aehrenthal's agreement that this exchange would be formally ratified by a conference of all European powers before being implemented. Aehrenthal, however, declared the annexation unilaterally on October 6, 1908. Izvolsky tried desperately to organize a conference at which he might collect the Russian side of the bargain but failed to interest any of the other major powers. A crisis developed over the Serbian demand for compensation and an Austrian threat of military action against Serbia unless it withdrew its demand, recognized the annexation, and canceled mobilization measures. Russia and Great Britain supported Serbia and refused to recognize the annexation.

The Germans were surprised and, moreover, rather unhappy about the Austrian action, since it struck a blow against Turkey, where German economic interests had been growing rapidly, and it would probably deepen British suspicions of the Central Powers. Anglo-German relations were already at a low ebb because of the naval race. The Germans were also irritated at not being informed or consulted. Nevertheless, Germany supported Austria unequivocally throughout the crisis. Both Bülow and Holstein feared that Austria might defect to the entente if not supported. As Bülow explained to the Kaiser: "Our position would indeed be dangerous if Austria lost confidence and turned away. So long as we stand together, we form a bloc that no one will lightly attack. In eastern questions above all, we cannot place ourselves in opposition to Austria, who has nearer and greater interests in the Balkans peninsula than ourselves. A refusal or a grudging attitude in the question of annexation of Bosnia and Hercegovina would not be forgiven."[50]

Aehrenthal wrote to Bülow on September 26, with a pointed reference to Algeciras: "We reckon with complete confidence on the support of Germany, who has received proofs that we stand by our friends at critical moments."[51] Bülow replied, "Our ally can count on us should difficulties and complications ensue."[52]

The German support of Austria was aimed not just to preserve the alliance but also to shore up Germany's resolve reputation, which had been damaged in the Morocco crisis, and to loosen ties in the opposite alliance. Bülow believed Britain was about to join the Franco-Russian alliance. The crisis presented an opportunity to block this development and perhaps to break up the Triple Entente. His calculation was that France would not support Russia if Germany supported Austria; this would cause Russia to doubt French reliability and perhaps to defect.[53]

Germany's support went well beyond being a "brilliant second." On March 22 Germany demanded that Russia accept the annexation: "We expect an answer—yes or no; we must regard an evasive, conditional or unclear answer as a refusal. We should then draw back and let things take their course."[54] This could only mean that if the Russian reply were deemed unsatisfactory, Germany would make no effort to restrain Austria from attacking Serbia. The Russians, whose military forces had not yet been rebuilt since the war with Japan, had no choice but to back down. Without their Russian backing, the Serbs could only do likewise, although they held out for a time with dogged British "diplomatic" support.

Bülow thought he had scored a great success, one that not only repaired the damage to Germany's resolve reputation suffered at Algeciras and underscored his loyalty to his ally but also weakened his enemies. He had "torn the encirclement net to pieces." But the effects on the Triple Entente were just the opposite. Alexander Nelidov, the Russian ambassador in Paris, reported that "the Cabinets of Paris and London have concluded from this that Russia, France and England must pay more attention than ever to action in common and must at the same time proceed to the necessary military measures in order to convince their opponents that they are dealing with a political combination which knows how to make itself respected and to carry through its demands."[55] As for the Russians, they were resolved to build up their strength so that they would never again have to capitulate to German threats. They drew closer to Britain and France. Of course, the crisis finally wrote finis to the detente between Austria and Russia that had prevailed since 1897.[56]

It was a pyrrhic victory for Austria also. Austria had demonstrated an ability to take the initiative, but the German ultimatum revealed that it needed allied help to finish the job. The wrecking of the detente with Russia, the strengthening of the Anglo-Russian connection, the alienation of Britain, and the worsening of relations with Serbia all reduced Austria's security and increased its dependence on Germany.

Germany's dependence had also increased, owing to increased Russian hostility and greater solidarity between Russia and Britain, but less so than Austria's. The balance of dependence in the alliance, and hence relative bargaining power, had actually shifted somewhat in Germany's favor, not by a reduction in German dependence but by an increase in Austria's.

At first glance, our calculus of alliance bargaining power does not seem applicable to this crisis because there does not appear to have been any bargaining: Germany simply supported the Austrian position without trying to change it. Superficially, it seems to have been a game of "pure coordination," in which the parties' preferences over the possible outcomes are identical and their only problem is to coordinate on their joint maximizing strategy. This was not quite the case, however: there was some, though not much, conflict of interest between the allies, which made it an example of tacit bargaining. Austria had a positive interest in annexing the provinces for security and prestige reasons. The interest of the Germans, however, was negative, as shown by their initial reaction to the Austrian move: dismay. They had no interest in Austrian annexation of Bosnia-Herzegovina, which, they feared, would disturb their relations with other powers and/or entrap them in an Austro-Russian war. During the crisis they generated certain motives to justify their support of Austria—preserving the alliance, strengthening their own and Austria's resolve image, and exacting revenge on Russia for entering into the entente with Britain—but these positive interests were not sufficient to overcome fully their negative interest in the Austrian initiative. Germany supported Austria because of dependence on the alliance, not because it shared Austrian interests or approved the Austrian policy in its own interest.

Thus the German interest in a firm stance toward Russia was, on balance, negative but low. Its dependence on the alliance was high and its commitment was also high, having been increased during the crisis. These estimates give Germany a bargaining power score of 3. Austria had a moderate positive interest, moderate dependence, and moderate commitment, which works out to a bargaining power rating of 6. These scores are consistent with the outcome, in which Austria's demands were fully backed by Germany.

In sum, this case supports our general Hypothesis A: the ally with the greatest bargaining power, calculated as a combination of interests, dependence, and commitment, indeed prevails. It also supports all three of our specific hypotheses: the outcome might be explained by asymmetries in interests, dependence, or commitment. Technically, we are unable to say which of these factors was the more weighty; the evidence strongly suggests, however, that it was the greater German sense of dependence.

Joint Military Planning Resumed

Joint military planning was resumed during the Bosnian crisis after a hiatus of twelve years. Franz Conrad von Hötzendorf, the Austrian chief of staff, took the initiative, apparently sensing an opportunity, in the signs of German solicitude for the alliance, to strengthen and expand the German commitment. The civilian leaders, Aehrenthal and Bülow, only reluctantly approved the exchanges. Aehrenthal insisted that they be limited to written communications between the two chiefs of staff, with no contacts at lower levels.[57]

Conrad and Moltke, the German chief, exchanged nine letters between January and March 1909. Their most significant political result was Moltke's response to Conrad's blunt question: What would Germany do if Austria invaded Serbia and Russia intervened? Moltke replied unequivocally that "this would constitute the *casus foederis* for Germany." As soon as Russia began to mobilize, Germany would call up its entire fighting force.[58] He had cleared this statement with the Kaiser and Bülow, he informed Conrad. Aehrenthal declared it to be a "loyal and binding declaration" by the German government.[59]

By these few words, Moltke substantially broadened the scope of the German commitment to Austria and changed the meaning of the alliance, making it potentially an offensive as well as a defensive instrument. The new meaning was contrary to the one Bismarck had always given it: that Austria could expect military assistance from Germany only if it were directly attacked by Russia. True, the great chancellor had always qualified this statement by assuring Austria that Germany would never permit its status as a great power to be imperiled, however the war might start. But this qualifier implied that German aid might come late. Moltke was now saying, apparently, that Austria could count on German aid from the beginning in an Austro-Russian war provoked by itself. The change reflected Germany's increased dependence. It opened up new vistas for Austrian activism in the Balkans.

Moltke also told Conrad, however, that any war would have to be fought in accordance with the Schlieffen Plan. If Russia mobilized, France would also mobilize, and this would require that the bulk of the German forces be sent initially against France, while Austria took the offensive against Russia. Victory over France would be obtained quickly, however, before events in the east had reached the crucial stage. Then the full weight of German forces would be sent against Russia.[60]

Conrad agreed that if Russia entered the war at the outset, the bulk of Austria's forces would have to be directed against Russia, in support of Germany. But personally he was far more interested in attacking Serbia than in fighting Russia. The "most probable case," he insisted, was a Russian entry into the war only after Austria had engaged considerable forces against Serbia. In that event, Austria could mount an offensive against Russia only if supported by a simultaneous German offensive in the east. If Germany could not ensure such an offensive, he told Moltke, Austria would have to go on the defensive against Russia and concentrate on fighting Serbia.[61]

This prospect did not suit Moltke at all, for he was counting on Austria to do most of the fighting against Russia in the east while Germany was taking care of France in the west. Evidently, the Austrian demand would have to be satisfied. The upshot was an agreement on parallel offensives against Russia. Moltke promised that the German Eighth Army in East Prussia would take the offensive into northern Poland, although with fewer troops than Conrad would have liked and subject to an escape clause.[62] Conrad promised a simultaneous attack into southern Poland by Austrian forces in Galicia.[63] Moltke evaded a precise answer to Conrad's query as to when reinforcing troops from the western front would arrive, "since the enemy will have a voice in it." Depending on whether the French forces took the offensive or not, the issue might be decided in the west in three or four weeks and the transfer of troops would take another nine or ten days. He refused to discuss the number of troops that would then be shifted to the eastern front and how they would be used.[64] Although the military discussions continued intermittently, Conrad never succeeded in getting further and better assurances, though he repeatedly pressed for them. In the end, in 1914, both men reneged on their promises: Moltke failed to carry out an offensive from East Prussia, and Conrad attacked Serbia before making good his promise to attack Russia.[65]

Loosening Ties: The Potsdam Interlude

The year 1909 saw more centrifugal tendencies in the alliance. Germany negotiated with France a further agreement on Morocco, one that recognized Germany's economic rights and France's political preponderance. Italy and Russia reached an agreement to "view with goodwill" each other's interests in Tripolitania and the Straits, respectively, and to make no fresh agreements concerning the Near East without each other's consent.[66] This agreement was implicitly directed against Austria and contradicted Italian obligations under the Triple Alliance.

Despite Germany's success in the Bosnian crisis, the experience had vividly demonstrated the danger of entrapment. Austria had taken a unilateral initiative that could well have embroiled Germany in a war for strictly Austrian interests—had Russia been ready to fight. Alfred von Kiderlen-Wächter, who succeeded Wilhelm von Schön as German foreign secretary, was determined to reassert control of Austria and leadership of the alliance. He sought to do this by a conciliatory move toward Russia. Contrary to the worries of Bülow and Schön, Kiderlen had little fear that such a move would lead to Austrian defection: the conflict between Austria and Russia was too deep for that. It would usefully demonstrate German independence of Austria and thus improve Germany's intra-alliance leverage.[67] Kiderlen also hoped to sew dissension in the Anglo-Russian entente.[68]

The opportunity came when the Czar and Sergei Sazonov, the Russian foreign minister, visited the Kaiser and German governmental leaders at Potsdam on November 4 and 5, 1910. Kiderlen and Bethmann-Hollweg, who had succeeded Bülow as chancellor, promised Sazonov that Germany would not support any aggressive plans by Austria in the Balkans. In return, Sazonov pledged not to pursue an anti-German policy or to support England in one. Germany acknowledged Russia's sphere of influence in Persia, on condition that German trade there not be disturbed. Russia dropped its opposition to Germany's Baghdad Railway project. Sazonov refused to put all this in writing, however, except for the agreement on Persia and the Baghdad Railway, which was signed on August 19, 1911.[69] German-Russian relations improved after these talks, reducing somewhat the German dependence on Austria.

News of this meeting caused some irritation in Vienna; the Emperor, especially, was deeply hurt by the German promise regarding Austrian "aggression." Austro-German relations deteriorated as a result of Potsdam, partly also because of contradictory policies the two governments were pursuing in Turkey.

1910–1914

The general trend in dependence relations between 1910 and 1914 was a rise in Austria's dependence as Germany's remained stable under offsetting military and diplomatic tendencies. German dependence on military grounds declined, owing to a marked increase in its military strength and potential. As Table 7-1 shows, the German share of great-power resources increased from 27.9 percent in 1910 to 30.1 percent in 1913, and the gap between the German share and the combined French-Russian share declined from 11.6 percent to 9.2 percent. Meanwhile, the Austrian share increased modestly, from 9.5 percent to 10.2 percent of the total, and the difference between Austria's and Russia's resource shares declined from 15.1 percent to 14.7 percent. Thus, as measured by military strength and potential compared to their principal opponents, the alliance dependence of both allies fell, but Germany's fell more than Austria's.

Diplomatic trends increased both allies' dependence, Austria's somewhat more than Germany's. Although German-Russian tension had been reduced somewhat by the Potsdam agreements, it flared up again during the Liman von Sanders crisis in 1913. The Agadir crisis of 1911 sharply increased conflict between Germany and France, and the conflict did not significantly ease with the compromise settlement. On the other hand, German hopes for British neutrality picked up with the experience of collaboration during the Balkan Wars and the negotiation of modest colonial agreements. The Russian option for Austria had disappeared for good in 1909; Austro-Russian tension increased markedly with the outbreak of the Balkan Wars in 1912 and continued rising.

The combined effect of the military and diplomatic dimensions of dependence was to leave Germany's overall dependence virtually unchanged from the beginning of the decade and to increase Austria's substantially, making the allies nearly equally dependent in 1914. There were five salient bargaining encounters between the allies during this period, all of them crises.

Alliance Bargaining: The Agadir Crisis

A second crisis over Morocco, the Agadir crisis, occurred in the summer of 1911. France attempted to consolidate its hold on Morocco and was again resisted by Germany. As in the first crisis, England solidly supported France, and Germany was defeated, getting only a small piece of the French Congo as compensation. A factor in the German decision to retreat was the lack of support from Austria. Aehrenthal vowed his perfect loyalty to the alliance but pointed out that Morocco lay beyond its scope.[70] Germany could count on Austrian support only when "questions of European importance were at stake."[71] In Morocco, Austria would follow strictly its own interests, which were the maintenance of the open door and the preservation of peace.[72] Aehrenthal repeatedly sought to impress on Germany its responsibility for keeping the peace, and he sought to mediate between France and Germany to this end. He told the French government from the start that he sympathized with their aims in Morocco; he was anxious to keep the French money market open for the support of Austria's economic interests in the Balkans.[73]

Thus the principal Austrian preoccupation throughout was to urge moderation on both sides so as to avoid having to fulfill its alliance obligations.[74] Beyond this rather vague effort, it made no attempt to influence Germany on specific issues or occasions. Nor did it offer any support beyond avowals of loyalty to the alliance. There were, indeed, some flashes of friction between the allies. Aehrenthal was irritated at not having been informed beforehand about the "Panther's spring"[*] or about German objectives in the crisis.[75] In instructing his ambassador in Berlin to "be reserved," he invoked the logic of tit-for-tat: since Germany had told Russia (in the Potsdam conversations) that it would not support Austria in an aggressive policy, why should Austria support Germany?[76] Aehrenthal gave Germany little or no credit for its support in the Bosnian crisis.[77] The attitude of the Austrian press ranged from indifference to outright hostility.[78]

The Austrian attitude was resented in Germany and tended to confirm Bethmann's opinion, expressed to the Kaiser the previous year: "Let us hope that if there is a war the attack will be aimed against Austria, which

---

[*] The *Panther* was a German gunboat that dropped anchor in the port of Agadir as a threat during the crisis.

will then need our assistance, and not against us, so that it is not left to Austria to decide whether to be loyal to the alliance or not."[79]

Vienna was also concerned about German policies external to the crisis, notably the increasing German enthusiasm for *weltpolitik* and its naval building program, both of which not only alienated England but also shifted German resources away from the army, which, of course, was the dimension of German capability the Austrians valued most. Other areas of Austrian dissatisfaction in 1911 were Germany's aggressive economic penetration of the Balkans and its lack of understanding of Austria's internal South Slav problem.

Austria's nonsupport during the crisis is probably explained best by the relatively narrow focus of its interests, on the Balkans and the Near East. Germany might have global concerns, but Austria's were limited to a particular nearby piece of Europe. Such matters as rebellion in Albania and the Italian challenge to Turkey in Tripoli weighed far more heavily than German prestige interests in Morocco.[80] Austria was even relieved that Germany was involved in Morocco, for this tended to limit its irritating meddling in the Balkans.[81]

In our calculus of bargaining power, the interest of Germany in the issue at stake was high, it was feeling highly dependent on Austria, and its commitment (since the Moltke extension) was high, generating a score of 5. Austria's score is also 5, based on low negative interest, moderate dependence, and moderate commitment. These scores imply modest German concessions to the Austrian position—that is, a compromise—and the outcome might superficially be interpreted that way, in support of Hypothesis A. We must code the outcome as ambiguous, however, since there is no way of knowing to what extent Germany's concessions to France were the result of pressure from Austria. The evidence suggests that they were far more the result of French (and British) firmness. Of course, the results for Hypotheses 1, 2, and 3, which posit independent effects of asymmetries in interest, dependence, and commitment, are also ambiguous.

Concert versus Alliance: Treating the "Sick Man"

The Agadir crisis was the first in a series of crises that would lead to the collapse of the Ottoman Empire and eventually to world war. These crises also produced the last gasp of the nineteenth-century Concert of Europe. By the early twentieth century, the concert process had fallen into disuse except with respect to the European possessions of Ottoman Turkey. There the powers still were in the habit of calling conferences, or otherwise collaborating, to put down disturbances or to force the Ottoman sultans to execute reforms to satisfy grievances of the people, who were largely Christian. The alternative to such propping up, it was widely believed, was the demise of the "sick man of Europe," followed by a mad rush to collect pieces of the carcass, which might very well produce a European war.

Until 1911 the powers cooperated, more or less, in refraining from raids on the "sick man." In that year and the following one, however, the temptation to defect began to overwhelm the incentives to cooperate. France made the first defection in establishing full control of Morocco. This was the signal for Italy to move into Tripoli (Libya), thus "cashing in" its previous agreements with France and Russia wherein Italy had been granted a free hand in Tripoli in return for similar privileges for France in Morocco and for Russia at the Straits.

This action by Italy precipitated action by the small states of the Balkans—Serbia, Greece, Montenegro, and Bulgaria—which were quite aware that Italy also had ambitions on their side of the Adriatic. These four states formed an alliance, the Balkan League, under Russian auspices and attacked Turkey on October 8, 1912.

Alliance Bargaining: The First Balkan War

For a brief time, this first of the Balkan Wars threatened to involve Russia and Austria, the two great powers with the most at stake. Russia supported the aims of the Balkan states; Austria opposed them. Both countries mobilized forces on their common border, and Austria also mobilized against Serbia. Although their allies, France and Germany, counseled caution and restraint, Germany also assured Austria of its full military support in the event of an Austro-Russian war, and France gave a similar assurance to Russia in case Germany intervened. Peace was saved, partly because neither Austria nor Russia wanted war [82] and partly because the Balkan allies achieved a quick victory. An armistice was reached on December 3, 1912, after the allies had divested Turkey of most of its European possessions.

Another crisis occurred, however, over the division of the spoils. According to Austria, its Balkan nemesis, Serbia, had gained far too much during the fighting. Austria proposed to reduce these gains by creating the new state of Albania on the eastern shore of the Adriatic, thus not only reducing Serbian territory but also denying Serbia an outlet to the sea. (Albania, as a province of Turkey, had been in virtually continuous revolt for several years and had recently been granted a degree of autonomy.) Serbia, at first supported by Russia, was naturally opposed, although it was willing to accept a smaller Albania provided it got a port on the Adriatic. To deal with these issues, the powers institutionalized the Concert in the form of a conference of their ambassadors in London.

As early as October, Sir Edward Grey and Bethmann had informally agreed to exchange opinions and act together in the developing Balkans crisis.[83] Cooperation between Britain and Germany continued during the conference, but it was in some tension with the demands of their alliance relationships. Their incentives to cooperate in restraining their more directly involved allies—mainly Russia and Austria—were countered by incentives to support the allies, in order to avoid the risk of abandonment that restraining them would entail.

The game was complicated on Germany's side by its desire to wean England away from the Triple Entente and even to gain a pledge of British neutrality. This was an incentive in Germany's alliance game which tended to contradict and neutralize its incentive to support Austria. It increased Germany's net payoff for cooperation in the concert game with Britain. England, on the other hand, anticipated no such bonus, since it had no thought of weaning Germany away from the Triple Alliance.

Britain and Germany managed to cooperate during the conference. By the exercise of cooperative cajolery on their allies, and by the latter on their Balkan clients, they produced a settlement on December 31, 1912. Russia and Serbia accepted the Austrian demand for a new autonomous Albania, thus giving up much of Serbia's war gains. Serbia was to have a commercial outlet to the Adriatic through a neutral Albanian port. Austria accepted the Serbian commercial outlet under German pressure; Serbia accepted it, in lieu of a naval port of its own, after "advice" from Russia, itself the result of Anglo-French pressure. The conference failed to reach agreement on the exact boundaries of Albania, however. Austria wanted Albania to be as large as possible; Russia wanted it as small as possible so as to maximize Serbian and Montenegrin gains. Austria wanted it to include the town of Scutari; Russia wanted the town to go to Montenegro. The concert had prevailed so far, but the alliance game was still operative.

On February 3, 1913, the Balkan allies resumed fighting, and a new crisis arose between Austria and Russia, principally over Scutari, on the Albanian-Montenegrin border, which was under siege by Montenegrin troops. In Vienna, the foreign minister, Leopold von Berchtold, came under heavy pressure from his military to intervene, but he also received strong messages from Berlin counseling restraint. Bethmann advised Berchtold to control his "war party" and attempt to reach a settlement with Serbia. England, he said, was restraining Russia. To attempt a forcible solution would be "an error of incalculable magnitude," since a "re-orientation" of British policy might be expected if the crisis were resolved peacefully.[84] Moltke urged Conrad to make concessions; after Serbia's concession on the matter of the port, he said, "the justifiable demands of Austria had been satisfied." In urging Gottlieb von Jagow, the German state secretary, to "prevent Austrian follies," he also expressed some doubt whether that would be possible, since Germany had "fallen into a certain dependence on Vienna through our treaties and from the necessity of preserving Austria."[85] Berchtold, embittered by the lack of German support, commented sarcastically, "The German point of view that we must not move lest the tender plant of German-English rapprochement is trampled underfoot is expressed here with what one might call impertinent frankness."[86]

Bethmann and Moltke need not have worried, since none of the civilian leaders in Austria-Hungary was thinking of war. The Hungarians, as usual, were loath to approve any action that might add more Slavs to the empire. Berchtold was fully committed to preserving the peace and with the Emperor's backing was able to veto Conrad's desire to attack Serbia.[87] In an attempt both to respond to his ally's concern and to ease the tension, Berchtold, on February 22, proposed to Russia a reduction of troops. On March 11 the two powers announced reciprocal troop reductions.

The powers were able to resolve the Scutari issue among themselves, chiefly through an Austro-Russian deal brokered by Germany and Great Britain. Russia gave up its insistence that Scutari go to Montenegro in return for an Austrian concession of four other towns—again, after heavy pressure from Berlin. But the Montenegrins refused to stop their bombardment. Although Berchtold was under strong internal pressure to invade, he acceded to Grey's proposal for a joint naval demonstration by the Concert powers. The demonstration, carried out by British, French, German, Austrian, and Italian ships, persuaded the Serbians to withdraw their troops but failed to impress the Montenegrins, who proceeded to occupy the town on April 22, after buying off the Turkish commander. The powers then considered a joint land expedition to oust the Montenegrins but could not agree on who was to participate.

With the crisis now at its peak, the Concert, and its Anglo-German nucleus, began to come apart. Berchtold, tired of German restraints and under military pressure, insisted he would make no more concessions and threatened unilateral action. Jagow informed Grey that Germany could no longer restrain Austria, since any results this might produce had already been achieved.[88] Unless the powers acted immediately to enforce their decision, he warned, Germany must give Austria a free hand. The unstated reason for the German shift was that costs in Germany's alliance game with Austria were beginning to exceed the benefits of the Concert. When Grey equivocated, Austria, with German acquiescence, drew up a note demanding Montenegrin withdrawal and began military preparations for an invasion.

News of these measures induced Montenegro to give way on May 4, and troops from the international fleet occupied Scutari on May 14. A peace treaty between Turkey and the Balkan states was signed on May 30, 1913.

Alliance Bargaining: The Second Balkan War

The Balkan alliance soon collapsed in a struggle over the distribution of spoils. Deprived of much of its gains by the creation of Albania, Serbia determined to make good the loss at the expense of Bulgaria's gains in Macedonia. It organized, for this purpose, an alliance with Greece, Montenegro, and Rumania, which Turkey eventually joined. Bulgaria's forces attacked preemptively on June 28 to begin the Second Balkan War. As in the first war, Austria and Russia found themselves on opposite sides diplomatically—Austria supporting Bulgaria, and Russia, Serbia.

The renewed prospect of an enlarged Serbia naturally worried the Austrians. On July 3 Berchtold informed the German ambassador that if Bulgaria were beaten decisively, Austria might have to intervene on its behalf. Bethmann responded that if Austria followed this course, "it would mean a European war. This would most seriously affect the vital interests of Germany and I must therefore expect that before Count Berchtold makes any such resolve, he will inform us of it."[89] This statement fell short of an outright threat of abandonment but, added to other factors (principally domestic) that were working against Austrian intervention,[90] it was enough to hold Austria back.

This attitude on the part of its ally produced a mood of pessimism and resentment in Vienna. Berchtold told the German ambassador that "recently the policy of the Berlin cabinet seemed systematically designed to do the work of the [Franco-Russian] Dual Alliance."[91] Actually, the German motives in this instance had little to do with Concert norms and more to do with a desire to gain Serbia and Greece as allies. Austria and Germany were in disagreement about the most desirable allies in the Balkans. Rumania had been allied with both Austria and Germany since 1883. Berlin wished to keep Rumania's allegiance, while also recruiting Serbia and Greece as Triplice clients. Austria also wanted to keep Rumania but preferred Bulgaria, which had no irredentist claims on Austro-Hungarian territory, over Serbia, which did. The German motives came partly from the Kaiser's dynastic connections with the thrones of both Greece and Rumania and partly from a strategic aim: free Austria from threats on its southern border so that in case of a major war, it could send all its forces against Russia.[92]

The Second Balkan War was brief—only one month—and resulted in the complete defeat of Bulgarian forces. A peace conference in Bucharest redistributed most of Bulgaria's previous winnings among the victorious allies. It was a serious blow for Austria, which was left with the bitter feeling of having been deserted by Germany.[93] Berchtold complained to the German ambassador that Austria might as well have belonged "to the other grouping," for all the good Germany had been.[94]

Alliance Bargaining: The October 1913 Crisis

Thus it was in a mood of disillusionment that Austria discovered in September 1913 that Serbian troops had reoccupied parts of Albania. After a preliminary warning, which produced no results, Vienna informed Berlin and Rome that it was determined to enforce the London decisions and asked for their support. The Germans were now keenly aware of Austria's resentment over being restrained during the previous war. Fearing defection if Austria were restrained again, Germany promised support, as did Italy. The Kaiser told Conrad that Austria's value to Germany would diminish "if we did not brace ourselves to do a manly deed."[95] Without further consulting his allies, Berchtold dispatched an ultimatum to Belgrade on October 17. It demanded the evacuation of Albanian territory within eight days; otherwise, Austria would "have recourse to proper means to assure the realization of its demands."[96] Lacking Russian support, the Serbs had no alternative but to comply, which they did by October 26. Berchtold gloated to Archduke Franz Ferdinand: this action had "cleared the air," showing Europe that Austria could act independently "and that our allies will stand closely behind us."[97] In terms of our theory, Germany had definitely chosen to defect in the concert game in order to discourage Austrian defection in the alliance game.

On the surface, the Austrian ultimatum could be reconciled with the Concert, since Austria could claim to be merely enforcing a prior Concert decision. In reality, however, it marked the end of the Concert. Alliance ties henceforth predominated over the ideal of great-power unity, especially in the Triple Alliance, mostly because of German concern over Austrian loyalty. Germany would not restrain Austria again, and the Anglo-German detente would become increasingly illusory.[98]

The changed German attitude was colorfully expressed by the German Kaiser, who appeared in Vienna on the day of the Serbs' capitulation, October 26, and had a long conversation with Berchtold. According to the latter, whenever an opportunity arose to mention the alliance, "His Majesty made a point of assuring me that we could count fully on him . . . and that whatever came from the Vienna foreign ministry was for him a command."[99] Clapping his hand on his sword hilt, he declared that he was fully prepared to draw the sword for Austria.[100]

Austro-German Relations during the Balkan Wars

The Balkan Wars period may be divided into four episodes of Austro-German bargaining: the First Balkan War, the Scutari crisis, the Second Balkan War, and the October 1913 crisis. We now examine each of those events for consistency with our alliance bargaining hypotheses.

During the First Balkan War and the attendant negotiations about the creation of Albania and the Serbian outlet to the sea, the Austrian interest in preventing Serbian gains was high, its dependence on Germany was high, and its commitment to the alliance was moderate, giving Austria a bargaining power score of 6. Germany had little or no interest in the Albanian and port issues but had a substantial interest in avoiding war and in maintaining the friendship of Britain. These values gave Germany a strong net interest in restraining Austria. Its high dependence on the alliance and strong commitment to it, however, worked against that interest; overall, Germany has a bargaining power score of 5. Hypothesis A predicts German restraining pressure on Austria but a bargaining outcome slightly favoring Austria.

That is a fair description of the actual outcome. Germany sought to restrain Austria, but it was weak restraint since it was accompanied by a pledge of ultimate military support. Austria got an independent Albania although it had to compromise on the port issue. Austria refrained from intervention but it is unclear whether because of German restraining pressure or its own reluctance to risk war with Russia. Theoretically, such ambiguity may occur in any attempt to restrain an ally; it is analogous to the problem, in deterrence between adversaries, of determining whether the nonoccurrence of war is due to successful deterrence or to a lack of aggressive intent by the state being "deterred."[101]

The same composite scores prevailed during the Scutari crisis. This time, however, Germany brought more restraining influence to bear on Austria, at least in the early part of the crisis when the issue was the Albania-Montenegro border. Austria capitulated to this pressure. Later, when the issue was whether and how to force Montenegro out of Scutari, Germany stopped holding Austria back and instead supported an Austrian ultimatum. These outcomes—first a clear German win, then an Austrian—are hard to reconcile with the bargaining power scores. Apparently, the Germans, frightened that their success had reduced the Austrian value for the alliance, resolved to repair that weakness by supporting Austria on the next issue.

Germany shifted back to restraining Austria during the Second Balkan War and apparently was successful—only apparently, because it is not clear whether the Austrian inaction, despite an interest in protecting Bulgaria, was the result of German pressure or Austrian pusillanimity, or simply the brevity of the war. On the surface, the outcome, favoring Germany, does not seem consistent with our bargaining power estimates and Hypothesis A. However, the German interest in restraining Austria, and hence German bargaining power, was stronger in this case because it was supplemented by a German desire for alignment with Bulgaria's enemies, Serbia and Greece.

The October 1913 crisis brought another marked shift in German strategy: support for an Austrian ultimatum to Serbia. By this time, Germany's interest in restraining Austria had declined, owing to increased concern about its ally's internal political health and a desire to shore up its morale. At the same time, the Germans again were worried that their earlier restraint might have weakened the Austrian commitment to the alliance. These changes (we estimate) reduced Germany's bargaining power score to 3, while Austria's remained constant at 6. The outcome—an Austrian success—is consistent with this revised estimate.

It is impossible to say which of the components of bargaining power—interests, dependence, or commitment—were most influential during the first three of these episodes, since interests and dependence are rated high for both parties. The German commitment is rated higher than Austria's in each case, indicating an Austrian bargaining advantage, but that does not explain the virtual draws in the First Balkan War and Scutari cases and the German success in the second war. In the October 1913 crisis the outcome, an Austrian win, could be explained either by the greater Austrian interest at stake or the German fear of Austrian defection.

Alliance Dependence

The Balkan Wars shifted the balance of power in Europe against the Central Powers and increased their mutual dependence, but especially the Austrian dependence on Germany. The Ottoman Empire was eliminated as a power factor in Europe and replaced by a strengthened group of Balkan states, several of which, such as Serbia, were hostile to Austria. Developments during the fall of 1913 and spring of 1914 further increased the mutual dependence of the Central Powers. The Liman von Sanders affair (see next chapter) increased tensions between Russia and Germany; Italy and Rumania drifted closer to the Entente; Russia and Britain began negotiations for a naval convention; France was showing increased military confidence and popular xenophobic tendencies.

Friction between the allies also increased. Austrians resented the restraint Germany had exercised during the Balkan Wars. The Serb threat was still alive, and the men in Vienna felt that military action against it would ultimately be necessary, but they were unsure of German support. The allies continued to differ about which Balkan states to support or align with. Competing economic and imperial ambitions in Turkey and the Balkans further disturbed the relationship.

The Austrians need not have worried, for the men in Berlin were now resolved to support Austria through thick and thin. Never again would they subject themselves to the reproaches of disloyalty the Austrians had directed toward them after the Second Balkan War. The Germans had little respect for Austria-Hungary as a state or as a military ally: Heinrich Tschirschky, their ambassador in Vienna, wondered whether it was worthwhile to continue supporting that "ramshackle" entity. But they had little choice, since Austria was their only reliable ally in view of the de facto defection of Italy and the wavering of Rumania. They had to protect and, if possible, strengthen Austria's questionable status as a great power.

Meanwhile, a great arms race had gotten under way on the continent. At the end of 1913 Russia announced a massive military buildup, including an increase in its army to three times the size of Germany's and an enlarged network of strategic railways to be completed by 1917. France had just increased its army substantially by adopting three-year compulsory service. In July 1913 the Reichstag approved the largest military bill in German history, providing for a 15 percent increase in the German army. In Austria a law of March 1914 called for a similar increase.[102]

Joint Military Planning

Joint military planning, which had been more or less in abeyance since 1909, was stepped up after the First Balkan War. Conrad and Moltke continued to differ, however, in their choice of war strategies: Conrad preferred an Austrian war against Serbia alone, with Germany deterring Russian intervention; Moltke thought in terms of a great-power war, with Germany and Austria fighting Russia side by side but with the bulk of the German forces being deployed against France. Each of the allies had a two-front war problem, but the fronts were different: for Germany, it was France and Russia; for Austria, Serbia and Russia. Russia was the common opponent of both but the primary opponent of neither. Germany wanted to concentrate its initial efforts against France; Austria, against Serbia. Each hoped that, while it was disposing of its primary opponent, the other would bear the brunt of holding the secondary opponent—Russia—at bay. That is, each tried to pass the buck to the other for dealing with Russia.

The Moltke-Conrad correspondence in 1909 had only imperfectly resolved this conflict by an exchange of promises: Moltke pledged to take the offensive against Russia immediately from East Prussia with thirteen divisions; major reinforcements would arrive after the defeat of France, which, he estimated, would take three to four weeks. Conrad, in return, promised an immediate offensive from Galicia with twenty-eight divisions, even while simultaneously engaged in war with Serbia. Both men apparently harbored mental reservations rooted in mistrust, however. In their subsequent annual correspondence, Conrad always insisted, as the first item of business, on a reaffirmation of the German pledge.[103] Although the 1909 agreements were thus confirmed every year up to 1914, Conrad continued to maintain an alternative plan for an offensive against Serbia and a defensive holding action against Russia. Moltke's estimate of the time it would take to defeat France and move forces to the eastern front gradually lengthened, from four weeks to seven weeks.[104] Conrad repeatedly pressed for more German troops to be deployed initially in the east, but without success.

Alliance Bargaining: Austria and Germany in the July 1914 Crisis

Whether German-Austrian relations during the July 1914 crisis are to be characterized as "bargaining" depends heavily on how one perceives the dominant motives of Germany. The central question is whether Germany supported Austria in the hope of deterring other European powers from intervention, thus avoiding general war while gaining a significant diplomatic victory; or whether Germany wanted war and deliberately manipulated the crisis (including its ally's policy) so as to bring it about. The question is still a matter of furious debate among historians,[105] with the weight of opinion seemingly leaning toward the latter, "preventive war" interpretation of German motives.

If this interpretation is accepted, there was hardly any bargaining between the two allies, or whatever appeared to be bargaining was simply camouflage for Germany's aggressive intentions. In the first interpretation, however, there was some real bargaining, although most of it occurred during the latter part of the crisis. The following analysis tries to strike a middle ground: Germany hoped for a "localized" Austro-Serbian war—with no intervention by Russia and the Triple Entente—thus yielding a substantial diplomatic victory, but it was willing to accept, as a close second-best, a continental European war, which was thought to be inevitable and which Germany believed it could win in 1914 but not in two or three years, after Russia had completed its arms buildup.

The assassination at Sarajevo removed some important constraints on Austrian policy. First, it tended to legitimize the military action against Serbia that many Austrian leaders, notably Conrad, had been advocating for years. Second, it provided an ideological cover: if Russia perceived the action as a defense of monarchical values, it would be less likely to intervene. Third, the assassination sharply dramatized the internal threat to the state that was posed by the Serbian attraction to its Slav minorities. Since the autumn of 1913 Berchtold and other civilian leaders had come to believe that only war could eliminate this threat.[106] It was now or never; Austria must act both to remove the Serbian danger and to restore its waning prestige as a great power. But it could not act alone, for Russia would probably support Serbia. Hence it was necessary to ascertain whether Germany, as Conrad put it, "will cover our rear against Russia or not."[107]

The Blank Check

The Austrian leaders were at first unsure of German support. Recent experience in the Balkan Wars was mixed: Germany had restrained as much as it had supported. Thus the first Austrian move was to probe its ally's intentions. The Austrian ambassador in Berlin, Count Szögyény, met with Wilhelm II at noon, July 5. He carried a letter from Emperor Franz Joseph to the Kaiser calling for the elimination of Serbia "as a political power factor in the Balkans."[108] The Kaiser assured the ambassador of Germany's full support, including military support in case of Russian intervention, which he did not think likely. Austria should "take advantage of the present moment" and act without delay. The chancellor, Bethmann-Hollweg, gave a similar assurance to the Austrian ambassador the next day, also urging "immediate action."[109]

Why this unequivocal assurance, after the Germans had been at pains to restrain Austria during earlier Balkan conflicts? Clearly, like the Austrians, they were attracted by the window of opportunity created by the assassination. They were worried about the internal condition and declining external status of their ally. Here was a chance, perhaps the last chance, for Austria to restore its position as a great power. This was in Germany's interest as well as Austria's own. Germany was heavily dependent on its ally as a result of recent external developments: rising German-Russian hostility, the growth of Russian military power, the news of Anglo-Russian naval collaboration, the de facto defection of Italy, and the growing tension between the two alliance systems. The Germans, in particular the Kaiser, had been stung by Austrian reproaches for their equivocation during the Balkan Wars; they worried that any further restraint of their ally would lead to its defection or realignment.

The Germans at first believed an Austro-Serbian war could be localized: Russia, Serbia's ally, would protest but probably would not fight, since it was not prepared for war. Even if Russia wished to take a stand, it would be restrained by France and Britain. This, in turn, would weaken and perhaps lead to the breakup of the Entente. If it came to war with Russia, France would join its ally—this, of course, was the underlying political assumption of the Schlieffen Plan—but England probably would stand aside. The assumption or hope of English neutrality had been strengthened by recent diplomatic agreements and by Anglo-German collaboration in containing the crises in the Balkans.

Even if localization failed and the crisis led to a European war, this was acceptable to Germany (and positively desired by some of its leaders), because it was better to fight that "inevitable" war in 1914, when Germany could win, than two or three years later, when Russia would be much stronger. Supplementing this argument was the thought that if there was to be a general war, better that it begin with an Austro-Russian clash than a Franco-German one, from which Austria might very well abstain.

Thus the Germans had two general aims in issuing their blank check to Austria, and they accepted two risks in doing so. The aims were to restore Austria's external prestige and halt its internal decay, through a resounding military chastisement of Serbia, and to score a dramatic diplomatic success by facing down and dividing the Entente powers. The first risk—a war against Germany's continental opponents—was tolerable, since it would "prevent" a later war under much less favorable conditions. The second risk—a war against England as well as against Russia and France—was worse, but its probability was thought to be low.[110]

The Austrian Response

The Germans had assured the Austrian government of their support "whatever its decision." The blank check was not really blank, however: the Germans made quite clear that they expected military action, and without delay, although it was up to the Austrians just how it was to be carried out. It took the Austrian government two and a half weeks to prepare and deliver an ultimatum to Serbia, and even then it was not ready to act. There were some good reasons for the delay, including timing its delivery so that French leaders, who had been visiting Russia, would be on their return journey and thus out of touch with events and their government. But it was extremely frustrating to the German government, which feared that every day or hour that went by reduced the chances of localizing an Austro-Serbian war. German pressure for action was unremitting, backed up by broad threats of abandonment. For example, Tschirschky, the ambassador in Vienna, impressed on Berchtold, in the latter's words, that "Germany would not understand our letting the opportunity slip by without striking a blow" and "would interpret any compromise on our part with Serbia as a confession of weakness, which would not remain without repercussions on our position in the Triple Alliance and the future policy of Germany."[111]

These urgings and threats were not without effect in Vienna, where they tended to buttress an Austrian resolve that was initially somewhat tentative. Thus Berchold told Conrad on July 10 that "on account of Germany, if for no other reason, there could be no hanging back now."[112] In persuading the reluctant Hungarian premier, Count Stephen Tisza, to support the ultimatum, Berchtold argued that Germany would consider Austria "unfit for alliance" if it did not act against Serbia.[113] When Berchtold and Tisza decided on July 14 to delay sending the ultimatum to Serbia until after the departure of Poincaré and René Viviani from Russia, they both "begged" Tschirschky (according to the ambassador's report) to reassure Berlin that there was no other reason for the postponement and that it reflected "no question of hesitancy or indecision."[114] Berchtold told his colleagues on July 19 that further postponement was undesirable, since "Berlin was beginning to feel edgy."[115]

There was no consultation between the Austrian and German governments concerning the content of the ultimatum or any other details of Austrian policy. This was as the Germans desired. They were at pains to claim, in their conversations with Entente diplomats, that they were innocent of any complicity in Austrian decision making. There were two related reasons for this arm's-length attitude. One was their extreme sensitivity to Austria's declining strength and prestige. As a great power, they kept saying, what Austria did toward the upstart, Serbia, was entirely its own business. Germany had no "competence" to intervene in Austria's affairs. In support of this pretense of unconcern were physical demonstrations: the Kaiser was sent on his usual summer cruise, and Moltke left on vacation.

Another reason for the pretense was its link to the notion of localization. This, of course, was simply a euphemism for giving Austria a free hand. If Germany expected the other great powers to stand aside while Austria cleaned up on Serbia, it would hardly do for Germany itself to be implicated in that enterprise.

This constraint seriously hindered any German attempt to restrain or influence Austria, however, or even to gain information about Austrian intentions. Thus Jagow, the German foreign secretary, on July 16 instructed Tschirschky to ascertain Austrian views about the "future shape of Serbia," since this would decisively influence the attitudes of Italy and England. But in asking this question the ambassador was to "avoid giving the impression that we had any wish to stand as a hindrance in the way of Austrian action or to prescribe definite limits or aims for it."[116]

The contents of the Austrian ultimatum, delivered to the Serbian foreign ministry at 6 P.M. on July 23 with a forty-eight-hour time limit, are too well known to require recounting here. It had been deliberately drafted so as to render it unacceptable to Serbia. The Wilhelmstrasse received a copy only on July 22, but it had been aware of the general contents since July 11. The Germans made no effort to change it; indeed, the Austrian ambassador was assured that "the German government is entirely in agreement with the contents of the note."[117]

By prearrangement, the conciliatory Serbian response on July 25 was judged unacceptable by Austria. Accordingly, Austria severed diplomatic relations and began military mobilization.

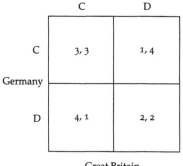

Figure 7.2. German-British relations during the Balkan Wars

	C	D
C	3, 3	1, 4
D	4, 1	2, 2

Germany

Great Britain
(numbers are ordinal;
4 is highest)

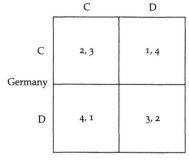

Figure 7.3. German-British relations in the Sarajevo crisis

	C	D
C	2, 3	1, 4
D	4, 1	3, 2

Germany

Great Britain
(numbers are ordinal;
4 is highest)

Bethmann's Duplicity

In Great Britain the Austrian ultimatum brought home to Sir Edward Grey that a major war was looming. His first reaction was to try to reestablish the Concert of Europe, operating around the core of Anglo-German collaboration as in the Balkan Wars of 1912–13. On July 24 he proposed to Germany that the four states not directly interested—Britain, Germany, France, and Italy—undertake mediation between Russia and Austria and that the time limit of the ultimatum be extended.[118]

A difference between the Balkan Wars conference and what Grey was now proposing was that two great powers—Austria and Russia—which had earlier been participants in Concert peacekeeping, would now be its objects. This, however, was only a formal difference. In 1912–13 the essential restraints had been exercised by Britain on Russia and by Germany on Austria; that was also what seemed to be required in the present situation. The essential structure of the Anglo-German relationship was similar in both cases: it was that of a prisoner's dilemma, as shown in Figure 7-2. Mutual cooperation (CC) meant that Germany would restrain Austria while Britain restrained Russia. Unilateral defection (DC or CD) meant that one party would support its ally while the other party restrained its. Bilateral defection (DD) meant that both parties would support their allies rather than restrain them. The outcome of the game during the Balkan Wars was essentially CC—the parties collaborated in restraining their allies at some risk to their alliance ties.

By the summer of 1914, however, the situation had changed, especially for one of the parties—Germany. The change is shown in Figure 7-3. Germany had become more dependent on Austria and more fearful that not supporting Austria would lead to its defection or defeat. Thus the alliance risk involved in exercising collaborative restraint with Britain (CC) was greater. Partially offsetting this was the fact that another element in the German CC payoff—possible British neutrality in a European war—was valued as highly in 1914 as it had been earlier. But still another change had further increased the German incentive to defect: Germany's payoff for general war (DD) had increased relative to war in the future. This was the incentive for "preventive war" generated by awareness of the Russian military buildup, in progress since 1913. The incentive was not strong enough to motivate a deliberate attack on Russia but it increased the German willingness to risk war. In other words, in game theory lingo, by increasing DD relative to CD and CC, it increased the German readiness to defect from Concert collaboration.*

As a result of these changed preferences, Germany was motivated to pretend to cooperate with England in restraining allies—thus keeping alive the possibility of English neutrality—while secretly egging Austria on—thus preserving and strengthening the alliance. This is indeed what happened. To the British ambassador, Sir Horace Rumbold, on July 25, Jagow indicated acceptance of Grey's proposal for four-power mediation and an extension of the time limit, but he delayed communicating the proposal to Vienna until after the ultimatum had expired.[119] And in so doing he did not recommend accepting it but merely commented that he was "communicating" the proposal because he had told London he would do so.[120] That same day, Germany urged Austria "immediately" to declare war and begin military operations.[121] On July 26 the German ambassador in London, Prince Lichnowsky, repeated the German acceptance of Grey's proposal and, at Bethmann's instruction, urged Grey to use his influence to restrain Russia.[122]

Responding the next morning, Grey indicated that he would try to restrain Russia, even at the risk of "reproaches," but that Germany should likewise use its influence with Austria. Specifically, Germany should persuade Vienna either to regard the Serbian reply as satisfactory or to consider it a basis for negotiation. Bethmann passed on this proposal to Berchtold, via Tchirschky, commenting drily that an outright rejection would mean that "we should be held responsible for the conflagration by the whole world." He asked for Berchtold's views on the matter.[123] The real German attitude, however, was made clear to the Austrian ambas-

---

*The change in Germany's preferences changed the structure of Germany's game from prisoner's dilemma to "bully." Since Britain remained in prisoner's dilemma, the overall game was a hybrid: bully–prisoner's dilemma. In both bully and prisoner's dilemma, the dominant strategy is D—defection—but the dominance is much stronger in bully. For a fuller comparison of these and other games, see Snyder and Diesing, *Conflict among Nations*, chap. 2.

sador, Szögyény, by Jagow. The German government, said Jagow, "in no way associates itself" with British mediation proposals and only "passes them on to conform to the English request. In doing so the Government proceeds from the standpoint that it is of the greatest importance that England at the present moment should not make common cause with Russia and France."[124] At about the same time, the evening of July 27, Bethmann was assuring Grey, through Lichnowsky, that "in the sense desired by Sir Edward Grey we have at once begun mediatory action at Vienna."[125] Bethmann, incidentally, knew Austria planned to declare war the next day but made no mention of this in his messages to either Vienna or London. Tschirschky in Vienna knew perfectly well the real desires of his masters in Berlin: he waited until the Austrian declaration of war had gone off at 11:00 A.M. on July 28 before delivering Bethmann's message.[126] Berchtold's predictable response was that the English move came "too late."[127]

The German government found it necessary even to deceive its own sovereign. Kaiser Wilhelm returned from his cruise on July 27 and read the text of the Serbian reply the next morning. In stark contrast to his earlier bellicose language, he pronounced it a "brilliant achievement" and asserted that "a reason for war no longer exists." Instead, Austria should exercise only "gentle violence" by occupying Belgrade temporarily as surety for Serbian execution of its promises. Declaring himself ready to mediate on that basis, he instructed Jagow to communicate the proposal to Vienna.[128]

Nevertheless, Jagow and Bethmann were still committed to supporting "strong" (not "gentle") Austrian action against Serbia; consequently, they evaded their sovereign's instructions. They delayed implementing them until 10:15 P.M., so that the proposal did not reach Vienna until after the Austrian declaration of war had been issued. Moreover, they changed the proposal: the occupation was to guarantee "integral fulfillment" of all the ultimatum's demands, whereas the Kaiser had suggested "negotiation" of the points on which Serbia had expressed reservations. Finally, Bethmann told Tschirschky that in presenting the proposal he was to "carefully avoid giving the impression that we wish to restrain Austria."[129] This behavior and language did not square with Bethmann's statement to the British ambassador the same evening that he was doing "his utmost to maintain general peace."[130]

Austrian Declaration of War and Russian Partial Mobilization

Berlin had been urging Vienna to declare war on Serbia immediately after expiration of the ultimatum and to begin military operations.[131] The Emperor, Franz Joseph, authorized mobilization on July 25. But it was impossible to heed the advice to begin military operations, because, as

Conrad informed Berchtold, the army would not be ready for action until August 12. Conrad preferred to hold up the declaration of war until that date, but Berchtold told him the "diplomatic situation will not hold so long."[132] The "diplomatic situation" no doubt meant German pressure, even though Berchtold explained to the German ambassador that its purpose was "principally in order to forestall any attempt at mediation." Accordingly, the declaration was issued on July 28.

In Russia the Czar had contingently authorized partial mobilization—mobilization against Austria alone—on July 25, to be put into effect whenever Sazonov, the foreign minister, thought it necessary from a diplomatic point of view. News of the Austrian declaration of war and mobilization against Serbia persuaded Sazonov that the time had come to make this move.[133] Accordingly, he informed the German government on July 29 that mobilization of Russian forces in the military districts facing Austria would be ordered that day. However, measures preliminary to general mobilization were already under way and known to the Germans.

Bethmann's Reversal

On the evening of July 29–30 the German chancellor abruptly changed his stance and began to work actively and forcefully to restrain Austria. He sent a series of six telegrams to Vienna, requesting in increasingly urgent tones that it halt the move toward war. The first four generally urged Austria to negotiate and suggested limiting military operations to the occupation of Belgrade as hostage, as Grey and the Kaiser had suggested. The fifth used stronger language, in part:

> Austria's political prestige, the honor of her arms, as well as her just claims against Serbia, could all be amply satisfied by the occupation of Belgrade or of other places. . . . Under these circumstances we must urgently and impressively suggest to the consideration of the Vienna Cabinet the acceptance of mediation on the above-mentioned honorable conditions. The responsibility for the consequences that would otherwise follow would be an uncommonly heavy one both for Austria and for us.[134]

The sixth telegram, sent at 3 A.M., said, in part: "We are, of course, ready to fulfill the obligations of our alliance, but must decline to be drawn wantonly into a world conflagration by Vienna, without having any regard paid to our counsel. . . . Please talk to Count Berchtold at once with all impressiveness and great seriousness."[135]

Historians attribute Bethmann's shift to two items of information that reached him that day. One was that Russia had declared partial mobilization. The other was a somewhat more explicit statement by Grey that Britain would fight on France's and Russia's side in a European war.

Most authors give more weight to Grey's warning. There are two problems with this interpretation, however. One is that what Grey actually said was not much different from language he had already used several times. He told the German ambassador "not to be misled by the friendly tone of our conversation . . . into thinking that we should stand aside" in the event of war between Germany and France. In that event, "the situation would immediately be altered, and the British Government would, under the circumstances, find itself forced to make up its mind quickly. In that event it would not be practicable to stand aside and wait for any length of time. If war breaks out, it will be the greatest catastrophe that the world has ever seen."[136] Coming from Grey, this was indeed fairly strong language; but its meaning was not markedly different from previous statements he had made to the ambassador. Bethmann may have accorded it greater weight because Grey himself had given it special emphasis by calling it a "private communication" and by the earnestness and candor of his tone. Certainly, the Kaiser interpreted it as a new departure for the British, to judge from his near-hysterical marginal notes.

A second and related problem with this interpretation is that English neutrality was only a hope, not a fundamental assumption of German government planning. Military plans simply assumed British participation, though they underestimated its significance. Bethmann himself had, several times before the crisis, indicated he believed Britain would come to France's aid. He knew that Germany's war plan called for violating Belgian neutrality[137] and, given his sensitivity to British moral values, as displayed in his efforts to avoid putting Germany "in the wrong," he must have recognized that implementation of the plan was likely to bring Britain into the war. Thus, although the German government hoped for British neutrality, it was only a slim hope whose extinguishment by Grey's warning could not have been solely responsible for Bethmann's sharp turnabout.

A case can be made, as Marc Trachtenberg has,[138] that it was the Russian partial mobilization, news of which reached Berlin at 5 P.M. on July 29, that was the greater cause of Bethmann's change of heart. This was a tangible military development and one with a heavy bearing on whether there would be a great war or not, not merely on who would participate in the war. Given the logic of the Schlieffen Plan and the Austro-German alliance, it meant that war had become distinctly closer. Earlier that day, Bethmann had received a sobering memorandum from Moltke. It warned that if Austria and Russia mobilized against each other, "the collision between [them] will become inevitable. But that, for Germany, is the *casus foederis*. If Germany is not to be false to her word and permit her ally to suffer annihilation at the hands of Russian superiority, she, too, must mobilize. And that would bring about the mobilization of the rest of Russia's military districts as a result." This would bring into operation the Franco-Russian alliance, "and the mutual butchery of the civilized nations of Europe will begin." Moltke went on: "Germany does not want to bring about this frightful war. But the German government knows that it would be violating in ominous fashion the deep-rooted feelings of fidelity which are among the most beautiful traits of German character and would be setting itself against the sentiments of the nation, if it did not come to the assistance of its ally at a moment which was to be decisive of the latter's existence."[139]

This statement was merely an elaboration of the commitment Moltke had given Conrad on January 21, 1909.[140] But the civilian leadership apparently did not know of this commitment. The foreign minister, Jagow, had told the French ambassador on July 27 that Germany "would only mobilize if Russia mobilized on the German frontier."[141] According to Albertini, the civilians did not realize that mutual mobilization by Russia and Austria, "under the terms of the alliance and the interpretation given to them" and "because of the assurances given to Austria in July, would call forth German mobilization and consequently war."[142]

Moltke's sobering scenario apparently was on Bethmann's mind at his meeting with military leaders the evening of July 29 to consider the news of the Russian partial mobilization. The chancellor argued, contra Moltke's memo, that the Russian move did not activate the *casus foederis* of the German-Austrian alliance, since Sazonov had said that Russian mobilization did not necessarily mean war. Therefore, Germany should hold off on its mobilization until Russia actually attacked Austria, because then England would not be able to side with Russia. After only slight opposition from Moltke, the military officers accepted this interpretation as the political prerogative of the chancellor.[143]

But Bethmann must have realized that war was very close, as indicated by his telegram to his ambassador in St. Petersburg later that evening: "Russian mobilization on the Austrian frontier will, I assume, lead to corresponding Austrian measures. How far it will still be possible to stop the avalanche then it is hard to say."[144] Bethmann's telegrams to Vienna the night of July 29–30 can be interpreted as a desperate attempt to "stop the avalanche" before it became unstoppable because of a spiral of mobilizations. The warning from Grey, which was received in Berlin at 9:12 P.M. on the 29th, provided an additional incentive to hold Austria back, but a strong motive for doing so already existed. A balanced assessment of the reasons Bethmann reversed course on July 29 and tried to restrain Austria ought to place at least as much emphasis on the Russian partial mobilization as on the message from Grey. The former ruined the hope of localization; the latter destroyed the hope of British neutrality. Localization, the notion on which the Germans had bet everything, now was exposed as impossible; the only way to avoid a general European war was to head off the local one.

The Outbreak of War

The German ambassador communicated Bethmann's messages to Berchtold during the morning and early afternoon of July 30. The foreign minister's reaction was to decide for general mobilization against Russia, perhaps in order to preempt further German restraining pressure. Berchtold and Conrad met with the Emperor late that afternoon and received his approval for this measure. It was also decided to go ahead with the war against Serbia, to reply "courteously" to the English proposal without accepting it, and to order general mobilization (against Russia) on August 1.[145] In effect, Bethmann's pleas were simply rejected. The Austrian leaders were determined to prosecute their war against Serbia even while taking a decision that brought war with Russia distinctly closer. One can only conclude that they were so committed to war—not least because of earlier German pressure and German indications to ignore contrary German advice—that Bethmann's words were simply not dramatic enough to move them. Bethmann would have had to threaten to denounce the alliance, in words going well beyond the bounds of normal diplomatic prose, to get their attention.

During the evening Conrad received two messages from Moltke that sharply contradicted Bethmann's. In the first, sent through the Austrian military attaché in Berlin, Moltke said the Russian partial mobilization had created the necessity for Austro-Hungarian mobilization "at once.... This would give the *casus foederis* for Germany . . . Reject renewed English *démarche* for maintenance of peace. Last means of preserving Austria-Hungary is to fight out a European war. Germany with you unconditionally."[146] In a second telegram, sent directly to Conrad, Moltke said, "Austria-Hungary must be preserved, mobilize at once against Russia. Germany will mobilize." Apparently, Moltke had reached these conclusions because of reports of Russian preparedness measures against Germany, received during the morning of July 30.[147] This put the situation in a different light: it was no longer a case of Germany's coming to Austria's aid but a matter of getting ready for an imminent Russo-German war in which Austria had an important supporting role to play. It was now imperative that Austria mobilize against Russia and not commit large forces against Serbia.

Bethmann stopped trying to restrain Austria after his early morning efforts on July 30, but the Kaiser made one last try. In a telegram sent to the Austrian Emperor at 7:15 P.M., Wilhelm reminded Franz Joseph of his Halt-in-Belgrade proposal designed to "avert a world conflagration and preserve world peace," and requested a "decision as soon as possible."[148]

The Austrian leaders (without the Emperor) considered both the Kaiser's and Moltke's messages at another meeting in the morning of July 31. When Conrad read out those from Moltke, Berchtold exclaimed: "How odd! Who runs the government, Moltke or Bethmann?" After a reading of the Kaiser's telegram he turned to Conrad and said, "I have sent for you because I had the impression that Germany was beating a retreat; but now I have the most reassuring pronouncement from responsible military quarters."[149] His words have two significant implications: (1) He considered the message from the German emperor, along with the previous ones from the chancellor, important enough to warrant a special meeting of Austrian leaders—perhaps, one wonders, to consider changing the decisions of the previous day? (2) He gave more weight to the words of the German military leader than to those of the head of state and the top civilian official. Austrian decisions may have gone so far that they could not be reversed even if Germany was "beating a retreat"; nevertheless, it is tantalizing to speculate about what might have happened (or not happened) had Moltke not contradicted the communications of his superiors.

Later that day a formal Council of Ministers decided to continue military operations against Serbia and to reject the British proposal for mediation after a halt in Belgrade. Interestingly, Berchtold did not tell the ministers that Germany, as well as Britain, had proposed a halt in Belgrade; thus he gave the impression that the rejection was directed not so much to Germany as to England. As Luigi Albertini observes, "Thus they were not able to discuss the fundamental feature of the situation on that day, which was that Germany was extremely worried and unwilling to plunge into a European war opening under bad auspices for both the Central Powers and that Berlin no less than Britain was pressing for a conciliatory formula."[150]

Any remaining hope in Berlin that war might yet be avoided was quenched by news about noon on July 31 of the Russian order for general mobilization—that is, against Germany. This was answered by a German ultimatum, Russian rejection, and German declaration of war. Thus the immediate and ostensible cause of the German decision for war was a threat to Germany itself, but it seems clear that this threat was not a necessary cause; the mutual mobilization of Austria and Russia, and certainly the outbreak of war between Austria and Russia, would have been sufficient.

It is difficult to interpret the July 1914 crisis through our composite index of bargaining power because there was so little conflict between the allies until the last phase of the crisis. It was almost a game of pure coordination, in which the only problem is to converge on the strategy preferred by both parties. Germany fully agreed with Austria's aims, protesting only at the slow pace at which they were carried out. The allies' interaction can hardly be called bargaining until the final phase after Germany decided to oppose the Austrian policy. At that point (we may estimate), Germany's interests in the Austrian policy shifted to moderately negative because Germany now recognized its probable high cost. Along with its high dependence and high commitment, this gave Germany a bargaining power score of 4, which was weaker than Austria's score of 6, calculated from its high interest engagement, high dependence, and moderate commitment. Hence the German pressure was insufficient to persuade Austria to change course. Our Hypothesis A is consistent with this final phase of the crisis, although it is irrelevant to earlier phases.

It is difficult, probably impossible, to explain the outcome in terms of any one of the component variables separately. German support of Austria through most of the crisis may be attributed largely to a positive interest in Austria's Balkan problems. A rising sense of dependence on Austria, reflected in the fear of Austrian defection, also reduced Germany's capacity to restrain Austria, as did its recent strong statements of commitment to the alliance, culminating in the blank check. The Austrian alliance "victory"—if such it can be called—in the final phase of the crisis, when the allies' interests were opposed, may be attributed either to the greater Austrian interest at stake or to a perception of the increased German dependence and firm commitment (or both), but it is impossible to say which had the greater impact on the outcome.

Certain factors other than those in our bargaining power index deserve mention in this case. We have learned from the study of adversary crises that once decision makers become committed to a particular strategy, they tend to ignore or downplay evidence that the strategy is not succeeding.[151] In this case, Austria was thoroughly committed, not only through its own sense of desperation but also because of the unequivocal support it had received from Germany until the last days of the crisis. Thus it would have found it very difficult to change course when urged to do so by its ally. Bethmann did not realize that he needed to use much more forthright language, amounting to a clear threat to abandon Austria, to get its attention; or, if he did realize it, he could not bring himself to issue such a threat.

Yet Berchtold suspected that Germany was "beating a retreat," and the suspicion was strong enough to warrant calling a meeting of his advisers. Bethmann's restraining words might have received more serious consideration had Moltke's telegrams not supervened. Thus Germany's inability to sway Austria in this last-minute alliance bargaining can be attributed not just to its relative weakness on our bargaining power index but to two cognitive factors as well: Austria's inertia stemming from its "motivational bias," and the ambiguity of German communications. A normative factor—the German sense of alliance loyalty—may have contributed to Bethmann's inability to make the blatant threat of defection that was necessary to restrain Austria.

[8]

The Franco-Russian Alliance, 1894–1914

This chapter continues the empirical analysis of alliance management, shifting the focus to the Franco-Russian alliance, with some comparative reference to the Triple Entente. Ten case studies of alliance bargaining are presented, with intervening material intended to highlight changes in the parties' dependence, commitment, and interests. The impact of these factors on outcomes is assessed through the hypotheses stated in Chapter 6.

Figure 8-1 displays the four dimensions of alliance bargaining for France and Russia, from 1890 until the outbreak of World War I in 1914. As in the previous diagram for Germany and Austria (Fig. 7-1), the top graph (part A) shows variations in the relative dependence of the allies. The X and O lines show dependence as a function of the allies' power resources relative to their principal opponents. The principal opponent of Russia is taken to be Great Britain from 1890 to 1905[1] and Germany-Austria from 1905 to 1914; the principal adversary of France is Germany throughout the period. The comparative power resources of the states are their percentages of aggregate European great-power military and economic resources, operationalized as iron and steel production, energy consumption, population, military appropriations, and military personnel, as shown in Table 7-1.

As measured by these "hard" resource data, Russia was more dependent on the alliance than was France at the beginning of the period. Russia's dependence was declining and France's was increasing, however, so that they became about equally dependent, on grounds of military potential, around 1895. Thereafter France was the more dependent until about 1904, when Russia again became equally dependent; both allies' resource dependence then increased gradually until 1913. Russia's principal opponents became Germany and Austria after its defeat in the Far East at the

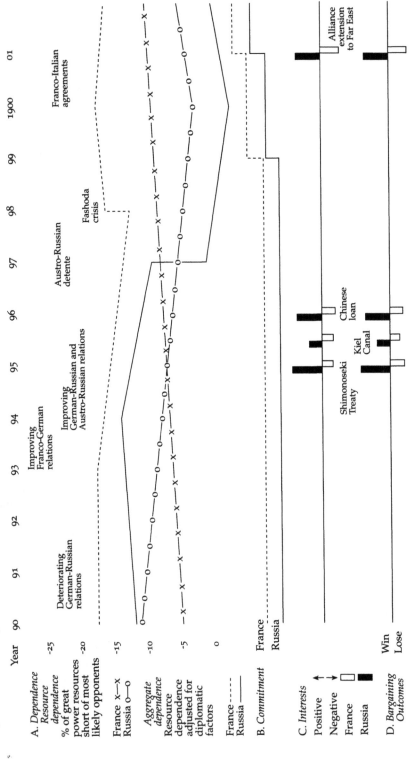

Figure 8.1. Franco-Russian relations and bargaining outcomes, 1890–1914

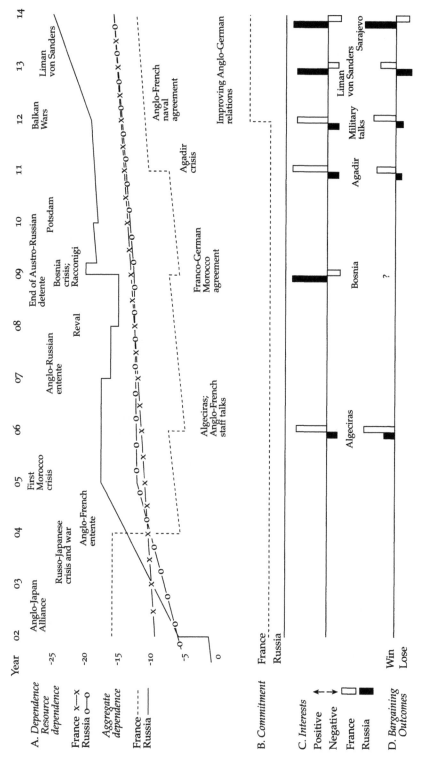

Figure 8.1. Franco-Russian relations and bargaining outcomes, 1890–1914 (*Continued*)

hands of Japan in 1905, which redirected its diplomatic energies to the Balkans and Near East. Thus the ascending line for Russia's resource dependence after 1905 reflects a gradually widening gap—from 11.6 percent in 1905 to 15.4 percent in 1913—between Russia's share of great-power resources and the greater share of Germany and Austria together. France's deficit vis-á-vis Germany increases from about 11 percent of total resources to 15.7 percent during the same period.[2]

As before, the solid and dashed lines in part A of Figure 8-1 represent modifications in estimated dependence to take account of changes in degree of conflict with adversaries and availability of alliance alternatives. These factors change the picture considerably. France's overall dependence in 1890 was higher than it would be on resource grounds alone because of its lack of alliance alternatives and the relative severity of its conflict with Germany. Russia, by contrast, still had the German option, despite the nonrenewal of the Reinsurance Treaty, and it had the possibility of settling its conflicts with Austria. Because of Russia's relatively favorable diplomatic position, its dependence was no higher than it would be on a strict resource comparison. Russia's overall dependence increased gradually until 1894 because of deteriorating relations with Germany. Then it declined as relations with Germany and Austria improved, especially after 1897. Russia continued to be the less dependent ally until 1904, when the Russo-Japanese war and its aftermath made Russia the more dependent party until 1914.

The second graph, part B of the figure, shows variations in alliance commitments during the period, and the third, part C, displays the comparative interests at stake in salient bargaining episodes between the allies. The bottom graph, part D, shows the outcomes of those episodes in terms of the relative gains or losses of the partners.

Intra-alliance bargaining events during the period come in three types: crisis confrontations with adversaries, alliance extensions, and burden-sharing negotiations. The crisis confrontations are basically instances of coercive bargaining between adversaries, but they include also bargaining between allies, centered on the issue of the stance to be taken toward the adversary. We now turn to a closer look at these ten minicases to ascertain (1) whether the outcomes matched those predicted by the parties' scores on our bargaining power index (Hypothesis A), and (2) which of the three central components of bargaining power was the most influential (Hypotheses 1–3). Four episodes of Anglo-French and Anglo-Russian bargaining are considered briefly for comparative purposes.

1894–1904

Alliance Bargaining: The Shimonoseki Treaty

The first test of the alliance's solidarity occurred in the Far East. A war between China and Japan in 1894–95 had resulted in certain territorial gains for Japan on the mainland, codified in the Treaty of Shimonoseki. Russia coveted the same areas, including the Liaotung Peninsula, with its valuable Port Arthur, and conceived the idea of a joint protest by the European powers to force Japan to give it up. Germany readily agreed, in order to foreclose a Russian-French-English combination or a consolidating exercise for the Franco-Russian alliance. France was reluctant but agreed to participate, in order to please Russia and to demonstrate the alliance's solidarity. Great Britain was also reluctant, because of its common interest with Japan in holding the Russians at bay, and finally decided to abstain.[3] So it turned out to be a Franco-Russian-German action, which succeeded in coercing Japan into disgorging its gains. It was a precursor of the rather ghostly project for a "continental league" against Britain which would later appear from time to time in response to anti-British sentiments of one or the other of the three parties.

The outcome in this case was a clear bargaining success for Russia: France, with no positive interest involved (indeed, a negative interest in avoiding participation), supported its ally nevertheless. France's low negative interest, moderate dependence, and moderate commitment to the alliance produces a bargaining power score of 5. Russia's score, from its high interest, low dependence, and moderate commitment, is 8. Hypothesis A is supported: the party with the higher score on this index prevails.

As for the three components of these scores, commitment explains nothing, since the parties were equally committed. The explanation lies either in relative interest at stake or in relative dependence (or both), with both these indicators favoring Russia. Which of these was the more potent factor cannot be stated unequivocally, but we may hazard that it was the interest asymmetry: Russia's positive stake was far greater than the French desire to avoid participation, whereas the difference in their degrees of dependence was smaller. Thus Hypothesis 2, with interests as the causal variable, is strongly supported; Hypothesis 1, on dependence, only weakly so.

Alliance Bargaining: The Kiel Canal

Early in 1895 the German government invited the French to send some warships to ceremonies marking the opening of the Kiel Canal in June.

The French cabinet first decided to decline, not wishing to appear so friendly to Germany so soon after making the alliance with Russia. But when the Czar learned of the French intention, he abruptly vetoed it: "The French government is wrong in hesitating to reply to the German invitation. Once all the powers have accepted, the participation of France, along with ours, is indispensable."[4] Reconsidering, the cabinet agreed to participate, but only if the event included some clear demonstration of Franco-Russian solidarity. Gabriel Hanotaux, the premier, suggested that the number of vessels and the grade of the commanding officers be identical and that the two squadrons rendezvous at sea and arrive at the Kiel Harbor together.[5] The Russians waited until two weeks before the ceremony before they agreed to the rendezvous; as if to atone for the delay, the Czar announced that the Cross of St. Andrew would be presented to French president Félix Faure on the opening day. Hanotaux countered criticism of his policy in the French chamber by referring, for the first time in public, to the "alliance" with Russia, thus violating the pledge of secrecy that had been made to Russia at the time of the alliance's negotiation. To his ambassador in St. Petersburg, he explained that "after the effort which has been demanded of us in the Sino-Japanese affair, the Kiel sacrifice, coming just on the eve of the Chinese loan, demanded a new formula."[6] In other words, Russia was making so many demands of France that France deserved some compensation in the form of a public commitment.

The rendezvous of the ships came off without a hitch. The French squadron left before the Kaiser's tour of inspection, however, on the pretext that it was due at home for ceremonies on the anniversary of the death of a former French president.[7]

Despite their comic opera flavor, these events precisely dramatized the distribution of influence in the alliance during its early years. The French gave in rather easily to the Russian desires, although they managed to exact compensation in the form of a marginal tightening of the Russian commitment while minimizing the cost of appearing to dance to the German tune. Overall, it was a compromise, somewhat favoring Russia. This outcome is consistent with Hypothesis A and the relative bargaining power of the allies. Russia had a low positive interest in the issue at stake—participation of French warships—while its dependence on the alliance was low and its commitment moderate, for a bargaining power score of 6. France had a low negative interest, a moderate degree of dependence, and a moderate commitment, for a score of 5. It seems clear that the outcome favoring Russia was entirely the result of asymmetrical dependence, since the parties' ratings are equal on the other two components. On the other hand, the French negative interest was strong enough to force a degree of compromise.

Alliance Bargaining: The Chinese Loan

The Japanese capitulation on the Shimonoseki Treaty opened the way for Russian designs on Manchuria and Korea.[8] Russia hoped to realize these designs by a process of nonviolent penetration and coercion of China. This venture, however, required money, which Russia, as ever, lacked. The French were glad to oblige. French money, via a loan to the Russian government, enabled China to pay off an indemnity owed Japan. French capital also founded a Russo-Chinese bank, which the Russian government was to use as an imperialist instrument, notably to finance a railroad through Manchuria. These loans were initial installments in a flood of French capital to Russia, which was to become a hallmark of the alliance. They marked the Russian financial dependence on France, which to some extent offset the French military dependence on Russia.

Although, superficially, this might seem to be a case of shared positive interests, Russian expansionism in the Far East was contrary to the interests of France. It necessitated the concentration of Russian military strength far away from Europe. It threatened to embroil Russia (and entrap France) in conflicts with Japan and Britain. It required Russo-German friendship in order to relieve pressure on Russia's western border. Consequently, it turned the point of the alliance against Britain rather than Germany, against Russia's principal enemy rather than France's.

The case was therefore one of opposed interests, although France could have seen some offsetting positive value in increasing the Russian financial dependence. The French overall interest, we may estimate, was negative and low, while its dependence on the alliance was moderate. Russia had a strong interest in getting the money, while its dependence on the alliance, in a politico-military sense, was low. These ratings, along with the moderate commitments of both parties, produce bargaining power scores of 5 for France and 8 for Russia. This is consistent with Hypothesis A: France provided the loan without demurral because it was unwilling to risk the collapse of the alliance. The outcome can be explained by either, or some combination of, the asymmetry of interests or the asymmetry of alliance dependence, both favoring Russia. Hypothesis 1 and Hypothesis 2 are both plausibly supported.

Alliance Dependence

The dependence of Russia on the alliance declined during the late 1890s because of improving relations with Austria and Germany. An important complement to the Russian imperialist surge in the Far East was an agreement with Austria, on May 5, 1897, not to disturb the status quo in the Balkans. The agreement freed Russian resources for use elsewhere. Its effect on the Franco-Russian alliance was to reduce Russian dependence on France, thus reducing French and increasing Russian bargaining leverage.

Similar in its effects was the British decision in the wake of the Franco-Russian alliance to give up the goal of holding the Straits (since the British Mediterranean fleet was weaker than the combined French and Russian fleets in the Mediterranean) and to concentrate instead on holding Egypt. By reducing pressure against Russia and increasing British power dedicated against France, Britain also redistributed dependence in the Franco-Russian alliance—again, to the disadvantage of France. This was an ironic outcome, since the French had made the alliance with Russia in the first place partly to strengthen their position against England in Egypt.[9]

For France, however, deteriorating relations with Britain were offset by an improvement in relations with Germany. Under Hanotaux as foreign minister, French foreign policy after 1894 shifted in a colonial direction, where it inevitably collided with Britain. The corollary was a more conciliatory policy toward Germany to protect France's continental rear. The combined effect of the two policies was to leave French diplomatic dependence on the alliance unchanged until the Fashoda crisis of 1898 brought a sharp rise in conflict with Britain.

Treaty Revision, 1899

Russia failed to support France during the Fashoda crisis, in which Britain forced a humiliating French backdown over a colonial issue.[10] This crisis, although it increased French dependence on Russia, marked a low point in French valuation of the alliance. Apparently, it had no political "halo," no practical value as a diplomatic instrument beyond the contingency of actual military attack. Russia, it seemed, was unwilling to support its ally unless its own interests were heavily involved. Moreover, Russia's suggestion of a disarmament conference in 1899, without previously consulting France, revealed a disturbing tendency toward unilateralism.[11]

Thus Théophile Delcassé, the French foreign minister, was in a pessimistic mood when rumors reached him that the Kaiser was seeking a meeting with the Czar. Delcassé suspected that the Kaiser's purpose was to make an agreement with Russia on the contingent partition of Austria-Hungary. The suspicion was entirely without foundation, but it was consistent with widespread speculation that after the death of the aged Emperor, Franz Joseph, the monarchy would collapse into its German, Magyar, and Slav segments. Germany could plausibly wish to incorporate the German and Magyar portions, leaving the Slavs to Russia. Germany might gain control of Hungary's Adriatic coastline and consequently a direct naval access to the Mediterranean.[12] To preempt a German-Russian agreement to this effect, and incidentally to line up Russian support for the recapture of Alsace-Lorraine in the diplomatic cataclysm that would follow the collapse of Austria-Hungary, Delcassé set out for St. Petersburg in August 1899.

Delcassé persuaded the Russian government to accept a rewording of the alliance contract. A new purpose was added to the political agreement: "to maintain the balance of power in Europe." This addition would permit activation of the alliance to prevent German absorption of the greater part of Austria-Hungary. It also potentially increased the scope and flexibility of the alliance, since "maintenance of the balance of power" would permit of many interpretations. In particular, it would serve to justify French compensation in Alsace-Lorraine if Germany and Russia were to divide the corpse of Austria-Hungary between them. In a second change, the military convention was given an indefinite duration, whereas the original text had made it coterminous with the Triple Alliance. This ensured that the alliance's military obligations would survive the dissolution of Austria-Hungary.[13] The Russians were amenable to these changes not so much because they shared the French concerns about the collapse of Austria-Hungary but for more immediate reasons. They were increasingly worried about German economic and political penetration of the Turkish empire, in particular via the project of the Baghdad Railway.[14] This was reason enough for them to desire a strengthening of their alliance with France. In addition, however, the Russians were alarmed about the internal conflicts in France that had been revealed by the Dreyfus affair and by the increasing tendency of the French press to favor a rapprochement with Germany. Their willingness to accept the specific changes desired by Delcassé also reflected their personal confidence in him due to the improvement in Franco-Russian relations that had occurred since he took office.[15]

This case does not fit our bargaining framework well because there was no discernible conflict. Both parties had an interest in strengthening the alliance, although their motivations for doing so were somewhat different. There is no reason to believe that the gains from the revision were other than roughly equal.

Alliance Bargaining: Treaty Revision, 1901 and 1902

In 1901 the scope of the alliance was extended formally to cover the contingency of war with Great Britain. As noted earlier, the alliance in practice had operated more against Britain than against Germany during the 1890s, simply because of the imperial orientation of Russian and French policies. This anomaly was now corrected. The change was more to the satisfaction of the Russians than the French, since Britain was more prominent in Russia's than in France's pantheon of enemies. Indeed, Russia had always wanted the alliance to cover war with England, whereas it took the Fashoda crisis to persuade France that such broadening was desirable.[16]

The change was negotiated in two meetings of the French and Russian chiefs of staff in July 1900 and February 1901. In case of a British attack on Russia, France would mobilize one hundred thousand men on the Channel coast and threaten an invasion of the British Isles. In the event of a British attack on France, Russia was to deploy three hundred thousand men on the borders of India and Afghanistan. The agreement was ratified by an exchange of letters between Delcassé and Lamsdorff, the Russian foreign minister, on May 16–17, 1901. An integral followup was a new French loan specifically for the construction of an Orenburg-Tashkent railroad, which was necessary for the Russians to carry out their promised mobilization.[17]

Russian penetration of China activated common interests of Great Britain and Japan, both of which had imperial agendas there. England in 1898 had tried to negotiate a settlement with Russia, to no avail. It had also tried to enlist Germany in the anti-Russian enterprise, but this effort foundered on the stubborn facts that had blocked earlier attempts at Anglo-German cooperation or alliance: Germany, unlike Britain, had no real interests in Asia and, moreover, was loath to antagonize Russia. That left Japan, whose own imperialist hunger remained unsatisfied after the deprivation of 1895.

An Anglo-Japanese alliance was signed on January 30, 1902. It was a classic "holding the ring" arrangement: the parties agreed to remain neutral if the other were attacked by one other power, and to come to the other's aid if attacked by more than one power. For Japan, this was a guarantee against French intervention in a Russo-Japanese war, a war Japan was already contemplating. For Britain, it meant a sharing of the task of defense against Russia, thus releasing some of its Far Eastern naval forces for other tasks and/or reducing its overall defense burden. It also blocked a possible Russo-Japanese deal partitioning Manchuria, Korea, and northern China, a possibility the Japanese exploited masterfully during the alliance negotiations.

The news of this alliance between Russia's two principal opponents reinvigorated its interest in the alliance with France. Lamsdorff, the foreign minister, proposed responding to the Anglo-Japanese alliance with "a similar agreement which would neutralize its effect," committing France and Russia to take "all the measures which they considered necessary" in the event of "joint military action" by England and Japan. Delcassé countered with milder wording: "if the occasion arises, to consider measures necessary" to the maintenance of the status quo and open door in China. An agreement to this effect was signed on March 19, 1902.[18] As with the earlier change, this one worked to Russia's advantage, if only because its interests

[270]

in China were far greater than France's. An engagement to consult did not necessarily mean fighting; nevertheless, Russia could expect French military assistance with a greater probability than before, and presumably so would Russia's enemies in Asia—Britain and Japan. Delcassé's domestic opponents railed against his incurring unnecessary risks of entrapment for no compensating gain. The minister replied that France's "prestige" would require its intervention in any case.[19] The real reason was unequal dependence: France needed the alliance more than Russia did; hence the Russian request could hardly be denied.

The similarity of these two changes permits their analysis together. Russia's interest in both revisions was high, its dependence was low, and its commitment moderate, for a score of 8. The interest of France in the 1901 revision was low though positive (since it still considered Britain an enemy), its dependence was moderate, and its commitment moderate, giving it a positive score of 5. These scores predict that France will support Russian interests simply because it shares them. France's interest in the 1902 revision was probably moderately negative (France had no interest in risking war with Japan). This gives it a negative score of 6, compared to Russia's positive 8. Since the outcome favored Russia, Hypothesis A is supported. The evidence bearing on the specific subhypotheses is ambiguous: France preferred not to extend the scope of the alliance to the Far East but went along with Russian desires because of either the higher Russian interest or the higher French dependence. A cost for France in both these revisions was a greater risk of conflict with Great Britain. Delcassé now turned his attention to that problem and found a solution in Africa.

Morocco and the Entente Cordiale

The issue of Morocco materialized at the intersection of several lines of policy: Russia's imperialist drive in the Far East and the British-Japanese resistance to it; France's desire to expand its North African domain and Germany's resistance to that; and Britain's desire to reduce its international commitments and thus to lighten its defense burden. The most significant result of this intersection would be the informal adherence of Great Britain to the Franco-Russian alliance.

France had long coveted Morocco. Tucked away in the northwest corner of Africa, it would nicely round out the French North African empire already established in Algeria and Tunis. The problem was that others— notably Britain, Germany, Italy, and Spain—were also interested, although French economic interests were preeminent. Delcassé set about buying off his rivals, one by one. First he tried Germany, without success. He succeeded with Italy. Two agreements, in January 1901 and June 1902, exchanged French claims in Tripoli for Italian claims in Morocco. The second agreement also contained pledges of neutrality that blatantly contradicted Italy's existing obligations under the Triple Alliance with Austria and Germany. This agreement lowered French dependence on Russia by reducing its need to maintain forces on the Italian frontier, thus increasing forces available against Germany. Indirectly, the Italian defection from the Triple Alliance also reduced Russia's alliance dependence, since it meant that Austria would have to deploy forces against Italy, leaving fewer for the Russian front.

Delcassé turned next to Spain, but the Spanish procrastinated, basically because they feared British disapproval. So Delcassé moved on to England, with which the obvious trade was French interests in Egypt for British interests in Morocco. France had little to lose by this exchange, since Fashoda had made crystal-clear that French ambitions in Egypt were futile. France shared with Britain a further incentive to agreement: reducing the risk of entrapment in the Russo-Japanese conflict that was clearly impending. Although neither was formally committed to participate in such a war, they might be dragged in by the halo effect of their alliances—that is, by their allies' expectations of support and the risk of the alliances' collapse were these expectations to be dashed. An Anglo-French agreement would create a plausible excuse for refusing to participate.

England had another incentive to reach a colonial settlement with France: it suffered from "imperial over-stretch."[20] For several years, England had been trying to get its overseas commitments more in line with its resources, either by settling conflicts with opponents or by negotiating alliances against them. In 1898 it attempted a settlement with Russia, concerning Turkey and China, without success. In the same year and again in 1901 it sought an alliance with Germany, failing both times. It succeeded, finally, with Japan in 1902; this alliance gave England a helpmate in defending its Far Eastern interests, reducing the strain on its naval resources. But this was not enough, particularly after the Boer War had painfully demonstrated the limits of England's overall resources. A colonial settlement with France, by reducing the interests that needed defending, would further reduce the strain and would ease the way, the British hoped, to a similar agreement with Russia.

France, too, had an overcommitment problem. Unique among the great powers, France was both a great continental and a great colonial power. On the continent, its enemy was Germany; in the colonies, the enemy was generally England. The Fashoda crisis had brought home to Delcassé that France was not strong enough to balance simultaneously against both Germany and Britain.[21] One of the enmities had to be liquidated. Immediately after Fashoda, Delcassé sought a rapprochement with Germany, but the Germans did not respond to his overtures. The entente with Britain, by which the parties settled most of their colonial differences, solved the problem. An important incentive for France, although it was not emphasized during the negotiations, was security against Germany. The lack of Russian support at Fashoda, and the Russian involvement in the Far East, had convinced Delcassé that he needed more help against Germany.[22] Constant coquetry between Germany and Russia pointed to the need for a hedge against the possible defection of Russia.[23]

Nevertheless, balancing Germany was not a prominent motive in the British government, even though public hostility toward Germany was high.[24] It was present consciously for only some decision makers, such as Joseph Chamberlain, that erstwhile protagonist of alliance with Germany, who had now switched 180 degrees because of anger and disappointment over being rebuffed, and some Foreign Office and military officals who were beginning to be concerned about German naval plans and colonial bullying. Arthur Balfour, the prime minister, and Lansdowne, the foreign minister, were more worried about the Russian than the German threat and viewed an agreement with France as a first step toward an improvement of relations with Russia.[25] Only later, during the Morocco crisis of 1905, did the British begin to perceive their entente with France as a quasi-alliance against Germany.

The agreement was signed on April 8, 1904. France agreed not to obstruct British policy in Egypt, and Britain accepted French preponderance in Morocco. The parties agreed to provide each other "diplomatic support" should these arrangements be challenged by any other state.[26] Other clauses settled conflicts over Newfoundland fishing rights and certain colonial boundaries in Africa, Siam, and the New Hebrides. Obviously, the accord created an entente, not an alliance. Aside from the clause about "diplomatic support" on Egypt and Morocco, the parties undertook no explicit obligations for joint action of any kind. Nevertheless, the general liquidation of colonial conflicts made it much easier for them to act as allies in the future. In particular, the settlement over Egypt ended a conflict that had barred truly friendly relations since 1882.

The parties incurred a mutual dependency, although this effect was more prominent for France, given its greater sensitivity to the German threat. It was balanced for France, however, by a reduction of its dependence on Russia—ceteris paribus, acquiring a new ally reduces dependence on existing ones. In time, of course, with a clearer perception of the German threat, the British dependency would rise. Britain's underestimate of the German threat during the negotiations tended to minimize both its subjective security benefits from the agreement and its perception of long-run costs—that is, neither the positive effect of balancing against Germany nor the negative effect of stimulating German hostility was appreciated.

The agreement successfully achieved its immediate aim for both parties—staying out of the Russo-Japanese war. Russia's disastrous defeat drastically weakened its military strength and increased its dependence on France. In turn, Russia's new weakness made France more dependent on its new partner, Britain, and the end of Russia's ambitions in the Far East significantly improved the chances of the Entente's being extended to Russia. The defeat refocused Russian attention on the Near East and eastern Europe, where it collided with Austria. The rising salience of this conflict significantly increased Russian dependence on France.

The German government saw in the war, and the Dogger Bank incident during the war,[27] a golden opportunity to split up both the Franco-Russian alliance and the Anglo-French entente and to organize the Kaiser's favorite project, a continental league against Britain. In October 1904 the Kaiser suggested a Russo-German alliance to the Czar, and Holstein, the German idea man, made a similar proposal to the Russian ambassador. Holstein's logic was that Russia would accept out of disillusionment with France because of the French move toward Britain. France would then have to choose between Russia-Germany and Great Britain and would choose the former. The Czar, however, insisted that France be consulted first. The Kaiser was just as insistent that the alliance be signed first and presented to France as a fait accompli. Since these demands were incompatible, the project collapsed.

When France dropped its foreign minister, Delcassé, under German pressure during the Morocco crisis, the Kaiser took it as a sign that France was ready for alliance, so he reopened negotiations with the Czar in 1905. At a famous meeting at Bjorko aboard his yacht, he actually persuaded Czar Nicholas to sign an alliance document promising mutual defense. Nicholas thought the anti-German orientation of the Franco-Russian alliance was passé, that England was the true enemy of both parties and Germany their friend, and that France could be persuaded to join an alliance against Britain, perhaps with the help of a nice pourboire in Morocco. Again, however, the Russian foreign office thought otherwise and persuaded the Czar that an agreement with Germany was not only incompatible with the alliance with France but also inconsistent with Russian interests. The Czar was forced to tell the Kaiser that the deal was off, much to the latter's chagrin. The Bjorko episode was the last gasp of the dream of a continental league. The Russians' realization that such an arrangement was out of the question increased their sense of dependence on France. Russia thereafter moved closer to France and began to look with more favor on British overtures.

Alliance Bargaining: The Dual Alliance and the First Moroccan Crisis

Russia provided far more support to France during the first Moroccan crisis in 1905–6 than it had at Fashoda, even though it had no more interest in Morocco than in the Sudan. Russia's support went beyond mere voting at the Algeciras conference. The Russian government made frequent petitions through regular diplomatic channels to get Berlin to yield to French desires. The Czar also appealed directly to the Kaiser. The Russian finance minister, Sergei Witte, a booster of the continental league, persuaded Bülow and the Kaiser to accept a French proposal for the conference's agenda, arguing that such a German concession would make the French more likely to adhere to the treaty that the Kaiser and the Czar had just negotiated at Bjorko.[28] During the conference the Russian delegates supported France at every turn, in a considerable show of alliance loyalty. It might perhaps be sufficient to attribute this support to Russia's defeat in the Far East, which had seriously weakened its military and naval strength and thus increased its military dependence on France. In addition, however, Russia's financial needs had increased, and France skillfully exploited them during the crisis. Russia requested a large loan to deal with domestic economic disruption caused by the war and the subsequent revolution. France agreed but only after satisfactory conclusion of the Moroccan crisis and on two further conditions: that Russia support France at the conference and that much of the loan proceeds be used to build up the strategic railway network in European Russia. At one point, Lamsdorff urged France to make concessions to prevent the breakdown of the conference. But France insisted on complete support, and Lamsdorff capitulated.[29] Financial leverage may also have helped France persuade its ally, in April 1906, to drop the clauses in the Franco-Russian military agreement of 1901 that envisaged a possible war against Great Britain.[30]

All this added up to an intra-alliance bargaining victory for France. Such a victory is predicted by our Hypothesis A. France had a strong interest at stake in the crisis. It was still moderately dependent on the alliance: the growing German belligerence had heightened French dependence on Russia, while the entente with Britain had reduced it. Russia had no direct interest in providing support but a negative interest in not risking war with Germany. Its dependence on the alliance had increased substantially, however, owing to the defeat in the Far East. Because of military weakness, the alliance had become strategically more valuable to Russia, and because of dire economic straits, Russia had also become financially dependent. The alliance commitments of both states were still moderate, although they had been extended geographically, as noted above. These factors combine to produce a bargaining power score of 7 for France and

4 for Russia, consistent with the supportive Russian behavior during the crisis. The outcome might be explained, more specifically, by the disparity of interests or the asymmetry of dependence, both of which favored France, or by some combination of these factors.

Alliance Bargaining: The Entente Cordiale and the First Moroccan Crisis

During the first Moroccan crisis Britain provided strong support to France, although it varied slightly in different stages of the crisis and with changes in the British government. In the early phase the Conservatives, with Lansdowne as foreign minister, stiffened the French when they exhibited a tendency to cave in to German bullying. Lansdowne wished to preserve the Entente, but his principal worry was that the French might appease the Germans by giving away a British interest, such as permitting a German port on the Moroccan coast. He gave a strong warning to Germany and requested full consultation from the French, a request they (mistakenly) interpreted as an offer of alliance.[31] The Liberals under Grey, assuming office in January 1906, were even more determined than Lansdowne to support the Entente as a bulwark against the German threat on the continent, but they were more willing to countenance concessions in the colonial realm, such as a German port on the (Atlantic) coast of Morocco. Grey suggested this concession and later advised acceptance of the Austrian compromise proposal for the police power in Morocco. But when these suggestions drew French expressions of annoyance and doubts about British loyalty, Grey drew back. As the German threat came into focus during the crisis, British support firmed and joint military talks got under way.[32]

There was little bargaining between Britain and France, since there was little conflict; yet there was some during the Grey phase. Considering the risk of war, Britain had a marginal negative interest in the tough French demands; it would have preferred concessions to Germany. Britain was at least moderately dependent on the Entente, however, and it is clear that this factor provides most of the explanation for the British stance; Grey was not about to desert the Entente in its first real test. Britain's commitment, limited to "diplomatic support" on the specific issue of Morocco, might be considered moderate. These ratings in our bargaining power index give Britain a score of 5. France's interest at stake was high; its dependence on Britain, especially in view of Russia's weakness, was also high; and its commitment was low, yielding a score of 7. These scores are consistent with the bargaining success of the French in resisting Grey's attempts to moderate their stance.

The elements in their success were their stronger interests at stake and

the British treaty commitment to diplomatic support. These factors overcame the greater French dependence due to the weakness of Russia. Still,
Britain may have capitulated to French desires to a greater degree than it
"should" have, given the relative bargaining power of the two governments. There is some evidence that the British exaggerated their own dependence and underestimated France's. Another possible explanation
might lie in the commitment factor: Britain may have felt more committed
by the "diplomatic support" clause of the treaty than our moderate rating
would allow.

The Triple Entente

The Anglo-French entente created an anomalous situation in the relations of both countries with Russia. France and Russia were formally allies,
France and Britain were quasi-allies, but Russia and Britain were still at
odds. France, being deeply committed to alliance or entente with the other
two, took the lead in trying to bring them together. The task was greatly
facilitated by the defeat of Russia in the Far East, which eliminated its
capacity to challenge British interests there and increased its willingness
to settle other imperial conflicts with Britain. The defeat also made Russia
more vulnerable to French pressure and redirected its energies toward
southeast Europe and the Ottoman Empire, where it was more likely to
come into conflict with Germany and Austria. Thus the change in the
geographic arena of conflict tended to produce a corresponding shift of
alignments.

Moreover, the situation in the Near East had changed during the past
decade. Previously, Russia had been opposed there by England. But now,
having downgraded the strategic importance of the Straits and Constantinople, England had become more or less indifferent to the fate of the
Turks. Germany, which had formerly stood aloof from or even supported
Russia's ambitions in the Ottoman Empire, had developed strong financial
and commerical interests there and had emerged as the Turks' best friend.
German activities in the Near East, especially the project for a Berlin-to-
Baghdad railway, had aroused deep Russian suspicions.

The British had been trying to get a colonial agreement with Russia at
least since 1895. The project received new impetus from conclusion of the
Anglo-French entente: British leaders saw the latter as a step toward a
rapprochement with Russia, and the French repeatedly urged their two
allies to bury their differences. The British and Russian governments had
been able to maintain fairly cordial relations during the Russo-Japanese
war, despite being on opposite sides. Izvolsky was initially reluctant (because of his deference to German wishes, the French thought)[33] but finally

agreed to talks. He and Nicolson, the British ambassador to Russia, opened formal negotiations on May 29, 1906.

Russia had four principal incentives for an agreement with Great Britain. First, after the defeat by Japan, Russia needed a period of peace and quiet during which to rebuild its forces and its economy; a settlement with its primary rival was therefore necessary. Second, such a settlement would usefully supplement the alliance with France in building security against Germany (the Russians had noted the French weakness in the Morocco crisis before they were sure of British support). Third, Russian liberals, their influence increased by the revolution of 1905, greatly admired the British political system. Fourth, the Russian government hoped to tap the London money market for some of the huge sums it needed for military and economic rebuilding.

The primary British motive, as in the earlier agreement with France, was to reduce imperial commitments and conflicts so as to ease the strain on its military and economic resources. Constructing a balance of power against the German threat was an important secondary motive, however, in contrast to the entente with France in 1904, when this motive was barely present. By 1907 the naval race and the experience of the Morocco crisis had brought a clear perception of Germany as an enemy. Settling Anglo-Russian differences in Asia would release resources of both countries for balancing Germany in Europe. A related motive was to head off a possible Russo-German deal and to banish once and for all that old bogey, the continental league.

Not only was the balancing of German power a stronger motive for Britain than it had been in the French entente; it was also a stronger motive for Britain than it was for Russia. This was a reversal of the comparative incentives in the entente with France, when France was much more strongly motivated than Britain to balance the German threat. In 1907 Russia was primarily interested in settling conflicts so as to save resources for internal purposes, not in forming a quasi-alliance against Germany.[34] Indeed, in Russia a strong current of opinion favored a German over a British connection, so that the choice for the latter was politically difficult. During the negotiations, and afterward, the Russians sought to keep the German option open by reassuring the Germans that the agreement was not directed against them. That was not the case in Britain, where the earlier enthusiasm for a German alliance had been completely dissipated.

The agreement, signed on August 31, 1907, was similar to the Anglo-French entente in that ostensibly it was merely a settlement of colonial issues. In Persia the parties awarded each other spheres of influence—Russia in the north, Britain in the southeast. Russia recognized British preponderance in Afghanistan, and both agreed to abstain from political penetration in Tibet. Izvolsky tried to get British approval of Russian control of the Straits but had to be content with a vague promise from Grey that this issue might be settled in Russia's favor after agreements had been reached on other issues and public opinion had gotten used to the idea of Anglo-Russian friendship.

In terms of the specific issues involved, Russia's gain was marginally greater than Britain's. Russia's sphere in Persia was the larger, and the Afghan and Tibetan settlements simply ratified the status quo. Britain's previously unyielding attitude on the Straits had been dropped. On the larger strategic issues, however, the advantage fell to Great Britain. The easing of Asiatic conflicts between the two countries was of greater benefit to Britain because the Russian threat to British possessions in that part of the world was greater than vice versa. Since Britain was the more concerned about the German threat, the containment of that threat meant more to it than to Russia. Britain, therefore, was the more dependent on the Entente, subjectively speaking; it had more to lose if the relationship should weaken or break up. This asymmetry would work to Britain's disadvantage in bargaining with Russia in subsequent years.

The agreement reduced Russian dependence on France and thus increased Russian bargaining power in the Dual Alliance. For France, however, this debit was more than offset by the reduction of conflict between its two partners and the elimination of the potential need to choose between them, and by the general strengthening of the bulwark against Germany.

The Russians went out of their way to assure Germany that it was not the target of the pact. Izvolsky kept the German government informed on the progress of the negotiations and promised that no decisions would be made affecting German interests without Germany's consent. He indicated soon afterward that he was ready to negotiate a German-Russian understanding similar to the Anglo-Russian one. He informed the British government that it was "imperative ... that Russia should act with the greatest prudence toward Germany and give the latter no cause for complaint that the improvement of relations of Russia with England had entailed a corresponding deterioration of the relations of Russia toward Germany."[35]

Deterioration of British relations with Germany in the years after 1907, largely due to the naval race, increased the British sense of dependence on both Russia and France. This sense of dependence had led Grey, earlier, to refrain from conciliatory gestures toward Germany for fear of alienating France; he now had further reason in the danger of Russian defection. This risk would affect his behavior in the next great crisis, over the Turkish province of Bosnia-Herzegovina in 1908-9.

Alliance Bargaining: The Triple Entente and the Bosnia Crisis

Russia's allies differed markedly in the amount of support they gave in the major crisis over the Austrian annexation of Bosnia-Herzegovina in 1908–9. France provided virtually no support. England, while making clear it would not fight over the issue and demurring on the Russian demand for compensation at the Straits, nevertheless backed the Russian position. Russia refused to recognize the annexation until Serbia's demand for compensation had been satisfied.

The French government, in a strongly worded note, pleaded that Russia do everything possible "to avoid the risk of a conflict over a matter in which her vital interests are not involved and from which, in consequence, French public opinion would not understand that a war could result, in which the armies of France and Russia would have to take part under the terms of the alliance."[36] The French foreign minister, Stéphen Pichon, told the Russians their position was untenable because of the Bosnian occupation rights granted to Austria by the Treaty of Berlin. France would support Russia's demand for an international conference, he said, but beyond that it could not go.[37] During the crisis France agreed with the German view that collective pressure should be brought against Serbia to drop its demand for territorial compensation, and then unilaterally exerted such pressure.[38] Grey, on the other hand, refused to put pressure on Serbia without Russian consent and would not even ask for Russian consent unless Germany agreed to urge Austria to make economic concessions.[39]

One reason for the French attitude was simply anxiety about entrapment in a Balkan war at Russian or British initiative. Georges Clemenceau, the premier, was haunted by the fear of being dragged into war via the Anglo-German rivalry.[40] French leaders were feeling acutely vulnerable because of the military weakness of their allies, particularly Russia, whose military forces had still not been rebuilt after the defeat by Japan. Consequently, the French sought not only to restrain Russia but also to appease Germany. During the crisis, without consulting Britain or Russia, they negotiated an agreement with Germany over Morocco: France was to have political preponderance in return for German commercial freedom. However necessary or justified the agreement was on grounds of realpolitik, it left France's allies feeling that France had exploited the Bosnia crisis for its own gain.[41] France also entertained hopes of weaning Austria away from the alliance with Germany, much as it had already done with Italy. Nicolson thought France had moved "a quarter of the way towards a fuller understanding with Germany." He would not be surprised, he said, if both France and Russia now gravitated toward Germany out of their mutual mistrust.[42] Izvolsky regarded the Morocco agreement, together with the lack of French support on the Bosnia issue itself, as almost amounting to a denunciation of the Franco-Russian alliance.[43] "I want to believe in the good faith of your government," he told the French ambassador, "but your diplomacy at Berlin and Vienna did not give us the support we expected. Since the conclusion of the Franco-German accord (over Morocco) Austria has dared everything because it believed that no one would stand in its way."[44]

Izvolsky also accused the French of having sold out to Austria and bitterly rebuked them for having agreed to the German suggestion to apply pressure on Serbia before applying it against Austria, turning Serbia over to Austria "bound hand and foot." This was his reward, he complained, for the strong support he had given France at the Algeciras conference.[45] In the face of pressures from his ally as well as his enemies, Izvolsky had no alternative but to advise Serbia to give up its demand for compensation, and Serbia could only acquiesce. To the French ambassador, Izvolsky contrasted "the loyal attitude of [the British] government, the friends of Russia, with that of Russia's ally."[46]

Britain's support was motivated almost entirely by the need to maintain and strengthen the entente with Russia. Its fragility had been revealed by Izvolsky's dealings with Aehrenthal. The British were aware that Russia still had the German option, as evidenced by Izvolsky's sensitivity to German feelings during the entente negotiations. Thus they reacted quickly when Izvolsky warned that he would have to reconsider his European alignments if forced to stand by and watch Austria invade Serbia.[47] Grey sent a rather stiff telegram to Vienna asking what concessions the Austrians were prepared to make, and, as noted, he refused to bring similar pressure on Serbia.

Other British motives were moral and ideological. Grey felt that Aehrenthal had unilaterally upset an internationally agreed status quo; he had thereby violated a tacit rule of the Concert of Europe. The ideological motive was sympathy for the liberal Young Turk regime, which had just taken power in Turkey and was thus legally the suzerain power in Bosnia-Herzegovina.

Eventually, of course, Russia had to give in to German-Austrian pressures, in view of its weakness and the lack of military support from its allies. Nonetheless, Grey resented Russia's sudden capitulation to the German "ultimatum." Neither Britain nor France had been consulted. The Russian action left Grey "out on a limb" from which he crawled back by continuing to support the Serbian demand for compensation until this, too, was dropped. Nicolson was dejected and worried that mutual mistrust engendered by the crisis would cause both France and Russia to drift toward the Central Powers. This might be avoided, he suggested to Grey, by turning the entente into an alliance.[48] Though rejecting the idea of alliance, Grey reaffirmed his support of the entente, and Nicolson assured the Czar, contrary to what he had just told Grey, that the British government "did not for one moment believe that in taking the course which she did, Russia had any desire to separate herself from her two partners."[49]

The Russians were quite aware of the British dependence. Sazonov said in October 1910: "We may rest assured that the English, engaged in the pursuit of political aims of vital importance in Europe, may, in case of necessity, be prepared to sacrifice certain interests in Asia in order to keep a Convention alive which is of such importance to them. This is a circumstance which we can, of course, exploit for ourselves, as, for instance, in Persian affairs."[50]

The Bosnia crisis definitively ended the ten-year-old Austro-Russian detente. Russia's humiliation and the personal animus of Izvolsky toward Aehrenthal guaranteed that henceforth the two countries would be on opposite sides of most Balkan issues. The Russian government resolved never again to concede to Austrian and German pressure.

It is difficult to assess the French-Russian interaction in this case, since it is not possible to know which factor was most responsible for the ultimate Russian backdown: French restraint or Austro-German pressure. France, in effect, demanded that Russia drop its support of Serbia and accept the Austrian annexation, and implicitly threatened to withhold military support if the intransigent position of Russia involved it in war. Germany made the same demand and threatened war. There is no hard evidence as to how much Russia's capitulation was due to the absence of support from France. Chances are the German threat was sufficient; Russia, even with French assistance, was in no military condition to fight Germany and Austria. Thus the alliance bargaining in this case was overwhelmed by the interaction between adversaries. Our calculus of alliance bargaining power gives France and Russia scores of 6 each, Russia's greater interest at stake being offset by its greater dependence. This result predicts an alliance compromise, that is, a moderate Russian concession to French wishes, but there is no way to estimate whether this would have occurred had not the German démarche supervened.

Alliance Loosening, 1909–1911

The period from 1909 to 1911 brought some loosening of the Triple Entente. Although its relations with Austria were irreparably damaged by the Bosnia crisis, Russia took significant steps toward accommodation with the other members of the Triple Alliance. In both cases, a prominent aim was to separate them from Austria. With Italy, Russia signed the Racconigi agreement in October 1909, guaranteeing the status quo in the Balkans and pledging mutual support to Italian colonial aspirations in North Africa and Russian interests at the Straits. The agreement was precipitated by the Bosnia crisis and was clearly aimed at blocking further Austrian expansion in the Balkans, in which the signatories had a common interest. It was another step in the detachment of Italy from the Triple Alliance, although Izvolsky vehemently denied to the Germans that this was its purpose.[51]

A change of foreign ministers in 1910, with Sazonov replacing Izvolsky, who moved to the Paris embassy, brought a more conciliatory Russian policy toward Germany. Sazonov's first official act was to negotiate the Potsdam agreement with Germany in November 1910.[52] His principal motive was to mend fences with Germany in order to avoid another Balkans defeat at the hands of Austria. He chose to conciliate his opponent's ally rather than move closer to his own allies, since the latter had provided only slim support during the recent crisis. The German promise not to support any aggressive Austrian behavior in the Balkans was a considerable increment to Russian security. It also reduced Russia's dependence on its allies, although it disturbed its relations with them. Neither Paris nor London was informed of these negotiations beforehand, and both were much irritated and anxious when they learned of their results, especially the Russian promise not to support any British policy hostile to Germany and Sazonov's departure from the understanding that all negotiations about the Baghdad Railway should include all four interested powers. (Now that Russia had broken ranks, the British and French governments felt free to enter into separate negotiations with Germany on this issue.) Sazonov's refusal to put into writing the declarations about not supporting aggressive Austrian or British policy only partly eased their worries. France compensated by resuming military conversations with England, which had languished since 1908.[53]

Racconigi and Potsdam raised questions about Russia's loyalty in the minds of its partners. But Russia also had reason to be concerned about a relaxation of tension between France and Germany, which had been proceeding under Pichon since 1907 and was notably advanced via the 1909 modus vivendi about Morocco. French movement away from Russia was motivated, in part, by worries about being entrapped in Russian initiatives to control the Straits. There was a good deal of friction between France and England over implementation of various parts of the entente agreement of 1904. Russian-British tension rose over Russian attempts to militarize its sphere of influence in northern Persia. In 1909 Germany and Britain renewed their discussions about naval limitations, causing some anxiety in Paris and a brief French attempt to tighten up the Entente. In their alliance games, on the whole, all three partners were playing moderate "defect" strategies, and it seemed that the entente was in trouble. Another crisis with Germany revived it, however.

Alliance Bargaining: Agadir

When Germany raised the Morocco issue again in the Agadir crisis of 1911, the pattern of support in the Entente was the mirror image of the pattern during the Bosnia crisis. The immediate protagonist (France) received moderate support from the entente partner (Britain) but little or none from the formal ally (Russia). Unlike Russia, Britain was an interested party: it had direct interests in the disposition of the Moroccan issue and was formally pledged to support France diplomatically.[54] Throughout the crisis British spokesmen made a clear distinction between their particular interests in Morocco and their more general interest in preserving the entente with France. They had two main worries: that France, by not conceding enough, might push the crisis to the point of war, but that, if it were not supported, it might sacrifice British interests (e.g., by granting Germany a naval base on the Moroccan coast or by partitioning Morocco with Germany) or desert the entente entirely. The first was the fear of entrapment; the second, of abandonment. Each fear was emphasized by a different group in the British government: of entrapment, by the Radical Liberals in the cabinet, who favored a hands-off policy; of abandonment, by most of the senior officers in the Foreign Office, who urged strong support of France. Grey sought a mixed strategy: restrain France from pushing the issue to the point of war but support it enough to retain its confidence in the entente. He advised France to make concessions (e.g., a commercial port on the Atlantic coast of Morocco), suggested a conference in case the bilateral negotiations broke down, insisted on consultation or full participation on any issues involving British interests, and firmly refused all French requests for an explicit pledge of military assistance.[55] He also asserted, however, that Britain would "in all circumstances" fulfill its obligations to France,[56] and he tried to convince the Germans that Britain would aid France if it were attacked by Germany. The French, for their part, sought to keep Britain engaged by reiterating that the real German objective was to get a piece of Morocco, where British interests were directly involved, and by failing to inform the British government of German concessions.[57]

The principal British threat was made (however vaguely) in a speech by David Lloyd George, the chancellor of the exchequer, after which the main axis of conflict shifted from Paris-Berlin to London-Berlin, and a brief war scare between Germany and England ensued. It was this British move that persuaded the Germans of the need to compromise. Soon thereafter they retreated from their initial demand for the entire French Congo and accepted a much smaller portion as compensation for allowing the French to consolidate their hold on Morocco. Yet it was also Grey's cautionary private statements to France—somewhat contradictory to the impression

[284]

made by Lloyd George—that left the French somewhat uncertain about British reliability and encouraged them to make the necessary compromises.[58]

The Russian stance during the Agadir crisis was less supportive than the British. The first messages from St. Petersburg after the "Panther's spring" in July were positive but formal and reserved. Russia would, of course, stand by its treaty obligations, but it hoped war would be avoided. The Russian government acceded to a French request that Russia express its "surprise and astonishment" in Berlin.[59] In carrying out this mission, however, the Russian ambassador turned it into a mere request for information, acknowledging that Russia was interested in Morocco only "as it could become an object of strife through which Russia could be drawn into joint suffering by virtue of the treaties of alliance."[60] Later, after a meeting of the Council of Ministers on August 19, Russia began actively to urge French concessions.[61] Izvolsky told Justin de Selves, the French foreign minister, that it would be unfortunate if the Franco-German talks broke down over a French refusal to concede a few more square kilometers of colonial territory. He urged France to exercise "prudent compliance" with Germany's wishes, including relinquishing the port of Agadir.[62] He compared the situation to that of February 1909, when France had urged him to do everything possible to avoid war over Bosnia. Russia now had the right to advise prudence "in a similar friendly way."[63] The Russian ambassador in Berlin, Nicholas Osten-Sacken, was instructed to remonstrate with the Germans, but only in the "mildest possible form."[64] The Czar told the French ambassador in St. Petersburg that "if all else failed he would honor his signature, but that Russia was not ready, that we must be prudent and try to reach an accommodation with Germany."[65]

The mildness of the Russian representations in Berlin no doubt reflected, besides military unreadiness and lack of interest in Morocco, a reluctance to jeopardize the improved relations with Germany that had been established at Potsdam. The main results of that meeting—the agreements on Persia and the Baghdad Railway—were formalized in August 1911 during the Agadir crisis, and pro-German sentiment in the Russian government was quite strong at this time.[66] These agreements, plus the one with Italy at Racconigi, reduced somewhat Russia's dependence on the French alliance.

In terms of our interest-dependence-commitment framework, Russia's interests during the Agadir crisis were negative and low, its dependence was high, and its commitment moderate, for a bargaining power score of 4. The French interest was high, its dependence moderate, and its commitment moderate, yielding a score of 7. These scores suggest a Russian strategy of mild restraint and a French policy of firmness in the intra-alliance bargaining, resulting in a French "victory." This fairly accurately portrays the policies of both countries and the outcome of the bargaining. In terms of specific components of bargaining power, the outcome may be explained by either the disparity of interests or the greater Russian dependence, or some combination of both. Commitments were not a factor, since they were equal.

Strengthening of the Anglo-French Entente, 1912

The Agadir crisis was the most serious of the several crises that punctuated the European diplomatic scene in the decade before World War I. All capitals had felt the hot breath of war, and this concentrated their minds on their preparations for war—their armaments, their alliances, and their relations with opponents. Allies on both sides began to feel more dependent. Significant repairs were made to both the Triple Alliance and the Triple Entente, military conversations became more serious and more detailed, and an arms race in land forces got under way.

The formal German acceptance of a French protectorate over Morocco eliminated that particular issue as a source of conflict between France and Germany and, by association, between Britain and Germany. Nevertheless, Anglo-German and Franco-German tension did not ease. Many Germans blamed England for what they saw as the measly compensation they had received. In Britain the Foreign Office and the Liberal Imperialists in the cabinet saw their view of the German threat confirmed; consequently, they felt more dependent on France and fearful of French abandonment. Talks between the British and French military staffs were revived and expanded at British initiative.

The Radicals in the cabinet, however, were alarmed at how close they had come to war, and they urged Grey to do something to improve relations with Germany. The foreign secretary decided to have one more try at a naval arms control agreement. Great Britain and Germany had negotiated for such an agreement between 1908 and 1910, but their talks had always foundered on the German demand for a British declaration of neutrality as quid pro quo for any significant reduction in the rate of shipbuilding. Lord Haldane was appointed on Feburary 3 to go to Germany and reopen discussions. He was armed with a new proposal: in return for a halt to the naval race, Britain would neither pursue an aggressive policy toward Germany nor join in an unprovoked attack on it.[67] This was not sufficient for the Germans, however; they continued to insist on a declaration of unqualified neutrality. Grey's refusal to issue such a declaration underscores the extent to which the colonial settlement of 1904 had, in eight years, been transformed into a quasi-alliance.

For France, however, the Haldane mission revealed the fragility of the Entente Cordiale. Poincaré and Paul Cambon, the ambassador in London, decided it needed shoring up, and they saw their opportunity in an impending change in British naval deployments—ironically, the result of the German naval buildup.[68] The Admiralty had proposed a reorganization of the fleets, involving the transfer of forces based on Malta to Gibraltar, where they would be available to reinforce other squadrons in the North Sea and the Atlantic. This move would considerably weaken British naval strength in the Mediterranean, but the admirals were confident the French would take up the slack. Tentative discussions between British and French naval authorities had begun in the summer of 1911, but no formal agreement about such a division of labor had been reached.

Although the French had already concentrated most of their fleet in the Mediterranean, they insisted on a diplomatic quid pro quo. They first proposed a naval convention under which Britain would defend the Channel and France's northern ports, while France looked after both countries' interests in the Mediterranean. When this was rejected, they proposed an exchange of notes calling for joint consultation in case of a threat to the peace or to the two countries' interests. Grey and the cabinet reluctantly agreed to such an exchange, containing three points: (1) that military and naval conversations had occurred, (2) that neither these talks nor the dispositions of the fleets bound the governments to assist each other, and (3) that in case of a threat to the peace, the two governments would consult about joint measures to be taken. If action was deemed necessary, the plans of the general staffs would be taken into account.[69]

This outcome was a clear bargaining victory for the French: they had achieved a British commitment to consult and at least a moral commitment of British seapower in case of war with Germany. Above all, the Entente had been given a written definition. Although Grey stressed the absence of any obligation to action and the innocuous nature of the agreement to consult, it was clear that the Entente had been significantly strengthened. One effect was to reduce French dependence on Russia. But Poincaré was determined to tighten the alliance with Russia as well.

Strengthening of the Franco-Russian Alliance, 1912

Between 1908 and 1912 the ties between France and Russia had distinctly weakened. In two major crises, Bosnia and Agadir, the allies had reciprocated indifference to each other's need for support. Russia had made deals with the opponents, at Racconigi and Potsdam. In France a succession of weak and inexperienced foreign ministers, constrained by a continuing public distaste for the Russian autocracy, had done nothing to correct these tendencies.

The advent of Raymond Poincaré to the French foreign ministry in January 1912 brought a surge of vigor to French foreign policy and new life to the alliance. Poincaré perceived three dangerous trends in Russia's policy: its support of Italy in the Italo-Turkish war, its attempts to organize alliances among the small Balkan states that might be employed offensively against Turkey, and its tendency to take unilateral initiatives.

Russia was supporting Italy in the hope of exploiting a Turkish defeat to get control of the Straits. This created a danger of either French entrapment in a Russian initiative or a collapse of the Ottoman Empire, resulting in a general war or the loss of French interests in Syria and the Lebanon. Furthermore, French ambassadors were reporting that Russia was moving toward an entente with Austria as well as Italy, or even a resurrection of the *Dreikaiserbund*.[70] Thus Poincaré was beset by rumors and fears of both entrapment and abandonment by his ally. The fear of abandonment was dominant, however, and he moved to avoid it by strengthening the French commitment to Russia. He dealt with the danger of entrapment not by the standard method of weakening his support of the ally but by insisting on close consultation and agreement before any major foreign policy initiative. In short, he sought to resolve the alliance security dilemma by dealing with the risk of entrapment in a way that did not automatically increase the risk of abandonment.

Poincaré repeatedly sought to impress on the Russians the need for consultation and joint decision making.[71] For instance, when he learned of a Russian buildup of troops on the Turkish border, he summoned Izvolsky and told him that according to the terms of the alliance, Russia could take no major initiative in the Near East without first reaching agreement with France. Simply to "inform" France would not be enough; it was necessary to "concert beforehand." He did not want another surprise like Potsdam.[72]

At the end of March, Poincaré received news of the formation of an alliance between Serbia and Bulgaria for mutual defense and maintenance of the status quo in the Balkans. He suspected, correctly, that Russia had engineered this alliance and that it had an implicit aggressive purpose against Turkey.[73] He instructed the French ambassador in St. Petersburg, Georges Louis, to complain to Sazonov about his carrying out these negotiations without informing France and about his angling for an Austro-Italo-Russian entente. Sazonov must be warned that France would not be content with "*a posteriori* information" on such serious questions.[74] To Izvolsky, he pointed out that intrigues by Sofia or Belgrade must be nipped in the bud before Vienna had a chance to react to them.[75]

Yet the French foreign minister was less concerned about being entrapped by Russia's Balkan machinations than about being abandoned through a Russo-German rapprochement. His suspicions were aroused by the news that the Russian and German emperors were to meet in the Gulf of Finland on July 3. Poincaré asked Sazonov for formal assurance that no political questions would be discussed and for a public declaration of Russia's allegiance to the Triple Entente. Sazonov refused both requests.[76]

Poincaré decided he should go to Russia to iron out the various frictions that were disturbing the alliance. He wanted to improve the alliance in two aspects: cohesion and restraint. Its cohesion had suffered by Russian dallyings with the enemy and French indifference; more basically, by an underlying divergence of interest. Russia had to be restrained from Balkan adventures that might entrap France. As Poincaré saw it, both these goals could be met by closer ties and fuller consultation. Greater Russian confidence in French loyalty would reduce the Russian temptation to defect or mend fences with opponents; fuller and more frequent consultation would increase the French ability to influence Russian policy and thus to reduce its unilateral tendencies.

After arriving in St. Petersburg in early August, Poincaré had interviews with the Czar, Vladimir Kokovstov (the Russian premier), and Sazonov. When Sazonov showed him the text of the Serbo-Bulgarian treaty, Poincaré exclaimed, "But it's an agreement for war!" To Sazonov's assurance that Serbia and Bulgaria could not declare war or even mobilize without Russia's consent, Poincaré pointed out that Pan-Slav opinion would force Russia to acquiesce and to go to their aid if they met Austrian resistance.[77]

Far more significant were the exchanges that took place over the general obligations of the parties, in particular France, under the terms of the alliance. According to Sazonov:

> M. Poincaré considered it his duty to emphasize the point that public opinion in France would not permit the government of the Republic to decide on a military action for the sake of purely Balkan questions if Germany did not take part and if she did not provoke on her own initiative the application of the *casus foederis*. In this latter case we could certainly count on France for the exact and complete fulfillment of her obligations toward us.[78]

In a later statement to Izvolsky, Poincaré clarified this position by saying that if Austria attacked Serbia, and Russia went to the defense of Serbia, France would provide only "diplomatic support," but if Germany then intervened, that "would constitute the *casus foederis* and [France] would not hesitate a minute in meeting its responsibilities toward Russia."[79] This was an extension of the earlier statement, since it did not restrict the *casus foederis* to the case where Germany provoked it "on her own intiative." Moreover, it went beyond the text of the military convention of 1892, since that agreement applied only to a direct attack by Germany or by Austria supported by Germany; it did not mention a war that began with a Russian attack on Austrian forces that had invaded Serbia. Although this clarification verbally enlarged the French commitment, the enlargement hardly went beyond French interests, for it is difficult to imagine that France would have been passive in any Russo-German war, including one initiated by Russia. Enlargement of the French commitment in this way certainly contributed nothing to the restraint of Russia, but as noted above, Poincaré hoped to keep Russian initiatives under control by a process of close consultation. He could at least argue that if, after such consultation, France failed to approve a proposed Russian action, it was not responsible for the consequences.

Albertini comments:

> It is evident that, from the summer of 1912, there came into operation a broadened interpretation of the Franco-Russian alliance analogous to that which had transformed the nature of the Austro-German alliance in 1909. Just as Germany, during the Bosnian Annexation crisis, had taken her stand at the side of Austria, ready to aid her against Russia if the latter had made a *casus belli* of an Austrian attack on Serbia, reversing the practice of Bismarck in his alliances, so now, during the Balkan wars, France in a similar way promised armed assistance to Russia if Russia deemed it necessary to intervene against Austria in defense of Serbia, thus going beyond her obligations under the alliance as Poincaré himself had interpreted them in the spring of 1912.[80]

Poincaré's various statements during 1912 amounted to a change in the spirit if not the letter of the alliance. They permitted the alliance to be used for an offensive purpose. Russia could henceforth be confident that France would be at its side in any war involving Germany, regardless of the circumstances that brought the war about. Russia could also be sure of French diplomatic support in a crisis confrontation with Austria. The positive and supportive (rather than restraining) tone of Poincaré's statements implied that France approved Russian firmness in any dealings with the Central Powers. The allies moved closer through agreement on a naval convention and the start of naval staff talks in July 1912.

The change toward unequivocal French support of Russia may be partly explainable by the personality and opinions of Poincaré himself. Since the Agadir crisis, however, the view had become widespread within the French government that war with Germany was virtually inevitable. Thus entrapment by Russia was no longer a significant risk; abandonment was by far the greater danger.

France and Russia in the Balkan Wars

It cannot be said that France exercised much restraint on Russia during the Balkan Wars. Certainly, French restraining efforts were less energetic and less effective than the British, because they were more qualified by assurances of ultimate loyalty to the alliance. The burden of France's communications to Russia was a firm avowal of military support in case Russia should become involved in war with Germany. The effect of this message, had Russia been willing to countenance war between the two alliances, would have been to urge it forward. But Russia was not so willing, especially without full confidence in British support, and this reluctance, more than French admonitions, accounted for Russia's willingness to compromise. Whatever effective restraint was exercised by France was accomplished through the process of consultation and persuasion, not through threats of nonsupport.

Some of Poincaré's moves were clearly directed toward stiffening rather than restraining Russia. For instance, during the fall of 1912, Poincaré made repeated inquiries as to what steps Russia intended to take to counter the Austrian troop deployments. This moved Izvolsky to write Sazonov:

> While not long ago the French Government and press were inclined to accuse us of egging Serbia on and the dominant note was: "France does not mean to go to war for a Serbian port," at the present moment, on the contrary, our indifference towards the Austrian mobilization is viewed with amazement and unconcealed apprehensions.... The conclusion drawn is: either we do not sufficiently realize the aggressive attitude of Austria, or else, for some particular reason, we do not at this moment want to take counsel with France.... It is no longer the idea that France might see war forced on her for foreign interests that I shall have to combat, but rather the fear that we are too passive in a question touching the position and prestige of the whole *Entente*.[81]

There was another side to French diplomacy, however. Although Poincaré was firmly behind Russia and wanted Russia to be resolute on all issues involving a potential confrontation with the Triple Alliance powers, he sought to prevent or modify Russian moves that might escalate to such a confrontation. Thus he blocked a Russian plan to intervene as Bulgarian troops approached Constantinople and urged Russia to restrain Serbia. Russia did restrain Serbia, notably in persuading it to give up its demand for a port on the Adriatic.[82] Poincaré often spoke up for the use of concert diplomacy to settle points in dispute.[83] Behind all these "soft" positions, however, was a determination to preserve the cohesion and resolve of the entente at all costs. When there was tension between the "soft" and the "hard" elements of his policy, the latter usually prevailed.

When Poincaré became president of the republic in January 1913, he continued to exert a general direction on foreign policy despite the change in his formal role. His successors as foreign minister, Charles Jonnart and Pichon, modified his policies somewhat, however. Pichon, in particular, sought to improve relations with Germany and was less supportive of Russia in the Balkans than Poincaré would have wished.[84]

On the British side of the *Entente* triad, London exercised a restraining influence on Russia during the Balkan Wars, consistent with the understanding with Germany on collaborative mediation. This policy incurred some risk of alienating Russia and of exacerbating the persistent conflict between the two governments in Persia. Britain sought to alleviate this danger by appeasing Russia on Persian issues. The Foreign Office perceived Britain as more dependent on Russia than vice versa.[85] Nicolson wrote in October 1912, "This understanding is more vital to us than it is to Russia, though of course it is not necessary to let them know this."[86] That the Russians already knew it is clear from Sazonov's remark to Izvolsky (quoted earlier) that Russia could exploit Britain's need for the Entente to make gains in Persia.

Alliance Bargaining: Franco-Russian Military Conversations

Military conversations in the Franco-Russian alliance were sporadic and inconclusive until after the Russo-Japanese war. The war not only virtually destroyed the Russian navy but also weakened the army and revealed serious defects in its strategy, organization, and equipment. Formal joint talks were resumed in April 1906. At this meeting and at subsequent sessions, held annually after 1910, the French generals exerted constant pressure on the Russians to remedy their military deficiences, build more strategic railroads in western Russia, and commit themselves to early offensive action against Germany with maximum forces. The French were well aware of the German Schlieffen Plan for a two-front war, which called for sending the bulk of the German armies against France initially. Therefore, they were anxious that the Russians commit large forces early to the eastern front, and to the German portion of that front, to force the Germans to weaken their thrust to the west. The French used their financial leverage to forward this aim; thus French loans to Russia, in 1906 and subsequent years, usually came with the condition that the money be used to build strategic railways and to increase the strength of the army.

The French soldiers exploited the Russian dependence and bargaining weakness to correct what they regarded as a serious defect in the 1892 military convention: the requirement to mobilize if Austria or Italy alone mobilized. It was agreed that French and Russian mobilization would be required only if Germany or the entire Triple Alliance mobilized. If only Austria or Italy mobilized, the allies were obligated only to consult.[87] The Russians also agreed to regard Germany as the principal enemy and accepted the assumption that the main thrust of the German attack would be against France.

The Russians were in no position to make specific operational commitments for several years, owing to the sorry condition of their army. In 1906 and 1907 they refused to commit themselves to an early offensive against Germany and spoke of the need to maintain superiority against Austria. They resisted French pressures until 1910, when a major army reform plan got under way, stimulated by the humiliating defeat in the Bosnia crisis. Even then they made only vague promises to accelerate mobilization. Of course, the Russians had their own two-front war problem: should they send most of their forces against their primary but weaker enemy, Austria, or against their stronger but secondary enemy (but France's primary enemy), Germany? Alliance considerations counseled the latter, not only to meet alliance obligations and to discourage French abandonment (Russia did not become confident of French loyalty until 1912–13) but also to prevent France's defeat. From this perspective, it was in Russia's interest to slow down German military progress against France long enough to permit completion of Russian mobilization before the bulk of German forces could be transferred to the eastern front. But many in the Russian high command preferred to concentrate against the traditional enemy, Austria. At the joint conferences they resisted the French argument that Austria posed no serious threat to Russia, and they only gradually conceded to the French view that the defeat of Germany should have priority.

Of central importance to Russian planning and in the joint conferences were the Russian forces in the salient of Russian Poland, which lay between German East Prussia on the north and Austrian Galicia in the south. This position offered the opportunity of a decisive offensive into central Germany, toward Berlin. On the other hand, it posed the danger of being cut off and surrounded by a German-Austrian pincer from East Prussia and Galicia. The French were impressed by the offensive opportunity, but most of the Russian generals regarded such a maneuver as far too risky, given the superior speed of concentration of the Central Powers' armies.[88] In the Russian war plan devised in 1909–10, these exposed forces were to be pulled back to a more defensible line. This plan was conceived as a defensive hedge against the possibility of Germany's sending large forces against Russia at the beginning of the war. It was also a hedge against the uncertainty of French support in a German-Austrian-Russian war over a Balkan issue.[89] It avoided the risk that the forces in the salient would be cut off and encircled by a combined offensive of Austrian and German armies. It assumed that the German attack would initially push the Russian armies back but that they would counterattack successfully against both Germany and Austria after their mobilization was completed.[90]

The French general staff had also embraced a defensive strategy until 1911. Then, under General Joseph Joffre and his doctrine of "offense de l'outrance," it adopted an offensive plan. In the joint staff conference of August 1911, at the height of the Agadir crisis, the French persuaded the Russians to adopt it as well. Both allies were to throw all their forces into a simultaneous counterattack against Germany as soon as possible after the outbreak of war. The Russians agreed to undertake offensive action by the sixteenth day of mobilization, without waiting for the full concentration of their army on the twentieth day. They hoped thereby to tie down five or six German army corps, as the French desired. During this conference the French complained about the Russian withdrawal of troops from the Polish salient without consulting them. They would have preferred that the forces remain in western Poland as a springboard for an offensive westward.[91] The French misgivings were assuaged by a promise from General Sukhomlinov, the Russian war minister, that a Russian offensive against Germany would take place, and with a million men, rather than the seven to eight hundred thousand mentioned in the military convention.[92] The 1911 agreement was signed by the war ministers of the two governments, thus giving it a quasi-legal character.

These arrangements were confirmed in the July 1912 conference. General Joffre reiterated his prediction that Germany would commit most of its troops against France, leaving only a minimum holding force against Russia. He recognized that Russia would also have to deal with an Austrian attack, but he urged that the major effort be directed against Germany.[93] Although they concurred for the record, the Russian generals had just made changes in their war plan that did not jibe well with Joffre's words and the existing agreements for joint action. The modification said that in case of a German attack on France, Russia would send the larger part of its forces against Austria, on the assumption that it would still be possible to conduct a successful offensive in East Prussia with a reduced force.[94] This optimistic appraisal was based in turn on a perception of increasing French strength, which would force the Germans to reduce their deployments on the eastern front.[95]

With the help of financial pressure, however, the French were able to shift the Russian plan back in line with their own. At the joint staff conference of 1913, they successfully demanded that the eastward deployment of Russian forces, called for in the war plan of 1910, be changed to concentrate more troops around Warsaw.[96] The Russian planners agreed once again to give priority to an offensive into East Prussia. General Zhilinsky, the Russian chief of staff, reiterated that at least eight hundred thousand troops would be deployed against Germany and that an attack would be mounted on the fifteenth day of mobilization, even though an offensive in full strength would not be possible until the twenty-third day.[97]

Apparently, the French were able to exert leverage by linking their strategic desires to Russian financial needs. In April 1906 Russian acceptance of French changes in the military convention was probably helped by the fact that a huge French loan was being negotiated in Paris.[98] In June 1913 the French government offered Russia annual loans of four hundred to five hundred million francs, over five years, subject to two conditions: construction of more strategic railway lines in western Russia and an increase in the strength of the Russian army. The Russian prime minister, Kokovstov, accepted these terms but was able to modify the railways condition to strengthen the entire Russian railroad system, not just the strategic lines in the west as the French desired. A program to reorganize the army and to enlarge its peacetime strength by 39 percent was prepared in October 1913.[99]

Nevertheless, the role of French money can easily be exaggerated. Russian compliance in the staff talks can also be plausibly attributed simply to military weakness. Moreover, the French military negotiators had the strong and active support of their civilian leaders, especially Poincaré and Delcassé, and the Russian soldiers had developed a high respect for the French army and the French commitment to the alliance, especially after the introduction of three-year military service.[100]

The general pattern of bargaining in the staff conferences is that the French demanded and the Russians acquiesced. The French views were accepted on virtually all issues: identification of Germany as the main enemy and priority target in war, an early Russian offensive against Germany, and consultation rather than mobilization in response to Austrian or Italian mobilization alone. It is true that actual Russian war plans did not fully reflect these agreements; the Russians planned to send more forces against Austria than the French would have liked; the seven to eight hundred thousand men they had promised to deploy against Germany in the 1892 convention was half the Russian army at that time, but only one-fifth in 1913. Nevertheless, their concessions to the French views were substantial, and they did almost all the conceding. The costliest concession was their acquiescence to the French demand for a hasty attack in East Prussia, before the logistical mobilization of the attacking forces would be complete—a concession that contributed to the disastrous Russian defeat at Tannenberg. Of course, it can plausibly be argued that this concession was not coerced: it was in the Russian interest to engage the Germans quickly in order to enhance the chances of French victory in the west or delay a German victory. Still, it was a risky strategy that probably would not have been adopted in the absence of French pressures.

It is always a condition of any assertion about power, of course, that the target of the power is led to do something it would otherwise not wish to do. From that perspective, the French influence may have been less than it seems. By and large, the Russian military leaders wanted many of the same things the French did: greater Russian military efficiency, coordinated early offensives, even primary concentration against Germany. Certainly, they had nothing against the construction of more strategic railroads in western Russia. Their chief conflict on this point was not with the French generals but with their own finance ministers, who, like finance ministers everywhere, were reluctant to grant the military a larger share of the government's budget. The finance ministers resisted the tying of French loans to strategic railway construction and pushed for general railway improvement for economic reasons. Thus, to some extent, the Russian generals "mobilized" the French generals in the service of their own domestic ends.[101] If this required some verbal concessions about strategic doctrine, these need not be fully incorporated in private planning. It is noteworthy that neither party was given full access to the other's detailed war plans.

Although the military talks reflected mostly the common interest in effective coordination of planning, there was enough conflict to warrant considering them one of our bargaining cases. The French had strong interests in what they were demanding. They were moderately dependent on and highly committed to the alliance. These three factors combine to produce a bargaining power score of 6. Russia's score was 4, calculated from a low interest in resisting the French demands, high dependence, and moderate commitment. The scores predict a French bargaining success, to be attributed, apparently, to the superior French interest and the higher Russian dependence, on financial if not other grounds. France was the weaker party on grounds of commitment, so this factor cannot explain the outcome.

Cross-Cutting Alignments

During 1913 and early 1914 a certain blurring of alignments occurred, chiefly because of great-power involvement in the Ottoman Empire and an improvement in Anglo-German relations. The Balkan Wars had settled the fate of Turkey-in-Europe. Attention now shifted to Turkey-in-Asia, where alignments ran somewhat counter to the European alliances. France and Germany both had large economic stakes in Turkey and thus found themselves harmoniously committed to the empire's survival. Russia, as usual, had no such commitment, nor had Britain, whose strategic interests had largely shifted to Persia. But Britain was beginning to challenge France's traditional preeminence in Syria and the Lebanon.

Meanwhile, an Anglo-German detente had gotten under way, beginning with the Haldane mission in 1912 and further nourished by the two powers' collaboration during the Balkan Wars. Although the mission failed to resolve the naval rivalry, and the Germans failed to get their pledge of British neutrality, it led to negotiations on less momentous issues. In June 1913 Britain and Germany signed an agreement provisionally dividing between them the Portuguese colonies in Africa when they escaped the hold of the mother country, an event that was thought to be imminent. Later they agreed on a formula for British participation in the German project for a railroad across Turkey to Baghdad and the Persian Gulf. Naturally, these developments generated the usual anxieties in France and Russia about British allegiance. And they revived German hopes of British abstention in case of a continental war.

Alliance Bargaining: The Liman von Sanders Crisis

Entente solidarity received another blow in the Liman von Sanders affair of 1913–14. It became known in the fall of 1913 that a German general, Otto Liman von Sanders, had been appointed to head a German military mission to Turkey. His duties and powers were far-reaching, including the title of inspector-general of the Turkish army and the direct command of an army corps at Constantinople. The Russians immediately took alarm and declared the arrangement unacceptable, especially the general's control of Turkish forces in the capital. Kokovstov suggested to German Chancellor Bethmann that the general's command powers be relocated at some venue other than Constantinople, where Russian interests were less sensitively involved, but Bethmann refused. On November 25 Sazonov called on his allies for support, insisting that it was a test of the Triple Entente. The new Doumergue government in France gave a mixed response: while maintaining its loyalty to its treaty obligations, it warned against precipitate action and indicated that French policy would follow the British lead.

The British government was initially supportive, despite the fact that one of its men, Admiral Limpus, commanded the Turkish navy. The British drew back, however, when they researched the full extent of Limpus's powers and learned that he, not Liman von Sanders, commanded the Straits. At Grey's insistence, a joint démarche, which the three governments had earlier agreed on for delivery in Constantinople, was watered down to an oral "enquiry." Sazonov was furious at what he regarded as a British betrayal.

Sazonov now proposed a joint protest by the Entente powers in Berlin. The British and French governments both advised waiting, since the Germans were showing some willingness to compromise and a protest might stiffen them. Poincaré refused Sazonov's request to bring financial pressure against Turkey in view of the "great sacrifice" this would mean for French economic interests.[102] Britain and France inquired of Russia what action it proposed the three powers take "in case their common action at Berlin and at Constantinople should not have found the peaceful solution which they seek."[103] In particular, the British added, "did Russia contemplate pressing her demands to the point of a war with the Triple Alliance?" Sazonov replied, in substance, that the Entente powers, acting together, should be willing to risk war to avoid a major political defeat for Russia, but that a firm stand would not lead to war.[104] Of course, it was quite clear that Britain and France were not willing to take that risk.

Eventually, the Germans devised a compromise with some help from Grey: General Liman von Sanders would be promoted, and, by a technicality, this would divest him of command of the corps at Constantinople. Sazonov was hardly satisfied, but lacking wholehearted backing from his allies, he decided not to push matters further.

This crisis is different from the earlier ones in that two allies were about equally active in exercising restraint on the ally directly engaged with an adversary. Presumably, the total pressure brought against Russia was the sum of the British and French pressures. Therefore, in checking our hypotheses, we should add the British and French bargaining power scores and compare them to Russia's. Russia had a strong positive interest in frustrating the German plans. Since it had considerably repaired its military deficiencies, it was now only moderately dependent on the alliance. These factors, along with its moderate commitment to the alliance and the Entente, gave Russia a bargaining power score of 7. Britain and France had only weak interests in resisting the German plans, and they had negative interests in not antagonizing Germany. France had a common interest with Germany in strengthening Turkish finances and was in the middle of negotiations with Germany about the Baghdad Railway. The position of England was weak because of its role vis-à-vis the Turkish navy and because it wished to preserve its recently developed detente with Germany. Both France and Britain were moderately dependent on the alliance. France's commitment to it was strong (after Poincaré's declarations), and England's was weak. These considerations aggregate to a bargaining power score of 4 for France and 6 for Britain, a total of 10, compared to Russia's 7. According to our Hypothesis A, these scores predict that Russia will concede to its allies' restraining pressures, and that is a fair description of what occurred. Judging from what Sazonov said during the crisis, he was far more disillusioned, and apparently influenced, by the British restraining advice than by the French, which is consistent with Britain's higher bargaining power score. He was willing to compromise under pressure from both allies, and probably from England

[298]

alone, but probably not from France alone. England's leverage was greater because of its lack of explicit commitment.

As for the separate elements in bargaining power, the crucial one, apparently, was commitment, especially the absence of a firm British commitment. Comparative dependence did not play a role, since it is rated as equal for all parties. Nor did comparative interests, since Russia's interests at stake were far greater than those of either of its allies.

From this crisis and recent colonial agreements between Britain and Germany, Sazonov drew the conclusion that the entente with Britain needed strengthening. "One must recognize," he wrote, "that the peace of the world will only be assured when the Triple Entente, whose real existence is no more proved than that of the sea serpent, is transformed into a defensive alliance."[105] Therefore, he launched a diplomatic campaign to bring about this transformation. It drew the usual cool response from Britain, although it was supported by Nicolson in the Foreign Office and by Sir George Buchanan at the embassy in St. Petersburg. Grey and others pointed out that an Anglo-French-Russian alliance would merely encourage the "hotheads" in France and Russia; the uncertainty of the Entente would keep them cautious. Nevertheless, Grey felt that something should be done to reassure the Russians and to restore the solidarity of the Entente. Thus he was receptive when the Russians suggested, and the French supported, the idea of Anglo-Russian naval staff talks. Yet when the news of this decision broke in the French press, Grey worried that it might destroy the Anglo-German detente and lead to a resumption of the naval arms race. When a subordinate suggested that closer ties between Britain and Russia might help deter Germany, Grey retorted: "We are on good terms with Germany now and we wish to avoid a revival of friction with her, and we wish to discourage the French from provoking Germany." He added that Germany was dangerously frightened of Russia and that therefore the very power of the Triple Entente was a problem.[106] Grey found reasons to postpone the start of the talks to August 1914. Even so, the Russians were grateful and showed it by making several concessions in Persia. They also made concessions to France in negotiations for a large loan, agreeing to the condition that the strategic railway network called for in the military staff talks be completed within four years.[107]

By the summer of 1914 the Triple Entente had closed ranks from the comparative disarray of 1910–11. The Anglo-French naval agreement, the Anglo-Russian agreement on naval talks, and the Franco-Russian military conversations had each added an important new element of cohesion to the alliance. The French and the Russians were now reasonably sure of each other's and of Britain's loyalty. Although the Central Powers had made more progress in strengthening their armies, the overall balance of power still favored the Entente, and its advantage was increasing. The French, especially, were confident of military victory should war occur. The military modernization undertaken by Russia, although not yet complete, had advanced far enough to restore its pre-1904 military position and to make it willing, once again, to risk war to protect important interests.

Alliance Bargaining: The Triple Entente in the Sarajevo Crisis

France-Russia

By a historical accident, the two leading French decision makers—Poincaré and Viviani—happened to be in St. Petersburg on a state visit when the July 1914 crisis broke. Their presence was fortunate for alliance consultation but unfortunate for French decision making, especially when the two were on the high seas on the way home. As we have seen, the Austrians had delayed their ultimatum to Serbia until they could be sure the Frenchmen had set out on their homeward journey, hoping thus to prevent effective alliance coordination. But the Russians had broken the Austrian diplomatic codes, so they knew at least the main points of the planned ultimatum. Thus they had plenty of opportunity to discuss countermeasures with their guests and undoubtedly did so. Although they made no record of what they discussed, the British ambassador, Buchanan, was given a summary by Sazonov and by the French ambassador, Maurice Paleologue. According to Buchanan's report, agreement was reached on the following points: (1) peace and the existing balance of power would be preserved, (2) diplomatic action would be taken at Vienna to prevent Austrian demands on Serbia that would provide an excuse for intervention or violate Serbian sovereignty, and (3) the obligations of the Franco-Russian alliance were reaffirmed.[108]

Consistent with these points, Sazonov told the German ambassador, Count Pourtales, on July 21, as he had previously warned the Austrian ambassador, that Russia would not condone any infringement of Serbian sovereignty; it would not "allow Austria-Hungary to make any threats against Serbia or to take any military measures."[109] That same day, Poincaré told the Austrian ambassador, "Serbia has a very warm friend in the Russian people, and Russia has an ally, France."[110]

These warnings had no effect, for the Austrian ultimatum was delivered on July 23, just after the Frenchmen had left for home. Informed of its text by the Austrian ambassador on the morning of July 24, Sazonov responded, "You are setting fire to Europe!" Meeting for lunch with the French and British ambassadors immediately afterward, he heard from Paleologue that France would provide strong diplomatic support and would fulfill all its obligations under the alliance. Buchanan could give no similar pledge; indeed, he expressed his personal doubt that any British declaration entailing the use of force would be forthcoming.[111]

Later that day Sazonov presided over a ministerial council at which it was decided to ask Vienna to extend the time limit of the ultimatum, to urge Belgrade to be conciliatory within the limits of Serbian independence, and to request the Czar's permission for partial mobilization—of military districts opposite Austria—and for certain measures preliminary to general mobilization. After this meeting Sazonov advised the Serbian ambassador to exercise utmost moderation in replying to the ultimatum but assured him that Russia would permit no violation of Serbian sovereignty or independence.

The Czar authorized partial mobilization the next day, July 25, to be implemented, however, only when Sazonov thought it desirable for political reasons. Sazonov met again with the French and British ambassadors and informed them of this decision. Buchanan said he hoped Russia would not precipitate war by mobilizing before the British government had had a chance to work for peace. Sazonov replied that Russia would take no action until forced to do so. Paleologue said he had received authority from Paris to say that "France placed herself unreservedly on Russia's side."[112] Sazonov then turned to Buchanan: "And your government?" Buchanan replied that Britain could best play the role of friendly mediator that "might one day be converted into an ally." According to Buchanan, Sazonov retorted that Germany was convinced of British neutrality, that "her attitude was decided by ours. If we took our stand firmly with France and Russia there would be no war." The foreign minister concluded by declaring, "Russia cannot allow Austria to crush Serbia and become [the] preponderant power in the Balkans," and "secure of the support of France she will face all the risks of war." Thus the pattern of alliance support to Russia was established: England enjoining prudence and refusing commitment; France declaring unequivocal support. Buchanan warned his government that it would have to choose between "actively" supporting Russia or renouncing its friendship.[113]

French policymaking was hindered during the six days Poincaré and Viviani were at sea. Subordinate officials at the Quai d'Orsay were inexperienced and essentially let things drift.[114] Their superiors on shipboard were short of information but telegraphed fresh declarations of support to Sazonov. Once back in Paris, the leaders tried to shift the balance somewhat toward caution. For example, Viviani on July 29 urged Sazonov not to do anything that would give Germany a pretext for mobilization, though he added, as usual, that France would fulfill its obligations.[115]

But any restraining advice had been outrun by events. The Austrian declaration of war against Serbia on the July 28, and the subsequent bombardment of Belgrade, decided Sazonov to use his standby authority for partial mobilization. But his generals told him that mobilization against Austria alone would disrupt a later general mobilization against Germany.

A telegram from Bethmann on July 29, threatening German mobilization and war if Russian mobilization continued, finally convinced Sazonov that war with Germany was unavoidable. He then persuaded a vacillating Czar to order general mobilization on July 30.

French military officers apparently threw their weight on the side of general rather than partial Russian mobilization. On July 27, after partial mobilization had been authorized but before it was ordered, Marshall Joffre and General Messimy, the minister of war, urged the Russian military, in case of war, to take the offensive in East Prussia as soon as possible, as had been previously agreed on. Russian generals also persuaded Sazonov that partial mobilization, without consulting France, was a violation of the alliance and would give Germany an opening to demand a promise of neutrality from France.[116] Thus the partisans of general mobilization in Russia had available not only the technical argument about the incompatibility of partial with general mobilization, and the political argument that war with Germany had become inevitable, but also pressure from the French military and the supposed moral-legal weight of the alliance itself.

The French civilian leaders did not object to the Russian partial mobilization, nor were they consulted in advance, as required by existing agreements. They did counsel against provocative measures on the German frontier. But these counsels were over-balanced by the repeated assurances of support that the Russians heard from the French ambassador, Paleologue. The French government was also hindered by Paleologue's sloppy, if not deceptive, reporting. For example, Paleologue reported the final Russian decision for general mobilization on July 30 as a decision "to proceed secretly to the first measures of general mobilization."[117] This was interpreted in Paris as preliminary measures, not total mobilization. Paleologue entirely failed to report that the order had first been canceled, then reinstated. When finally, the morning of July 31, he reported the Russian decision straightforwardly as "general mobilization," the message was delayed twelve hours by a circuitous transmission route. Thus his superiors were in the dark about the imminence of Russian mobilization against Germany.[118] Consequently, their efforts to delay or discourage this momentous decision lacked vigor and precision, and they were surprised when they finally learned of it on the evening of July 31.

In sum, France did not issue a blank check to its ally, as Germany had done, but neither did it exercise much restraint. It was, of course, caught in the familiar supporting ally's dilemma of how to restrain without alienating the partner. A third "horn" of the dilemma was that in the event of war with Germany, it was in the French interest that the Russian army be ready for an immediate offensive into East Prussia. The Russian knowledge of this French interest helps explain the alacrity with which the Russians moved toward mobilization. The French leaders would have wished to favor the restraint option a little more, but they were foiled by the supportive bias of their ambassador, both in communicating their wishes to Russia and in informing them about Russian decisions. The result, in terms of Russian perceptions, if not quite in reality, was unqualified French support.

In our crude analytic scheme, this outcome has to be coded as a Russian "win" in the alliance interaction. Russia followed its own interests, took a firm stand, and was fully supported by France, even though France had little or no interest in Serbia per se. This is consistent with the allies' comparative bargaining power scores. The very strong interest, moderate dependence, and moderate commitment of Russia give it an aggregate score of 7, compared to France's 4, based on low interest, moderate dependence, and high commitment. Hypothesis A is supported. Of the specific dimensions of bargaining power, dependence cannot explain the outcome, since the parties are judged to be equally dependent. Otherwise, the outcome could be explained by the difference in commitment or in the interests engaged. Since the latter asymmetry was by far the greater, the greater effect probably should be attributed to interests. Thus Hypothesis 2 is strongly supported, Hypothesis 3 weakly so, and Hypothesis 1 rejected. Russia was not restrained by France—indeed, France did not seriously attempt restraint—primarily because of Russia's stronger interest at stake and secondarily because of France's strong commitment.

Britain-Russia

Sir Edward Grey's first instinct as the crisis broke was to reactivate the Concert of Europe. On July 24, the day after Austria presented its ultimatum to Serbia, he suggested to Germany that the four least interested powers—Britain, Germany, France, and Italy—undertake mediation between Austria and Russia and that the ultimatum's time limit be extended to permit this effort. From the outset, however, he was bombarded with conflicting pressures, from Russia and France on the one hand that he declare solidarity with them and from Germany that he exercise a restraining influence on Russia. Grey refused any outright commitment to his allies, citing his lack of authority and arguing that such a declaration of solidarity would only stiffen Germany and ruin his mediation efforts. He replied to Germany that he would restrain Russia if Germany restrained Austria. He hoped to resuscitate the Anglo-German cooperation of the Balkan Wars, not realizing that this was now impossible because of changed German preferences. The story of how Germany pretended to cooperate but double-crossed England has been told in the previous chapter. Grey appears to have been misled, until late in the crisis, by his incorrect belief that Germany was cooperating. He was also hampered by his ignorance of the dangers inherent in military mobilization.

[303]

By July 28, after the Austrian declaration of war and the collapse of talks between Austria and Russia, Grey began to lose confidence in Berlin and to move somewhat closer to Russia and France. Even on July 27, Alexander Benckendorff, the Russian ambassador, was able to report that there was "no foundation" to the German and Austrian belief that Britain would be neutral and that Grey's language supporting Russia had become "more unambiguous, noticeably more decided."[119] Grey made no attempt to hold Russia back from mobilizing; indeed, he said he "assumed" Russia would mobilize.[120] He was apparently oblivious to the provocative effect on Germany that Russian mobilization would have. His ambassador, Buchanan, was not, however, and he urged Sazonov to refrain from military measures that would "challenge" Germany.[121]

Several times before July 29, Grey had told the German ambassador, Lichnowsky, albeit in rather prolix diplomatic prose, that England could not be expected to stand aside if Germany attacked and attempted to conquer France. His ambiguity was dictated by his wish to avoid antagonizing Germany while there was still some hope for his mediation efforts. On the 29th, however, he called in Lichnowsky and, shifting to the mode of a "private communication," told the ambassador that in the event of war between Germany and France, "it would not be practicable [for the British government] to stand aside and wait for any length of time."[122] These were blunter words than he had previously used and, when added to other factors,[123] were apparently instrumental in triggering Bethmann's attempt to restrain Austria. But they came too late to stop the mobilization juggernaut.

SUMMARY: BARGAINING IN ALLIANCE MANAGEMENT

Table 8-1 summarizes the results of the bargaining case analysis as they bear on our hypotheses. The strongest finding is in the support found for Hypothesis A: that the outcome of alliance bargaining will favor the party with the greatest bargaining power, as calculated from an index of comparative dependence, commitment, and interests. Predictions derived from

Table 8-1. Alliance bargaining case results: Austro-German and Franco-Russian alliances

	Support			Nonsupport			Ambiguous		
	A-G	F-R	Total	A-G	F-R	Total	A-G	F-R	Total
Hypothesis A	9	9	18	2	0	2	1	1	2
Hypothesis 1	5	8	13	6	1	7	1	1	2
Hypothesis 2	7	7	14	4	2	6	1	1	2
Hypothesis 3	5	2	7	6	7	13	1	1	2

this indicator were correct in eighteen of the twenty-two cases, or 82 percent of the time. They were clearly incorrect in only two cases.[124] Two cases produced ambiguous, thus uncodable, results, because the effects of alliance bargaining could not be separated from the effects of simultaneous bargaining between adversaries. A more detailed compilation, showing the calculation of bargaining power scores for each case, may be found in Appendix B.

The results were less satisfactory in revealing the independent effects of the three variables in the bargaining power index. It became clear that the commitment variable was much less potent than had been assumed in giving it equal weighting with the other three. Only in seven of the cases was the least committed ally favored in the outcome, as hypothesized; in thirteen cases, the least committed got the worst of the bargaining, and two cases were ambiguous in this respect. This is suggestive, although not conclusive, evidence that our hypothesis about commitment—that it detracts from bargaining power—is incorrect.

If we set aside the commitment variable and look just at the other two factors—dependence and interests—only in seven cases was it possible to infer that one or the other was the determining factor: dependence in three cases, interests in four. In eleven cases, 50 percent of the sample, both dependence asymmetry and inequality of interests could have contributed to the outcome, but it was not possible to judge which was the more weighty. Outcomes were consistent with Hypothesis 1 (comparative dependence) in fourteen cases and inconsistent in six cases. They were consistent with Hypothesis 2 (comparative interests) in fifteen cases and inconsistent in five. In three cases, the outcome was inconsistent with both Hypothesis 1 and Hypothesis 2.

What is the significance of these findings? First, they inspire confidence that at least two of the three factors emphasized as components of bargaining power are in fact the central factors, the primary determinants of outcomes in alliance bargaining. Second, they show that the third factor—commitment—actually exerts much less impact on outcomes than hypothesized. Finally, they demonstrate that these factors can be isolated empirically and crudely measured and compared. They cannot be measured exactly enough to permit statistical treatment, but something worthwhile can be accomplished short of that.

Certain deficiencies and difficulties must be noted, however. In the crisis cases, it was sometimes not possible to separate the effects of bargaining with the ally from the effects of interaction with the adversary. Each ally, in a crisis, is interacting with the enemy as well as the partner, and its own behavior will necessarily be a response to both sets of pressures. Reality does not conform to the neat separation of the "alliance game" and the "adversary game" that is implied in most expositions of N-person game theory. That is, the sequence of (1) allies negotiating a payoff distribution, then (2) playing a game against an adversary which yields the joint payoff to be distributed, is rarely to be found in international political life. Usually, the two sets of negotiations occur simultaneously, or nearly so. I have dealt with that problem here by estimating from the context, where the evidence permitted, whether and to what extent either ally adjusted its policy to suit its partner. Where such a judgment was not possible—when the pressure from adversaries was so great as probably to overwhelm alliance bargaining effects—these cases (two of them) were coded as "ambiguous."

Although dependence and interests clearly are the most crucial variables, the data unfortunately do not permit us to isolate the effects of each, except in the few cases mentioned. Of course, this only reflects the fact that the ceteris paribus clause in the hypotheses did not hold most of the time. Strictly speaking, therefore, the hypotheses have not been fully tested in a scientific sense. Nevertheless, the results lend confidence to the common-sense prediction that both interest inequalities and dependence asymmetries are likely to influence bargaining outcomes between allies.

There was little difference between the Austro-German and Franco-Russian sets of cases. In the Austro-German set, nine of the twelve cases supported the amalgamated hypothesis (Hypothesis A), two did not, and one yielded ambiguous results. In only four cases was it possible to say that either relative interests or relative dependence was the primary determinant of the outcome: interests were determining in three and dependence in one. Both factors could have contributed to the outcome in five cases. In two cases, neither the interest nor the dependence hypothesis was supported.

The Franco-Russian cases supported Hypothesis A nine times out of the ten cases and yielded ambiguous results in one case. In only three cases could it be said that one of the three constituent factors in the bargaining power index was solely responsible for the outcome: interest inequality in one instance and asymmetrical dependence in two. In six cases, apparently both these variables contributed to the result.

The Anglo-French and Anglo-Russian cases yield similar results. Hypothesis A is supported in four cases involving Britain in bargaining with its entente partners. The outcomes could be explained by either Hypothesis 1 or Hypothesis 2—that is, they were consistent with both relative dependence and comparative interests. In a deviation from the pattern of the continental alliances, the outcomes were also fully consistent with relative commitments, as predicted by Hypothesis 3.

The next chapter again turns to the historical data for illumination of a different phenomenon: the alliance security dilemma.

[9]

Conclusions: Alliance Management

The principal purpose of this chapter is to summarize the findings from the case studies that bear on the alliance security dilemma, that is, how the pre-1914 states dealt with their fears of abandonment and entrapment. A related purpose is to explore the interplay between alliance and adversary relations. The final section covers several subsidiary themes, including the role of alliance norms and the tension between concerts and alliances.

The theory of the alliance security dilemma holds that states in an alliance are subject to two opposing fears: the fear of abandonment and the fear of entrapment. Often, but not always, reducing one of these fears incurs the cost of heightening the other. Thus the risk of abandonment may be eased by increasing one's support of or tightening one's ties to the ally, but this heightens the risk of entrapment in the ally's quarrels with its opponent. Vice versa, reducing the risk of entrapment by dissociating oneself from the ally may provoke it to abandon the alliance.

Fears of abandonment or entrapment are generic in an anarchic and multipolar system. Allies are free to realign at will, their interests are diverse, and they may become highly dependent on each other. Flexibility of alignment maximizes the probability of abandonment; diversity of interests increases the cost of entrapment. Dependence heightens both the potential cost of abandonment and the probability of entrapment. Thus the alliance security dilemma tends to be severe in a multipolar system.

The several dimensions of the alliance security dilemma were discussed at length in Chapter 6. Here they may be summarized according to whether they affect the cost or the probability of abandonment and entrapment. The cost of abandonment turns largely on a state's own dependence on the alliance; the likelihood of abandonment is mostly a function of its ally's dependence and commitment, although the state's estimate of this likelihood must also consider the ally's recent behavior. The overall risk of abandonment, obviously, involves a combination of the cost and probability estimates. The fear of entrapment, likewise, is a product of costs and likelihood. The costs of entrapment are a function of the divergence of one's own interests from those of the ally, and the estimated cost of war; the likelihood of entrapment turns mainly on the severity of the ally's conflict with its adversary and its confidence in one's own support in that conflict, as well as on one's own degree of commitment to the alliance. Of course, "fears" of abandonment or entrapment will depend on statesmen's perceptions of these variables.

Fears of Abandonment in the Triple Entente

The fear of abandonment was more prominent in the Franco-Russian alliance and the Triple Entente than in the Triple Alliance. There were two primary reasons: the vagueness of the commitments between Great Britain and the other two members of the Entente, and the divergence of particular interests between Russia and France. Lacking an explicit alliance pledge, England and France, but especially England, worried constantly about each other's fidelity. France, although it had the benefit of a written contract with Russia, also was concerned about abandonment by Russia, because Russia's direct conflicts with Germany were considerably less than France's own. Russia might just decide to sit out a war that began on the Franco-German border. Russia was less anxious about being deserted, apparently because it recognized France's high level of dependence. Late in the period Russia became somewhat concerned about Britain's loyalty.

Worries about Russian defection prompted France to increase its commitment in 1899, 1901, 1902, and 1912. In 1899 the purpose of the alliance was generalized to cover "maintenance of the balance of power." This revision in effect broadened the *casus foederis* implicitly to include virtually any aggressive move by the alliance's adversaries and hence broadened the commitments of both parties. In 1901 and 1902 the scope of the alliance was expanded to cover the Far East, and its domain or target was extended to include Britain. Since Russia was more involved than France in the Far East and more in conflict with Britain, the changes chiefly operated to increase French commitments and risks and to increase the alliance's benefits to Russia.

The Russo-German talks at Potsdam in 1910 renewed French fears of Russian abandonment, especially since the French knew the Russians resented their lack of support in the Bosnia crisis of the previous year. French fears were reinforced by the Russian pressure for concessions (implicitly portrayed by Russia as "tit for tat" for Bosnia) during the Agadir crisis. After Agadir, French fears of abandonment by Russia increased still more, especially as the idea took hold that war with Germany was virtually inevitable. In 1912 Poincaré worried about Russian support of Italy in North Africa and signs of a new Austro-Russian detente. His fears were heightened by the dramatic increase in Russian military strength after 1911 which reduced Russian dependence on the alliance. His reaction was to strengthen the French commitment to Russia and to insist on no dealings with opponents without prior agreement.

Repeated French requests to transform the Anglo-French entente into an alliance reflected a persistent worry about British abandonment. Such concern became especially strong during the Haldane mission in 1912, since the French knew the Germans were seeking a neutrality agreement. These worries were largely behind the French insistence on a diplomatic formalization of the naval division of labor. Still, after 1904, the French were more confident of British than of Russian loyalty, chiefly because Britain no longer had the German option, whereas Russia did. The quite different behavior of the two allies in 1914—the Russians leaping into war before they were prepared, while the British cabinet dithered—indicates that the French may have misplaced their confidence.

Russian leaders were quite worried about French reliability during the latter half of the 1890s, mostly because of internal developments in France: the Dreyfus affair, governmental instability, and the increasing tendency of the French press to favor a rapprochement with Germany. These concerns did not move them to support France in the Fashoda crisis, however. Their fears must have been eased by the alliance revisions of 1899, 1901, and 1902, increasing French commitments. The Russians saw France's passivity during the Bosnian crisis as a virtual renege on its alliance obligations, however. They responded by moving closer to Germany at Potsdam, apparently preferring to hedge against a collapse of the alliance rather than attempt to strengthen it. Their failure to support France during the Agadir crisis is consistent with this conjecture: not only did they withhold support, but they urged the French to make more concessions to Germany. Russian confidence in France increased markedly during the Balkan Wars because of Poincaré's strong and explicit reiterations of French loyalty.

Britain's loyalty to the entente with Russia was strongly demonstrated in the Bosnia crisis; by its behavior in Persia, Russia showed that it harbored few worries about British defection. It developed doubts during the Liman von Sanders crisis, however, and sought to alleviate them by asking for an upgrading of the entente to alliance. In lieu of this, and being sensitive to the Russian worries, Grey agreed to naval talks.

British fears of abandonment by France were particularly intense during and immediately after the Morocco crisis of 1905. They inhibited Grey's attempts to restrain France during the crisis. On a few occasions he attempted to persuade France to make concessions, but he quickly withdrew these suggestions when the French protested. Grey's fear of abandonment was stronger than his fear of entrapment. The fear of abandonment was all the greater (and for the French as well) in view of the vagueness of their mutual commitment. Since they were tied only by the uncertain and still-developing links of interest and expectation, their alliance security dilemma was severe.

In the aftermath of the crisis the newly awakened sense of threat from Germany combined with the newness and vagueness of the Entente Cordiale to produce an almost pathological fear of offending France by any sign of friendliness toward Germany. Germany was kept at arm's length; its overtures were rejected. The British were afraid that if France became disillusioned with the Entente, it might very well listen seriously to the German siren calls for a continental league. During the Agadir crisis these fears seemed to have diminished; Grey seemed less worried about French defection than that France would give away British interests in negotiations with Germany. (Of course, this latter behavior would be a kind of abandonment.) Still, Grey chose to send Lord Haldane to Germany for naval talks in 1912, rather than going himself, which "might arouse suspicion and distrust in Paris."[1]

The British also worried about Russian defection. The Czar's willingness to sign alliance agreements with Germany in 1904 and 1905, even though they were disavowed by his government, indicated the reality of the danger. The Foreign Office also feared a renewal of the Russian threat to India if Russia became dissatisfied with the Entente.[2] Britain's response to its concern about Russian abandonment was to appease Russia in Persia and to agree, reluctantly, to naval talks. On the whole, however, the British were less concerned about Russia than about France. One reason was that their strategic interest in Russia was lower. That is, a German alliance with or defeat of Russia was seen as less damaging to British security than a German defeat of or alliance with France. Another reason was France's comparative weakness: Russia could probably survive if it lost its allies; France could not and therefore was more likely to defect if it feared losing them.[3]

That Britain was more fearful of losing its allies than they were of losing it can be attributed to the greater British sense of dependence. Britain was doubly dependent on its ententes: not only for security against the German threat but also for the continued security of its empire against possible depredation by its own partners. If the ententes were to collapse, Britain would once again have to face colonial challenges from France and Russia, and it doubted whether it was up to the challenge, especially from Russia.[4] In other words, Britain's alternatives to the ententes (e.g., isolation or alignment with Germany) were rendered singularly unattractive because they would be accompanied by the reemergence of conflicts that the ententes had submerged.

It is noteworthy that even though British fears of abandonment were greater than French and Russian fears of British defection, it was Britain that persistently refused to transform the Entente into an alliance, despite its partners' importunings. The explanation for this anomaly is to be found, no doubt, in domestic politics and traditions. Formal alliance with a European power for other than colonial purposes was simply unacceptable to Parliament and public opinion.

Fears of Abandonment in the Austro-German Alliance

The alliance security dilemma was less severe in the Austro-German alliance. Because of the high degree of common interest between the partners and their lack of alliance alternatives after 1904, there was little reason for either to contemplate defection. Still, fears of abandonment arose at several critical points. During the Bismarckian period Austria felt abandoned when Germany failed to support it in its Balkans disputes with Russia, but this feeling did not extend to worries about outright German defection or realignment; Bismarck's protestations of loyalty in the event of direct Russian attack on Austria were believed. The immediate effect of Bismarck's fall and the dropping of the Reinsurance Treaty was to increase Austrian confidence in German support. This confidence was somewhat dissipated, however, by the Russo-German rapprochement that began about 1894. The Austrians also worried about British loyalty under the Mediterranean Agreements after the Russians announced they would maintain a naval presence in the Mediterranean; the British themselves indicated they could not challenge the combined Russian and French fleets. These doubts about the loyalty of its two primary allies led Austria, first, to request a firmer alliance commitment from Germany; when this failed, it negotiated a far-reaching detente with Russia in 1897. In short, fear of abandonment produced, ultimately, a move away rather than toward the ally.

Austrian confidence in German support received a big boost from the dramatic German démarche to Russia during the Bosnia crisis of 1908–9 and from Moltke's broadening of the German alliance commitment. It declined again with the German promise to Russia at Potsdam not to support Austrian aggressive designs in the Balkans. It declined further with the

German attempts to restrain Austria during the Balkan Wars. Although confidence was again somewhat restored by the firm German support received in the 1913 Albanian crisis, Berchtold still feared in July 1914 (before receiving his blank check) that if Austria attacked Serbia, Germany might "leave us in the lurch."[5] In all these cases, however, the Austrian doubts applied only to the German willingness to support Austrian aggressive ventures in the Balkans, not to the ultimate German commitment to defend Austria against aggressive attack.

German worries about Austrian defection were minimal during Bismarck's chancellorship. Although the Austrians grumbled about getting no support on Bulgaria and other issues in the Balkans, Bismarck knew they had no real alliance alternatives. After Toulon, in 1893, the Germans became somewhat concerned about possible British defection, and consequently Austrian defection, from the Mediterranean Agreements. After the Algeciras conference in 1906, which dramatized their political isolation in Europe, they worried more about Austrian abandonment, not because it had become more likely but because of their increased dependence on Austria. With the defection of Italy, Austria was their only reliable ally. The Anglo-Russian entente of 1907 further augmented the Germans' dependence on Austria and their worries about losing it. This time, their response was to increase their own alliance commitment, by firmly supporting Austria in the Bosnia crisis and by broadening the alliance *casus foederis*. For about two years, during Bülow's tenure at Berlin and Aehrenthal's in Vienna, Austria was able to seize the leadership of the alliance, owing to the German sense of dependence. Kiderlen, during his short term as German foreign minister, seized it back again, professing not to be worried about Austrian defection. But the fears resumed when Austria sat on its hands during the Agadir crisis and later when it complained about being restrained during the Balkan Wars. There followed the unequivocal German support in the October 1913 crisis and then the decisive blank check on July 5, 1914.

German and Austrian worries about abandonment by Italy were chronic during the life of the Triple Alliance. The result was a series of concessions to Italy in periodic renewals of the alliance. Germany, in particular, steadily increased its commitment to support Italian interests against France in North Africa. Austria made fewer concessions, since it had fewer illusions about Italian loyalty and considered Italy as likely to be an enemy as an ally in war. Germany and Austria continued renewing the alliance with Italy long after they knew Italy would not be with them in a war; a facade of alliance had some value for deterring adversaries and for preventing Italy from throwing in its lot entirely and publicly with France.

Our theory predicts that when fears of abandonment dominate fears of entrapment, the state will move toward its ally, increasing its general commitment or indicating support on a specific issue, in order to enhance the attractiveness of the alliance to the partner. A possible exception would be when the state believes its partner is irrevocably in the process of defecting; then the state might be motivated to defect itself and seize its best available alternative. In a less drastic variant, fears of abandonment might so depress the value of the alliance as to motivate the state to negotiate a settlement with its opponent rather than increase its solidarity with its ally.

By and large, the cases support the main hypothesis, that fears of abandonment produce movement toward the ally. There were only one or two instances of the counterhypothesis—for example, Austria's negotiation of detente with Russia in 1897 as German support wavered. There were some ambiguous episodes, such as Russia's accommodation of Germany at Potsdam and its nonsupport of France in the Agadir crisis after France had leaned toward Germany during the Bosnia crisis in 1909. These cases are ambiguous because it is unclear whether Russia was motivated by fears of French defection. In most instances, a state that feared its partner's defection increased its support. Even when abandonment was clearly imminent or under way, as with Italy and Rumania, the response of the defectors' allies was to do everything possible to retain their allegiance, or at least its appearance.

Generally, statesmen's fears of abandonment by allies went well beyond the actual possibilities. Except for the case of Italy, there was no real likelihood of defection by any of the major powers. Such fears were exaggerated, perhaps, because they arose from apprehension of the high cost of losing an ally more than from a sober assessment of its likelihood. The cost of an ally's defection could be estimated with some confidence, since it involved detraction from one's own interests, whereas its likelihood, a function of the ally's interests, was inherently uncertain and therefore was consigned to worst-case analysis. A consequence of the exaggerated fears of abandonment was that almost all statesmen underestimated their own bargaining power.

Loyalty Reputations

Statesmen often expressed concern for their general loyalty reputations. Here the concern went beyond worries about abandonment by present allies, to fear of losing general alliance value or losing others' trust generally, consequently making it difficult to negotiate agreements with anyone in the future. As one example among many, Sir Edward Grey warned during the Algeciras conference that failure to support France in a war with Germany would lead to "a general feeling . . . that we had behaved meanly and left France in the lurch. Russia would not think it worth while to make a friendly arrangement with us in Asia."[6]

In the Russian ministerial council of July 24, 1914, which decided to authorize partial mobilization against Austria, Sazonov justified the move by saying that after the "immense sacrifices" Russia had made on behalf of the Balkan Slavs, if she now abandoned "her historic mission," she would lose "all her authority" and allow Russian prestige in the Balkans "to collapse utterly."[7]

Do states actually gain or lose loyalty reputations by their supportive or nonsupportive behavior? By and large, Jonathan Mercer's finding is reinforced: states acquire reputations for disloyalty more easily than for positive loyalty.[8] Three examples of the former involve England, Germany, and France. In 1893 England appeared to back down to France in a crisis over Siam after having requested German assistance. The German government took this as evidence of England's unreliability and worthlessness as an ally. In 1901 Germany interpreted a previous agreement with Britain about maintaining the integrity of China as excluding Manchuria from "China." That contributed to the British lack of faith in Germany and rejection of a German alliance proposal. After the French government fired its foreign minister, Delcassé, on German demand, in 1905, Lord Lansdowne said the incident had "undoubtedly shaken peoples' confidence in the French nation."[9]

Although these and other examples confirm that loyalty reputations can be damaged, there is little evidence that the damage is long-lived or that the damaged state suffers much. If a state acquires a reputation for disloyalty, its ally does not react by leaving the alliance. It may, however, punish the disloyal state by refusing support the next time the latter needs it. Russia, for example, withheld support from France in the Agadir crisis explicitly as a payback for the French abstention in the Bosnia crisis. These tit-for-tat exchanges permit the exaction of punishment around the political periphery of the alliance, thus leaving its military core, or basic commitment, intact.

Mercer's finding that reputations for alliance disloyalty are more easily acquired than reputations for loyalty has implications for the alliance security dilemma. It implies that a danger of entrapment is easier to correct than a danger of abandonment. A reputation for not living up to commitments is useful for avoiding entrapment; the opposite reputation is desirable for avoiding abandonment. Since a positive reputation is more difficult to develop than a negative one, the risk of abandonment is less easily reduced than the risk of entrapment. This implication is supported in our cases, which show that decision makers are usually more worried about being abandoned than about being entrapped.

Fears of Entrapment

The fear of entrapment, although inescapably present for systemic reasons, was less overtly prominent among pre-1914 European statesmen than the fear of abandonment. This asymmetry was especially marked in the years immediately before the outbreak of war in 1914: rising tension—that is, increasing probability of war—increased the fear of being isolated and defeated more than the fear of war costs. Indeed, the widespread belief that war was inevitable took most of the edge off the fear of entrapment: if war was going to happen in any case, it was better that it break out over the ally's interests than over one's own, since that would at least ensure the engagement of the ally's forces. The common prediction of a short war also tended to reduce cost estimates and thus to ease entrapment anxieties.

Still, throughout the period the divergence of the allies' particular interests provided materials for entrapment fears. The French disliked the prospect of fighting for Russian interests in the Balkans and sought to minimize the risk by insisting (with little success) on consultation before any Russian initiatives there. The Russians worried about French adventures in North Africa and especially about the possibility that France might exploit the alliance to recover Alsace-Lorraine. Britain had most reason to fear entrapment, since both its allies had revisionist aims, whereas it did not. Divergence between German and Austrian interests in the Balkans and the Near East was a constant source of entrapment worries for the Germans.

Our theory predicts that when fears of entrapment dominate fears of abandonment, states will either loosen their general alliance commitment or withhold support from their allies in the latter's specific disputes with an adversary. There were no instances, in our cases, of the first type of response: all revisions of general alliance commitments were in the direction of tightening, not loosening.[10] There were several examples, however, of failure to support the ally in specific disputes or crises—Russia at Fashoda, Italy in both Morocco crises, France in Bosnia, Russia in the Agadir crisis—and other instances when the ally provided only lukewarm support—England and Germany (to Russia and Austria, respectively) during the Balkan Wars; France (to Russia) and England (to Japan) during the Russo-Japanese war; Germany (to Austria) in the Bulgarian crisis in the 1880s. All these instances are consistent with the theory's predictions.

We can only speculate as to why there were so few instances of reducing commitment by treaty revision and so many examples of withholding support in specific crises. Revising a treaty commitment is a rather momentous act that bears directly on the core of the alliance: the parties' promise to each other and their expectations concerning future support. States no doubt shy away from such formal loosening for fear of creating a perception that the alliance is unraveling. To withhold support to the ally in a crisis has less drastic future implications because it may be motivated simply by the withholder's lack of particular interest in the issue. Moreover, the basic military commitment of the alliance is not in question, merely its political halo. Nonsupport on the present occasion can usefully warn of less support in the future, but the signal can be modulated by reassurances of loyalty to the basic commitments.

Overall, the alliance dilemma was less severe in the Triple Alliance than in the Triple Entente. Because of the high degree of common interest between Germany and Austria and their lack of alliance alternatives after 1904, there was little objective reason for either to contemplate defection. Germany worried about being entrapped by Austrian adventures in the Balkans and occasionally attempted to dissociate itself, but with little success in view of its well-known strategic interest in Austria. Italy, of course, was another matter. It had the French and British alternatives throughout the period and actually exercised them partially in 1900 and 1902. The existence of these options yielded Italy enormous bargaining power in successive renewals of the alliance treaty. Yet Italy did not present a serious allliance dilemma to its partners because it did not command enough resources to make its defection a disastrous loss.

Some Variations

There were a few instances when the supporting ally acted contrary to the theory's predictions. France provides a good example. Poincaré dealt with his entrapment fears not by dissociating France from Russia but by moving closer and insisting on close consultation. He believed dangerous Russian initiatives could best be guarded against by personal persuasion, from a background of firm commitment, rather than by threats of defection or nonsupport. This attitude may be explainable in terms of a sense of high dependence, which made Poincaré worry more about abandonment than about entrapment.

But it is worth noting that France was entrapped in the Balkans as much by the German military's response to the Franco-Russian alliance as by the alliance itself. The French were entrapped in any Austro-Russian quarrel by the Germans' decision to implement their alliance with Austria by attacking France. The Schlieffen Plan weakened the credibility of any French attempt to restrain Russia by threatening nonsupport and rendered illusory any French hope of abstaining from an Austro-Russian war. Entrapment was virtually inescapable.

In another variant, the French military and some civilian leaders positively desired to be entrapped by a Russian adventure in the Balkans: this would at least ensure that the Russians would be involved in the war from the beginning. Similar thoughts were voiced by German military figures regarding the desirability of the war's breaking out over Austrian rather than German interests. In these cases, however, the dominant concern was that of abandonment, not entrapment, so the theory is not contradicted: the actors simply were willing to accept entrapment as the price of insurance against abandonment.

The point can be generalized: when allies have a common enemy, the alliance security dilemma is softened by the unlikelihood of abandonment and the low cost of entrapment—since a war precipitated by either ally would be fought in the other's interest as well. When they face different enemies, the dilemma is more acute, since each is more likely to stand aside when the other is attacked, and the cost of being entrapped is higher because they do not share each other's interests. The dilemma is somewhat eased in this situation, however, as in the examples given above, because entrapment in the ally's war simultaneously reduces the risk of abandonment by getting the ally's forces engaged.

Still another wrinkle is provided by the British and French fears about being pulled into the Russo-Japanese war. Rather than dissociating themselves from their allies, they aligned with each other. Thus each acquired an excuse for not intervening, should their intervention be requested by the ally.

A variation on the fear of abandonment is the fear that the ally will give away some of one's own interests in negotiations with its adversary. This concerned the British government, for example, during both Moroccan crises: it worried that France might grant Germany a slice of Morocco or a naval port on the Morocco coast, to the detriment of British commercial or strategic interests. Consistent with our theory, Lansdowne in 1905 sought to reduce this danger by moving toward France, suggesting that the two governments "discuss in advance any contingencies by which they might in the course of events find themselves confronted."[11]

Easing the fear of abandonment does not necessarily mean accepting an increased risk of entrapment; it merely requires adapting one's policy more closely to the ally's desires. The notion of the alliance security dilemma evokes an image of one ally being involved in a crisis or dispute with an adversary over an issue in which the other ally has little interest. The latter provides reluctant support, fearing abandonment if it does not. But it may be that the supporting ally is more desirous of a firm stand than the ally that is directly involved, and that the latter fears abandonment if it does not make such a stand. An example is Austria, after having received the blank check from Germany in July 1914. Berchtold said on July 8, "I could see that Germany would interpret any compromise on our part as a confession of weakness, which would not remain without repercussions on our position in the Triple Alliance and the future policy of Germany."[12] Thus the trade-off is not necessarily between the risks of abandonment and entrapment but, more broadly, between the risk of abandonment and the costs of tailoring one's policy to the ally's wishes. The point is illustrated in reverse by the French and British relationship during the 1930s: when France feared abandonment by Britain, the perceived remedy was not to accept a greater risk of entrapment but to join Britain in a policy of appeasement of Germany.[13]

Incitement

Abandonment and entrapment are not the only alliance risks that states have to manage. Another is the danger of incitement. Incitement may be defined as encouraging two other states to fight, one of the others being an ally and the other an opponent, and then withdrawing one's own support to the ally after the fight begins. Britain was often accused of playing this game, tricking others into "pulling its chestnuts out of the fire." Incitement is, obviously, a form of abandonment, related to buck-passing.[14]

There was only one good example in the cases of actual incitement: German encouragement of both Russia and Japan to go to war in the early 1900s. The German aims were to stimulate Anglo-Russian antagonism, block French efforts to create a French-Russian-English alliance, and keep Russia tied down in the Far East and away from Europe.[15] However, the fear of being incited, or suspicion of incitement motives in others, occurred several times. For example, in the 1880s and 1890s Germany and England mistrusted each other's overtures for alliance for fear of "being used as a cat's-paw."[16] The Germans suspected Salisbury of trying to precipitate a continental war by his proposals to partition Turkey; Salisbury said in 1898, "The one object of the German emperor since he has been on the throne has been to get us into a war with France."[17]

However unscrupulous, incitement is a logical strategy in a multipolar system. When one faces several possible opponents, it may seem desirable to trick two of them into "bleeding each other white." War between others removes them as threats to the self and also magnifies one's own bargaining power over them. The tension between the fear of incitement and the need for allies is one of the central tensions in a multipolar system and a source of domestic division. An especially striking example is Germany's pursuit of an alliance with England around the turn of the century while demanding ultratight commitments to guarantee against English "perfidy."

A mild kind of incitement is to foster conflict with others short of war, thus blocking their alignment with each other and increasing their dependence on oneself. This tactic might be called political incitement. Despite much talk of a peaceful division of the Balkans between Austria and

Russia, Bismarck really wanted to maintain a moderate degree of tension between them; he showed the greatest alarm when any serious settlement proposals were made.[18]

Fostering a moderate degree of tension between other states was one of Bismarck's general goals in manipulating the system. Langer comments: "Bismarck's object was not to precipitate a conflict, for he regarded any war between two great powers as a menace to Germany. His ideal, rather, was to keep the relations between England and France and between England and Russia in a certain state of rivalry or tension sufficient to prevent their uniting against Germany and sufficient to make them look to Germany for support and friendship."[19]

An antidote to the fear of incitement is to get the ally committed before committing oneself; then one need not worry about being left alone in the field. Of course, if both allies play this "Alphonse and Gaston game," nothing gets done. England and Austria played it repeatedly in the Near East before the turn of the century when they were tacit or formal allies. In September 1886, for example, it seemed that Russia might take action against Bulgaria. Bismarck advised Austria to "take great care not to rush matters, but so to maneuver that the initiative should come from England's side." The Austrians should "wait until they hear the English cannon."[20] One contemporary observer remarked that the situation was "one in which Austria declares that she will be delighted to take the first step, as Lord Salisbury proposes, if Lord Salisbury will begin by taking the second."[21] Note that the idea here is not to incite or pass the buck to the ally but to guard against the ally's pursuing such a strategy.

A similar defense against incitement or buck-passing is to make one's own commitment formally dependent on prior action by the ally. Thus the Soviet treaty with Czechoslovakia in 1935 committed Russia to act only after France, Russia's other ally, came to Czechoslovakia's defense.

This game may be formally represented as "stag hunt," as in Figure 9-1.

Figure 9-1. Stag hunt

	C	D
C	4, 4	1, 3
D	3, 1	2, 2

(numbers are ordinal; 4 is highest)

Both parties prefer cooperating (CC) over defecting while the other co-operates (DC), but they are unsure of each other's preferences. Each fears that the other may prefer to defect, that is, to pass the buck to the cooperating ally (DC). Therefore, each chooses to hang back, play D provisionally, and commit to a cooperative strategy (C) only after the partner does. Of course, that risks that neither commits and nothing gets done (DD), but that is the price to be paid for mistrust.*

The Politics of Restraint

Although the primary purpose of most alliances is to gain security against an opponent, an important secondary goal is to restrain or control the ally. Indeed, it can and has been argued that this is the primary function of many alliances and the leading motive for entering into them in the first place.[22] The idea appears occasionally in the utterances of statesmen, as in Bismarck's explanation why it was better for Germany to ally with Austria than with Russia in 1879: Germany could be the "rider" to Austria's "horse," whereas Russia, with its strength and its alliance option with France, would be the dominant partner.[23] And we are familiar, in more recent times, with the idea that a secondary purpose of NATO is to control Germany.

At first glance, this argument seems illogical. Restraint of the ally is a bargaining problem, and success in bargaining requires leverage. Leverage over any state would seem to be maximized before one has allied with it; afterward one has less to offer. True, one can threaten to leave the alliance if the ally misbehaves, but why is that threat any more effective than holding out the prospect of alliance with the state if it behaves? As A. J. P. Taylor remarked, "Bismarck's strongest weapon with Austria-Hungary was to threaten to repudiate his alliance—a curious reason for making it."[24]

There are at least three possible solutions to this puzzle. First, an alliance increases the ally's security. Feeling safer, the ally may be less aggressive, less inclined to run risks, and more willing to make concessions to its

---

* In the stag hunt, as described by Kenneth Waltz following Rousseau, several hunters surround a stag. If they all keep their positions, the stag will be caught. There are rabbits in the neighborhood, however, and although each hunter prefers venison to rabbit meat, he is not certain about his buddies' preferences. Therefore, in order to be sure of getting at least something to eat, each goes after a rabbit and the stag escapes. See Waltz, *Man, the State, and War: A Theoretical Analysis* (New York: Columbia University Press, 1959), pp. 167–68.

opponent. The dynamic involved here is the opposite of entrapment: instead of giving the partner the courage to confront or attack its opponent, dragging in its allies, the alliance pacifies the ally by satisfying its security needs. Thus one of Britain's objects in making its alliance with Japan in 1902 was to restrain, in the words of I. H. Nish, "a willful Japan whose strength was acknowledged but whose self-control was thought to be doubtful."[25] The British thought that by increasing the security of Japanese interests, the alliance would reduce Japan's incentives to attack, at the same time reducing the likelihood that Japan would make excessive concessions to Russia.

A second explanation is that the alliance makes the ally dependent in some degree. It is dependent on the alliance for the increased security it now enjoys or perhaps for the reduction in arms expenditures the alliance made possible. This dependence logically is no greater than the ally's need or desire for the alliance before it was made and thus would seem to yield no greater leverage to the partner. But there are psychological and political consequences of alliance formation which make the costs of losing the alliance, once it is formed, somewhat greater than its anticipated value beforehand. Policies will have been adjusted to alliance requirements, and readjustment would be costly. Commitment to the alliance will have increased the values subjectively associated with that alliance and reduced the attractiveness of alternatives. Formation of the alliance may also have damaged some alternative alliance options by antagonizing third parties. Psychologists have demonstrated that we tend to value potential losses more highly than potential gains.[26]

Third, making an alliance activates certain alliance norms that may facilitate controlling the ally—for instance, the norm of consultation. Even if it is only tacit, the consultation norm derives considerable force from the thought that since each state's policies may involve its allies in war, the allies ought to have a say in them. And such verbal persuasion may be sufficient to modify the policy even when little or no coercive leverage is employed.

In terms of the alliance security dilemma, the chief purpose of restraining the ally is to avoid entrapment.[27] The exercise of restraint between allies, like the exercise of deterrence between adversaries, is essentially a bargaining process. Thus it consists of a demand and a threatened sanction or promised reward. A typical demand is that the ally refrain from military action or make concessions to its opponent so that military action is avoided. A typical sanction is the threat of abandoning the alliance, of military inaction in case the ally precipitates war, or of withholding diplomatic support in a crisis. The ally might also be rewarded in some way— say, by territorial compensation—if it submits to restraint.

Methods of Restraint

An obvious method of restraint is to threaten defection or realignment. This method takes the greatest risk of precipitating the ally's defection, which perhaps explains why there are so few instances of it in the case studies. The only explicit threats of defection came from states that were being restrained or not supported, not from those seeking to restrain them. One is Izvolsky's statement to the British ambassador during the Bosnia crisis that "if Russia were compelled . . . to passively assist at an Austrian occupation or invasion, . . . the question would of necessity arise whether she ought not to change entirely her course and abandon her alliance and entente." There had been "frequent hints" from Berlin, he said, that Russia "was steering a wrong course."[28] Of course, the anarchic and multipolar structure of the system presents a continuous existential threat of defection, which can be heightened by the merest of hints or by friendly moves toward another state, including the adversary. Threats of this kind were more numerous than explicit ones in the cases.

A less provocative method than threatening outright defection is to withhold diplomatic support from the ally in a particular dispute with its opponent, or to threaten to do so. Prominent examples in our cases are France's withholding support from Russia during the Bosnia crisis, Russia's reciprocating during the Agadir crisis, and Germany's denying support to Austria during the Second Balkan War.

Still less provocative or coercive is to insist on consultation during a crisis or before any major policy initiatives. Many alliance treaties explicitly stipulate consultation before going to war or when the danger of war is present. This type of restraint, first, guarantees against being surprised by a fait accompli. Second, it places its bets on one's ability to persuade, rather than coerce, the ally to change its policy, although of course, coercive threats, such as those mentioned above, are not ruled out during the consultation. Restraint by consultation relies heavily on "good atmospherics" to generate influence; a friendly atmosphere of mutual respect and confidence is thought more likely to induce compliance than threats to withhold support, which may merely antagonize the ally. Instead of coercion, the restraining ally employs persuasion, defined as attempting to change the ally's own preferences in the direction of restraint. The restrainer may argue from normative grounds—for example, that allies should, to a degree, incorporate each other's interests into their own. Or the restraining ally may point to various undesirable consequences of not being restrained, such as third-party reactions. For example, Bethmann warned Austria, during the Scutari crisis of 1913, that an Austrian military move would provoke Russian intervention. He also suggested a desirable consequence of restraint: the prospect of a "reorientation" of British policy if war could be avoided.[29]

Restraint by consultation is an example of what Albert Hirschmann calls the exercise of "voice" in partners' decision making, as distinct from influence by the threat of "exit"—the threat of defection.[30] An interesting example of the use of consultative restraint was that of Poincaré, who attempted to combine declarations of absolute fealty to Russia with insistence on close consultation; the former eliminated his coercive leverage, so the only means of restraint he had left were his own considerable powers of verbal persuasion.

Entrapment may be avoided by urging the ally to make concessions to its opponent. Thus Great Britain, during the 1903 crisis between Japan and Russia, urged its ally, Japan, to drop its insistence that Russia give a pledge to respect Chinese sovereignty in Manchuria. (Japan, incidentally, did not follow this advice.) Sir Edward Grey, during the Agadir crisis, tried to persuade the French to make more generous offers to Germany. He backed this up by refusing to promise aid to France if the negotiations collapsed.[31]

Restraint may be accomplished not only with the "stick" of threatened nonsupport but also with various kinds of "carrots." Thus Bismarck restrained Austria by emphasizing his Russian alternative but also by offering Austria various compensations in the Balkans for his very strict interpretation of the German defense commitment to Austria.[32]

To take the coercive edge off an attempt to restrain the ally, a state may employ reassurance as counterpoint. One assures the ally of one's loyalty on the central contingency of the alliance contract—attack by an adversary—even though one would like the the ally to modify its policy in the current political situation. This ploy was standard practice in virtually all the instances of attempted restraint in our cases. Its intent, apparently, is to make it easier for the ally to accommodate the adversary, by assuring the ally that its basic security needs are met. The ally need not run excessive risks or worry obsessively about relative power gains by its opponent, if it can count on being supported on critical issues.

One way to restrain an ally from aggressive initiatives is to point out that the alliance is defensive only. This was Bismarck's constant refrain when the Austrians sought backing in their conflicts with Russia in the Balkans. The message becomes disingenuous when the supporting/restraining partner has a strategic interest in the ally's independence, as Germany had in this case. The Austrians knew well enough that Germany would have come to their assistance even in a war started by Austria. Bismarck tried to surmount this contradiction by making a distinction between the common interests and the "special interests" of allies. The "whole existence of each country as a great power is a necessity to the other in the interest of European equilibrium," he told the Reichstag in 1887, "but these relations do not . . . rest on the principle that one of the two nations puts itself and its whole strength and policy completely at the service of the other. . . . There exist specifically Austrian interests which we cannot undertake to defend and specifically German interests which Austria cannot undertake to defend. We cannot each adopt the other's special interests."[33] Privately, Bismarck admitted the deception. He told a Crown Council in May 1888: "We could not look on passively if Austria got into a war with Russia, even though our *casus foederis* were not fulfilled. We should be obliged at first to *faire le mort*, play dead, but not so long as to allow Austria to be destroyed."[34]

Bismarck was not alone in employing this kind of casuistry. It was often specified in alliance treaties of the pre–World War I era that they applied only to cases of "unprovoked attack" on an ally. There was no obligation to assist the ally if it had itself started the war. This was an attempt to portray the alliance commitment as resting on moral principle, to be applied and judged in particular instances by the supporting state, even though that state might be committed to the ally by its own interests, whoever started the war. Grey repeatedly told the French and Russian ambassadors that whether England came to their aid in case of war would depend on the "circumstances" of its outbreak, which was taken to mean that England would not support the aggressive party. This pretense was useful to Grey for restraining his allies, since they could never be sure that England's strategic interests would dominate its well-known moral predilections. It also cost him, however, in fostering the miscalculation among German leaders, until very late in the July 1914 crisis, that England would remain neutral if Russia or France could be made to appear the aggressive party. Of course, Grey's circumlocutions were also useful, indeed necessary, for reasons of domestic politics.

A similar casuistry, perhaps inadvertent, is involved when a policymaker says that certain minor interests of the ally are not "worth" a war—for example, a Serbian port on the Adriatic or "a few square miles of desert in the Congo." Of course, once the ally goes to war, the issue is no longer a bit of seacoast or desert but the very existence of the ally. Kiderlen unmasked the pretense in a speech on November 28, 1912: "It has often been said that Germany does not need to fight for the Albanian or Adriatic interests of Austria or for the harbor of Durazzo, but that is not the point. . . . If Austria, whatever the reason, is forced to fight for her position as a great power, we must stand at her side in order that we do not afterwards have to fight it alone."[35] Grey complained to the German ambassador about Kiderlen's implication that "Germany would support Austria in whatever the latter said her interests required, apart altogether from the merits of the case."[36] The complaint was justified, but as a complaint about the logic of the international system, not about German policy.

Apparently, such pretenses are credible enough to have some effect, or at least to be worth trying, because the ally can never be certain about one's strategic interest or about the importance one attaches to nonstrategic interests, such as alliance norms. When the alliance rests primarily on the latter, it will be much more credible to claim that one will fight in some contingencies and not in others, depending on, for example, whether the ally or its opponent is "in the wrong."

When strategic interest is low or absent—when the ally would not be defended were it not for the alliance commitment—then of course the threat of nonsupport is more credible and likely to be more effective. In that case, it can plausibly be claimed that one's commitment is contingent on the circumstances in which the war starts. If the alliance is "defensive," there is no obligation if the ally is the attacker. Even then, of course, there will be political costs in failing to fulfill the commitment, given the usual ambiguity about who was the aggressor. The ally cannot be expected to fulfill its side of the alliance bargain if one is attacked later; one may also suffer some reputational costs with other allies and potential allies. There may even be some normative costs. But all these costs will be small compared to the cost of failing to defend a strategic interest. Moreover, they are highly subjective costs. Thus it can be plausibly claimed that in one's own eyes they are minimal (or zero, given the wording of the contract), and, of course, for bargaining purposes that is all that matters.

A Calculus of Restraint

It is possible to isolate the factors that determine whether restraint of the ally will be attempted and whether it will be successful. Whether a restraining attempt is made will depend centrally on the restrainer's fear of abandonment and the extent to which its interests in the situation at hand diverge from the interests of the restrainee. The restrainer's motive usually is to evade entrapment; the principal constraint on the effort, according to the theory of the alliance security dilemma, is the risk of abandonment. The restraining party will not make the attempt if the reduction in its expected cost of entrapment is less than the increase in the expected cost of alienating the ally and causing its defection. Thus in 1908–9, during the Bosnia crisis, Bülow and the Kaiser feared that Austria might drag Germany into a serious confrontation with Russia. They refrained from holding Austria back, however, because their fear of Austrian defection was greater. They were feeling very dependent on the alliance after the formation of the Triple Entente, the apparent loss of Italy, and the defeat at Algeciras in 1906. As Bülow said, "Aehrenthal (and the dynasty behind him) must gain the impression that we shall remain loyal," no matter how precarious the position into which they might maneuver themselves.[37]

Restraint is more likely to be attempted when the two allies have somewhat different interests in conflict with the adversary than when their interests are similar. Thus, in the Agadir crisis, Austria made a stronger effort to moderate the German position than Britain did to soften France's, largely because Austria did not share the German interest in Morocco, whereas Britain had interests similar to, if not identical with, France's.

The success of a restraining effort will depend essentially on three factors: (1) the credibility of the restrainer's threat, (2) the restrainee's interests in conflict with the adversary, and (3) the restrainee's dependence on the alliance. The credibility of the restraining threat will depend, in turn, on the restrainer's dependence on and commitment to the alliance and on its interest in whatever is involved in the conflict with the adversary—all as perceived, of course, by the restrainee. If the restrainer is highly dependent on the alliance, it will have difficulty making its threats of nonsupport credible. Thus its restraining attempts will be ineffective when it is weak relative to its opponent and when it lacks alternatives to the alliance. For example, Germany lost much of its restraining influence over Austria when it gave up the Russian alternative in 1890.

Restraining threats will be more credible when the allies have different interests in conflict with the adversary than when their interests are similar. In the latter case, the restraining ally cannot credibly say it will support some bargaining positions but not others. It can do so when its interests diverge from the ally's. Thus, in the Agadir crisis of 1911, Britain brought restraining pressure on France by revealing that it could accept an unfortified German port on the west coast of Morocco, something France had refused to concede. This reduced the apparent British strategic interest and cast some doubt on the firmness of its support. France still refused to concede a port in Morocco, but it made concessions in the Congo which resolved the crisis.

On grounds of credibility, it is likely to be easier to restrain a strong ally than a weak one. It is credible to threaten nonsupport of a strong ally if the ally can defend itself. Obviously, this is not credible vis-à-vis a weak ally. The vulnerability of the weak ally gives it bargaining leverage in another way: it can more credibly threaten to realign with the enemy than if it were capable of its own defense.[38] Thus, when Russia and France together were weaker than the Central Powers after Russia's defeat by Japan in 1904–5, England could not afford to seem unreliable for fear its allies would go over to the German side; but after these two states had achieved equality with Germany and Austria, they were less likely to defect if they became unsure of Britain. Thus England by 1914 was able to take a less committed stance than before without great risk of abandonment. Britain was then freer to exercise restraint in order to escape entrapment, owing to the reduced risk of being abandoned.[39]

The credibility of restraining threats will also be affected by the restrainer's degree of commitment to the alliance. Firm, explicit commitment can be a hindrance to restraining the ally because the threat of nonsupport may not be credible. A vague or ambiguous commitment, as in an entente, has the advantage of fostering uncertainty and thus maximizing the credibility of hints or threats of defection. Thus restraint is likely to be more successful when the alliance's terms are vague or ambiguous than when they are explicit and precise. Grey seemed to entertain this hypothesis when he remarked during the Liman von Sanders crisis, "It is precisely because Russia knows that an *entente* is not an alliance, and that an *entente* does not entail any obligation upon us, that she is so sensitive and anxious to know how she stands as regards our support of her respecting the German command at Constantinople—a point on which I have been very careful to avoid committing H. M. government."[40] Russian and French uncertainty about British support several times exercised a moderating effect on their policies. Russia accepted a compromise settlement of the Liman von Sanders affair; France made important concessions during the Agadir crisis. In 1914 France was very careful not to appear bellicose lest British support be lost. In these instances, the uncertainty arose largely from the ambiguity of the Entente relationship. There is less evidence that France and Russia, or Germany and Austria, linked as they were by formal alliances, were restrained in crises because of uncertainty about each other's loyalty.

On the other hand, vagueness of commitment may inhibit restraining attempts through the restrainer's fear of abandonment. Although restraining threats are more credible, the restrainer will hesitate to make them for fear of precipitating the partner's defection. This risk is higher than when commitments are explicit and firm, for two reasons: first, one's own dubious loyalty makes the ally's alternatives look better; and second, the ally itself is not tied down by a formal pledge. Thus restraint is less likely to be attempted. Great Britain, for example, hesitated to restrain its entente partners in crises between 1905 and 1914, whereas France and Russia, although bound more explicitly, withheld their support and attempted to restrain each other several times. France and Russia, unlike Britain, could dare to practice mutual restraint on issues short of war because they could each be confident of the other's loyalty on the military contingencies covered by their treaty.

The success of restraint will depend not only on the credibility of re-

straining threats but also on (1) how much the ally must give up in suc-
cumbing to restraint, and (2) how much it would be harmed if it does not
succumb and the threat is carried out. The first is a function of the ally's
interests in dispute with the adversary; the second is related to its dependence on the alliance. Even if the threat (say, of nonsupport in a crisis)
is credible, it may still not be effective if the ally would have to sacrifice
important values in being restrained or if it has little need of help.

Thus it was difficult for England and France to restrain Russia in the
summer of 1914 because of Russia's strong interest in Serbian independence and its resolve never to back down again to the Central Powers
after the humiliation of 1909. Although Russia was quite dependent on
the alliance, and restraining threats of nonsupport, especially by England,
would have been quite credible, by this time being restrained would have
cost Russia too much.

There are times when a state positively wants to be restrained by its
allies. For example, being restrained by one ally may facilitate disengagement from another. Thus, during the Balkan Wars, Russia hinted broadly
to France that it would like to be taken off the hook of its commitment to
Serbia by a French denial of support. But Poincaré refused to accept the
responsibility for restraining Russia's client and continued to assert French
loyalty. Alexandre Millerand, the French minister of war, told the Russians, "We are not to be blamed; we are prepared and that fact must be
borne in mind."[41] The incident illustrates that passing the buck between
allies can involve the avoidance of reputational costs as well as more tangible ones. Russia sought to shift the reputational cost of restraining Serbia
to its ally, France, but France refused to accept the buck.

Restraint of allies is problematical in a multipolar system when dependence relations are relatively symmetrical. The dependence of the restrainee makes it vulnerable to restraint, but the dependence of the
restrainer makes it reluctant to attempt restraint or the attempt is ineffective. Evidence from our cases indicates that when tension in the system,
and hence mutual dependence, is on the rise, the restrainer's reluctance
will rise faster than the restrainee's vulnerability. Thus Germany's will and
ability to restrain Austria, and France's to restrain Russia, steadily declined
from 1911 to 1914 as adversary tensions increased and alliance ties hardened. Logically, it might seem that, in 1914, the rearward allies—France,
Britain, and Germany—could have exploited the dependence of the front-
line states to restrain them, rather than follow them into war like prisoners
in a chain gang. Austria's and Russia's high dependence made them quite
restrainable. For the states in the rear, however, the risk of alienating their
allies overbalanced the possible success in restraining them. Losing allies
was the worst case; war was only second worst; the fear of abandonment
trumped the risk of entrapment.

ALLIES, ADVERSARIES, AND THE COMPOSITE SECURITY DILEMMA

As discussed in Chapter 6, the separation of intra-alliance relations from relations between adversaries is only an analytical convenience. In reality, the two realms—the two "games," to recall the earlier terminology—are closely intertwined. I have tried to capture some of the interplay in the model of the composite security dilemma, as summarized in Table 6-2. The model shows how choices in the alliance security dilemma produce side effects in the adversary security dilemma and vice versa. That some statesmen at least are aware of this fourway interplay is demonstrated by an assertion Poincaré made in 1912:

> On us rested two duties, difficult to reconcile but equally sacred: to do our utmost to prevent a conflict, and to do our utmost in order that, should it burst forth in spite of us, we should be prepared. And there were still two other duties which, also, at times ran the risk of being mutually contradictory: not to break up an alliance on which French policy has been based for a quarter of a century and the break-up of which would leave us in isolation at the mercy of our rivals; and nevertheless to do what lay in our power to induce our ally to exercise moderation in matters in which we are much less directly concerned than herself.[42]

The four objectives, in brief, are to conciliate the adversary, to deter or otherwise coerce the adversary, to preserve the alliance (avoid abandonment), and to restrain the ally (avoid entrapment). Chapter 6 described how they are interrelated and how they may be mutually contradictory. The following discussion presents evidence from the case studies about how pre-1914 statesmen sought to resolve these contradictions. The principal contradictions or tensions considered are between Poincaré's second and fourth—deter the adversary versus restrain the ally—and his first and third—conciliate the opponent versus support the ally.[43]

Deter versus Restrain; Conciliate versus Support

When a state wishes to deter an opponent and also to restrain an ally from provoking the opponent, the two goals may work against each other. Deterrence requires a firm stance, which may indirectly encourage the ally to excessive belligerence; restraint of the ally may mean threatening to withhold support, but that may undermine deterrence if the adversary "overhears" the threat. Obversely, the state may want to conciliate the adversary in order to keep the peace and at the same time support its ally in order to keep the alliance intact. But conciliating the opponent risks alienating the ally, whereas supporting the ally against the opponent ob-

[329]

viously is incompatible with concessions to the opponent and may provoke the opponent to greater firmness or even war. In short, if peace is
the objective, it might be obtained by deterring or conciliating the opponent, but efforts in either direction may be canceled out, respectively, by
efforts to avoid entrapment or maintain alliance solidarity. Strategies in
the alliance game and the adversary game may easily get in each other's
way.

One way of dealing with these dilemmas is to reassure the party that
may be frightened or alienated by one's move. In our cases, it was almost
automatic that when an alliance member made a conciliatory move toward
the alliance's opponent, it would at once reassure the ally that the move
was not a prelude to realignment. For instance, after the Potsdam conversations between Russia and Germany in 1910, Germany reassured Austria
that the alliance remained intact, and Russia made a similar declaration
to France. Sometimes the anxious ally will demand reassurance, as Poincaré did after the British announcement of the Haldane mission in 1912.
He requested and got, and made public, a reassuring statement from
Grey.[44] In 1914, after having restrained Russia during the Balkan Wars and
having given only weak support during the Liman von Sanders incident,
Grey was persuaded (by the French) to reassure Russia by agreeing to
naval conversations.

Sometimes it is the opponent that needs reassuring, as after a move to
strengthen one's alliance or support the ally which risks further antagonizing the opponent or provoking it to countermeasures. For example,
Sazonov was careful to assure the German government that his 1907
agreements with Britain did not imply hostility toward Germany.

An obvious way to deal with these dilemmas is to say one thing to the
opponent and something else to the ally. Grey employed this strategy
masterfully during the first Morocco crisis. To the German government he
emphasized that Britain very probably would intervene on France's side
in case of war. To France he promised full diplomatic support in accordance with the Entente agreement but refused any firm assurance of military aid. He even refused to repeat to the French ambassador the same
language he had used in speaking to Germany, explaining that Germany
would not be "disappointed" if British actions did not match his words,
"but I could not express so decidedly my personal opinion to France,"
implying that this would constitute a commitment of honor to an ally. In
short, Grey alternately emphasized opposite sides of the uncertainty concerning British behavior—whether it would or would not fight for
France—to deter Germany and restrain France.[45]

A variant is to make public declarations to one party and private ones
to the other. Tough deterrent declarations are directed publicly to the adversary, and restraining advice is given privately to the ally. The ally then

knows that one is doing one's best to resolve the issue in its favor but that one would like it to do some accommodating. Grey used this strategy successfully during the Agadir crisis: his public firmness caused Germany to concede, and his private pressure on France led to French concessions, resulting in a compromise settlement.

Restraining the ally is least likely to damage one's resolve reputation with the adversary if restraint can be exercised before the ally's policy becomes publicly known. Kiderlen, the German foreign minister in 1912, insisted that Austria consult with Germany before taking any initiatives, because "reasons of policy would make it hard to separate from our ally once his intentions are known to the powers of the so-called *Triple Entente*—for this very reason we must desire urgently that the Austrian government keep us informed of their intentions *in advance* and not as has so often happened, face us with a *fait accompli*."[46]

The support-versus-conciliate dilemma may also be eased by strengthening one's formal commitment to the ally; the ally then feels sufficiently confident of one's future support that it is willing to accept some dallying with the adversary. Thus Grey felt that once French fears of abandonment had been quieted by the exchange of notes in 1912, he could continue his efforts to improve Anglo-German relations. He concluded agreements with Germany about the ultimate disposition of the Portuguese colonies and about the Baghdad Railway without serious damage to the French entente. After the 1912 agreement the entente was sufficiently firm that Britain no longer had to prove itself by avoiding deals with the opponent.

Strategies in the Composite Security Dilemma

There appear to be four possible ways to deal with the alliance-adversary composite security dilemma. One is simply to choose one "horn" or the other, another is to choose a middle ground between the horns, a third is to grab both horns by saying different things to the adversary and the ally and hoping they do not find out, and a fourth is simply to vacillate between the horns. France chose the first, Britain the second and third, and Germany the fourth.

Poincaré's Choice

The purest example of the straightforward choice of one horn of the dilemma is furnished by Poincaré between 1912 and 1914. Poincaré recognized the tension between his determination to deter and resist Germany and to maintain his alliance with Russia and Britain, on the one hand, and, on the other hand, his desire to restrain Russia from dangerous adventures. He chose the first option: firm resistance to Germany and virtually unequivocal support to Russia, at least on the main contingency covered by the alliance—a German attack on Russia. If Russia needed restraining, he would do it not by threats of defection or nonsupport but by insisting on close consultation before any major policy initiatives. He hoped to accomplish both sets of objectives by "clinging" to Russia, as he put it.[47]

Poincaré also rejected firmly any suggestions of conciliating or negotiating with Germany and other members of the Triple Alliance. Such "interpenetration" of alliances, he maintained, would only produce confusion about the lines of enmity and amity and thus destabilize the system. Far better that everyone be absolutely clear about alliance lineups and loyalties and that the loyalties be unsullied by dealings with members of the opposing side.

When the French ambassador to Vienna, Philippe Crozier, sought to encourage a rapprochement with Austria-Hungary by promoting a French loan to Hungary, a move that Russia opposed, Poincaré squelched the idea and promptly fired Crozier. The task of the Triple Entente, he believed, was to contain Germany and Austria; any attempt to isolate Germany by trying to drive a wedge between it and its allies would lead to conflict. Crozier's subordinate at Vienna, Count de St. Aulaire, expressed Poincaré's own sentiments when he wrote:

> We could not [make such an agreement with Austria] without falling prey to the deadly system of the penetration of the alliances, of which it has been said, so rightly, that it is "a cause of international decomposition just as pacifism is a cause of national decomposition." The penetration of alliances, in fact, corrupts and dissolves them. By upsetting the balance and by obscuring the clarity of the situation, in reality it leads to ambiguity and instability. In doing so, it eventually weakens the guarantees for peace while claiming to increase them by the chimera of universal harmony.[48]

In terms of our theoretical categories mentioned earlier, Poincaré and St. Aulaire favored deterrence of opponents and solidarity among allies over conciliation of opponents and restraint of allies. They were willing to accept risks of conflict spirals and entrapment, but not risks of appearing irresolute or of being abandoned by allies. Restraint of allies, if necessary, would be accomplished not by bargaining or threats of nonsupport but by verbal cajolery from a stance of firm support. Vis-à-vis adversaries, peace would be preserved through deterrence rather than through negotiation.

Grey's Straddle

There was no one more sensitive to the composite security dilemma than Sir Edward Grey. Nevertheless, his responses to it went through several phases. During and immediately after the Morocco crisis of 1905–6 he was determined to be firm toward Germany and to maintain the Entente with France. There was no contradiction between these objectives, and he sometimes went to extreme lengths to protect the Entente, turning aside German overtures and refraining from any moves that might lead France to question British loyalty. For instance, in the summer of 1907 it became known that Chancellor Bülow was planning to accompany the Kaiser on a state visit to England in the fall. Grey perceived this as a German attempt, by transforming the meeting into a political demonstration, to sew suspicion in France that Britain was drawing toward Germany. "I am particularly anxious," he said, "that nothing should occur that would lend any color to the idea that we are wavering by a hairspread from our loyalty to the *entente* and are contemplating a new departure."[49] Grey was able to dissuade the Germans from sending Bülow, thus keeping the visit a private one between royalty.

From 1906 to about 1911 Grey followed consistent strategies of deterring the opponent and supporting the allies. He became gradually aware, however, that this posture was contributing to German feelings of encirclement and might encourage the French to "beard" the Germans. Therefore, he modified these strategies with an admixture of their opposites: conciliation of Germany and restraint of France. For example, he held out to Germany the prospect of improved relations if Germany would be flexible at the Algeciras conference, restrained France during the Casablanca crisis in October 1908, and publicly welcomed the Franco-German agreement about Morocco in 1909. On the whole, however, Grey's posture during these early years of the Entente amounted to solid support of France and the Entente. His primary worry was that of French defection and appeasement of or realignment with Germany; behind this fear lay a strong sense of dependence on France.

By 1911 British fears of French abandonment had lessened somewhat, owing to several years of experience with the Entente. Worries about French entrapment had comparatively increased, suggesting that support of France ought to be tempered with restraint. The German threat had increased, however, pointing to a firm posture in support of France. Grey's composite security dilemma had become more severe: there was increasing tension between constraints in the alliance game and those in the adversary game. In the Agadir crisis of 1911 Grey sought to manage this tension by maintaining a firm stance against Germany while moderating the French position. He urged the French to make concessions, while warning Germany that "public opinion" would not permit England to remain neutral in case of war between Germany and France. Both lines were effective: Germany reduced its demands, and France made concessions.

By 1914 the nature of Grey's dilemma had again shifted. Having had the experience of cooperating with Germany during the Balkan Wars and settling certain colonial disputes in the spring and summer of 1914, Grey had changed his image of Germany and was now more ready to accommodate it. He believed that Germany, although "formerly . . . aggressive," now was "genuinely alarmed" at Russia's increasing military strength.[50] At the same time, he was less fearful of French or Russian defection, because the bonds of the Entente had been tightened and because, with the revival of Russia's strength, there was an apparent equilibrium of power on the continent. This lessened Britain's need to swear or demonstrate loyalty to its allies: if they could hold their own against the Central Powers, they were less likely to defect out of fear of British defection. He found the growing spirit of xenophobia in France "very unwholesome," suggesting possible British entrapment in a war to recover Alsace-Lorraine.[51]

Thus Grey had about evenly balanced incentives for all four options in the composite security dilemma. His worries about the intransigence of his allies were at least as strong as his fears of their desertion, and he was as eager to avoid provoking Germany as to deter it. Therefore, he adopted a straddle—a mixed strategy—in both the alliance and the adversary games. He gave only vague reassurances to France and Russia, rejecting their pleas for an unambiguous declaration of support. He accepted Anglo-Russian naval talks only with reluctance and insisted on keeping them secret so as not to provoke Germany. He issued a few mild warnings to Austria and Germany during the July crisis but concentrated on reviving the joint Anglo-German mediation of the Balkan Wars. Only very late in the crisis, when war appeared to be imminent, did he issue an unequivocal warning to Germany, but even then he refused to repeat this statement directly to the French ambassador, because it would amount to a "guarantee."[52] It was Grey's hope that Russia and France would be restrained without being alienated, while Germany would be deterred without being provoked. The strategy failed because France-Russia and Austria-Germany, all thinking wishfully, drew opposite conclusions from it. France and Russia counted on British armed support, while Germany and Austria hoped for British neutrality until the very last moment. Thus, in striving for the best of all worlds, Grey got the worst. If, early in the crisis, he had declared his firm support of Russia and France and warned Germany unequivocally, *or* if he had clearly declared to France and Russia that Britain would not fight, the war might have been averted. This is not to argue that Grey's ambiguity was *the* cause of World War I or even a central one. Nevertheless, England was the only power that still had both polar options available; in failing to exercise either one, it gave up a chance to prevent the war.[53]

Germany's Vacillation

Under Bismarck, Germany pursued a straddle policy, building up alignments against Russia and at the same time conciliating it. This carried some risk of abandonment, since supporting Russia in Bulgaria and at the Straits disheartened Austria, Italy, and Britain, but it also minimized the risk of entrapment and kept the Russians and the French apart. After Bismarck's departure in 1890, however, Germany shifted from one horn of the composite security dilemma to the other. Between 1890 and about 1895 it firmly grasped the deter-support horn. The "new course" policy called for clear-cut opposition to Russia (in place of Bismarck's ambiguous stance) along with unqualified support of Austria and friendliness toward Britain. In mid-decade, however, Germany shifted to the policy of the "free hand," which meant holding the balance between Britain and the Franco-Russian alliance, eschewing commitment or enmity toward either, and loosening alliance ties with Austria. The change played havoc with its alliances. When Germany refused to challenge Russia in the Balkans and denied support to Britain in the Mediterranean, Italy and Austria turned elsewhere. Italy moved toward France, gaining approval for its ambitions in Tripoli in return for recognizing French preponderance in Morocco. Austria negotiated a detente with Russia.

The Morocco crisis of 1905 brought another reversal. Germany's isolation at the Algeciras conference induced a strong feeling of dependence on allies and encirclement by adversaries. From 1906 to 1911 Germany clung to Austria and stood up to Britain and Russia. Then, in 1911 and 1912, especially after the Haldane mission in 1912, Germany began to hope for British neutrality. In another switch, it started conciliating Britain in colonial affairs and qualifying its support of Austria in the Balkans. In September 1912 Bethmann refused Austria's request for joint diplomatic action against the Balkan League and counseled Austria against intervention. Germany collaborated with Britain in restraining Austria and Russia during the Balkan Wars. But by the fall of 1913, smarting under Austrian reproaches and fearing abandonment by its only reliable ally, Germany had returned to four-square backing of Austria. Continuing to hope for British neutrality into the July 1914 crisis, Germany then found itself in a contradiction that it was able to negotiate only by deception: saying one thing to Britain and another to Austria. Finally, when it became clear that conciliation of Britain was not working—Britain was not going to be neutral—Bethmann switched back to the restrain-Austria horn of the dilemma, but by then it was too late; military imperatives had taken over.

Choosing among Strategies

Which of these strategies for dealing with the composite security dilemma—choice, straddle, or vacillation—has the most to recommend it?

One can be dealt with summarily: vacillation hardly ever pays off. Vacillation is different from the straddle, of course, in that it is a shifting between policy goals rather than an attempt to optimize across a mixture of goals. It is "choosing," à la Poincaré, but not sticking to one's choice. The problem with German policy, fundamentally, was that it failed to confront trade-offs—between, say, friendship with England and friendship with Russia—but sought to have it all. This failure occurred partly because domestic factions pulled in opposite directions and the government lacked the power to reconcile them; partly it was due to intellectual deficiencies; and partly it followed from Germany's geographic and systemic position.

Assessment of choice-versus-straddle strategies is more difficult. No unequivocal judgment can be made, for the appropriateness of one or the other depends on a range of contextual factors. One is the nature of the opponent; as Jervis points out, the choice between deterrence and conciliation depends on whether the adversary has major revisionist aims: if it does, unqualified deterrence is necessary; if it does not, it can be conciliated to avoid a spiral of hostility.[54] Another factor is the nature of the ally: if the ally is known to be an exploiting opportunist—eager to take advantage of one's support for aggressive aims—it must simply be restrained; any watering down of firm restraint risks encouraging it in a too-forward policy. Conversely, if the ally is a weak-kneed appeaser, it may need unequivocal stiffening. Thus Poincaré's prescription of making a clear choice is indicated when the adversary or the ally, or both, has strongly undesirable tendencies that require countering.

A second and related factor is whether the adversaries and allies are "wishful" or "careful" thinkers, whether they are risk-acceptant or risk-averse. Grey's straddle was foiled by the wishful thinking of both his adversaries and his allies: adversaries focused on the conciliatory aspects of his strategy mixture, while allies paid attention to the supportive components. The straddle works best, one supposes, when the reverse is true, when adversaries and allies both are risk-averse; then, for any given strategy mixture, adversaries are most likely to be deterred and allies to be restrained. In that case, the dilemma itself is less severe. When both adversaries and allies are risk-acceptant, only a Poincaré-type pure strategy will work, for that is the only one that will pose high enough risks for the target, whether adversary or ally.

A third factor has to do with the systemic context: what is the level of tension in the system? A straddle works best when tension is low: when adversaries and allies are not yet firmly committed to a confrontation, the conciliatory and restraining elements of the strategy are most likely to overcome the spiral-inducing effects of deterrence and/or support. An unmixed choice is more appropriate after a spiral of tension has already occurred and adversaries and allies are firmly set in a confrontation; then the need is to send a clear message to the adversary or the ally that will maximally deter the one or maximally restrain the other. From this point of view, Poincaré's choice and Grey's straddle were both ill-timed: if Poincaré had not declared his complete fealty to Russia as early as 1912, the spiral of tension in the system might have been slowed down. Or if Grey had chosen an unmixed strategy in 1914, the clarity of British intentions might have defused the tension that had already built up.

DIVIDE AND RULE

The logical corollary of the task of keeping one's own alliance intact is that of weakening or dividing the opposing alliance. By far the most active in pursuing this strategy was Germany. The Germans used several methods. One, in line with their belief in bandwagoning, was to demonstrate the weakness of the other alliance by bringing pressure against one of its members. They tried this in the first Morocco crisis, anticipating that Britain would fail to support France and that France then would give up on the Entente and move toward Germany. Of course, the result was the opposite of their expectation. A second method was to negotiate an agreement with one state on the opposite side, hoping that would sew dissension and foster defection by that state's allies. This method may be illustrated by Germany's promise to Russia, during the Potsdam talks in 1910, not to support Austrian aggression in the Balkans, in return for a Russian pledge not to support hostile British policy toward Germany. The Germans hoped this demonstration of Russian disloyalty would lead to British defection and a neutrality agreement with Germany.[55] This hope, too, went unfulfilled, although Grey cited the Russian move to justify his own negotiations with Germany (the Haldane visit) a little over a year later.[56] Germany pursued divide-and-rule with more success in 1909, when it kept France from supporting Russia in the ongoing Bosnia crisis, by offering an accord over Morocco.[57]

Still another maneuver was simply to propose an alliance to a state on the other side, as in the Kaiser's offers of an alliance to the Czar in 1904 and 1905. The Czar was willing, owing to his resentment over the lack of French aid in his war with Japan, but his government refused to abandon France.

By 1912 France had already detached Italy, de facto, from the Triple Alliance and had made overtures to Austria. After Poincaré took over the Quai d'Orsay, however, France eschewed any attempts to divide the opposing alliance, as did England under Grey. Grey and Poincaré both disliked the divide-and-rule strategy, but for somewhat different reasons. The principal danger, for Grey, was that it might provoke the adversary to attack. Thus he declared that any attempt to separate Austria from Germany would be "fraught with considerable danger. The balance of power in Europe would be completely upset and Germany would be left without even her nominal allies." This might provoke her to "risk everything in defense of her honor, dragging Europe into what would be the most terrible war in all history."[58] Moreover, intriguing to break up the Triple Alliance would destroy the contention that the Triple Entente was defensive.[59]

Poincaré agreed with Grey that any attempt break up the Triple Alliance would be dangerously provocative. In line with his doctrine of no interpenetration of alliances, he also warned that it would foster miscalculation and instability and disrupt the balance of power. He vetoed all proposals by his subordinates aimed at fully separating Italy or Austria from Germany. In the case of Italy, he argued that its movement to the Triple Entente would rupture the equilibrium in Europe and lead England to withdraw, since its weight would no longer be needed to maintain the balance. Berlin would regard it as an act of hostility.[60]

A subtle difference between Grey's and Poincaré's views was that whereas Poincaré opposed any significant accommodative moves toward opponents on the principle of no interpenetration,[61] Grey was willing to negotiate agreements with the Triple Alliance powers so long as they were not intended to divide that alliance.[62] Poincaré's policy fostered inflexibility, the hostility-integrative spiral, and chain-gang effects, although it minimized the chances of miscalculation. Grey, on the other hand, sought flexibility, which tended to dampen the spiral but at the risk, and eventual cost, of miscalculation by others.

What the two men had in common was rejection of any attempt to disrupt the opposing alliance. There seemed to be two separate hypotheses underlying this position. In the first, Grey's, any such attempt is a hostile act that will provoke an opponent to react similarly, or perhaps even to attack preemptively before a realignment is consolidated. In the second, Poincaré's, conciliatory negotiations across alliances introduce uncertainty about who stands with whom and thus risks miscalculation. The first argument resonates with Jervis's spiral model;[63] the second, with the deterrence model and Waltz's theory about the instability of multipolar systems.[64] Underlying the Grey-Poincaré view was the conviction that the balance of power was superior to any alternative and must be preserved to the letter: not only must the opponent be balanced by one's own strength, but the opponent's side of the balance should be left undisturbed.

Spirals, Chain Gangs, and Passed Bucks

In the adversary security dilemma, strategies of firmness, played between rivals that believe each other to be potentially agressive but that really are not, produce an insecurity spiral, a spiral of power/security competition that feeds on each party's fears that the other's moves are aggressively motivated.* An analogous spiral in the alliance security dilemma is an integrative spiral, in which allies move progressively closer out of mutual fears of abandonment. The alliance integrative spiral and the adversary insecurity spiral are mutually generating and reinforcing. The process may be illustrated by the interplay between the two alliance systems in Europe between 1905 and 1914.

Until about 1905 the two major European alliance groupings were rather loose and flexible. Alignments on particular issues often cut across the formal alliances; lines of amity and enmity were not fully clear. There were contradictions between the Austro-German alliance and the Three Emperors' League and between the alliance and the Austro-Russian detente of 1897–1908. It was some years before France and Russia (and bystanders) could make up their minds whether their alliance was directed at Germany or England. German and Russian attempts to form a continental league against Britain were not, at the time, regarded as totally fantastic. Britain itself was, until around the turn of the century, firmly wedded to "splendid isolation."

Around 1905, however, there began an integrative spiral within the two alliance systems that proceeded *pari passu* with the insecurity spiral between them. The two spirals were mutually reinforcing in the following ways. Although it was not so intended, Germany perceived the 1904 entente as a threat to itself and tried to break it up by coercive behavior during the Morocco crisis. This move only drew Britain and France closer together; it also increased their coolness toward Germany, not only because they began to see Germany as a threat but because friendliness toward Germany might be misinterpreted by the partner as incipient realignment. As a result, Germany began to feel threatened and more dependent on Austria, especially after the Anglo-Russian rapprochement of 1907. It tightened its ties with Austria, dramatically so during the Bosnia crisis of 1908–9. This and the subsequent Agadir crisis further sharpened the Entente powers' image of a German threat and drove them closer together. After a brief interlude during the Balkan Wars, when Britain and Germany collaborated in holding back their allies, Germany reverted to unqualified support of Austria in the fall of 1913, followed by the blank

---

*I am using the term "insecurity spiral" for what is usually called the "security dilemma." For reasons stated earlier, I believe the latter is a mislabeling.

check of July 1914. By then the Franco-Russian alliance had further solidified and Britain and Russia were moving toward naval collaboration. Thus a spiral of insecurity between adversaries and a spiral of solidarity between allies reinforced and exacerbated each other until they became so tightly wound by the summer of 1914 that war could no longer be avoided.

One thread running through this sequence of events is a steadily increasing dependence between allies. The ability to restrain allies declined commensurately. Dependence grew on two related counts: perceptions of increased threat from adversaries and foreclosure of alliance options. With increased dependence, allies became more and more fearful of abandonment and so were driven to swear greater fealty and to bind their partners closer. Of course, the fears of abandonment were exaggerated, much as threats from adversaries tend to be exaggerated in the adversary security dilemma. In the alliance game, as in the adversary game, anarchy plus uncertainty tend to encourage a focus on the worst possible contingency. This focus in the decade before 1914 produced an especially virulent integrative-insecurity spiral.

Other threads reinforced the threat-dependence core of the spiral. One was the Russian switch from a focus on the Far East to a concentration on Europe after the defeat by Japan in 1905. Italy's attack on Tripoli in 1912, followed by the Balkan states' attack on Turkey, greatly increased the level of tension in the system. The Anglo-German naval race blocked any real detente between these two powers. The fact that the two alliance systems were about equal in military strength exacerbated fears of abandonment on both sides. The widespread belief that war was inevitable further heightened fears of abandonment and tended to neutralize worries about entrapment, thus reducing incentives to restrain allies. A sharp rise in nationalistic sentiment in France and Germany after the Agadir crisis reciprocally stoked feelings of hostility and insecurity.

Against a background of continued tension, any letup in one's support of allies, far from slowing the spiral, tended to tighten it in a kind of backlash effect. Thus Russia's failure to back Serbia's demand for an Adriatic port in 1913 caused Russia to feel it had to support Serbia in the summer of 1914, lest it lose all its credibility and influence in the Balkans. Similarly, Britain and France felt constrained to support Russia, as Germany felt bound to stand by Austria, after having restrained their allies during the Balkan Wars. This effect is the alliance analogue to the "never again" effect between adversaries—for example, as Russia felt it could never again back down to Austria after doing so in the Bosnia crisis of 1909.

Integrative spirals can start from small beginnings, analogous to the "little sins" Herbert Butterfield says can trigger a security dilemma between opponents.[65] Thus, when British leaders rather casually agreed to give France "diplomatic support" for its claim to preeminence in Morocco, they thought it meant something like "moral support." It turned out, however, that the implementation of this promise in the crisis of 1905–6 was an important step in the German perception of enmity in the Entente, and the reciprocal perception on the Entente side.[66] The crisis also clarified alignments that previously had been ambiguous: that Italy could no longer be counted a reliable member of the Triple Alliance and that Britain had thrown in its lot with France and probably with Russia.

Nevertheless, the Morocco crisis, although it contributed, was neither a necessary nor a sufficient trigger for the spiral. The ententes of 1904 and 1907 very probably would have been sufficient. Before 1900 there were three power centers: Germany, France-Russia, and Great Britain. Insecurities and tensions were diffused; none of the three had reason to believe that either of the other two was an ineluctable opponent. But around the turn of the century tensions rose enough that all three felt the need to join one of the others. Previous chapters have described the jockeying that took place between Britain and Germany, Germany and Russia, and finally, Britain with France and Russia. The two British ententes transformed the system from triadic to dyadic; amity-enmity was no longer diffused in two directions for each power center but concentrated in one direction. Once Britain had settled matters with France and Russia, Germany was the only remaining candidate for the role of enemy, so Britain placed it in that role. Germany accepted the role and began to perceive Britain as the chief engineer of encirclement. Thus the process of elimination by which Britain divested itself of two enemies automatically gave it another. Arguably, it was simply this reduction in the number of power concentrations that triggered the integrative spiral within the two alliance systems and the insecurity spiral between them. Once under way, the spiral fed primarily on the systemic rivalry between the two alliances and only secondarily on particular conflicts of interest between their members.[67]

The spiral included not only a tightening of alliance bonds but also increases in alliance membership and a broadening of the scope of alliance commitments. The British connection with France logically required a rapprochement with Russia as well.* Both sides stepped up their efforts to recruit smaller states: Bulgaria and Turkey attached themselves to the Triple Alliance, and Rumania switched from its Austro-German connection,

---

*See Jervis, *System Effects*, chap. 6, for a discussion of "balance theory" which explains why positive relations on two sides of a triangle, with negative relations on the third, is an unstable pattern that tends to become either three positives or two negatives and a positive. The Germans predicted the latter transformation among Britain, France and Russia: formation of the Anglo-French entente would not bring Britain and Russia together but would break up the Franco-Russian alliance.

first to neutrality and finally to an alliance with Russia and France. Japan and Spain lined up with the Entente powers. James Joll observes, "Once the governments of Europe came to believe that they were aligned in two rival camps, then the winning of an additional small state to their side seemed to be of great importance, while the wooing of partners in an alliance whose allegiance seemed doubtful or wavering, such as Italy, came to be a major objective of diplomacy."[68]

Alliance commitments were extended—between Austria and Germany in 1909 and between France and Russia in 1912—to include support of semiaggressive initiatives. The Franco-British entente was tacitly broadened from mutual support on two colonial issues to an expectation of support on almost any issue in conflict with Germany. Issues became more and more contests of relative power gains or losses between the two alliance systems, their "merits" more and more incidental. As enemies and allies became more clearly identified, joint military planning was intensified, further tightening commitments, both in general and in detail.

Finally, as the spiral tightened, all foreign offices became increasingly sensitive to events throughout the system. With the rise in tension and the cruciality of allied support, statesmen and diplomats became alert to small happenings that nevertheless might affect the cohesion of alliances or the balance of power between them. Reforms in Macedonia, the boundaries of Albania, changes in government personnel in any country, shifts in the size and allocation of military spending, the allegiance of Rumania and Bulgaria, social or state visits of monarchs, and the like all entered into the calculus of capabilities and intentions.

At first glance, there seems to be a contradiction between the ideas of balance of power and the integrative spiral. Balancing alliances are said to play a stabilizing role: aggressors are either deterred or put down when they appear. The integrative spiral is destabilizing: states are driven to cling to their allies up to and over the brink of war. The contradiction seems particularly striking when it is noted that balancing and spiraling can occur simultaneously. Very probably it was the spiral effect that gave both alliances and balance of power such a bad reputation, and not only among liberal idealists, in the aftermath of World War I.

The apparent contradiction can be resolved, however, by placing both notions in the context of Jervis's "deterrence versus spiral" dichotomy.[69] The balancing idea emphasizes deterrence and defense; it works as theoretically specified when one or more states with large revisionist intentions need to be deterred and defended against. But when there is no such state, when all are interested primarily in defensive security, an attempt to balance tends to set off a spiral, in relations between allies as well as between adversaries. Between adversaries, defensive measures by others, including defensive alliances, appear as potentially aggressive, requiring countering moves, in the familiar logic of the security dilemma. Between allies, any move toward restraint raises intolerable fears of abandonment; hence allies provide unwavering mutual support.

Christensen and J. Snyder label the integrative spiral before World War I the "chain gang" effect and attribute it primarily to the offensive military doctrines that were prevalent at the time. The doctrine of the superiority of the offensive drove states to bind themselves closer to their allies, and support them unstintingly, because an ally could easily be defeated by an opponent that had the initiative.[70] If military planners and statesmen had recognized the true state of technology—that the advantage lay with the defense—they would have felt less pressured to support their allies, since the allies could more easily defend themselves. Scott Sagan has argued, however, that this thesis reverses cause and effect: the fact that they were committed to allies forced the states to adopt offensive doctrines, since only by employing offensive strategies could they effectively aid an ally that was the victim of attack.[71]

Without entering into the specifics of this debate, I would argue that, although offensive doctrines may have exacerbated the spiral, its basic causes were systemic anarchy and multipolarity, balanced alliance lineups, and the interests that underlay or were generated by those alliances. The spiral was latent in system structure and the high alliance dependence that is characteristic of a multipolar system. Once the system had divided into two power groups, it required only one or two "little sins" by particular states (German aggressive diplomacy, Grey's ultrasensitivity to French feelings) to get the spiral going, and once under way, it fed on itself. The existence of an alliance balance contributed by maximizing dependence; it meant that loss of an ally, through conquest or defection, was perceived as a disaster; hence states were driven to support their allies, whatever the risk or cost.

Christensen and Snyder also invoke military doctrines to explain why European states behaved so differently in the 1930s than they did in the early 1900s. In the 1930s, rather than allowing themselves to be dragged one after another, into war, they tended to pass the buck—to shunt the burden of war-fighting onto others. Thus the French passed the buck to the British, Chamberlain passed it to Stalin at Munich, and Stalin passed it back by making a deal with Hitler in 1939. In this case, the western powers (and the Soviet Union later) all embraced defensive military doctrines based on the (erroneous) assumption that defense had the technological advantage over the offense. This led statesmen to believe that their allies could defend themselves and, furthermore, that their own state did not urgently need military aid from allies.

It could well be argued, however, for the 1930s as well as the early 1900s, that systemic factors were more basically causal than technological assumptions. Thus in the 1930s the European states were unable to form a balance against Hitler's Germany: the United States was abstaining, and the Soviet Union was considered unreliable and weak. The only feasible strategy, it seemed, was to appease Hitler, and a consequence of appeasement was to shift the burden of resistance to someone else. By contrast, a balance was possible before 1914, so attention centered on the support of allies and resistance to opponents, in order to create and maintain the balance. Beliefs about military technology may have contributed to the differences, especially the prevalent belief in 1914 that the war would be short, compared to the opposite belief in the 1930s, but they were less central than systemic factors.*

Although chain-ganging was the rule in the pre-1914 period, there were some instances of buck-passing, especially in the early part of the period, and in joint military conversations. Bismarck, for example, was a master buck-passer. He passed to Britain the burden of supporting Austrian aspirations in the Balkans and resisting Russian designs on the Straits. Austria passed to Germany the job of coercing Russia on the Bosnia issue. In the Austro-German staff talks, Germany persuaded Austria to assume the bulk of the task of fighting Russia in the early part of the war, although Austria ultimately "dropped the buck" by sending too many forces into Serbia. Similarly, France persuaded Russia to undertake a major offensive against Germany early in the war; in this case, Russia "kept the buck" but with unsatisfactory results.

Germany's extreme wariness about Britain's supposed buck-passing proclivities was one reason an Anglo-German alliance never materialized. "Perfidious Albion" would get its allies involved in a crisis, then withdraw, leaving them to deal with the adversary and incidentally to protect British interests.

The Franco-Russian alliance provides an example of a guarantee against buck-passing. Poincaré assured the Russians in 1912 that France would launch an immediate offensive against Germany on the outbreak of war and demanded that Russia give a similar assurance in writing. The Russians gave such a promise during the joint staff talks of 1911, 1912, and 1913.[72] These assurances took the form of addenda to the original military convention of 1892.

A disintegrative alliance spiral is conceivable as the extreme of buck-passing. When one state passes the buck to an ally, the ally perceives this move as a prelude to abandonment and decides to hedge against it by conciliating the opponent. The first party then takes this move as an in-

---

*I do not wish to imply (nor did Christensen and Snyder) that either systemic factors or technological beliefs, or even their combination, would exhaust the explanation of war in 1914 or appeasement in the 1930s.

dication that the ally is getting ready to defect or realign and then realigns with the opponent preemptively. A disintegrative spiral would be facilitated by a spiral of decreasing tension between adversaries. That would encourage buck-passing by decreasing interdependence between allies.

There was no prolonged disintegrative spiral in the pre-1914 alliances. Certain states, such as Italy and Rumania, switched sides, but for other reasons. There was a weak tendency toward such a spiral, however, between 1909 and 1911. The Moroccan agreement between Germany and France in 1909 and the Potsdam agreements between Germany and Russia in 1910 caused allies on both sides to worry about being abandoned and to reassess their options. Had another crisis, Agadir, not intervened, some realignment, or at least further loosening, might have occurred. After Agadir, however, the tightening spiral resumed and continued up to the outbreak of war.

Logically, a disintegrative spiral is most likely to take place when the tension between adversaries (and adversarial alliances) is low. Thus the most obvious examples of such spirals are those that occur in the aftermath of major wars, when victorious alliances tend to collapse for lack of an opponent. Gunter Hellmann and Reinhard Wolf argue that a reduced adversary threat leads to alliance disintegration for two reasons. First, it changes the trade-off between security and autonomy in favor of autonomy, causing the partners to loosen their ties. Second, it increases the salience of relative gains between the allies themselves, making them less willing to cooperate when the result may be a comparative increase in the ally's power.[73] I would add that the first factor prevails when the parties still consider each other allies, even though their mutual dependence has declined; the second kicks in when they begin to perceive each other as possible opponents—that is, when the disintegrative process is fairly far advanced.

A disintegrative spiral may also get under way, however, as a consequence of high dependence between allies, when the dependence is not being "satisfied" because of weakness or mistrust. Such a spiral would be driven by motives of defensive bandwagoning. This is what Nicolson had in mind just after the Bosnia crisis in 1909, with its exposure of Russian weakness and the simultaneous French negotiations with Germany. He would not be surprised, he said,

> if we were to find both France and Russia gravitating rapidly towards the central powers, as neither of the former, distrustful of each other, feels that she can stand alone against the power of the central combination. Our *entente*, I fear, will languish and possibly die. If it were possible to extend and strengthen it by bringing it nearer to the nature of an alliance, it would then be possible to deter Russia from moving toward Berlin . . . and if we could

contract some kind of an alliance with Russia, we should probably also
steady France and prevent her from deserting to the central powers[74]

Despite the instances mentioned above, buck-passing and free riding
are more difficult and less frequent in a multipolar than in a bipolar system, because (1) the ally may not be able to provide the ride or accept the
buck, owing simply to a lack of capability, and (2) these strategies may
cause the ally to defect and realign. In a bipolar system the superpowers
can and will accept the buck and have no real option to defect or realign.
Conversely, chain-ganging, as in 1914, is more likely in a multipolar system, especially when adversarial tension is high, because the high and
symmetrical dependence among allies, and the structural availability of
realignment options, maximizes fears of allies' defection.

THE USES AND COSTS OF AMBIGUITY: ALLIANCES VERSUS ENTENTES

Our cases provide an opportunity to compare the advantages and disadvantages of ententes versus alliances.[75] The two may usefully be compared on three dimensions: relations with the opponent, relative
effectiveness in dealing with the risks of entrapment and abandonment,
and implications for alliance bargaining.

The alliance seems clearly preferable for deterrence of the adversary. Its
explicit commitments maximize the likelihood in the opponent's mind that
its aggression will meet the combined resistance of the allies. The lack of
formal commitment in the entente may tempt the opponent to gamble.

Against this view, it is sometimes claimed that the very uncertainty of
Britain's ententes exercised a deterrent effect on Germany. But this effect,
although greater than with no agreement at all, could hardly have exceeded the deterrent value of a firm alliance. A more sophisticated variant
of this argument is that an entente avoids defining the area within which
an opponent is free to act. A formal alliance maximizes the probability of
joint resistance in the contingency specifically mentioned but implies that
it is not required in other contingencies. An entente, or some other ambiguous understanding, preserves some threat of joint action across a
wider range of circumstances.

An entente preserves more flexibility than an alliance because it does
not entail a decisive choice of partners. The absence of decisive choice also
means that an entente is less provocative to the opponent than an explicit
alliance; it is less obviously a hostile act, since the opponent need not feel
irreversibly excluded. Moreover, since an entente is not based on explicit
pledges to use force, denials of its hostile intent are more plausible.

Vis-à-vis the ally, the entente seems preferable for minimizing the risk of entrapment. Since one is not fully committed, one is freer to abstain in a crisis between the ally and its opponent. But an entente maximizes the risk of abandonment, since the ally is not committed. Conversely, a formal alliance is superior for avoiding abandonment, though it carries a high risk of entrapment. It could be argued, however, that an alliance is also superior for avoiding entrapment, for the same reason that weakens it as a deterrent—the limits of commitment are clearly stated. One can withhold support on issues outside the limits without calling into question one's loyalty on issues inside them. The ally need not feel it is being abandoned regarding the ultimate contingency of military attack just because one fails to support it on a dispute or crisis short of war. And one can verbally emphasize that one's loyalty to the formal *casus foederis* remains undiminished, as most actors did in our cases.

But when commitments are vague or merely tacit, as in an entente, there are no clear limits. Then any show of reluctance to support the ally on any issue casts doubt on one's reliability over all issues and incurs a risk that the ally will defect in consequence. To ensure against this, one may feel compelled to support or acquiesce in the ally's policies on virtually any issue. Thus fear of abandonment drove Britain to keep proving itself by supporting France and Russia in crises and acquiescing in Russian violations of the Persian accord.[76] This need would have been much less with an explicit mutual commitment, as illustrated by the behavior of the French and the Russians, who withheld support from, or gave only niggardly support to, each other in the Fashoda, Bosnia, and Agadir crises. Confidence in an entente necessarily turns more on performance than on a verbal promise; in the alliance, by comparison, the promise carries more weight and validating performance is less necessary.

British statesmen also worried that France or Russia, being unsure of Britain's support, would concede too much to the opponent in a crisis or give away some of Britain's own interests. Sir Francis Bertie, the British ambassador to Paris, neatly compared this abandonment risk to the avoid-entrapment benefit during the Agadir crisis: "The French government . . . do not feel sure how far they could rely on [the Entente] if Germany became threatening or bluffed. This feeling is useful to us as a security against France committing imprudence in her discussions with Germany, but it is also a danger as France might, if hard pressed, give us away in a question important to British and not to French interests, as Sazonov gave away at the Potsdam interviews both France and England."[77]

An entente may yield more bargaining power over the ally than an explicit alliance: one's existential threat of defection is more credible. This could be useful for restraining an overly bold ally in a crisis. Moreover, not being committed enables one to hold out the prospect of firmer commitment or support as a reward for the ally's good behavior. If no commitment is formally stated, one has greater diplomatic flexibility; informal statements about one's actual or possible intentions can be varied to fit the occasion. Grey's various references to "public opinion," "circumstances," and so on in deflecting French and Russian pleas for a clear British commitment were a virtuoso performance in calculated ambiguity.

This logic applies, however, only when the means of restraint is the threat of abandonment—Hirschmann's threat of "exit." When the method of restraint being considered is that of consultation—Hirschmann's "voice"—the advantage shifts to the formal alliance.[78] The norm of consultation applies much more strongly to alliances than to ententes. The reason is that if one is committed to fight in consequence of the ally's policies, one has a right to participate in the making of those policies. Although the threat of exit is weaker in formal alliances, this may be more than offset by the greater opportunities for a voice in the ally's decision making. It was the absence of a British voice in French decision making that concerned Bertie, who worried that France might sacrifice British interests to appease Germany.

Winston Churchill nicely summed up the weaknesses of ententes when he wrote after the war that the entente with France gave Britain

> the obligations of an alliance without its advantages. An open alliance . . . would have exercised a deterring effect upon the German mind, or at least would have altered their military calculations. Whereas now we were morally bound to come to the aid of France and it was our interest to do so, and yet the fact that we should come in appeared so uncertain that it did not weigh as it should have done with the Germans. Moreover, as things were, if France had been in an aggressive mood, we should not have had the unquestioned right of an ally to influence her actions in a specific sense; and if, as the result of her aggressive mood, war had broken out and we had stood aside, we should have been accused of deserting her, and in any case would have been ourselves grievously endangered by her defeat.[79]

Britain's bargaining disabilities declined as the Entente gradually became more formal and explicit. Thus, after French anxieties had been calmed by the exchange of notes in 1912, the British government felt freer to try to improve Anglo-German relations. Agreements on disposition of the Portuguese colonies and on building the Baghdad Railway were concluded, and a spirit of detente developed between Germany and Britain. Britain could make these agreements without worrying about disturbing the French because the Entente had been quasi-formalized and more tangibly based via the military conversations. At the same time, Grey became less timid about restraining France and Russia. His language toward France during the Agadir crisis, though generally supportive, was noticeably less accommodating and more assertive than it had been during and immediately after the first Morocco crisis. Toward Russia, Grey was less supportive and more restraining during the Balkan Wars and the Liman von Sanders crisis than he had been earlier in the Bosnia crisis.

Of course, the effectiveness of any particular entente or alliance will depend on variables other than the presence or absence of formal commitment. It was not fully understood in the pre-1914 years, particularly in Germany, that the strength and cohesion of the Triple Entente was a function not merely of the settlement of specific conflicts between its members but also of the common strategic interests that underlay it. The Germans thought that settlement of the issues of the Portuguese colonies and the Baghdad Railway had created something like the Anglo-French and Anglo-Russian ententes, which justified an expectation of at least British neutrality. And Jules Cambon, the French ambassador in Berlin, could not understand why he should not be allowed to negotiate an entente with Germany based on a general colonial settlement, just as his brother Paul had done with Britain.[80] In both instances, it was not appreciated that whereas the Anglo-French conflicts in 1904 were entirely colonial and "strategically virgin," the German-British rivalry was strategic—the parties had already firmly identified each other as power rivals—so that any colonial agreement between them could only be "atmospheric."

On balance, the weight of advantage seems to lie with formal alliances over ententes in a multipolar system. There is a systemic reason for this that underlies most of the specific reasons suggested above. In a multipolar system the interests of states are quite likely to be ambiguous and cross-cutting, more so than in a bipolar system. Allies are less likely to have interests wholly in common than in a bipolar system, where the confrontation between the superpowers tends to homogenize the interests of the allies clustered around each pole. Because there are few "natural" alignments based on common interests, there is a greater need for explicit contracts that clearly define the enemy, the contingencies that will activate the alliance obligations, and the required responses. The requirements of joint action cannot be automatically read off from "interests"; consequently, they must be explicitly defined. The Franco-Russian alliance provides a vivid illustration: the initial agreement left unclear not only the identity of the enemy but also the strategies and means of joint action. These things had to be specified, first in a military convention, then in a series of revisions that of course reflected the interests and relative bargaining power of the allies on each occasion. The British ententes were anomalies, made necessary by domestic politics. As noted earlier, they tended to give Britain the worst of both worlds: their ambiguity both weakened its deterrence of opponents and failed to restrain its allies.

ALLIANCE NORMS

To say that alliance management is primarily a process of bargaining is to imply that it is driven mostly by self-interest. Alliance managers are seen as rational means-ends calculators, making choices now that they anticipate will maximize future values. Such actors, of course, are ideal types. It is time now to increase their realism by investigating to what extent they are subject to norms, principles, and rules that are separable from self-interested rationality. Norms are guides to behavior that either prescribe or proscribe certain actions in relevant situations, on grounds of their moral goodness or badness, without regard to selfish interests, under pain of external or internal sanctions.[81]

Alliance members are, of course, subject to all the standard norms and rules of international law and diplomacy. But some of these norms have a special relevance to alliances; in addition, there are a number of rules, of more or less stringency, that are specific to alliances.

Pacta Sunt Servanda: *Obligations versus Interests*

An alliance agreement usually is a treaty and thus partakes of all the bindingness and solemnity that international law accords all treaties. Undoubtedly, the strongest norm applicable to alliances is that the commitments and promises made explicitly in the alliance treaty must be kept. The rule of *pacta sunt servanda* expresses this rule in international law. And among the various commitments that the treaty may contain, the obligation is strongest for the *casus foederis*, the statement of the contingency or contingencies in which the parties are to use force on each other's behalf. There is much evidence in the pre-1914 period, in both the verbal utterances and the behavior of statesmen, that the *casus foederis* is considered virtually inviolable. Whatever qualifications and hedges diplomats may make regarding lesser commitments and agreements, they generally end by reassuring the partner that, of course, they will fulfill their obligations to fight.

Against this clear norm must be juxtaposed the conventional wisdom that allies will always act according to their interests, without regard to whatever they have promised in the alliance contract. This "wisdom" is incorrect, as I attempt to demonstrate. If it were correct, alliances would be either redundant or futile: if the pledge in the contract matched the parties' interests, the contract would be unnecessary; if it did not match, it would not be observed.[82] The prevalence of alliance treaties and the care with which they are negotiated suggest that they have real functions and carry real moral obligations apart from the preexisting interests of the parties. This does not mean, of course, that the opposite claim is true: that the obligations will always prevail over the underlying interests. It means only that when the two conflict, states do not automatically follow one or the other criterion but often face a difficult choice between them.

What do our cases show about how this choice is made? When alliance members fulfill their commitments, is it done out of a sense of obligation or simply because the commitments happen to express their interests? When they renege, how do they justify it—by arguing that their interests or circumstances have changed, according to the ancient legal doctrine of *rebus sic stantibus* (as long as things remain the same), or by finding language in the treaty itself that excuses them? How often do they renege? Before the *casus foederis* arises, are alliance members confident that it will be honored, by themselves and others, and if so, does the confidence arise from the sanctity of an alliance norm or from their knowledge that it is consistent with each other's interests?

These are hard questions, and it cannot be said that the cases provide definitive answers. They do yield clues, however. The moment of truth arrived for members of the Triple Alliance and the Dual Alliance in August 1914; it also arrived in a qualified moral sense for Great Britain. Germany met its alliance obligations but went well beyond them when it virtually goaded Austria into moving against Serbia; thus Germany followed both its duty and its interest, but the two did not coincide. Italy reneged but found justification in the alliance treaty: it came into force only when the ally was attacked "without direct provocation," whereas Austria had given provocation by attacking Serbia. Austria's alliance commitments (as distinct from the influence of its allies) had little to do with its behavior. On the Entente side, Russia followed its interest in supporting Serbia; it had no formal treaty with Serbia. It upheld to the letter its commitment to France (in the joint staff talks) to attack Germany on the fifteenth day of mobilization, however, even though its front-line forces lacked full logistical support and some of their weapons. Indeed, Russia went beyond its commitment by attacking not only in East Prussia but also against central Germany.[83] Of course, it might have been motivated in part by the need, in its own interest, to relieve the military pressure on France, but it appears that a sense of obligation was more influential. France followed its interest rather than its alliance obligations; since it was directly attacked, its obligations were not at issue. Still, it seems quite clear that France would have come to Russia's aid if Germany had attacked only Russia. It would have done so out of some combination of interest and obligation. Great Britain, too, with slightly less certainty, would have satisfied both its moral obligation to and strategic interest in France, even if Belgium had not been violated. Unfortunately, such counterfactuals do not permit us to divine exactly the relative influence of obligation and interest, but they imply that both motives were operative for most of the states involved.[84]

It is not true that alliance commitments contributed nothing to the outbreak of World War I, as recent conventional wisdom has it. Nor is it quite true, as A. J. P. Taylor maintains, that the Schlieffen Plan "makes nonsense" of the contrary view.[85] The political context in which the Schlieffen Plan was devised included the knowledge that France and Russia were allies and the belief that their alliance would be honored. If they had not been allied, the Germans might have developed separate plans for wars against France or Russia, one that left open the possibility of defeating the two seriatim. In that case, a war that began in the Balkans might have been localized in east-central Europe. Only "might," however, since even without the Russian alliance, France might have taken a German-Austrian-Russian war as an opportunity to take back Alsace-Lorraine, and it might also have seen a strategic interest in preventing a German despoilment of Russia. The alliance no doubt codified interests, but it also established an obligation beyond interest.

Moreover, alliances create not only obligations but also new strategic interests, beyond those that may have existed before the alliance. Germany's imperative need to maintain Austria as a great power was not written in the stars; it followed largely from the pattern of alliances. In the 1870s, before falling in with Germany, Austria had alliance options with France, Britain, and Russia which it seriously considered. If one of those options had been chosen—say, France and Britain—Germany probably would have turned to Russia, its strategic interest would have lain in defense of Russia rather than Austria, and France's would have been to defend Austria against the German-Russian threat. The only certain alignment by interests in the 1870s was the enmity between France and Germany. Austro-Russian rivalry was likely but not certain. All other alignments were quite indeterminate, but if and when they had materialized, the parties would ineluctably have developed interests in defending their chosen allies and resisting their designated opponents. The point is that even when states follow their interests, alliance commitments are not irrelevant, because they will have had a role in shaping the interests.

The issue of the responsibility of alliances for World War I centers on whether other states were drawn into the conflict between Austria and Serbia by their alliance obligations. This focus ignores the question of the extent to which that conflict itself was a function of alliance ties. It is quite clear that the conflict could not have materialized in July 1914 in the form in which it did if Austria had not been assured of German support. It was the alliance with Germany and the unqualified German backing that allowed Austria to send an ultimatum to Serbia, to word it so that it could not possibly have been accepted in full, to pronounce the answer unsatisfactory, and to declare war on Serbia. It might be objected that Germany supported Austria because it was in its interest to do so, but the interest, and its degree of intensity, derived from the fact that Austria was Germany's only reliable ally. Similarly, Russia was emboldened to stand up to Austria and Germany by its confidence in French support, a confidence that derived from the treaty itself, from many French reiterations of loyalty to its terms, and from the experience of the military staff talks—not from a belief that the German war plan was bound to bring France into the war in any case. France had a strategic interest in assisting Russia, apart from its alliance commitment, but it certainly is doubtful whether the perception of it by Russian leaders would have been sufficient to cause them to stand firm.

On the other hand, it has been argued that states were drawn into World War I not by the rigidity of their alliance commitments but, rather, because of the flexibility of alignments.[86] That is, allies were driven to stand by each other not by the force of their obligations but by the worry that these obligations had little force; the realignment possibilities offered by the system meant allies had to be supported lest they defect. In this argument the basic issue in 1914 was the comparative power of rival alignments and states' uncertainty about their allies' reliability.

Curiously, both these factors—commitments and flexibility—seem to have contributed, in complementary ways. States in the front line—Austria and Russia—were emboldened to stand firm by the knowledge that they had supportive allies; those in the rear—France, Germany, and England—provided support out of fear that if they did not, the alliances would collapse.* In an uncertain world, having allies made the former more assertive in the adversary game than they otherwise would have been; the possibility of abandonment made the latter more supportive in the alliance game.

These remarks do not solve the puzzle with which we started—whether alliance commitments carry any weight beyond the interests that underlie them—but some additional clues can be found in the verbal utterances of policymakers in the years before 1914. These statements typically attribute substantial legal and moral weight to alliance treaty commitments. Interests are less frequently mentioned. Of course, there may be some bias here, since it is more praiseworthy to act according to "duty" than out of self-interest. Yet there is a ring of sincerity to most of these utterances, and many of them are private statements to governmental colleagues rather than declarations to allies or publics. For example, Sazonov and the Rus-

---

*France was actually in a middle position: its resolve was stiffened by both the support of England and the fear of Russian defection.

sian military commanders believed in 1914 that a hasty offensive might fail; nonetheless, Sazonov enjoined his colleagues, "We have no right to leave our ally in danger, and it is our duty to attack at once, notwithstanding the indubitable risk of the operation as planned." Moltke told Bethmann on July 29, after learning that Russia had ordered partial mobilization against Austria, "If Germany is not to be false to her word and permit her ally to suffer annihilation at the hands of Russian superiority, she too must mobilize."[87] The words "right," "duty," "false to her word" are striking, even though a cynic might argue that duty was not much at variance with these actors' interests. Some statements imply that norms trump interests when the two are contradictory. Lord Hardinge said of the German attempt to get a British pledge of neutrality in 1911: "What they want is to get some arrangement with us by which our hands are tied for a few years, and then to have a go at France, Italy, Russia, and perhaps Austria."[88] Such examples could be multiplied.

Actors expect others—both allies and opponents—to act according to their alliance obligations. After the Agadir crisis Bülow said that if the crisis had erupted into war, Russia, but not Austria, would have been obliged to participate: "The complication would have begun with Britain; France would have remained passive, it would have forced us to attack and then there would have been no *casus foederis* for Austria—as Aehrenthal said to the Delegations—whereas Russia was obliged to join in."[89] One reason Russia signed the Reinsurance Treaty with Germany in 1887 was that France was not yet ready for alliance. Without such an alliance, argued foreign minister Giers, Russia had to have an assurance of German neutrality in case of an Austro-Russian war.[90] The implication was that both France and Germany could be counted on to live up to their commitments. Others in the Russian government argued that France would come in on Russia's side even without an alliance, but Giers responded that this was a possibility, not a certainty.[91] Presumably, he thought an alliance would make it a certainty, or nearly so. The actual wording of the Reinsurance Treaty implied that the parties would act according to their obligations rather than their interests. Thus Germany was obligated to remain neutral in an Austro-Russian war if Austria was the aggressor but not if Russia was; Russia's obligation was similar in case of a Franco-German war. The neutrality obligation of both parties was clearly contrary to their strategic interests. A dramatic demonstration of the weightiness of legal obligations was the revision of the Franco-Russian alliance in 1899 to extend its life beyond the duration of the Triple Alliance. Delcassé feared that a collapse of Austria-Hungary, by terminating the Triple Alliance, would also end Russia's obligations to France.[92]

There is some contrary evidence, however, that statesmen placed more confidence in others' interests than in their alliance commitments. Thus Bethmann-Hollweg observed to the Kaiser in September 1910, "Let us hope that if there is war the attack will be aimed against Austria which will then need our assistance and not against us, so that it is not left to Austria to decide whether to be loyal to the alliance or not."[93] On the other side, General Foch expressed to General Wilson the opinion that Russian loyalty could be counted on if the war began over Russian interests in the Balkans but not if it started with a Franco-German fight over Belgium.[94]

The Anglo-Japanese alliance is a case in which Britain's interests seemed to go beyond its commitments. The commitment was a modest one, calling for assistance only if the partner were attacked by two other parties. Yet, as Lowe and Dockrill note, "few ministers believed that Britain could stand aside while Japan was being crushed [by Russia]—it would be a terrible blow to British prestige as well as to her own interests. Thus, even if France remained neutral, England might still have to intervene in the conflict."[95] Apparently, British interests were more compelling than the commitment; they were strong enough to warrant defending Japan against only one attacker. This may be a case in which the act of allying, regardless of the exact nature of the commitment, created a strategic interest in aiding the ally against any serious threat.

As Schelling made clear in discussing commitments between adversaries, commitments engage elements of prestige, honor, and reputation that supplement more tangible interests.[96] These values are also engaged vis-à-vis allies and help lend credibility to alliance commitments. Thus states have strong incentives to fulfill their commitments even when they extend beyond their a priori interests, in order to maintain their political weight in the alliance.

A skeptic might wonder why, if alliance commitments were so ironclad, the principals thought it necessary to reiterate so frequently that they would stand by them. Were they not just restating the obvious? Why was it necessary, for example, for Paleologue and Poincaré to reassure the Russians so fervently and so often that France would defend Russia against German attack, when this was no more than what the treaty itself proclaimed? The answer probably is that even when states are certain they would honor their own alliance obligations, they cannot be absolutely sure the partner realizes this, since it is, after all, an anarchic world in which treaties cannot be enforced. Verbal repetition helps fill the gap between one's own certain intentions and the partner's necessarily uncertain expectations. In a political system without strong legal institutions to support promises and contracts, verbal repetition may be necessary to prevent their deterioration over time. Such repetition may be expected as a sign that one still considers one's previous declarations valid.[97]

The Halo

Allies' sense of obligation, and their expectations about each other's support, do not end with the *casus foederis* or the text of the treaty. Allies expect each other's diplomatic support on issues short of the *casus foederis*, even though such support is not explicitly commanded in the alliance contract. Conversely, there seems to be a norm that such interests of the ally should be supported, at least when it would not incur serious harm to one's own interests. We may call these expectations the alliance "halo," the political penumbra that surrounds the basic military commitment.[98] The military commitment itself seems to generate a cognate political commitment. Having tied their fates together on the most crucial issue—survival—it is only natural that the partners come to feel they ought to give each other mutual support on lesser issues, most especially those that relate somehow to the ultimate military contingency. It seems, however, that the expectation of support is stronger than the felt obligation to support, for there are several instances—Bosnia, Agadir, the Balkan Wars—in which support for the immediately involved ally was either meager or not forthcoming. Still, in all such cases, resentment was expressed by the ally whose expectations were dashed, indicating the presence of a norm. Thus, when the Russians expressed irritation because Bismarck seemed to be favoring Austria at the Congress of Berlin in 1878 and after, they apparently felt they were entitled to at least equal treatment because of their common membership in the Three Emperors' League.

The halo may extend not only to political issues but also to military contingencies beyond those specified in the alliance treaty. Although statesmen sometimes sought to minimize their military obligations by citing the letter of the agreement, they also realized that to permit the ally to be defeated, however the war might have started, would severely damage their reputational if not their strategic interests. Thus, as mentioned earlier, British leaders felt they would have to act to prevent Japan's being "crushed" by Russia, even though they were not obligated to do so.

When the agreement is an entente rather than a formal alliance, the halo may relate not to lesser issues but to larger ones. The agreement itself is a settlement of particular substantive issues between the partners; it is not an agreement to provide mutual military support. The latter, however, is tacitly understood. Thus underlying the Anglo-Russian agreement of 1907 was an understanding that it would form the basis for military action against Germany.

The idea of an alliance halo was succinctly expressed by Ribot, the French foreign minister in 1911, in a speech to the French senate:

When two great nations enter into a permanent bond of friendship they join forces in foreign policy, not merely with the object of maintaining the peace of the world, but also of dealing jointly with all sorts of eventualities which cannot at the moment be foreseen. . . . They accordingly keep a watchful eye on events with a view of framing a suitable joint policy which will secure the greatest advantages for themselves from any concatenation of circumstances that may arise. This is the kind of pact which we have concluded with Russia.[99]

Among the implications of this statement, and others like it, is, first, that the making of an alliance tacitly entails a recognition that the parties have a wide range of common interests going beyond the common interest in mutual defense. Second, the allies will strive, so far as possible, to agree on a common policy of joint action with respect to those interests. Third, they expect to consult and to be consulted before undertaking any significant unilateral moves toward the adversary. Fourth, in any dealings with the adversary, and indeed, in their foreign policy generally, they will consider and promote the interests of the ally, so far as this is consistent with their own vital interests. In short, the weight of the evidence shows that statesmen believe alliance formation incurs an obligation to support, or at least to avoid damaging, the interests of the ally, so far as is possible, on a wide range of peacetime issues.

If a state urges concessions on an ally that is negotiating with an adversary, the state may incur an obligation to support the ally if the concessions are rejected. Partly for this reason, Britain decided not to urge moderation on Japan in negotiations with Russia in 1903, to avoid entrapment in the impending war.[100] Thus a normative factor may qualify the standard prescription for avoiding entrapment—restrain the ally. Conversely, there is some evidence that, in return for allied support on its important interests, a state is expected to be conciliatory to its opponent on peripheral issues.

There is also a general belief that mutual support on issues within the halo is required continuously to validate the core alliance itself. The members must cultivate these tacit expectations of political cooperation so as to preserve each other's confidence and trust in their formal obligations. Thus there was an expectation in Russia that it would receive some help from France in the war with Japan in 1904–5, even though the letter of the treaty did not apply, and indeed France provided aid via the coaling of Russian ships en route to the Far East.

The alliance halo points to the possibility of political entrapment: being forced by the ally's initiative into undesirable diplomatic policies. The Kaiser bemoaned his political entrapment in the Bosnia crisis: "I only regret having been brought by Aehrenthal's frightful stupidity into the dilemma of not being able to protect and assist the Turks, our friends, because my ally has injured them."[101] The antidote, of course, is political abandonment: not supporting the ally's initiative, while maintaining one's basic commitment to the alliance.

Expectations Create Obligations

There appears to be a norm to the effect that allies' expectations of support must be satisfied, even when such expectations are not founded on any formal obligation. This rule, obviously, is most relevant to ententes. Thus Sir Edward Grey said, during the crisis over Morocco in 1905–6:

> If there is war between France and Germany it will be very difficult for us to keep out of it. The *entente* and still more the constant and emphatic demonstrations of affection (official, naval, political, commercial, Municipal and in the Press), have created in France a belief that we should support her in war. If this expectation is disappointed the French will never forgive us. There would also I think be a general feeling in every country that we had behaved meanly and left France in the lurch. The United States would despise us, Russia would not think it worthwhile to make a friendly arrangement with us about Asia, Japan would prepare to re-insure herself elsewhere, we should be left without a friend and without the power of making a friend.[102]

Grey was extremely sensitive to the moral cost of not fulfilling French expectations and the need to avoid encouraging them. He held a "clear view," he recalled after the war,

> that no pledge must be given, and no hope even held out to France and Russia, which it was doubtful whether this country would fulfill. One danger I saw as so hideous that it must be avoided and guarded against at every word. It was that France and Russia might face the ordeal of war with Germany relying upon our support; that this support might not be forthcoming, and that we might then, when it was too late, be held responsible by them for having let them in for a disastrous war. . . . This was the vision of possible blood guilt that I saw, and I was resolved that I would have none of it on my hands.[103]

French expectations of support received a big boost from the joint military staff conversations that began during the first Moroccan crisis. Although the British civilian leadership insisted the plans carried no political or moral obligation, the military leaders, and probably some of the civilians, in their secret hearts, thought otherwise. Their feeling was that the degree of detail and precision in the joint plans itself tended to create a commitment; the agreement on specific implementation procedures implied a seriousness and mutual trust that a more general plan might not have carried.

Several British statesmen were aware that the "diplomatic support" they had promised France on Morocco implied military support as well. For example, Lord Lansdowne thought it "not unfair to say that in a case of this kind, an undertaking to give diplomatic support may tend to bring about an obligation to give support of another kind."[104] The mechanism here might not be so much French expectations, however, as simple means-ends logic: diplomatic support could hardly be effective unless backed up by a willingness to use force.

Reciprocity

The notion of reciprocity is at the heart of most alliances. Alliances involve a contingent exchange of benefits. Each partner commits itself to confer certain benefits on its ally, with the understanding that the honoring of the commitment is contingent on the ally's honoring its. If one party fails to fulfill its pledge, the other is released from its own. Indeed, this is a general principle of international law and of most domestic legal systems. Such legal obligation, of course, applies only to contingencies explicitly mentioned in the alliance contract. In addition, there appears to be a more general norm that enjoins the members to reciprocate any favors (or injuries), even those unrelated to the alliance agreement.

According to Robert Keohane, the essential dimensions of reciprocity are contingency and equivalence, and it may be exercised positively or negatively: "Reciprocity refers to exchanges of roughly equivalent values in which the actions of each party are contingent on the prior actions of the others in such a way that good is returned for good and bad for bad."[105]

By this definition, reciprocity need not carry a moral injunction. Reciprocal behavior can be explained entirely in terms of its practical value. Its central value is the reduction of uncertainty and consequently the fostering of cooperation. If one is able to count, with fair confidence, on one's cooperative behavior being reciprocated, one is more likely than otherwise to initiate cooperation. Such confidence is especially critical in alliances, because if the partners have different adversaries or different interests, the exchange of benefits may occur in sequence rather than simultaneously. One's own cost of the alliance—depending as it does on the whim of an adversary—may be assessed before the enjoyment of one's own benefits.*

---

*In other arenas, such as tariff bargaining, reciprocal concessions can more easily be timed to be simultaneous.

The (net) gain from reciprocity thus hangs on trust, which may flow in part from a sense of mutual obligation but probably more from confidence that the partner will honor its own commitment out of self-interest. Thus agreements based on reciprocity can be "self-enforcing." But, of course, they will be even stronger if self-interest is reinforced by obligation.

Any act of benefit to the partner generates an expectation in the actor, and (perhaps) some sense of obligation in the partner, that the latter will respond with some benefit of roughly equivalent value. For example, Bülow explained to the Kaiser in 1908, during the Bosnia crisis, that Germany owed Austria a debt for its support at Algeciras: "Austria-Hungary behaved loyally towards us not only at Algeciras but also this summer in the naval question. Like should be paid for with like."[106] Austria was amply repaid in this case, but the record shows that expectations of reciprocity are not always realized: "gratitude" may be expressed by a beneficiary, but it is not often accompanied by "payment." Thus in 1878 the Russians expected Germany to take their side at the Congress of Berlin in payment for their service in deterring Austrian intervention in the Franco-Prussian war of 1870–71; they were angry when Bismarck more often than not seemed to support Austria. Similarly, the Austrians no doubt appreciated the German help they received during the Bosnia crisis, but they did not reciprocate in the Agadir crisis two years later. This may have been partly because they undervalued the German help: Aehrenthal attributed the Russian backdown more to his own threat to reveal documents that compromised Izvolsky than to the German "ultimatum."[107]

Reciprocation, in principle, works both ways: not only is good to be returned for good but also bad for bad.[108] There is more empirical support for the negative aspect. Russia withheld support from France in the Agadir crisis partly in retribution for the lack of French support on the Bosnia issue. When Austria denied support to Germany in the Agadir crisis, it was, in part, retaliating for the German declaration at Potsdam that Austrian "aggressive aims" would not be supported.[109] The fear of retaliation may be a potent stimulus to fulfilling one's obligations. For example, Kokovstov, the Russian premier, in blocking a Russian mobilization against Austria in November 1912, said the action "would have destroyed the military covenant and thus permitted France to repudiate her obligations to us."[110]

Finally, the principle of reciprocity may run counter to the logic of bargaining and bargaining power. Reciprocity calls for an exchange of equivalent benefits, but the distribution of bargaining power may be unequal, thus normally producing nonequivalent gains. When this is the case, we would expect outcomes to reflect some combination of bargaining power and reciprocity (and other norms as well), that is, unequal benefits but not as unequal as would have resulted from the distribution of bargaining power alone.

Inform and Consult

Whether or not it is written into the alliance contract, the very making of the agreement carries with it an implicit obligation to consult with, or at least inform, the ally before taking any major policy initiatives, especially those that impinge on the ally's interests. The obligation derives from three sources: (1) the basic treaty obligation to act jointly in certain contingencies, (2) the possibility that allies' interests may differ in the actual contingencies that arise, and (3) the further possibility that unilateral initiatives, military or political, might precipitate contingencies that activate alliance obligations. Each ally, therefore, has a right to express opposition to or attempt to modify any proposed initiative. Having committed itself to joint military action, it has the right to have a say in any move by the ally that may make the occasion for action more or less likely.

The consultation norm applies most stringently when the initiator's interest in the issue is less than the ally's. Thus in the Bosnian crisis Grey refused, without Russian consent, to advise Serbia to give up its claims. "If I did so," he said, "I should be open to the charge of having gone behind their backs and thrown them over."[111]

There is considerable variation, however, in the extent to which the consultation rule is observed or expected to be observed. For Poincaré and Grey, it was virtually equivalent to a biblical commandment; for Sazonov, it was something to forget about when forgetting was convenient. For example, Sazonov failed to inform Poincaré about the Russian role in organizing the Balkan League and thereby earned the latter's rebuke. But he found the obligation useful in internal decision making, as when he blocked a partial mobilization planned by the Russian military in 1912 partly on the ground that France had not been consulted.

When the alignment includes or is based on a settlement of substantive issues, the consultation norm applies to any attempt to change the agreed status quo with respect to those issues, especially through negotiations with a third party. Thus France and Britain were unpleasantly surprised in January 1911 when it became known that Russia was about to sign an agreement with Germany concerning the continuation of the Baghdad Railway into Persia. They considered this move a violation of an understanding that none of the Entente powers would negotiate unilaterally with Germany over the railroad. A British protest was successful in forcing consultation.[112]

The Triple Alliance partners were no more conscientious about consultation. Italy launched its invasion of Tripoli in 1912 without informing its allies. Similarly, Aehrenthal announced the Austrian annexation of Bosnia-Herzegovina in 1908 without prior consultation with Germany or Italy. In both cases, Germany expressed irritation but nothing more. Germany itself failed to consult with its allies more often than not; the Austrians were particularly annoyed at not being informed in advance of the "Panther's spring" in 1911. Apparently, a norm of consultation exists but is rather weak. It is not observed if there are clear benefits in ignoring it, and its violation incurs not much more punishment than a slap on the wrist.

It is likely to be violated, as the foregoing examples suggest, when the violator wishes to spring a fait accompli—to preempt either resistance by the opponent or restraint by the ally. A state that is determined not to be deflected will face a choice between the normative costs of not consulting at all and the political costs of ignoring the wishes of the ally after consulting with it.[113] More often than not, the first course is chosen. Consultation is most likely to be practiced by weak states that are dependent on their allies' support, as in Austria's consultation with Germany after the Sarajevo murders. Germany's distancing itself from Austria during the next phase of this crisis suggests there are times when allies would rather not be consulted: when they wish to avoid the appearance of responsibility for their partner's behavior.

Slightly different from the norm of consultation is the norm of participation. In crises or disputes an ally of one of the protagonists may perceive that its own interests are involved; it may then demand not just consultation but actual participation in the negotiations with the adversary. Thus, in the Agadir crisis in 1911, Britain demanded to participate in the Franco-German bargaining to make sure the French did not give the Germans a slice of Morocco or a fortified port on the Moroccan coast, which would have been contrary to British naval interests. The norm apparently is that all parties with an interest in an issue deserve to participate in settling it. Germany stood on this principle when it demanded a conference on the Morocco issue in 1905–6.

The Functions of Alliance Norms

To show that alliance norms exist and are observed does not explain why this is so. What is the function of such norms? How do they arise? Why are they observed?

The existence of alliance norms might be accounted for in two different ways: their intrinsic moral weight or their utilitarian value. All norms have at least some moral content, and some, in addition, have practical value, but the proportions of the two may vary. When statesmen cite the requirements of "honor" or "duty," they generally have in mind a moral injunction to honorable behavior apart from the practical value of such behavior. Intrinsic values of this kind appear to be mostly imported into international relations from other, probably interpersonal, realms of interaction. Thus the general rule that promises should be kept is a general rule of human interaction which is naturally carried into alliance relations because of the prominent place of promises in such relations.

Norms can also be accounted for (without denying their moral content) by their contribution to practical needs and ends. Thus the injunction to keep promises serves the need of having some basis for trusting others. This need is particularly urgent in the international system, where the absence of central authority generates a high degree of both insecurity and mistrust. The norm of promise-keeping helps states negotiate the central paradox of anarchy concerning alliances: the tension between the need and desire to ally and the inability fully to trust allies to keep their word.[114] Alliances promise great benefits but also high risks. Norms help tilt the balance in favor of the benefits.

The utilitarian value of norms may be both collective and individual. States have a collective interest in supporting norms that strengthen the general reliability of promises and the predictability of behavior. They also have a private interest in their allies' fulfillment of their particular promises, which is encouraged by the existence of a norm. It is encouraged not just by the direct moral constraint of the norm but also by the allies' norm-induced confidence in one's own reliability.

Norms tend to moderate the alliance security dilemma. For example, the rule of promise-keeping reduces anxieties about abandonment, and the norm of consultation protects against entrapment. Norms not only enhance alliance security but also serve as a substitute for the exercise of alliance bargaining power.[115] The stronger the norm of consultation, for example, the less it is necessary to coerce the ally into consulting on every policy initiative. Acquiescing to someone else's desires is easier if it is done in terms of a norm than in response to pressures. Thus the greater the potency of alliance norms, the less costly and more reliable alliance management will be.

Norms may also be useful for their salience as focal points in bargaining situations.[116] They help resolve the indeterminacy of bargaining outcomes, which, as noted earlier, is usually broader in alliance bargaining than in bargaining between adversaries. Here norms of equity or equality may be important.[117]

Norms are supported by the anticipation of sanctions when they are violated. Sanctions might include damage to one's reputation or nonsupport by partners when one's own interests are threatened. Probably the most potent sanction is emotional.[118] Statesmen wish to avoid being the target of an ally's anger and contempt: the Kaiser said in 1914 that he wanted no more "reproaches" for disloyalty to Austria. Sir Edward Grey movingly expressed the shame he would personally feel if Britain failed to support France in war, after having created the expectation that it would.

ALLIANCES, CONCERTS, AND BALANCE OF POWER

In addition to games that states play with their allies and their adversaries, they sometimes play a "community" game that cuts across both. The community game, known in the nineteenth century as the Concert of Europe, has as its objective the realization of interests that all members of the system, or at least the great powers in the system, have in common, whereas the alliance and adversary games are dedicated to the interests of only a subset of those states, in conflict with another subset. The primary interests in the concert game are the preservation of peace and the fostering of orderly change. The central interests of the (same) players in the adversary and alliance games are to preserve the security of the state, by resisting or conciliating adversaries or by keeping and controlling allies; peace and stability are secondary objectives. Interests in these games tend to be selfish and oriented to the short run; interests in the concert game are shared and focused more on the long run.[119]

Tension may arise between the cooperative concert game and the two competitive games, partly because of the difference in dominant interests and motives: the pursuit of peace and order may require the sacrifice of either one's own or the ally's self-regarding interests. Beyond this, behavior dedicated to concert goals often is hard to distinguish from behavior in the competitive games. Thus cooperating with an opponent to defuse a dispute in the interest of peace can easily be misinterpreted by others as appeasement to the detriment of one's resolve reputation in the adversary game or as defection at the cost of one's loyalty reputation in the alliance game. The realization of concert goals may be hindered by states' reluctance to jeopardize either their interests or their reputations in the two competitive games.

The Concert of Europe functioned fairly effectively from 1815 to 1854, settling several small-power disturbances that might have led to war and, in general, keeping the peace among the great powers until the Crimean War. After that it declined, both in terms of respect for its substantive principles and in the use of the conference method. It did not entirely expire, however; Concert ideas lived on, at least in some statesmen's aspirations, and conferences were occasionally held to deal with problems on the periphery of Europe, notably in the Ottoman Empire. The Balkan

[364]

Wars of 1912–13 saw the last gasp of the Concert. Its final days throw some interesting sidelights on the concert-alliance interplay.[120]

Alliances and the Concert of Europe in the Balkan Wars

When the European powers became aware that war was imminent, they sought both to prevent it and to localize it by joint diplomatic action. At the suggestion of France and Germany, the powers prepared a collective démarche that was to be presented to the Balkan states by Austria and Russia, as the most interested powers. It called for peace, reforms in European Turkey, and no changes in the territorial status quo if war should break out. The chief purpose of the exercise was not so much to avoid a Balkan war as to constrain Austria and Russia from competitive intervention by co-opting them into the role of "agents" of the Concert. Each accepted that role largely because (apart from pressure from their allies) the other was willing to accept it. The concept of "agent" of the Concert was to reappear later but with a different rationale as legitimator of unilateral action rather than as a restraining device.

The European powers failed to stop the Balkan allies from attacking Turkey on October 8, 1912. Subsequently, they concentrated on regulating the results of the war, chiefly through a conference of ambassadors in London. Great Britain and Germany, as the parties with least at stake in the local issues and as the leaders of their respective alliances, were the natural leaders of the Concert. They collaborated in setting up the conference and cooperated closely during the early months of its deliberations. Their payoffs in this role were somewhat different, however. Both sincerely wanted to pacify the Balkans and to discourage military intervention by any great power, notably Austria or Russia. But these community motivations were evidently stronger on the British side. Germany's payoff for collaboration included an important side effect in the alliance game: Germany hoped thereby to detach Britain from the Entente, at least to the extent of moving it toward neutrality. The Germans believed, in other words, that "friendship" dividends earned in the Concert game could be cashed in the alliance game. Despite this difference in the content of their payoffs, Britain and Germany found themselves in a prisoner's dilemma: they could make satisfactory joint gains by cooperating to restrain their allies, but they were each subject to the temptation to defect from cooperation in order to support the allies; if both defected, however, they would be worse off than if they had cooperated.

The Concert was successful on the Albania issue: Austria and Russia both made concessions under German and British pressure. It was also successful during the first part of the Scutari crisis, when the issue was whether the town should go to Albania or to Montenegro. Both Austria

[365]

and Russia gave ground, again, under heavy pressure from their allies. But the Concert began to unravel during the latter part of this crisis, when the problem was to liberate the town from its Montenegrin occupiers. Austria, with German approval, prepared its own invasion force and an ultimatum for delivery to Montenegro. Although the Montenegrin capitulation made the implementation of these measures unnecesssary, Concert unity had been breached. That fact was papered over by a tacit joint pretense that Austria had acted as "agent" of the Concert. Thus, up to a point, the powers were willing to pretend that defection was cooperation, in order to avoid the total collapse of Concert norms and procedures. But the pretense did not prevent Grey from privately coordinating his policy with his Entente partners, a step he had refused to take earlier in the crisis for fear of disrupting the Concert.[121]

Germany restrained Austria during the Second Balkan War, but whether this should be considered a Concert success is problematic, since Germany had motives other than Concert norms—again, motives related to its alliance game. Germany hoped to recruit Greece and Serbia as allies and consequently would not countenance Austria's taking action against them in support of Bulgaria.

This experience, and the bitter Austrian reaction to it, apparently increased the German apprehension of alliance costs, should Austria be held back again. Thus, in the next crisis, October 1913, when Austria chased Serbian forces out of Albania by means of an ultimatum, Germany fully supported its ally. Again, the appearance of Concert unity was preserved by the pretense, tacitly accepted by Britain and France, that Austria had acted as the Concert's agent.

After this crisis Concert cooperation in the Balkans gradually dissolved and the actors retreated to the shelter of their alliances. The locus of issues shifted southward, to the demarcation of the southern boundary of Albania and the disposition of the Aegean islands, where Austria and Italy were the principal interested powers. Having similar interests, these two states repeatedly took joint initiatives, usually coercive, against the smaller Balkan states, often on matters about which the Concert as a whole was still deliberating. Typically, Germany would agree to a Concert action proposed by Britain, then fail to call its allies to account when they preempted Concert action. Or it would agree to a Concert proposal, then refuse to pressure Austria and Italy to agree, citing the sensibilities of its allies.[122] In one case, Germany agreed to a Concert decision against Turkey but refused to take part in enforcing it. This was, of course, a kind of buckpassing: Germany shared in the benefits of the decision but escaped the "odium," as Grey put it, of coercing the target of the decision.[123]

This behavior naturally made Grey and others in the British government increasingly skeptical about German sincerity and the value of the Concert. Grey became more inclined to yield to French and Russian desires for a solidary Entente policy. He was reluctant to continue standing against Russia on this point in view of the pressure he had earlier brought against it and the persistent troubles he was having with it over Persia. The apparent German defection from the Concert made a British defection easier. By the spring of 1914 it had become routine for the Entente as well as the Triplice partners to determine common Balkan policies among themselves without reference to the members of the other alliance or to Concert norms.[124]

German defection from the Concert was motivated far more by solicitude for allies than was the British defection, which simply reflected a recognition that Concert cooperation was no longer paying off. Worries about Austrian and Italian loyalty had moved the balance of Germany's incentives decisively toward defection in the Concert and loyalty to allies. These incentives prevailed into the July 1914 crisis, although the British did not realize it and the Germans successfully nurtured their ignorance. Grey's misreading of the changed structure of the German "concert game," or, alternatively, his hope that the 1912 version could be revived, apparently contributed to his equivocal stance in that crisis.

The burden of the foregoing argument and case material is that the relation between the concert and alliance games is negative: concert cooperation risks alliances, and alliance cooperation risks the concert. That is not always the case, however; sometimes the side effects from alliance to concert are positive. If one is worried about entrapment, the concert may usefully dampen the ally's conflicts with its adversary. Concert procedures can be a valuable tool for controlling an ally. Thus, when Grey proposed to terminate the London conference in August 1913, Germany argued against it because the conference had helped discourage unilateral initiatives by Austria and Italy. Benckendorff, the Russian ambassador, was pleased at Grey's decision because it would mean more dissension in the Triple Alliance. Eyre Crowe, in the British foreign office, at a low point in the conference's deliberations, proposed dropping Albania from its agenda in the belief that this move would generate friction between Austria and Italy and force Germany to choose between them.[125] Thus the major actors were aware that concert procedures and obligations could be useful in resisting calls for support from their alliance partners and that the absence of such procedures could increase intra-alliance friction.

In short, concert procedures introduce a kind of two-level bargaining,[126] in which the bargainer—Germany in this case—can say to its partners at the alliance level that what they are demanding is unacceptable to its colleagues at the concert level. By showing that it would suffer losses at the concert level by giving in, its resistance to the allies gains credibility. Moreover, when the concert is in operation, concert norms can be appealed to in opposition to alliance norms—for example, the norm of systemwide collaboration can be adduced to resist calls for alliance solidarity.

The Balkan Wars testify to the value of institutions in fostering cooperation. After the London conference ended, cooperation among the great powers immediately began to deteriorate. Partly that was because the settlement of the most urgent local issues had reduced the value of cooperation compared to the longer-term value of alliance relationships.[127] But also, it seems that simply the absence of face-to-face contact and the reversion to traditional diplomatic machinery removed some of the incentive to agree. The most self-interested states—notably Austria—were no longer required to clear initiatives with others. Actors could less plausibly cite conference norms as leverage over their allies and were less subject to pressures from their rivals to exert such leverage. While it was in session, the conference served as physical evidence that other actors were committed to concert principles; thus it deterred preemptive defections, those motivated by anxiety that a rival was about to defect. The conference also maximized transparency, regarding both what others were doing and their motives for doing it. Allies could ascertain with some confidence that their partners' cooperation with adversaries was aimed at concert goals rather than realignment. Adversaries could be surer of detecting when their opposite numbers were giving precedence to alliance relations over concert goals.

Concert and Balance

The Balkan Wars experience sheds some light on the controversial question of the relation between "concert" and "balance of power." Some consider the two ideas virtually identical: concert collaboration is nothing more than joint efforts to preserve balance.[128] At the other extreme, some believe the two are opposed and irreconcilable. Both these views are incomplete.

As theoretical ideal types, the two concepts are indeed quite different. Concert is a small step in the direction of "government"; balance of power is the logical consequence of competition in an "anarchic" system. Concert emphasizes the preservation of peace and order through the negotiated adjustment of conflicts; balancing emphasizes deterrence and defense against the potential disturbers of order.

Difference does not necessarily mean incompatibility, however. In reality, the ideal types tend to fuse: a balance of power among the great powers is often said to be a necessary condition for the successful working of a concert. The balance operates as a safety net that permits states to trust others not to exploit their cooperation in the concert. Conversely, a balance of power must be managed, and such management may be accomplished through collective action and negotiation similar to that associated with a concert system.[129] The two processes, although different, are complementary. But they are also, under some conditions, opposed and contradictory. Whether they are complementary or contradictory depends largely on how "balance" and "balancing" are defined.

Concert and balance of power are most complementary when balance is defined situationally as a rough equality of resources among all the major states. If no potential aggressor can be sure of defeating even one of its fellow great powers, this should encourage and facilitate the settlement of disputes by negotiation—the heart of the concert method. The two ideas are also mutually supportive when balance is defined as a process of restoring an equilibrium that has been disturbed and when such balancing takes the form of military action. The prospect of such "action balancing" serves as insurance against failure of the diplomatic procedures of the concert. This safety net induces confidence that one's cooperation will not be exploited, thus making states more willing to subject their disputes to concert procedures. These ideas of resource equilibrium and action balancing were prominent in discussions of the relation between balance and concert among nineteenth-century theorists. Indeed, they were regarded as integral parts of the concert process.[130] Military balance and balancing underwrote the diplomatic aspect of the Concert of Europe and enhanced its prospects for success.[131]

Concert and balance are most likely to be contradictory when balancing occurs through the formation of competitive alliances in peacetime. Then both the process of balancing and the situational balance the process seeks to attain or restore are diplomatic more than military; an equilibrium exists between two groupings by virtue of political commitments and expectations among their members, and equilibrium is restored, if disturbed, by an adjustment of these commitments and expectations. Such peacetime alliance balancing became prevalent during the period covered by this book. It did so largely because of advances in military technology and logistics which increased the pace of warfare and thus made necessary the formation of alliances in advance of war. In addition, heightened arms competition, colliding with increased demands on governments for social welfare expenditures, brought pressure on governments to economize on arms budgets by signing up allies.[132] This burgeoning of alliances in peacetime added another competitive dimension—gaining and holding allies—to the traditional rivalry in the accumulation and employment of military force.*

One reason alliance balancing is partly incompatible with the concert

---

* The notions of resource, action, and alliance balancing are associated with the three arenas of security politics—preparedness, action, and diplomacy—discussed in Chapter 1.

ideal is that alliance formation activates a fear of the ally's defection. The need to avoid abandonment tends to conflict with the concert's injunction to cooperate with potential adversaries. Such cooperation may involve real sacrifices or risks to allies' interests, thus reducing the value of the alliance to the ally, and/or it may be interpreted by the ally as a sign that one is about to abandon it. Either way (or both) the ally may lose interest in the alliance and abandon it itself. Fear of this result may inhibit cooperation in the concert. In short, the central behavioral rules for the concert and the alliance balance—in the former, "cooperate with adversaries"; in the latter, "preserve the alliance"—may well be contradictory.

It is true, of course, that an alliance balance, like an action balance, provides a safety net in case the concert fails to prevent aggression and war. To that extent, Charles Kupchan and Clifford Kupchan are correct in saying that a concert is supported by a "subtle undercurrent of competitive balancing," by which they apparently have in mind balancing between alliances or alignments in peacetime: "Divergences of opinion and conflicts of interest not resolved through negotiation will trigger a set of balancing mechanisms."[133] But this view overlooks the fact that the safety net itself may get entangled in the concert machinery and frustrate its working. It may do so because it consists of a web of commitments, interests, and expectations whose maintenance and repair may conflict with the pursuit of concert goals. Paradoxically, although the *existence* of equilibrium theoretically underwrites the concert, the *preservation* of equilibrium may require policies at variance with concert principles.

In sum, although the principles of concert and balance are thoroughly compatible and reciprocally supporting when balance is defined as simple equality of resources among individual states or as an expectation that a grand defensive coalition will form once an aggressor reveals itself, that is not necessarily the case when balance is defined as the formation of opposing alliances in peacetime. Concert diplomacy and alliance balancing may be incompatible for two reasons: (1) the goals in the two processes may be contradictory; hence pursuing concert goals may entail sacrificing allies' interests and risking the alliance itself; and (2) means in the concert game and in the alliance game are behaviorally similar; hence moves to cooperate with adversaries in the concert are not easily distinguishable from moves toward realignment. The incompatibility between the concert and alliance games will be greatest on both counts when tension between rival alliances and dependence among allies are high; then states will be most sensitive to the interests of allies and most inclined to interpret uncertainties conservatively. This is consistent, of course, with the point often made that concerts are least likely to work when they are most needed.

Nevertheless, we need not conclude on so pessimistic a note: there are good reasons why the concurrent pursuit of concert diplomacy and alliance balance is both feasible and desirable, despite the tension between them. First, some goals in the alliance game are quite consistent with a concert. Notable among them are the aims of avoiding entrapment and restraining allies. A concert can facilitate disengagement from a reckless ally in a crisis. As our slice of Balkan history demonstrated, the existence of a concert can help a state control its allies. Second, concert principles and procedures may serve to moderate the tension normally generated in the alliance game by the struggle to recruit and keep allies: concerts are good prophylactics against security dilemmas and hostility-integrative spirals. Although alliance politics may hinder concert cooperation, the effort to cooperate through a concert may dampen the more extreme manifestations of alliance competition.

The alliance game tends to dominate the concert game because it is the more likely to engage the core interests of states. Nevertheless, the concert can be strengthened by judicious "engineering" in both games. For example, concert procedures can be tailored to increase the transparency of communications, thus enabling actors to distinguish more confidently between concert cooperation and alliance abandonment.[134] Formalizing alliance commitments, rather paradoxically, may help minimize the potential contradictions between the two games: formal allies need be less worried, than those less tightly bound, that their partners' ostensible concert cooperation is a cover for shifting alignment. Such worries might also be reduced by careful adherence to the alliance norm of prior consultation.

In a multipolar system control of allies ranks with the control of arms and the prevention and limitation of wars among the most desirable social objectives. Control of allies is (and was) less important as a community objective in a bipolar system because the superpowers themselves performed this task so well in their own interests. As earlier pages in this book have suggested, allies in a multipolar system are less able to control each other in the normal course of diplomacy; they find it much harder than do bipolar allies to surmount systemically induced dilemmas and uncertainties. A multipolar system needs a concert to help its members avoid the worst results of their own unavoidable rivalry, especially their rivalry in gaining and holding allies. This will be as true of the multipolar system that looms before us in the twenty-first century as it was for the system of the nineteenth and early twentieth centuries.

European Great-Power Military Resources, 1880–1913

An index of European great-power military resources was constructed from data on iron and steel production, energy consumption, population, defense appropriations, and defense personnel. Each country's percentage share of the five-country total for each of these components was calculated. These shares were then averaged, for each country, across the five components, to compute the country's share of aggregate military resources and potential. Table A-1 gives these shares at ten-year intervals beginning in 1880.

Table A-1. Military Resource Shares, 1880–1913

	Iron-steel production	Energy consumption	Population	Defense appropriations	Defense personnel	Average
1880						
Great Britain	60.7	57.4	14.3	21.0	15.5	33.8
France	13.3	13.3	15.1	26.0	22.9	18.1
Russia	3.7	2.5	38.0	24.8	33.0	20.4
Germany	18.7	21.6	17.6	17.0	18.0	18.6
Austria-Hungary	3.5	5.2	15.1	11.0	10.4	9.0
1890						
Great Britain	50.2	51.3	13.8	22.6	16.9	31.0
France	11.9	12.7	13.8	26.7	21.8	17.4
Russia	6.0	3.9	39.9	20.8	27.2	19.5
Germany	25.8	25.1	17.8	20.7	20.2	21.9
Austria-Hungary	6.1	7.0	14.9	9.2	13.9	10.2
1900						
Great Britain	31.1	43.9	13.1	26.9	18.5	26.7
France	9.3	12.3	12.4	22.5	21.2	15.5
Russia	13.7	7.7	42.4	21.7	33.2	23.7
Germany	39.1	28.8	17.8	21.8	15.6	24.6
Austria-Hungary	6.8	7.4	14.3	7.2	11.4	9.4

Table A-1. Military Resource Shares, 1880–1913 (continued)

	Iron-steel production	Energy consumption	Population	Defense appropriations	Defense personnel	Aver
1910						
Great Britain	22.3	38.6	12.5	26.0	15.6	23.
France	11.7	11.5	10.8	20.0	20.8	14.
Russia	12.0	8.6	45.3	23.9	33.2	24.
Germany	46.7	33.0	17.8	23.5	18.8	27.
Austria-Hungary	7.2	8.4	13.6	6.7	11.5	9.
1913						
Great Britain	20.6	35.6	12.1	20.8	13.0	20.
France	12.3	11.4	10.5	15.5	22.3	14.
Russia	12.9	9.9	46.0	23.9	31.9	24.
Germany	47.2	34.1	17.5	30.0	21.9	30.
Austria-Hungary	7.0	9.0	14.0	9.9	10.9	10.

SOURCE: Calculated from data in Paul M. Kennedy, "The First World War and the Internatic Power System," *International Security* 9 (Summer 1984), 7–41.

NOTE: Because of rounding, some columns do not add to 100.

Alliance Bargaining Cases: Bargaining Power and Outcomes

In each of twenty-two cases, a bargaining power score was calculated for each ally from its scores on three components: interests, dependence, and commitment. Scores ranged from 1 to 3 on each component, decreasing with greater dependence and commitment, increasing with greater interest at stake in the case. Table B-1 shows the scoring and the outcomes for twelve cases in the Austro-German alliance and ten cases in the Franco-Russian alliance. Outcomes are results of bargaining or influence attempts between allies, not between adversaries.

Table B-1. Bargaining Power and Outcomes

| | Austria–Germany | | | | |
	Interests	Dependence	Commitment	Bargaining Power	Outcome
Renewal of Three Emperors' Alliance, 1884[a]					
Austria	3	3	2	8	Austria wins
Germany	2	1	2	5	
Russia	2	1	2	5	
Renewal of Triple Alliance, 1887					
Italy	3	3	2	8	Italy wins
Austria	1	2	2	5	
Germany	2	2	2	6	
"Perfidious Albion," 1894					
Austria	3	2	2	7	Germany wins
Germany	2	2	2	6	

Table B-1. Bargaining Power and Outcomes (continued)

| | Austria–Germany | | | | |
	Interests	Dependence	Commitment	Bargaining Power	Outcome
Congo, 1894					
Austria	2	2	2	6	Austria wins
Germany	1	2	2	5	
Morocco, 1905					
Austria	1	3	2	6	Compromise
Germany	2	2	2	6	
Bosnia, 1909					
Austria	2	2	2	6	Austria wins
Germany	1	1	1	3	
Agadir, 1911					
Austria	1	2	2	5	Ambiguous
Germany	3	1	1	5	
First Balkan War					
Austria	3	1	2	6	Compromise
Germany	3	1	1	5	
Scutari					
Austria	3	1	2	6	Compromise
Germany	3	1	1	5	
Second Balkan War					
Austria	3	1	2	6	Germany wins
Germany	3	1	1	5	
October 1913 crisis					
Austria	3	1	2	6	Austria wins
Germany	1	1	1	3	
July 1914 crisis (final phase)					
Austria	3	1	2	6	Austria wins
Germany	2	1	1	4	

| | France–Russia | | | | |
	Interests	Dependence	Commitment	Bargaining Power	Outcome
Shimonoseki Treaty, 1895					
Russia	3	3	2	8	Russia wins
France	1	2	2	5	
Kiel Canal, 1895					
Russia	1	3	2	6	Russia wins
France	1	2	2	5	
Chinese loan, 1896					
Russia	3	3	2	8	Russia wins
France	1	2	2	5	
Alliance revision, 1902					
Russia	3	3	2	8	Russia wins
France	2	2	2	6	

Table B-1. Bargaining Power and Outcomes (continued)

	Interests	Dependence	Commitment	Bargaining Power	Outcome
		France–Russia			
Morocco, 1905					
Russia	1	1	2	4	France wins
France	3	2	2	7	
Bosnia, 1909					
Russia	3	1	2	6	Ambiguous
France	2	2	2	6	
Britain	1	1	3	5	
Agadir, 1911					
Russia	1	1	2	4	France wins
France	3	2	2	7	
Britain	1	2	3	6	
Military conversations					
Russia	1	1	2	4	France wins
France	3	2	1	6	
Liman von Sanders					
Russia	3	2	2	7	Britain and
France	1	2	1	4	France win
Britain	1	2	3	6	
Sarajevo					
Russia	3	2	2	7	Russia wins
France	1	2	1	4	

NOTE: "Win" means having one's proposal accepted, in the main, by the ally. "Compromise" means mutual adjustment leading to agreement roughly halfway between initial proposals. Outcomes coded "ambiguous" could not be attributed clearly to the influence or lack of influence of allies.

[a]Scores for "interest" in the case of the renewal of the Three Emperors' Alliance are estimated averages across the three issues involved in the bargaining. For the breakdown per issue, see Chapter 7.

Notes

1. Alliances are also sometimes made in order to control or influence the ally. See Chapter 9 for a discussion of this motive. Also see Paul W. Schroeder, "Alliances, 1815–1945: Weapons of Power and Tools of Management," in Klaus Knorr, ed., *Historical Dimensions of National Security Problems* (Lawrence: University Press of Kansas, 1975), pp. 227–63.
2. George Liska, *Nations in Alliance: The Limits of Interdependence* (Baltimore: Johns Hopkins University Press, 1962), p. 3.
3. Ibid., p. 12.
4. Ole R. Holsti, P. Terrence Hopmann, and John D. Sullivan, *Unity and Disintegration in International Alliances: Comparative Studies* (New York: Wiley, 1973). This book contains a valuable survey and classification of theoretical propositions in the literature.
5. Stephen M. Walt, *The Origins of Alliances* (Ithaca: Cornell University Press, 1987). Other classic traditional works are Arnold Wolfers, *Discord and Collaboration: Essays on International Politics* (Baltimore: Johns Hopkins University Press, 1962); Wolfers, ed., *Alliance Policy in the Cold War* (Baltimore: Johns Hopkins University Press, 1959); Robert E. Osgood, *Alliances and American Foreign Policy* (Baltimore: Johns Hopkins University Press, 1967); and Robert Rothstein, *Alliances and Small Powers* (New York: Columbia University Press, 1968).
6. The seminal article is Mancur Olson and Richard Zeckhauser, "An Economic Theory of Alliances," *Review of Economics and Statistics* 48 (August 1966), 266–79. Typical of the elaborations and critiques that followed are James Murdock and Todd Sandler, "A Theoretical and Empirical Analysis of NATO," *Journal of Conflict Resolution* 26 (June 1982), 237–65, and Bruce M. Russett and Harvey Starr, "Alliances and the Price of Primacy," in Russett, ed., *What Price Vigilance? The Burdens of National Defense* (New Haven: Yale University Press, 1970), pp. 91–127. For applications of the theory to pre-1939 systems, see

Wallace Thies, "Alliances and Collective Goods: A Reappraisal," *Journal of Conflict Resolution* 31 (June 1987), 298–332, and Barry Posen, *The Sources of Military Doctrine: France, Britain, and Germany between the Wars* (Ithaca: Cornell University Press, 1984).

7. J. David Singer and Melvin Small, "Alliance Aggregation and the Onset of War," in Singer, ed., *Quantitative International Politics: Insights and Evidence* (New York: Free Press, 1968). Also see Jack S. Levy, "Alliance Formation and War Behavior: An Analysis of the Great Powers, 1495–1975," *Journal of Conflict Resolution* 25 (December 1981), 581–613; Robert Rood and Patrick McGowan, "Alliance Behavior in Balance of Power Systems," *American Political Science Review* 79 (September 1975), 859–70; and Bruce Bueno de Mesquita and J. D. Singer, "Alliances, Capabilities, and War: A Review and Synthesis," *Political Science Annual* (1973), 230–37.

8. See Dina Zinnes, "Coalition Theories and the Balance of Power," in Sven Groennings, E. W. Kelley, and M. Leiserson, eds., *The Study of Coalition Behavior* (New York: Holt, Rinehart, and Winston, 1970), pp. 351–69, and James C. Hsiung, "Sino–U.S.–Soviet Relations in a Triadic-Game Perspective," in Hsiung, ed., *Beyond China's Independent Foreign Policy* (New York: Praeger, 1985), pp. 107–32. An early path-breaking effort was Bruce Russett's "Components of an Operational Theory of International Alliance Formation," *Journal of Conflict Resolution* 12 (September 1968), 285–301.

9. For the original theory, see Fritz Heider, *The Psychology of Interpersonal Relations* (New York: Wiley, 1958). See also Howard F. Taylor, *Balance in Small Groups* (New York: Van Nostrand Reinhold, 1970). For applications to international relations, see Robert Jervis, "Systems Theories and Diplomatic History," in Paul Gordon Lauren, ed., *Diplomacy: New Approaches in History, Theory, and Policy* (New York: Free Press, 1979), pp. 212–45; Brian Healey and Arthur Stein, "The Balance of Power in International History: Theory and Reality," *Journal of Conflict Resolution* 17 (March 1973), 33–61; and H. Brooke McDonald and Richard Rosecrance, "Alliance and Structural Balance in the International System: A Reinterpretation," *Journal of Conflict Resolution* 29 (March 1985), 57–83.

10. The seminal work applying N-person game theory to political science is William H. Riker, *The Theory of Political Coalitions* (New Haven: Yale University Press, 1962), but its emphasis is on legislative rather than international coalitions. An international application is Emerson M. S. Niou, Peter C. Ordeshook, and Gregory F. Rose, *The Balance of Power: Stability in International Systems* (New York: Cambridge University Press, 1989). Also see R. Harrison Wagner, "The Theory of Games and the Balance of Power," *World Politics* 38 (July 1986), 546–76.

11. See Michael F. Altfeld, "The Decision to Ally: A Theory and Test," *Western Political Quarterly* 37 (December 1984), 523–44; James D. Morrow, "On the Theoretical Basis of a Measure of National Risk Attitudes," *International Studies Quarterly* 31 (December 1987), 423–38; Michael D. McGinnis, "A Rational Model of Regional Rivalry," *International Studies Quarterly* 34 (March 1990), 111–37; and Alastair Smith, "Alliance Formation and War," *International Studies Quarterly* 39 (December 1995), 405–25.

12. Hans J. Morgenthau, *Politics among Nations*, 5th ed. (New York: Knopf, 1973),

pp. 181–98; Ernst B. Haas and Allen S. Whiting, *Dynamics of International Relations* (New York: McGraw-Hill, 1956), pp. 160–86.

13. On this distinction, see George Modelski, "The Study of Alliances: A Review," *Journal of Conflict Resolution* 7 (December 1963), 769–76; for a recent statement, see John J. Mearsheimer, "A Realist Reply," *International Security* 20 (Summer 1995), 83.

14. Steven David has introduced the term "omnibalancing" to stand for alliances against internal as well as external threats. See his *Choosing Sides: Alignment and Realignment in the Third World* (Baltimore: Johns Hopkins University Press, 1991). Also see Michael N. Barnett and Jack S. Levy, "Domestic Sources of Alliances and Alignments: The Case of Egypt, 1962–73," *International Organization* 45 (Summer 1991), 369–94.

15. This is Stephen Walt's usage in *Origins of Alliances*.

16. Cf. Charles W. Kegley and Gregory A. Raymond, "Alliance Norms and War: A New Piece in an Old Puzzle," *International Studies Quarterly* 26 (December 1982), 572–95.

17. On reciprocity, see Robert O. Keohane, "Reciprocity in International Relations," *International Organization* 40 (Winter 1986), 1–27; also Alvin Gouldner, "The Norm of Reciprocity," *American Sociological Review* 25 (April 1960), 161–78.

18. This paradox is posed by Arthur Stein in *Why Nations Cooperate: Circumstances and Choice in International Relations* (Ithaca: Cornell University Press, 1990), pp. 163–69.

19. Russett, ed., *What Price Vigilance?* p. 91.

20. Raymond F. Cohen, *International Politics: The Rules of the Game* (New York: Longman, 1981), pp. 118–23.

21. And agreements that are basically ententes may include some provision for mutual support against outsiders, as the Anglo-French Entente Cordiale of 1904 called for mutual "diplomatic support" of the agreement's provisions concerning Egypt and Morocco against opposition from third parties.

22. Paul W. Schroeder emphasizes the control function in "Alliances, 1815–1945." Robert L. Rothstein, *Alliances and Small Powers*, suggests that formal alliance establishes a right to be consulted.

23. For a thorough analysis, see Charles Lipson, "Why Are Some International Agreements Informal?" *International Organization* 45 (Autumn 1991), 495–538.

24. The leading neorealist text is Kenneth N. Waltz, *Theory of International Politics* (Reading, Mass.: Addison-Wesley, 1979).

25. Apparently, the earliest statement of the security dilemma (not counting Thomas Hobbes or Thucydides!) was by John H. Herz in *Political Realism and Political Idealism* (Chicago: University of Chicago Press, 1951), p. 4. For a further development, see Robert Jervis, "Cooperation under the Security Dilemma," *World Politics* 30 (January 1978), 167–214.

26. Glenn H. Snyder, "The Security Dilemma in Alliance Politics," *World Politics* 36 (July 1984), 461–96.

27. These remarks are not intended to imply any position on the empirical validity of the domino and bandwagon theories. For a thorough treatment, see Robert Jervis and Jack Snyder, eds., *Dominoes and Bandwagons: Strategic Beliefs and Great Power Competition in the Eurasian Rimland* (New York: Oxford University Press, 1991).

28. The classic exposition of such differences, and the effects of system structure generally, is Waltz, *Theory of International Politics*. See also Glenn H. Snyder and Paul Diesing, *Conflict among Nations: Bargaining, Decision-Making, and System Structure in International Crises* (Princeton: Princeton University Press, 1977), chap. 6, from which the propositions in this paragraph are largely taken.

29. Walt, *Origins of Alliances*, chaps. 3, 4.

30. Waltz, *Theory of International Politics*, pp. 169–70.

31. This section elaborates on some ideas Diesing and I first broached in *Conflict among Nations*, pp. 471–79.

32. See, for example, Waltz, *Theory of International Politics*, p. 80.

33. Barry Buzan suggests the labels "process" or "process formation" for "patterns arising from the interaction of units," such as war, alliance, the balance of power, arms races, the security dilemma, and patterns stemming from trade and monetary policies. I have in mind something different in the notion of relationships: not patterns of interaction but the more static situational patterns of alignment, interest, capability, and interdependence that exist before behavioral interaction or as the background context of continuing interaction. Barry Buzan, Charles Jones, and Richard Little, *The Logic of Anarchy: Neorealism to Structural Realism* (New York: Columbia University Press, 1993), pp. 48–50.

34. Waltz, *Theory of International Politics*, p. 80.

35. Ibid., p. 98.

36. Robert O. Keohane, "Institutional Theory and the Realist Challenge after the Cold War," in David A. Baldwin, ed., *Neorealism and Neoliberalism* (New York: Columbia University Press, 1993), p. 279.

37. Waltz, *Theory of International Politics*, p. 169.

38. Morgenthau, *Politics among Nations*, p. 5.

39. This classification differs from the one offered by Michael C. Desch. He divides strategic interests into four categories: the homeland, intrinsic and extrinsic interests beyond the homeland, and a residual without significant value. Apparently, his intrinsic and extrinsic interests would be major and minor strategic interests in my scheme. My intrinsic and reputational interests are not included in his classification. Desch, *When the Third World Matters* (Baltimore: Johns Hopkins University Press, 1993), pp. 9–12.

40. A similar point is made by Jervis in "Systems Theories," pp. 237–38.

41. Raymond Aron, *Peace and War: A Theory of International Relations* (New York: Doubleday, 1966), p. 28.

42. Charles L. Glaser makes a similar point in "Realists as Optimists," *International Security* 19 (Winter 1994/95), 50–91.

43. Waltz, *Theory of International Politics*, p. 131.

44. This benefit is emphasized by Glaser in "Realists as Optimists."

45. Thomas J. Christensen and Jack Snyder, "Chain Gangs and Passed Bucks: Predicting Alliance Patterns in Multipolarity," *International Organization* 44 (Spring 1990), 138–68. See also George H. Quester, *Offense and Defense in the International System* (New York: Wiley, 1977).

46. Debora L. Spar and David A. Welch, "Asset Specificity and Structural Theories of International Politics" (paper presented at the annual meeting of the American Political Science Association, New York City, September 1–4, 1994).

47. Kenneth N. Boulding, *Conflict and Defense: A General Theory* (New York: Harper and Row, 1962).
48. David A. Baldwin, *Paradoxes of Power* (New York: Blackwell, 1989), pp. 132–38.
49. Waltz, *Theory of International Politics*, p. 80.
50. For an analysis of the trade-off between armaments and alliances, see McGinnis, "Rational Model of Regional Rivalry."
51. Arnold Wolfers, "Alliances," in David L. Shils, ed., *International Encyclopedia of the Social Sciences* (New York: Macmillan, 1968), p. 268.
52. Evanesh Dixit and Barry Nalebuff, "Making Strategies Credible," in Richard Zeckhauser, ed., *Strategy and Choice* (Cambridge: MIT Press, 1951), p. 181.

CHAPTER 2. THEORY: ALLIANCE FORMATION

1. "Enhanced capability for defense of the ally" is not listed, because it is chiefly a benefit to the ally, not to the self. If one has a prior interest in defending the ally, one's own alliance commitment adds little of benefit to oneself, except possibly a reduction of potential costs by facilitating the coordination of plans and forces. "Enhanced deterrence of attack on the ally" is, however, beneficial to the self as well as to the ally, since it reduces the likelihood of having to fight.
2. Liska, *Nations in Alliance*, p. 27.
3. Liska refers to such conflicts and ideological frictions as alliance "handicaps." See *Nations in Alliance*, pp. 16–18. For a demonstration of the positive effects of tradition, culture, and ethnicity on alliance formation, see Raymond Dawson and Richard Rosecrance, "Theory and Reality in the Anglo-American Alliance," *World Politics* 19 (October 1966), 21–52.
4. Logically, such future discounts will be deeper in a multipolar system than a bipolar one, because of the relative instability of alliance lineups in the former. Joanne S. Gowa, "Bipolarity, Multipolarity, and Free Trade," *American Political Science Review* 83 (December 1989), 1250.
5. On the security-autonomy trade-off, see Morrow, "Measure of National Risk Attitudes."
6. A broader optimization, as stated in Chapter 1, would extend across the alliance and adversary games and the preparedness, diplomatic, and action arenas. A still broader calculus would, of course, have to weigh security gains and costs in these various dimensions against nonsecurity values.
7. Russell Hardin, *Collective Action* (Baltimore: Johns Hopkins University Press, 1982). Mancur Olson, *The Logic of Collective Action* (Cambridge: Harvard University Press, 1965).
8. The logic of certain resistance at this point, and the system stability that results, has been formally stated by Niou, Ordeshook, and Rose in *Balance of Power*, chaps. 2 and 3. Jervis has also discussed the logic of collective goods as compared to the balance of power theory and the domino theory. See "Systems Theories," pp. 221–22.
9. In a related argument, Joanne Gowa has demonstrated how the temporary quality of alliances in a multipolar system makes great powers less willing than in a bipolar system to tolerate free trade, with its power-security exter-

nalities, among their allies. Gowa, "Bipolarity, Multipolarity, and Free Trade." See also Gowa, *Allies, Adversaries, and International Trade* (Princeton: Princeton University Press, 1994). Arthur Stein gives a discussion of joint gains among allies in *Why Nations Cooperate*, chap. 6.

10. William A. Gamson, "A Theory of Coalition Formation," *American Sociological Review* 26 (June 1961), 373–82. Also see Theodore Caplow, *Two against One: Coalitions in Triads* (Englewood Cliffs, N.J.: Prentice-Hall, 1968).

11. Gamson, "Theory of Coalition Formation," p. 376. Gamson's reasoning is similar to William Riker's "size principle": that coalitions will be restricted to "minimum winning" size. See Riker, *Theory of Political Coalitions*.

12. Randall Schweller has pointed out that the third party also has the option of letting the others fight it out if they are evenly matched, thus improving its own postwar power position. To simplify, however, I set aside this possibility. In reality, one of the two contestants is likely to turn out to be weaker, thus activating the third party's interest in coming to its defense when this becomes clear. See Schweller, "Tripolarity and the Second World War," p. 79.

13. Schweller has proposed a tripolar model that, like mine, includes variation in both the military strengths and the interests of actors. He dichotomizes interests as "status quo" and "revisionist," however, whereas I conceptualize them as "conflicting" or "in common" in varying degree. His model emphasizes motivation for change, whereas mine centers on the degree of compatibility of interests. His version is more appropriate for the 1930s, which is his empirical case, whereas mine is more suitable for the pre-1914 period. I would also argue, however, that my version is more generally applicable, since it is not always clear, between states in conflict, which one desires change and which one wants to preserve the status quo. Even if one wants change, like France in the 1871–1914 period, it may not want it badly enough to be willing to contemplate attack or form an offensive alliance. Some states, such as Austria in the same period, may be revisionist on some issues (the Balkans) but status quo on others (Transylvania). Moreover, the status quo–revisionist dichotomy tends to orient the analysis around extreme cases; my continuum of conflict embraces all cases. It permits alliance between some states that have conflicts; the conflicts simply force some discount of the alliance's value. Unlike Schweller's scheme, it also permits enmities between status quo states, simply as a function of insecurities induced by anarchy. Finally, it more easily encompasses informal alignments (ententes) engendered by the settlement of existing conflicts. See Schweller, "Tripolarity and the Second World War," pp. 77–81.

14. Walt, *Origins of Alliances*, pp. 23–24.

15. R. J. Aumann and M. Maschler, "The Bargaining Set for Cooperative Games," in M. Dresher, L. S. Shapley, and A. W. Tucker, eds., *Advances in Game Theory* (Princeton: Princeton University Press, 1946), pp. 443–47; James P. Kahan and Amnon Rapoport, *Theories of Coalition Formation* (Hillsdale, N.J.: Lawrence Erlbaum, 1985), chap. 4. For a simplified treatment, see Morton D. Davis, *Game Theory: A Nontechnical Introduction* (New York: Basic Books, 1970), pp. 161–69.

16. This and the following three-party examples, and associated diagrams,

are adapted from John G. Cross, "Some Theoretic Characteristics of Economic and Political Coalitions," *Journal of Conflict Resolution* 11 (June 1967), 184–95.

17. See Cross, "Some Theoretic Characteristics of Economic and Political Coalitions," 191–95, for a summary of the linear programming procedure that was used to generate the "after bargaining" numbers in Table 2–3.

18. John C. Harsanyi, "Models for the Analysis of Balance of Power in Society," in Ernest Nagel, Patrick Suppes, and Alfred Tarski, eds., *Logic, Methodology, and Philosophy of Science* (Stanford: Stanford University Press, 1962), pp. 453–54; Harsanyi, "A Simplified Bargaining Model for the N-Person Cooperative Game," *International Economic Review* 4 (May 1963), 194–220.

19. Harsanyi, "Models," p. 452.

20. Alliance need and alliance alternatives were described in Chapter 1 as the central ingredients in alliance "dependence." I have avoided that term in this discussion of alliance formation because, strictly speaking, states can be dependent on an alliance only after it has formed.

21. Jon Elster, *The Cement of Society: A Study of Social Order* (New York: Cambridge University Press, 1989), p. 80.

22. The assumptions are: (1) Invariance with respect to utility transformations. I.e., a linear transformation of the utilities of one or both players does not change the outcome. (2) Independence of irrelevant alternatives. I.e., alternative proposals that are rejected by both parties do not change the outcome, provided they do not change the status quo point. (3) Symmetry. I.e., when the positions of the players are symmetrical, the solution gives them equal payoffs; in particular, changing the labels of the players does not affect the outcome. (4) Pareto-optimality. I.e., any improvement on one player's payoff reduces the payoff of the other; the solution cannot be one that can be improved on by both players. John F. Nash, "The Bargaining Problem," *Econometrica* 18 (1950), 155–162.

CHAPTER 3. AUSTRO-GERMAN ALLIANCE AND THREE EMPERORS' ALLIANCE

1. Harry Eckstein, "Case Study and Theory in Political Science," in Fred I. Greenstein and Nelson W. Polsby, eds., *Handbook of Political Science*, vol. 7, *Strategies of Inquiry* (Reading, Mass.: Addison-Wesley, 1975), p. 108.

2. Eduard Wertheimer, *Graf Julius Andrássy*, vol. 3 (Stuttgart, 1910–13); quoted in William L. Langer, *European Alliances and Alignments*, 2d ed. (New York: Knopf, 1950, p. 183.

3. *Die grosse Politik der europäischen Kabinette*, 3, no. 485; Langer, *European Alliances*, p. 183.

4. This summary is collated from *Die grosse Politik*, 3, nos. 455, 458, 461, 477, and 482.

5. Langer, *European Alliances*, pp. 184–85.

6. I realize I am subject to the suspicion of having "cooked the books" in order to make the model's predictions conform to history. I can only say that I have tried to avoid this. In any case, the main purpose of the model is not to test predictions about outcomes but rather to illustrate incentives and pro-

vide a framework for analyzing process. The process implications of the model are not so sensitive to variance in evaluations.

7. On bandwagoning as an alternative to balancing, see Walt, *Origins of Alliances*, esp. chap. 2; also Jervis and Snyder, *Dominoes and Bandwagons*.

8. Raymond J. Sontag, *European Diplomatic History, 1871–1932* (New York: Appleton-Century-Crofts, 1961), pp. 19–20.

9. W. F. Monypenny and G. E. Buckle, *The Life of Benjamin Disraeli*, vol. 6 (London, 1920), pp. 486–89; quoted in Langer, *European Alliances*, p. 187.

10. Bruce Waller, *Bismarck at the Crossroads: The Reorientation of German Foreign Policy after the Congress of Berlin, 1878–1880* (London: Athlone Press, 1974), p. 202; Paul Kennedy, *The Rise of the Anglo-German Antagonism, 1860–1914* (New York: Allen and Unwin, 1980), p. 35; Langer, *European Alliances*, pp. 190–91.

11. This interpretation is supported by relevant dates. Munster received his instructions to open talks with Britain on September 16, after Bismarck had had his first interview with Andrássy on August 27–28 but before the second, decisive, round of talks on September 22–24. It is plausible that Bismarck, having learned at the first meeting of Andrássy's grounds for objecting to a general treaty—that it would alienate England—was moved to sound out England in hopes of getting a "sweetener" for Austria. Then he dropped Britain when he learned at the second meeting that Andrássy was absolutely insisting on a treaty against Russia only. The British sweetener was no longer relevant. This interpretation is different from that accepted by most historians—that Bismarck dropped Britain when a deal with Russia appeared possible. Of course, the two explanations are not mutually exclusive.

12. Thomas C. Schelling, *The Strategy of Conflict* (Cambridge: Harvard University Press, 1960), chap. 3.

13. The anti-British motive is prominent in the memoirs of Peter Saburov, the Russian negotiator. See J. Y. Simpson, *The Saburov Memoirs* (London: Cambridge University Press, 1929).

14. Ibid., pp. 74–75.

15. Ibid., p. 83.

16. Langer, *European Alliances*, p. 199; W. N. Medlicott, *The Congress of Berlin and After: A Diplomatic History of the Near Eastern Settlement, 1878–1880* (London: Methuen, 1938), p. 398; Simpson, *Saburov Memoirs*, p. 122.

17. Langer, *European Alliances*, p. 201.

18. Medlicott, *Congress of Berlin*, p. 64.

19. The Treaty of Berlin, 1878, had divided Bulgaria into two parts: Bulgaria and Eastern Rumelia. The Russians wanted to reunify the country, which they expected to control.

20. F. R. Bridge, *From Sadowa to Sarajevo: The Foreign Policy of Austria-Hungary, 1866–1914* (London: Routledge and Kegan Paul, 1972), p. 116. The Sanjak was a strip of land lying between Montenegro and Serbia that Austria coveted as a land route to the Aegean Sea.

21. W. N. Medlicott, "Bismarck and the Three Emperors' Alliance, 1881–1887," *Transactions of the Royal Historical Society*, 4th ser., 27 (1945), 72.

22. Bridge, *Sadowa to Sarajevo*, pp. 116–17; Medlicott, *Congress of Berlin*, pp. 268–70; Medlicott, "Bismarck and the Three Emperors' Alliance," p. 75.

23. Bridge, *Sadowa to Sarajevo*, p. 118.
24. The localization idea, which was to achieve some notoriety in the 1914 crisis, meant deterring a fifth party from coming to the aid of a fourth party that was fighting a member.
25. Simpson, *Saburov Memoirs*, p. 226.

CHAPTER 4. THE FRANCO-RUSSIAN ALLIANCE

1. Frederick L. Schuman, *War and Diplomacy in the French Republic: An Inquiry into Political Motivations and Control of Foreign Policy* (New York: McGraw-Hill, 1931), pp. 135–36.
2. James Joll, *The Origins of the First World War* (London: Longman, 1984), p. 39.
3. A. J. P. Taylor, *The Struggle for Mastery in Europe, 1848–1918* (London: Oxford University Press, 1947), pp. 314–15.
4. George F. Kennan, *The Decline of Bismarck's European Order: Franco-Russian Relations, 1875–1890* (Princeton: Princeton University Press, 1979), p. 398.
5. John F. V. Keiger, *France and the Origins of the First World War* (New York: St. Martin's, 1983), pp. 11–12.
6. Kennan, *Bismarck's European Order*, pp. 415–16.
7. See Chapter 7 for a further discussion of these events. For a thorough account, see Erich Brandenburg, *From Bismarck to the World War: A History of German Foreign Policy, 1870–1914*, trans. Annie Elizabeth Adams (London: Oxford University Press, 1927), pp. 27–32.
8. William L. Langer, *The Diplomacy of Imperialism* (New York: Knopf, 1968), p. 7.
9. George F. Kennan, *The Fateful Alliance: France, Russia, and the Coming of the First World War* (New York: Pantheon, 1984), p. 29.
10. Ibid., pp. 45–49 (quotation from p. 49).
11. Ribot, in his memoir of the origins of the alliance, wrote: "We had no reason to pause along the path that led to an alliance; but we in Paris did not wish to force the pace. We did not find it desirable to show ourselves too eager. We thought it would be wiser on our part to give the Russians time to allow their decisions to mature." Alexandre Ribot, "L'alliance Franco-Russe," *Revue d'Histoire de la Guerre Mondiale* 15 (July 1937), 201–28. Passage quoted in Kennan, *Fateful Alliance*, p. 66. Later, however, as they became frustrated with the Russians' procrastination, the impatience of the French became too great to camouflage.
12. Kennan, *Fateful Alliance*, p. 57.
13. Ibid., pp. 58, 66.
14. Langer, *Diplomacy of Imperialism*, p. 19.
15. Kennan, *Fateful Alliance*, pp. 89–90. The quotations are from *Documents diplomatiques françaises* (cited hereafter as *DDF*), 1st ser., vol. 8, no. 430, pp. 589–91, letter, Laboulaye to Ribot, July 20, 1891.
16. Kennan, *Fateful Alliance*, pp. 93–96 (quotation from p. 93); *DDF*, vol. 8, no. 424, pp. 576–80.
17. Kennan, *Fateful Alliance*, pp. 97, 98.

18. Schuman, *War and Diplomacy*, p. 141.
19. Langer, *Diplomacy of Imperialism*, pp. 22–23. The text of the agreement is reprinted in Kennan, *Fateful Alliance*, pp. 260–62.
20. William L. Langer, *The Franco-Russian Alliance, 1890–1894* (Cambridge: Harvard University Press, 1929), p. 189.
21. Georges Michon, *The Franco-Russian Alliance, 1891–1917* (New York: Howard Fertig, 1969), p. 34.
22. Langer, *Franco-Russian Alliance*, p. 194.
23. Ibid., p. 209.
24. Kennan, *Fateful Alliance*, p. 142.
25. Ibid., p. 149.
26. Ibid., p. 153.
27. Ibid., pp. 264–68.
28. Ibid., pp. 167–68, 170.
29. Michon, *Franco-Russian Alliance*, pp. 42–43, 44.
30. Ibid., p. 46.
31. Langer, *Diplomacy of Imperialism*, pp. 34–35; Michon, *Franco-Russian Alliance*, pp. 47, 50.
32. Langer, *Franco-Russian Alliance*, p. 260.
33. Ibid.
34. Schuman, *War and Diplomacy*, p. 145.
35. Kennan, *Fateful Alliance*, p. 185.
36. Ibid., p. 186.
37. Sontag, *European Diplomatic History*, p. 53.
38. Kennan, *Fateful Alliance*, pp. 216–17.
39. Langer, *Diplomacy of Imperialism*, p. 47; Kennan, *Fateful Alliance*, pp. 220–223.
40. Kennan, *Fateful Alliance*, pp. 230–34.
41. Kennan, *Fateful Alliance*, pp. 124–25.
42. Samuel B. Bacharach and Edward J. Lawler, *Bargaining: Power, Tactics, and Outcomes* (San Francisco: Jossey-Bass, 1981), p. 78.

CHAPTER 5. CONCLUSIONS: ALLIANCE FORMATION

1. Langer, *European Alliances*, p. 21.
2. Waller, *Bismarck at the Crossroads*, p. 17.
3. For a thorough description of all these matters, see Waller, *Bismarck at the Crossroads*.
4. Kennedy, *Anglo-German Antagonism*, p. 159.
5. Jack Snyder, *Myths of Empire: Domestic Politics and Strategic Ideology* (Ithaca: Cornell University Press, 1991), p. 84.
6. Schuman, *War and Diplomacy*, p. 133.
7. Dominic Lieven, "Pro-Germans and Russian Foreign Policy, 1890–1914," *International History Review* 2 (January 1980), 34n.
8. Kennan, *Fateful Alliance*, pp. 7–12, 35.
9. Schuman, *War and Diplomacy*, p. 134.
10. George Monger, *End of Isolation: British Foreign Policy, 1900–1907* (London: Thomas Nelson, 1963), p. 44. See also Jervis, "Systems Theories."

11. Monger, *End of Isolation*, pp. 8–14.
12. Zara S. Steiner, *Britain and the Origins of the First World War* (London: Macmillan, 1977), p. 26.
13. Monger, *End of Isolation*, pp. 110–11.
14. On divisions in the Liberal party, see A. J. Anthony Morris, *Radicalism against War, 1906–1914* (London: Longman, 1972).
15. Monger, *End of Isolation*, p. 313.
16. Opposition from the Radicals was an important reason Grey in later years always rejected pleas from the French and the Russians to transform the ententes into formal alliances.
17. On the role of the army and the government of India in negotiating the Russian entente, see Beryl J. Williams, "The Strategic Background to the Anglo-Russian Entente of 1907," *Historical Journal* 9, 3 (1966), 360–73.
18. D. C. B. Lieven, *Russia and the Origins of the First World War* (New York: St. Martin's, 1983), pp. 118–39.
19. Ibid., p. 30.
20. Morris, *Radicalism against War*, p. 53.
21. Grey helped Izvolsky overcome this opposition by suggesting that Britain would consider an alteration in the Straits regime if the negotiations were concluded. Steiner, *Britain and the Origins of the First World War*, p. 81.
22. Geography may be subsumed in system structure as a partial determinant of the relative capabilities of states.
23. Robert Jervis, *System Effects* (Princeton: Princeton University Press, 1997), chap. 6.
24. King Edward had it right when he told the Kaiser in the summer of 1906, "There are no frictions between us; there exists only rivalry." *Grosse Politik*, 21, p. 453; quoted in Brandenburg, *From Bismarck to the World War*, p. 266.
25. For excellent discussions of the ideological component of alliances, see Holsti, Hopmann, and Sullivan, *Unity and Disintegration*, esp. chap. 2.
26. Kennan, *Bismarck's European Order*, p. 414.
27. Quoted in Monger, *End of Isolation*, p. 302.
28. Ernest L. Woodward, *Great Britain and the German Navy* (Oxford: Oxford University Press, 1935), p. 361.
29. I. H. Nish, *The Anglo-Japanese Alliance: The Diplomacy of Two Island Empires, 1894–1907* (London: Athlone Press, 1966), p. 338.
30. Langer, *European Alliances*, p. 194.
31. Lieven, *Russia and the Origins of the First World War*, p. 32.
32. Kennedy, *Anglo-German Antagonism*, p. 212.
33. "Better" means, of course, better in the state's own perceptions.
34. Jervis, *System Effects*, chap. 7; Snyder and Diesing, *Conflict among Nations*, pp. 426–27.
35. Riker, *Theory of Political Coalitions*. Schweller has argued that the size principle applies only to offensive alliances, since only these generate spoils to be divided. Since defensive alliances exist only to resist aggressive states, not to make gains, there is nothing to be lost in recruiting additional members. This view, however, overlooks the costs of adding members to a defensive alliance in terms of commitments to the defense of their interests. Schweller, "Tripolarity and the Second World War." The size principle is logically more

relevant to multipolar than to bipolar systems. In the latter, as in the cold war period, the superpower is committed by its own interests to defend all smaller states against the opposite superpower. There is no cost in codifying this commitment in an alliance. Note that peacetime alliances in the post-1945 period have been much larger than those in previous multipolar systems.

36. Robert Jervis, Richard Ned Lebow, and Janice Gross Stein, *Psychology and Deterrence* (Baltimore: Johns Hopkins University Press, 1985).
37. Nish, *Anglo-Japanese Alliance*, p. 354.
38. Monger, *End of Isolation*, pp. 158–59; Samuel R. Williamson, Jr., *The Politics of Grand Strategy: Britain and France Prepare for War, 1904–1914* (Cambridge: Harvard University Press, 1969), pp. 12–13.
39. Schelling, *Strategy of Conflict*, p. 45.
40. C. J. Lowe, *The Reluctant Imperialists: British Foreign Policy, 1878–1902*, 3 vols. (London: Routledge and Kegan Paul, 1967), vol. 1, p. 245.
41. Ibid., pp. 245–48.
42. Here I am agreeing with Harrison Wagner that "one could not construct a general theory of alliances based entirely on balance of power theory." R. Harrison Wagner, "The Theory of Games and the Balance of Power," paper presented at the annual meeting of the American Political Science Association, Washington, D.C., August 30–September 2, 1984, p. 16. See also Barry Buzan, *People, States, and Fear*, 2d ed. (Baltimore: Johns Hopkins University Press, 1991), p. 194.
43. Walt, *Origins of Alliances*, esp. chap. 2.
44. For the argument that the balance is unintended, see Waltz, *Theory of International Politics*, pp. 117–23; for the opposite, that it is intended as a matter of deliberate policy, see Hedley Bull, *The Anarchical Society: A Study of Order in World Politics* (New York: Columbia University Press, 1977), chap. 6; for a comparison of the two arguments, and a third, the "semi-automatic" theory, consult Inis L. Claude, Jr., *Power and International Relations* (New York: Random House, 1962), chap. 2 and 3.
45. Waltz, *Theory of International Politics*, pp. 117–23.
46. Walt, *Origins of Alliances*, chap. 2; Wolfers, *Discord and Collaboration*, p. 124; Waltz, *Theory of International Politics*, p. 126.
47. Quoted in Eugene N. Anderson, *The First Moroccan Crisis, 1904–1906* (Hamden, Conn.: Archon, 1966), p. 286.
48. Quoted in Steiner, *Britain and the Origins of the First World War*, p. 40.
49. G. P. Gooch and H. Temperley, *Britain Documents on the Origins of the War, 1898–1914*, vol. 5, p. 764 (hereafter cited as *British Documents*); quoted in Luigi Albertini, *The Origins of the War of 1914*, 3 vols. (London: Oxford University Press, 1952), vol. 1, p. 288.
50. Quoted in Michael Howard, *The Continental Commitment: The Dilemma of British Defense Policy in the Era of the Two World Wars* (London: Maurice Temple Smith, 1972), p. 36.
51. Jervis and Snyder, *Dominoes and Bandwagons*, pp. 36–38.
52. Walt, *Origins of Alliances*, p. 21.
53. Here I am disagreeing with Schweller, who argues that the notion of bandwagoning should be limited to the offensive type. See his "Bandwagoning

for Profit: Bringing the Revisionist State Back In," *International Security* 19 (Summer 1994), 72–108.

CHAPTER 6. THEORY: ALLIANCE MANAGEMENT

1. Baldwin, *Paradoxes of Power*, p. 206.
2. These factors were discussed in Chapter 2 as determinants of the relative bargaining power of the parties when they negotiate an alliance contract. Dependence after the contract is negotiated, however, is somewhat different and usually greater than before. After the alliance has formed, dependence manifests itself in the prospect of being deprived of something already possessed, which is generally more weighty than the prospect of acquiring the same values. (On this point, see Peter M. Blau, *Exchange and Power in Social Life* (New York: Wiley, 1964), esp. pp. 116–17.)
3. Jervis, *System Effects*, chap. 2.
4. Baldwin, *Paradoxes of Power*, p. 203.
5. R. M. Emerson, "Power-Dependence Relations," *American Sociological Review* 27 (1962), 31–40.
6. Franklin B. Weinstein has labeled these types "non-situational" and "situational" commitments, respectively. See "The Concept of a Commitment in International Relations," *Journal of Conflict Resolution* 13 (March 1969), 39–56.
7. Jervis, *System Effects*, chap. 5.
8. Emerson, "Power-Dependence Relations."
9. Jon Elster emphasizes time preference and risk aversion, as well as "disagreement utility," as determinants of bargaining power, in *Cement of Society*, p. 80.
10. On such pitfalls in international relations, there is no better source than Robert Jervis, *Perception and Misperception in International Politics* (Princeton: Princeton University Press, 1976).
11. J. V. Fuller, *Bisma. ck's Diplomacy at Its Zenith* (New York: Howard Fertig, 1967), pp. 44–45.
12. Patrick Morgan, *Deterrence: A Conceptual Analysis* (New York: Sage, 1977), p. 11.
13. James D. Morrow has discussed a similar trade-off between security and autonomy in "Measure of National Risk Attitudes." His definition of autonomy is different from mine, however.
14. There is a further trade-off, of course, between the tightness of alliance bonds and armament expenditures, since these are alternative sources of security. For theoretical treatments of this trade-off, see Altfeld, "Decision to Ally," and James D. Morrow, "Arms vs. Allies: Trade-offs in the Search for Security," *International Organization* 47 (Spring 1993), 207–33.
15. Michael Mandelbaum, *The Nuclear Revolution: International Politics Before and After Hiroshima* (New York: Cambridge University Press, 1981), chap. 6. See also Mandelbaum, *The Fate of Nations* (New York: Cambridge University Press, 1988), chap. 2, and G. Snyder, "Security Dilemma in Alliance Politics."
16. Arnold Wolfers, *Britain and France between Two Wars: Conflicting Strategies of Peace since Versailles* (New York: Harcourt Brace, 1940), pp. 234–35.

17. Paul M. Kennedy, *The Realities behind Diplomacy: Background Influences on British External Policy, 1865–1980* (New York: Allen and Unwin, 1981), p. 191.
18. Wolfers, "Alliances," p. 269.
19. Jonathan Mercer has used attribution theory to show that statesmen attribute undesirable behavior by adversaries and allies to their inherent characteristics, and their desirable behavior to the state's own policies. Thus, reputations can be acquired only for traits undesired by others, since reputations must logically attach only to innate characteristics. Consequently, reputations can be acquired only for alliance disloyalty, not loyalty; but in the case of adversaries, reputations attach to resolve, not irresolution. Hence the concern for loyalty image is realistic only in the negative sense: avoiding an appearance of disloyalty. In general, Mercer finds that statesmen are more concerned with their resolve and loyalty reputations than they need to be. See *Reputation and International Politics* (Ithaca: Cornell University Press, 1996).
20. Quoted in Albertini, *Origins of the War of 1914*, vol. 1, p. 338.
21. Blau, *Exchange and Power*, pp. 120–21.
22. Mandelbaum, *Fate of Nations*, chap. 2.
23. Mandelbaum, *Fate of Nations*, p. 101.
24. C. J. Lowe and L. M. Dockrill, *The Mirage of Power: British Foreign Policy, 1902–14*, 3 vols. (London: Routledge and Kegan Paul, 1972), vol. 1, p. 2.
25. Jervis, *Perception and Misperception*, chap. 3. Charles L. Glaser presents an elaboration of Jervis's theory in "Political Consequences of Military Strategy."
26. Herz, *Political Realism and Political Idealism*, p. 4; Wolfers, *Discord and Collaboration*, p. 84; Herbert Butterfield, *History and Human Relations* (London: Collins, 1951), pp. 19–20. Jervis has also written insightfully on the security dilemma in its standard, original sense. See his "Cooperation under the Security Dilemma."
27. Jervis points out that if allies and adversaries are told something they do not want the other to hear, they will be motivated to keep it secret. This supports the feasibility of trying to deter the adversary and restrain the ally simultaneously. See his *System Effects*, chap. 7.

CHAPTER 7. THE AUSTRO-GERMAN ALLIANCE

1. The numbers at the left of the resource graph in Fig. 7-1 show the difference between the shares of overall European great-power resources held by a state and by its principle opponent. Thus Austria's resource curve begins at −11.4 percent, which is the difference, in 1880, between the Austrian share of 9 percent and the Russian share of 20.4 percent. This is the resource gap that Austria is dependent on Germany to fill. Germany's curve begins at +0.5 percent, the amount of total great-power resources by which Germany's resources exceed France's in 1880. Thus Germany is not dependent in terms of resources until the beginning of the Franco-Russian alliance in 1891.
2. Alfred Kuhn, "Bargaining Power in Transactions: A Basic Model of Inter-

personal Relationships," *American Journal of Economics and Sociology* 23 (January 1964), 48–63.

3. Bridge, *Sadowa to Sarajevo*, p. 144.

4. F. R. Bridge, *The Habsburg Monarchy among the Great Powers, 1815–1918* (New York: Berg, 1990), p. 162.

5. Norman Rich, *Great Power Diplomacy, 1814–1914* (New York: McGraw-Hill, 1992), p. 243.

6. Langer, *European Alliances*, p. 398. For texts, see Alfred F. Pribram, *The Secret Treaties of Austria-Hungary, 1879–1914*, 2 vols. (Cambridge: Harvard University Press, 1920), vol. 1, pp. 94–104.

7. G. E. Buckle, ed., *The Letters of Queen Victoria*, 3d ser., vol. 1 (New York: John Murray, 1930), pp. 271–72; quoted in Langer, *European Alliances*, p. 400.

8. Langer, *European Alliances*, pp. 437–40; for texts, see Pribram, *Secret Treaties*, vol. 1, pp. 124–34.

9. Pribram, *Secret Treaties*, vol. 1, pp. 52, 59, 70.

10. Ibid., vol. 1, pp. 66, 67; Langer, *European Alliances*, p. 393; Albertini, *Origins of the War of 1914*, vol. 1, p. 53.

11. Fuller, *Bismarck's Diplomacy*, p. 195.

12. Erich Eyck, *Bismarck and the German Empire* (New York: Norton, 1958), p. 298.

13. Quoted in Bridge, *Habsburg Monarchy*, p. 186.

14. Gordon Craig, *From Bismarck to Adenauer: Aspects of German Statecraft* (Baltimore: Johns Hopkins University Press, 1958), pp. 232–35.

15. Quoted in Gerhard Ritter, *The Sword and the Scepter: The Problem of Militarism in Germany*, trans. Heinz Norden, 2 vols. (Coral Gables, Fla.: University of Miami Press), vol. 2, p. 243.

16. Taylor, *Struggle for Mastery*, p. 341.

17. Langer, *Diplomacy of Imperialism*, p. 40.

18. Kennedy, *Anglo-German Antagonism*, p. 214.

19. Langer, *Franco-Russian Alliance*, p. 297.

20. Langer, *Diplomacy of Imperialism*, p. 52.

21. Bridge, *Sadowa to Sarajevo*, p. 195.

22. Graydon A. Tunstall, *Planning for War against Russia and Serbia: Austro-Hungarian and German Military Strategies, 1891–1914* (Highland Parks, N.J.: Atlantic Research and Publications, 1993), p. 40.

23. Norman Stone, "Moltke and Conrad: Relations between the Austro-Hungarian and German General Staffs, 1909–1914," in Paul Kennedy, ed., *War Plans of the Great Powers, 1880–1914* (Boston: Allen and Unwin, 1979), p. 224.

24. Langer, *Diplomacy of Imperialism*, pp. 52–53; Arthur J. May, *The Hapsburg Monarchy, 1867–1914* (Cambridge: Harvard University Press, 1951), p. 298.

25. Bridge, *Habsburg Monarchy*, pp. 195–97; Langer, *Diplomacy of Imperialism*, pp. 53–54.

26. Rich, *Great Power Diplomacy*, pp. 259–60.

27. Quoted in Brandenburg, *From Bismarck to the World War*, p. 42.

28. Raymond J. Sontag, *Germany and England: Background of Conflict, 1848–1894* (New York: Russell and Russell, 1964), p. 281.

29. Ibid., p. 305.

30. Brandenburg, *From Bismarck to the World War*, p. 89.
31. Kennedy, *Realities behind Diplomacy*, p. 107.
32. Oswald H. Wedel, *Austro-German Diplomatic Relations, 1908–1914* (Stanford: Stanford University Press, 1932), p. 24.
33. May, *Hapsburg Monarchy*, p. 302; Bridge, *Sadowa to Sarajevo*, pp. 232–33; Albertini, *Origins of the War of 1914*, vol. 1, pp. 93–94.
34. Bridge, *Sadowa to Sarajevo*, p. 236.
35. Monger, *End of Isolation*.
36. Quoted in Sontag, *European Diplomatic History*, pp. 79–80.
37. The Franco-British negotiations are examined in more detail in the next chapter.
38. Anderson, *First Moroccan Crisis*, p. 355.
39. Ibid., p. 358.
40. Ibid., p. 374.
41. Ibid., p. 398.
42. Quoted in Wedel, *Austro-German Diplomatic Relations*, p. 38.
43. *Die grosse Politik*, 21, no. 7154; quoted in Wedel, *Austro-German Diplomatic Relations*, p. 37.
44. Bridge, *Sadowa to Sarajevo*, pp. 290–91.
45. May, *Hapsburg Monarchy*, p. 288.
46. Wedel, *Austro-German Diplomatic Relations*, p. 26.
47. Volker R. Berghahn, *Germany and the Approach of War in 1914* (New York: St. Martin's, 1973), p. 137.
48. Quoted in Brandenburg, *From Bismarck to the World War*, p. 312.
49. Wedel, *Austro-German Diplomatic Relations*, p. 56.
50. *Die grosse Politik*, 26 (1), p. 195; quoted in Gordon A. Craig, *Germany, 1866–1945* (New York: Oxford University Press, 1978), p. 322.
51. Quoted in G. P. Gooch, *Before the War: Studies in Diplomacy*, 2 vols. (London: Longmans, Green., 1936), vol. 1, p. 276.
52. Bülow to Szögyény, October 13, 1908; quoted in Brandenburg, *From Bismarck to the World War*, p. 322.
53. Fuller, *Bismarck's Diplomacy*, p. 421.
54. Albertini, *Origins of the War of 1914*, vol. 1, p. 286.
55. Quoted in ibid., vol. 1, p. 294.
56. The detente had already been damaged in 1908 by an Austrian plan to build a railroad through Turkish territory, which the Russians protested as a violation of the agreement to maintain the status quo in the Balkans.
57. David G. Herrmann, *The Arming of Europe and the Making of the First World War* (Princeton: Princeton University Press, 1996), p. 121.
58. Gordon A. Craig, *The Politics of the Prussian Army* (New York: Oxford University Press, 1964), p. 289.
59. Bernadotte Schmitt, *The Annexation of Bosnia* (New York: Howard Fertig, 1970), p. 97.
60. Ritter, *Sword and the Scepter*, vol. 2, p. 221.
61. Stone, "Moltke and Conrad," p. 227.
62. Bridge, *Habsburg Monarchy*, p. 293.
63. Stone, "Moltke and Conrad," p. 223.
64. Ritter, *Sword and the Scepter*, vol. 2, p. 244.

65. Stone, "Moltke and Conrad," p. 223.
66. Albertini, *Origins of the War of 1914*, vol. 1, p. 308.
67. Wedel, *Austro-German Diplomatic Relations*, p. 119.
68. Taylor, *Struggle for Mastery*, p. 463.
69. Wedel, *Austro-German Diplomatic Relations*, p. 121.
70. Ima C. Barlow, *The Agadir Crisis* (Chapel Hill: University of North Carolina Press, 1940), p. 250; Bridge, *Sadowa to Sarajevo*, p. 333.
71. Fischer, *War of Illusions*, p. 86.
72. Barlow, *Agadir Crisis*, p. 356.
73. Fischer, *War of Illusions*, p. 85.
74. Barlow, *Agadir Crisis*, p. 357.
75. F. R. Bridge, *Great Britain and Austria-Hungary, 1906–1914: A Diplomatic History* (London: Weidenfeld and Nicolson, 1972), p. 175.
76. Wedel, *Austro-German Diplomatic Relations*, p. 131.
77. Mercer, *Reputation*, p. 151.
78. Barlow, *Agadir Crisis*, pp. 236–50.
79. Quoted in Fischer, *War of Illusions*, p. 86, and Konrad Jarausch, *The Enigmatic Chancellor: Bethmann-Hollweg and the Hubris of Imperial Germany* (Princeton: Princeton University Press, 1972), p. 131.
80. Mercer, *Reputation*, p. 199.
81. Ibid., p. 200; Bridge, *Sadowa to Sarajevo*, p. 333.
82. In fact, war was only narrowly averted, late in November, when the Russian prime minister, Vladimir Kokovstov, and other civilian leaders vetoed a military decision for mobilization against Austria. This probably would have triggered Austrian mobilization and consequently German mobilization. See L. C. F. Turner, *Origins of the First World War* (New York: Norton, 1970), pp. 44–47.
83. R. J. Crampton, "The Balkans, 1909–1914," in F. H. Hinsley, ed., *British Foreign Policy under Sir Edward Grey* (Cambridge: Cambridge University Press, 1977), p. 260.
84. Fischer, *War of Illusions*, p. 206; Taylor, *Struggle for Mastery*, p. 495.
85. Albertini, *Origins of the War of 1914*, vol. 1, pp. 436–37.
86. Quoted in Fischer, *War of Illusions*, p. 208.
87. Samuel R. Williamson, *Austria-Hungary and the Origins of the First World War* (New York: St. Martin's, 1991), p. 135.
88. L. J. Crampton, *The Hollow Detente: Anglo-German Relations in the Balkans, 1911–1914* (London: George Prior, 1979), pp. 94–95.
89. Quoted in Turner, *Origins of the First World War*, p. 55.
90. The domestic factors were a backlash against the cost of the military measures taken the previous autumn, a scandal in the military establishment, and the opposition of Tisza, the Hungarian prime minister, to any military action. See Williamson, *Austria-Hungary*, p. 148.
91. Quoted in Fischer, *War of Illusions*, p. 218.
92. Fischer, *War of Illusions*, pp. 218–19.
93. Ibid., p. 218.
94. Williamson, *Austria-Hungary*, p. 149.
95. Quoted in Fischer, *War of Illusions*, p. 394.
96. Williamson, *Austria-Hungary*, p. 153.

97. Quoted in ibid., p. 155.
98. On these later developments, see Crampton, *Hollow Detente*, esp. chaps. 7 and 8.
99. Quoted in Fischer, *War of Illusions*, p. 225.
100. Turner, *Origins of the First World War*, p. 57.
101. On this problem, see Richard Ned Lebow and Janice Gross Stein, "Deterrence: The Elusive Dependent Variable," *World Politics* 42 (April 1990), 336–69.
102. R. J. Crampton, "The Decline of the Concert of Europe in the Balkans, 1913–1914," *Slavonic and East European Review* 52 (June 1974), 415.
103. Tunstall, *Planning for War*, p. 86.
104. Ibid., p. 138.
105. For a summary of the positions in the debate, see John W. Langdon, *July, 1914: The Long Debate, 1918–1990* (New York: Berg, 1991).
106. David Stevenson, *The First World War and International Politics* (New York: Oxford University Press, 1988), p. 15.
107. Quoted in Albertini, *Origins of the War of 1914*, vol. 2, p. 125.
108. Austrian emperor to German emperor, July 5, 1914, Document no. 13 in Max Montgelas and Walther Schucking, eds., *Outbreak of the World War: German Documents Collected by Karl Kautsky* (New York: Oxford University Press, 1924), pp. 68–69 (cited hereafter as *Kautsky Documents*).
109. Ibid., no. 15, p. 79.
110. Jack S. Levy, "Preferences, Constraints, and Choices in July, 1914," *International Security* 15 (Winter 1990/91), pp. 151–87, gives a thorough analysis of how the various possible outcomes were ranked by each of the states involved in the crisis.
111. Quoted in Albertini, *Origins of the War of 1914*, vol. 2, pp. 150–51.
112. Ibid., p. 170.
113. Ibid., p. 175.
114. Ibid., p. 263.
115. Ibid., p. 256.
116. Ibid., p. 262.
117. Ibid., p. 267.
118. *British Documents*, vol. 11, p. 99.
119. Ibid., p. 122; Albertini, *Origins of the War of 1914*, vol. 2, p. 341.
120. *Kautsky Documents*, no. 171, p. 195.
121. Bernadotte E. Schmitt, *The Coming of the War, 1914*, 2 vols. (New York: Howard Fertig, 1966), vol 2, p. 3.
122. *British Documents*, vol. 11, p. 145.
123. *Kautsky Documents*, no. 277, p. 256.
124. Quoted in Albertini, *Origins of the War of 1914*, vol. 2, p. 445.
125. *Kautsky Documents*, no. 278, p. 257.
126. Albertini, *Origins of the War of 1914*, vol. 2, p. 451.
127. Schmitt, *Coming of the War*, vol. 2, p. 75.
128. Albertini, *Origins of the War of 1914*, vol. 2, p. 468.
129. *Kautsky Documents*, no. 323, p. 289.
130. *British Documents*, vol. 12, p. 249.
131. Szögyény to Berchtold, July 25, 1914; cited in Schmitt, *Coming of the War*, vol. 1, pp. 304–6.

132. Albertini, *Origins of the War of 1914*, vol. 2, p. 455.
133. Schmitt, *Coming of the War*, vol. 2, p. 85.
134. *Kautsky Documents*, no. 395, p. 345.
135. Ibid., no. 396, pp. 345–46.
136. *British Documents*, vol. 11, p. 286; *Kautsky Documents*, no. 368, pp. 321–22.
137. W. J. Mommsen, "Domestic Factors in German Foreign Policy before 1914," *Central European History* 6 (1973), 38n; Gerhard Ritter, *The Schlieffen Plan : Critique of a Myth* (London: Oswald Wolff, 1958), p. 194.
138. Marc Trachtenberg, *History and Strategy* (Princeton: Princeton University Press, 1991), pp. 80–87.
139. *Kautsky Documents*, no. 349, pp. 307–8.
140. Moltke's exact words in 1909 were, "At the moment that Russia mobilizes, Germany will also mobilize and will mobilize her entire army." Trachtenberg argues it is not clear that this pledge applied to the case of Russian mobilization against Austria alone (p. 82). In my view, however, it clearly did. The Moltke-Conrad correspondence in 1909 centered mainly on the contingency of an Austro-Russian clash. If Moltke's statement was intended to apply only to a general Russian mobilization, the qualifying phrase "and will mobilize her entire army" would have been redundant. Apparently, Moltke wanted to reassure the Austrians that in case of a Russian partial mobilization (against Austria alone), the German response would be more than partial.
141. Albertini, *Origins of the War of 1914*, vol. 2, p. 482.
142. Ibid.
143. Ibid., vol. 2, p. 502.
144. Quoted in ibid., vol. 2, p. 505.
145. Ibid., vol. 2, p. 670.
146. Quoted in ibid., vol. 2, p. 673.
147. For an account of German knowledge of these measures, see Ulrich Trumpener, "War Premeditated? German Intelligence Operations in July, 1914," *Central European History* 9 (March 1976), 58–85.
148. *Kautsky Documents*, no. 437, p. 371.
149. Franz Graf Conrad von Hötzendorf, *Auf meiner Dienstzeit 1906–1918*, vol. 4, p. 153; quoted in Albertini, *Origins of the War of 1914*, vol. 2, p. 674.
150. Albertini, *Origins of the War of 1914*, vol. 2, p. 678.
151. Snyder and Diesing, *Conflict among Nations*, chap. 4. See also Jervis, Lebow, and Stein, *Psychology and Deterrence*.

CHAPTER 8. THE FRANCO-RUSSIAN ALLIANCE

1. Even though the Franco-Russian alliance named the Triple Alliance the enemy, England was actually Russia's primary antagonist in the early years of the alliance.
2. The comparisons for 1905 were estimated by extrapolating between 1900 and 1910.
3. Taylor, *Struggle for Mastery*, pp. 355–57; Langer, *Diplomacy of Imperialism*, pp. 184–85.

4. *DDF*, 1st ser., vol. 11, no. 483; quoted in Taylor, *Struggle for Mastery*, p. 358.

5. Thomas M. Iiams, Jr., *Dreyfus, Diplomatists, and the Dual Alliance: Gabriel Hanotaux at the Quay d'Orsay, 1894–1898* (Paris: Librarie Minard, 1962), pp. 81–82.

6. Quoted in ibid., p. 83.

7. Ibid.

8. The successful joint European action against Japan was the signal for a race between the European powers to carve up China. Germany began by seizing Kaio-chow. Russia then took Port Arthur and the Liaotung Peninsula. England, fearful of being left out, grabbed Wei-ai-wei, just across the Korea Bay from Port Arthur.

9. Taylor, *Struggle for Mastery*, p. 368; Monger, *End of Isolation*, p. 117.

10. Keiger, *France and the Origins of the First World War*, pp. 14–17; Roger Glenn Brown, *Fashoda Reconsidered: The Impact of Domestic Politics on French Policy in Africa, 1893–1898* (Baltimore: the Johns Hopkins University Press, 1969).

11. Christopher Andrew, *Théophile Delcassé and the Making of the Entente Cordiale: A Reappraisal of French Foreign Policy, 1898–1905* (London: Macmillan, 1968), pp. 242–46.

12. Christopher Andrew, "German World Policy and the Reshaping of the Dual Alliance," in Walter Laqueur and George L. Mosse, eds., *1914: The Coming of the First World War* (New York: Harper and Row, 1966), pp. 137–38.

13. Gooch, *Before the War*, vol. 1, p. 108; Andrew, "German World Policy," p. 132.

14. Andrew, *Delcassé*, p. 134.

15. Andrew, "German World Policy," p. 143.

16. Andrew, *Delcassé*, p. 125.

17. Gooch, *Before the War*, vol. 1, p. 110.

18. Andrew, *Delcassé*, pp. 237–38.

19. Michon, *Franco-Russian Alliance*, pp. 116–17.

20. Paul Kennedy, *The Rise and Fall of the Great Powers: Economic Change and Military Conflict from 1500 to 2000* (New York: Random House, 1987).

21. Jervis, "Systems Theories," p. 162.

22. Sidney B. Fay, *The Origins of the World War* (New York: Macmillan, 1929), p. 167.

23. M. B. Hayne, *The French Foreign Office and the Origins of the First World War* (Oxford: Clarendon Press, 1993), p. 103.

24. Gooch, *Before the War*, vol. 1, p. 153.

25. Andrew, *Delcassé*, p. 211.

26. Keiger, *France and the Origins of the First World War*, p. 19.

27. The Dogger Bank incident, in which the Russians mistakenly fired on and sank some British fishing trawlers in the North Sea, brought Britain and Russia close to war in October 1904. It also provided Delcassé, through his mediation of the crisis, with an opportunity to shore up the alliance with Russia, which might otherwise have been weakened by the entente with Russia's enemy, Britain.

28. Anderson, *First Moroccan Crisis*, p. 272.

29. D. W. Spring, "Russia and the Franco-Russian Alliance, 1905–14: Depend-

ence or Independence?" *Slavonic and East European Review* 66 (October 1988), 587. See also Anderson, *First Moroccan Crisis*, pp. 271–73.

30. Lieven, *Russia and the Origins of the First World War*, p. 29.

31. Delcassé sought to use this "offer" against his opponents in the cabinet who were seeking his ouster at German behest. The tactic backfired when Rouvier, the premier, reported that he had word from Bülow that alliance with England would provoke a German attack. The "offer" was not accepted, and Delcassé was forced to resign. Andrew, *Delcassé*, p. 297.

32. This brief account largely follows Monger's, in *End of Isolation*.

33. Donald R. Mathieu, "The Role of Russia in French Foreign Policy, 1908–1914" (Ph.D. dissertation, Stanford University, 1968), pp. 46–47.

34. F. R. Bridge and Roger Bullen, *The Great Powers and the European States System, 1815–1914* (London: Longman, 1980), pp. 157–60.

35. *British Documents*, vol. 5, pp. 237–45; cited in Gooch, *Before the War*, vol. 2, p. 31.

36. Raymond Poincaré, *Au service de la France: Neuf années de souvenirs*, vol. 1, pp. 295–96; quoted in Albertini, *Origins of the War of 1914*, vol. 2, p. 370.

37. Mathieu, "Role of Russia," p. 51.

38. Schmitt, *Annexation of Bosnia*, p. 70.

39. Ibid., p. 157.

40. Ibid., p. 159n.

41. E. W. Edwards, "The Franco-German Agreement on Morocco, 1909," *English Historical Review* 79 (1963), 483–513.

42. Nicolson to Grey, March 24, 1909, *British Documents*, vol. 5, no. 764, p. 736; quoted in Mercer, *Reputation*, p. 146.

43. Nicolson to Grey, February 26, 1909, *British Documents*, vol. 5, no. 612, p. 628; D. W. Sweet, "The Bosnian Crisis," in Hinsley, *British Foreign Policy*, pp. 188–89.

44. Touchard to Pichon, February 28, 1909, *DDF*, 2d ser., vol. 12, pp. 78–79; quoted in Mathieu, "Role of Russia," p. 51.

45. Touchard to Pichon, March 6, 1909, ibid., pp. 107–9; cited in Mathieu, "Role of Russia," p. 51.

46. Nicolson to Grey, February 27, 1909, *British Documents*, vol. 5, no. 617; quoted in Schmitt, *Annexation of Bosnia*, p. 163.

47. Nicolson to Grey, February 15, 1909, *British Documents*, vol. 5, no. 572; Albertini, *Origins of the War of 1914*, vol. 2, p. 277.

48. Nicholson to Grey, March 24, 1909, *British Documents*, vol. 5, no. 764; quoted in Schmitt, *Annexation of Bosnia*, pp. 201–2.

49. Nicolson to Grey, April 14, 1909, *British Documents*, vol. 5, nos. 835, 836; quoted in Schmitt, *Annexation of Bosnia*, p. 251.

50. B. de Siebert, *Entente Diplomacy and the World* (New York, 1921), p. 99; quoted in Keith Wilson, *The Policy of the Entente: Essays on the Determinants of British Foreign Policy, 1904–1914* (Cambridge: Cambridge University Press, 1985), p. 83.

51. Albertini, *Origins of the War of 1914*, vol. 2, p. 309.

52. See Chapter 7 for a fuller treatment of the Potsdam negotiations.

53. K. A. Hamilton, "Great Britain and France, 1911–1914," in Hinsley, *British Foreign Policy*, p. 131.

54. Barlow, *Agadir Crisis*, chaps. 11 and 12, gives a detailed account of British interests and behavior.
55. Lowe and Dockrill, *Mirage of Power*, vol. 1, pp. 44–45.
56. Williamson, *Politics of Grand Strategy*, p. 143.
57. Barlow, *Agadir Crisis*, pp. 283–92.
58. M. L. Dockrill, "British Policy during the Agadir Crisis of 1911," in Hinsley, *British Foreign Policy*, p. 285.
59. Barlow, *Agadir Crisis*, p. 246.
60. Ibid., p. 247.
61. Mathieu, "Role of Russia," p. 57.
62. Ibid., p. 358.
63. Dwight E. Lee, *Europe's Crucial Years: The Diplomatic Background of World War I, 1902–1914* (Hanover, N.H.: University Press of New England, 1974), p. 263; Michon, *Franco-Russian Alliance*, p. 195.
64. Lee, *Europe's Crucial Years*, p. 263.
65. Josephy Caillaux, *Agadir: Ma politique extérieure* (Paris, 1919), p. 143; quoted in Herrmann, *Arming of Europe*, p. 153.
66. Barlow, *Agadir Crisis*, pp. 246–47.
67. Hamilton, "Great Britain and France," p. 326.
68. Ibid., p. 328.
69. Williamson, *Politics of Grand Strategy*, pp. 295–97.
70. Keiger, *France and the Origins of the First World War*, p. 90.
71. Michon, *Franco-Russian Alliance*, p. 193.
72. Keiger, *France and the Origins of the First World War*, p. 91.
73. This was a perversion from the Russian purpose, however, which was to use the alliance as a defensive bulwark against Austria.
74. Keiger, *France and the Origins of the First World War*, p. 93.
75. Mathieu, "Role of Russia," p. 103.
76. Keiger, *France and the Origins of the First World War*, p. 96.
77. Ibid., p. 108.
78. Quoted in Fay, *Origins of the World War*, pp. 335–36.
79. Izvolsky to Sazonov, September 12, 1912, *Livre noir*, vol 1, p. 326; quoted in Mathieu, "Role of Russia," pp. 109–10.
80. Albertini, *Origins of the War of 1914*, vol. 1, p. 414.
81. Izvolsky to Sazonov, November 20, 1912, *Livre noir*, vol. 1, pp. 368–72; quoted in Albertini, *Origins of the War of 1914*, vol. 1, pp. 411–12.
82. This decision may have been domestically more than French-inspired, however. It came after the civilian leaders in Russia vetoed a military plan to mobilize against Austria-Hungary. Keith Neilson, "Russia," in Keith Wilson, ed., *Decisions for War, 1914* (New York: St. Martin's, 1995), p. 108.
83. Mathieu, "Role of Russia," pp. 121–22.
84. Hayne, *French Foreign Office*, pp. 248–49.
85. Taylor, *Struggle for Mastery*, p. 482.
86. Nicolson to Buchanan, October 22, 1912, *British Documents*, vol. 9 (ii), no. 57; quoted in Taylor, *Struggle for Mastery*, p. 482.
87. Fischer, *War of Illusions*, pp. 423–24.
88. Lieven, *Russia and the Origins of the First World War*, p. 102.
89. Jack Snyder, *The Ideology of the Offensive* (Ithaca: Cornell University Press, 1984), p. 168.

90. Dietrich Geyer, *Russian Imperialism: The Interaction of Domestic and Foreign Policy, 1860–1914*, trans. Bruce Little (New Haven: Yale University Press, 1977), p. 289.
91. Lieven, *Russia and the Origins of the First World War*, p. 102.
92. Herrmann, *Arming of Europe*, p. 136.
93. L. C. F. Turner, "The Russian Mobilization in 1914," in Kennedy, *War Plans*, p. 253.
94. Joll, *Origins of the First World War*, p. 78.
95. Snyder, *Ideology of the Offensive*, pp. 175–76.
96. Geyer, *Russian Imperialism*, p. 292.
97. Williamson, *Politics of Grand Strategy*, p. 223.
98. Lieven, *Russia and the Origins of the First World War*, p. 103.
99. Fischer, *War of Illusions*, pp. 426–27.
100. Lieven, *Russia and the Origins of the First World War*, p. 105.
101. Ibid., pp. 576, 581–82.
102. Gerd Krumeich, *Armaments and Politics in France on the Eve of the First World War: The Introduction of Three-Year Conscription, 1913–1914* (Dover, N.H.: Berg, 1984), p. 168.
103. Izvolsky to Sazonov, December 30, 1913; quoted in Robert J. Kerner, "The Mission of Liman von Sanders," *Slavonic Review* 6 (1927–28), 558.
104. Fischer, *War of Illusions*, p. 343.
105. Quoted in D. W. Spring, "Russia and the Coming of the War," in R. J. W. Evans and Hartmut Pogge von Strandmann, eds., *The Coming of the First World War* (Oxford: Clarendon Press, 1988), p. 65.
106. Quoted in Michael G. Ekstein, "Great Britain and the Triple Entente on the Eve of the Sarajevo Crisis," in Hinsley, *British Foreign Policy*, pp. 346–47.
107. Krumeich, *Armaments and Politics*, pp. 123–24.
108. Rich, *Great Power Diplomacy*, p. 446; Albertini, *Origins of the War of 1914*, vol. 2, p. 196.
109. Quoted in Rich, *Great Power Diplomacy*, p. 446.
110. Ibid.
111. Ibid., p. 447.
112. Ibid., p. 449.
113. Albertini, *Origins of the War of 1914*, vol. 2, pp. 306–7.
114. Ibid., p. 626.
115. Ibid. p., 604; Schmitt, *Coming of the War*, vol. 2, p. 232.
116. L. C. F. Turner, "The Role of the General Staffs in July, 1914," *Australian Journal of Politics and History* 11 (December 1965), 320–22.
117. Albertini, *Origins of the War of 1914*, vol. 2, p. 607, 620.
118. Ibid., p. 608, 621.
119. Ibid., p. 415.
120. Schmitt, *Coming of the War*, vol. 2, p. 41.
121. Ibid., p. 90.
122. *Kautsky Documents*, no. 368, pp. 320–21.
123. As noted in the previous chapter, the most important other factor, perhaps more influential than Grey's warning, was the news of the Russian partial mobilization.
124. The two cases were "Steering Clear of Perfidious Albion," when the Germans, against Austrian desires, rejected a British offer of collaboration in

the Near East; and the German restraint of Austria during the Second Balkan War. In both cases, Germany "won" the bargaining, although our index predicted otherwise, apparently because it irrationally exaggerated its interests at stake.

CHAPTER 9. CONCLUSIONS: ALLIANCE MANAGEMENT

1. Fay, *Origins of the World War*, p. 302.
2. Joll, *Origins of the First World War*, p. 165.
3. Jervis, *System Effects*, chap. 5.
4. Wilson, *Policy of the Entente*, p. 41.
5. Berghahn, *Germany and the Approach of War*, p. 188.
6. Quoted in Wilson, *Policy of the Entente*, p. 74.
7. Quoted in Lieven, *Russia and the Origins of the First World War*, p. 142.
8. Mercer, *Reputation*.
9. Lowe and Dockrill, *Mirage of Power*, vol. 3, p. 426.
10. A possible exception to this generalization might be the French success in getting a rescission, in 1906, of the earlier extension of the alliance to cover conflict with Great Britain. This was not a loosening of the alliance commitments, however, but a modification of their domain.
11. Delcassé interpreted this request as an offer of alliance, but the "offer" did not save him from being fired by a government fearful of war with Germany. Monger, *End of Isolation*, pp. 197–98.
12. Albertini, *Origins of the War of 1914*, vol. 2, pp. 150–51; Gary Shanafeld, *The Secret Enemy: Austria-Hungary and the German Alliance, 1914–1918* (New York: Columbia University Press, 1985), p. 26.
13. Mandelbaum, *Fate of Nations*, chap. 2.
14. Posen, *Sources of Military Doctrine*; Christensen and Snyder, "Chain Gangs and Passed Bucks."
15. Kennedy, *Anglo-German Antagonism*, p. 268.
16. Sontag, *Germany and England*, p. 238.
17. Quoted in Monger, *End of Isolation*, p. 17.
18. Medlicott, *Congress of Berlin*, p. 325.
19. Langer, *European Alliances*, p. 314.
20. Quoted in Fuller, *Bismarck's Diplomacy*, pp. 80, 47.
21. Quoted in ibid., pp. 72–73.
22. See Schroeder, "Alliances, 1815–1945."
23. Sontag, *European Diplomatic History*, p. 19.
24. Taylor, *Struggle for Mastery*, p. 265.
25. Nish, *Anglo-Japanese Alliance*, pp. 239–40.
26. Blau, *Exchange and Power*, pp. 97–106.
27. Conversely, the chief purpose of making the alliance in the first place (usually) is to avoid abandonment—i.e., to increase the chances of having the other state's support in war.
28. Nicolson to Grey, February 15, 1909, *British Documents*, vol. 5, no. 572, p. 601.
29. Fischer, *War of Illusions*, p. 206.

30. Albert Hirschmann, *Exit, Voice, and Loyalty* (Cambridge: Harvard University Press, 1970).
31. Dockrill, "Agadir Crisis," p. 280.
32. Liska, *Nations in Alliance*, p. 35.
33. Quoted in Albertini, *Origins of the War of 1914*, vol. 1, p. 271.
34. Quoted in Fuller, *Bismarck's Diplomacy*, pp. 78–79.
35. Quoted in Gooch, *Before the War*, vol. 2, p. 248.
36. Ibid., p. 249.
37. Quoted in Berghahn, *Germany and the Approach of War*, p. 138.
38. Jervis, *System Effects*, chap. 5.
39. Ekstein, "Great Britain and the Triple Entente," p. 343.
40. Grey to Harcourt, January 10, 1914; quoted in Lowe and Dockrill, *Mirage of Power*, vol. 3, p. 483.
41. Quoted in Taylor, *Struggle for Mastery*, p. 494.
42. Quoted in Albertini, *Origins of the War of 1914*, vol. 2, 605–6.
43. These are not the tensions Poincaré had immediately in mind; apparently, he was thinking of those peculiar to the adversary game and the alliance game, considered separately. He might have pointed to tensions across the games, and it is those I wish to focus on here.
44. Gooch, *Before the War*, vol. 2, p. 154; Steiner, *Britain and the Origins of the First World War*, p. 99.
45. Anderson, *First Moroccan Crisis*, pp. 345–47.
46. E. T. S. Dugdale, ed., *German Diplomatic Documents, 1871–1914*, 4 vols. (New York: Harper, 1931), vol. 4: *Descent into the Abyss, 1911–1914*, no. 92, p. 112 (italics in original).
47. Keiger, *France and the Origins of the First World War*, p. 98.
48. St.-Aulaire to Poincaré, May 17, 1912, DDF, 3d ser., III, no. 17; quoted in Keiger, *France and the Origins of the First World War*, p. 85.
49. Gooch, *Before the War*, vol. 2, pp. 39–40.
50. Ekstein, "Great Britain and the Triple Entente," p. 347.
51. Lowe and Dockrill, *Mirage of Power*, vol. 1, p. 138.
52. Albertini, *Origins of the War of 1914*, vol. 2, p. 649.
53. Historians are divided as to whether Grey could have prevented the war by taking a clear stance, one way or the other, earlier in the crisis. Albertini's opinion (*Origins of the War of 1914*, vol. 2, p. 514) is that he could have. Sean M. Lynn-Jones takes a similar position in "Detente and Deterrence: Anglo-German Relations, 1911–1914," *International Security* 11 (Fall 1986), 121–51. For a contrary view, see Taylor, *Struggle for Mastery*, p. 525. For Grey's dilemma, see Ekstein, "Great Britain and the Triple Entente." It is true that Grey felt constrained by domestic and constitutional considerations from issuing an unequivocal commitment.
54. Jervis, *Perception and Misperception*, chap. 3.
55. Fischer, *War of Illusions*, p. 68.
56. Gooch, *Before the War*, vol. 2, p. 82.
57. Mercer, *Reputation*, p. 131.
58. Quoted in F. R. Bridge, "Relations with Austria-Hungary and the Balkan States," in Hinsley, *British Foreign Policy*, p. 176.
59. Keiger, *France and the Origins of the First World War*, p. 55.

60. Hayne, *French Foreign Office*, pp. 243, 66.
61. Interestingly, Poincaré applied this principle only to European issues, not to colonial ones. Thus he collaborated with Germany in the Near East, where the economic interests of the two countries ran parallel. Keiger, *France and the Origins of the First World War*, pp. 122–23.
62. Keiger, *France and the Origins of the First World War*, p. 166.
63. Jervis, *Perception and Misperception*, chap. 3.
64. Kenneth N. Waltz, "The Stability of a Bipolar World," *Daedalus* 93 (Summer 1964), 881–909.
65. Herbert Butterfield, "The Tragic Element in Modern International Conflict," *Review of Politics* 12 (April 1950), 156.
66. Jervis, "Systems Theories," p. 235.
67. Jervis makes a similar argument in terms of consistency theory in *System Effects*, chap. 6.
68. Joll, *Origins of the First World War*, pp. 55–56.
69. Jervis, *Perception and Misperception*, chap. 3.
70. Christensen and Snyder, "Chain Gangs and Passed Bucks."
71. Scott D. Sagan, "1914 Revisited: Allies, Offense, and Instability," *International Security* 11 (Fall 1986), 151–77.
72. Ibid., p. 164.
73. Gunther Hellmann and Reinhard Wolf, "Neorealism, Neoliberal Institutionalism, and the Future of NATO," *Security Studies* 3 (Autumn 1993), 19.
74. Quoted in Wilson, *Policy of the Entente*, p. 38.
75. Robert E. Kann, "Alliances vs. Ententes," *World Politics* 14 (July 1976), 611–21; G. B. Berridge, "Ententes and Alliances," *Review of International Studies* 15 (1989), 251–60.
76. Paul W. Schroeder, "World War I as Galloping Gertie: A Reply to Joachim Remak," *Journal of American History* 44 (September 1972), 328–29.
77. Bertie to Nicolson, May 14, 1911; quoted in Lowe and Dockrill, *Mirage of Power*, vol. 3, p. 433.
78. Hirschmann, *Exit, Voice, and Loyalty*.
79. Winston S. Churchill, *The World Crisis* (London, 1923), vol. 1, p. 205; quoted in Albertini, *Origins of the War of 1914*, vol. 2, p. 202.
80. Keiger, *France and the Origins of the First World War*, p. 80.
81. Charles W. Kegley, Jr., and Gregory A. Raymond, *When Trust Breaks Down: Alliance Norms and World Politics* (Columbia: University of South Carolina Press, 1990).
82. Stein, *Why Nations Cooperate*.
83. Snyder, *Ideology of the Offensive*, p. 182.
84. At least in the case of Britain, most decision makers who, like Grey, argued for supporting France in 1914 on moral grounds also believed strategic interest required Britain to fight. What may have been operating here is the reluctance of people to make value trade-offs; the desired policy must be justified on all conceivable grounds. Nevertheless, the normative factor seems to have carried considerable independent weight, and not only in the British government. On value trade-offs, see Jervis, *Perception and Misperception*, pp. 128–43.
85. Taylor, *Struggle for Mastery*, p. 340n.
86. Jervis, "Systems Theories," p. 226; L. L. Farrar, *Arrogance and Anxiety: The*

Ambivalence of German Power, 1848–1914, (Iowa City: University of Iowa Press, 1981), pp. 66–67.

87. Both quotations are from Sagan, "1914 Revisited," 164–65.
88. Quoted in Wilson, Policy of the Entente, p. 101.
89. Quoted in Fischer, War of Illusions, p. 85.
90. Kennan, Bismarck's European Order, p. 331.
91. Ibid.
92. Andrew, Delcassé, p. 132.
93. Quoted in Fischer, War of Illusions, p. 86.
94. Sir Charles E. Callwell, Field Marshal Sir Henry Wilson (New York, 1927), vol. 1, p. 88; cited in Laney, "Military Implementation."
95. Lowe and Dockrill, Mirage of Power, vol. 3, p. 6.
96. Thomas C. Schelling, Arms and Influence (New Haven: Yale University Press, 1966), chap. 2.
97. Cohen, International Politics, p. 119.
98. Thibaut and Kelley define the halo effect as "the tendency for one's general attitude toward a person to influence more specific evaluations of him." Social Psychology of Groups, p. 76.
99. Quoted in Michon, Franco-Russian Alliance, p. 193.
100. Taylor, Struggle for Mastery, pp. 418–19.
101. Quoted in Brandenburg, From Bismarck to the World War, p. 322.
102. Quoted in Kenneth Bourne, The Foreign Policy of Victorian England, 1830–1902 (Oxford: Clarendon Press, 1970), p. 479.
103. Sir Edward Grey, Twenty-Five Years, 1892–1916 (London: Stokes, 1925), vol. 1, pp. 312–13; quoted in Schmitt, Coming of the War, vol. 2, pp. 34–35.
104. Quoted in Wilson, Policy of the Entente, p. 90.
105. Robert O. Keohane, International Institutions and State Power: Essays in International Relations Theory (Boulder, Colo.: Westview, 1989), p. 136.
106. Dugdale, German Diplomatic Documents, vol. 3: The Growing Antagonism, 1898–1910, no. 110, p. 305.
107. Mercer, Reputation, p. 150.
108. Robert O. Keohane, "Reciprocity in International Relations," International Organization 40 (Winter 1986), 8.
109. Helmreich, Diplomacy of the Balkan Wars, p. 180.
110. L. C. F. Turner, "The Russian Mobilization in 1914," in Kennedy, War Plans, p. 256.
111. Grey to Bertie, February 25, 1909; British Documents, vol. 5, no. 611, p. 627.
112. Cohen, International Politics, pp. 66–67.
113. Liska, Nations in Alliance, p. 86.
114. Kegley and Raymond, When Trust Breaks Down, p. 255.
115. Thibaut and Kelley, Social Psychology of Groups, pp. 130–35.
116. Schelling, Strategy of Conflict, chap. 3.
117. See Chapter 5 for a discussion of equity norms.
118. Elster, Cement of Society, pp. 99–100.
119. The seminal article on the theory of concerts is Robert Jervis, "From Balance to Concert: A Study of International Security Cooperation," in Kenneth A. Oye, ed., Cooperation under Anarchy (Princeton: Princeton University Press, 1986), pp. 58–80.
120. For a fuller discussion of the Balkan Wars, see Chapter 7.

121. Crampton, *Hollow Detente*, p. 93.
122. R. J. Crampton, "The Balkans as a Factor in German Foreign Policy," *Slavic and East European Review* 55 (July 1977), 380–84.
123. Crampton, "Decline of the Concert of Europe," p. 410.
124. Ibid., p. 418.
125. Ibid., p. 413.
126. Putnam, "Diplomacy and Domestic Politics."
127. Crampton, "Decline of the Concert of Europe," p. 415.
128. John J. Mearsheimer, "The False Promise of International Institutions," *International Security* 19 (Winter 1994/95), 34–37.
129. For an excellent analysis of the managed balance of power, with Britain the manager, see Mandelbaum, *Fate of Nations*, chap. 1.
130. On nineteenth-century theories, see Carsten Holbraad, *The Concert of Europe: A Study of German and British International Theory, 1815–1914* (New York: Barnes and Noble, 1970); for a valuable documentary collection, see René Albrecht-Carrié, *The Concert of Europe* (New York: Harper, 1968).
131. On the interplay of concert and balance, see Richard N. Rosecrance, *Action and Reaction in World Politics* (Boston: Little, Brown, 1963).
132. F. H. Hinsley, *Power and the Pursuit of Peace: Theory and Practice in the History of Relations between States* (London: Cambridge University Press, 1963), pp. 260–61.
133. Charles A. Kupchan and Clifford A. Kupchan, "Concerts, Collective Security, and the Future of Europe," *International Security* 16 (Summer 1991), 141.
134. During the Balkan Wars the British and German foreign offices exchanged large amounts of internal documentation, such as instructions to diplomats.

Index

Bethmann-Hollweg, Theobald von, 228, 235, 237, 240–42, 248, 252–59, 297, 302–4, 322, 335, 355

Bipolar system, 3, 12, 16, 19, 156n; compared to multipolar, 16, 18, 26, 145–46, 156, 184, 346, 349, 371, 383n, 390n. See also System structure

Bismarck, Otto von, 14, 80, 109, 133–35, 143, 147, 151, 319, 320, 323, 335, 360; as buck-passer, 344; and negotiation of Austro-German alliance of 1879, 46, 84–87, 88, 90, 95, 97, 99; and negotiation of Three Emperors' Alliance of 1881, 101–4; proposes alliance to Britain, 95–96, 216; and renewal of Three Emperors' Alliance (1884), 207, 209, 211–12; and renewal of Triple Alliance (1887), 213–15; resignation of, 111, 137, 217

Björko treaty, 145, 152, 159, 274

Boer War, 139, 145, 272

Boisdeffre, Colonel (General) Raoul Mouton de, 111–14, 118–20, 138. See also Franco-Russian alliance of 1891–94, formation of

Bosnia-Herzegovina, 104–07, 230–31, 233

Bosnian crisis (1908–9), 230–33; Austrian and German bargaining power in, 232–33; British policy in, 281; effects on Triple Entente, 232, 309; French policy in, 280–81; German support of Austria in, 231, 312, 325, 360–61

Boulanger, General Georges, 111–12, 138, 211–12

Boulding, Kenneth, 29

Buchanan, George, 299, 300–01, 304

Buck-passing, 29, 34, 113, 116, 184, 212, 221, 246, 319, 328, 343–46, 366

Bulgaria, 101, 104–7, 111, 158, 207, 341; in Balkan wars, 239, 242

Bulgarian crisis (1885–87), 144, 211–12, 215–16

Bülow, Bernhard von, 229–31, 233, 235, 312, 325–26, 333, 354, 360

Burden sharing, 34

Butterfield, Herbert, 340

Buzan, Barry, 382n

Cambon, Jules, 349

Cambon, Paul, 286

Capabilities, 6, 18, 21, 28–30, 32, 33, 37

Caprivi, Georg Leo von, 217

Chain-ganging, 28, 198, 343–44. See also Spirals: integrative

Chamberlain, Joseph, 225

Chamberlain, Neville, 343

Chinese loan, France to Russia, 267

Christensen, Thomas J., 28, 343

Churchill, Winston, 348

Clemenceau, Georges, 280

Coalitions, 12, 16

Coalition theory, 2, 3, 49, 54–55

Collective goods theory, 2, 49–51, 54

Commitment, 48–49; in Austro-German alliance, 204, 206; conditionality of, 36; as determinant of alliance bargaining power, 168–70; effects of, on alliance security dilemma, 188; in Franco-Russian alliance, 262–64; and restraint of ally, 327; role of, in alliance formation vs. alliance management, 169n; scope of, 14; sources of, 169; types of, 15

Concert of Europe, 103, 281; in Balkan wars, 238–43, 251; German defection, 366–67

Concerts: and alliance bargaining, 367; and balance of power, 368–71; tension with adversary and alliance games, 364, 367; value for controlling allies, 367–68, 371

Congo, the: French-German-British dispute over, 222–23

Conrad von Hötzendorff, Franz, 233–35, 246–47, 254, 257–58

Constantinople, 7, 115, 154, 207, 224, 291, 297–98. See also Straits, of the Bosporous and the Dardanelles

Consultation, as alliance norm, 13, 348; in French policy, 288; as method of restraining ally, 321–22; in Triple Alliance, 362; in Triple Entente, 361

Continental league, 149, 224, 265, 274–75, 278

Control of ally, as alliance benefit or motive, 13, 44, 381n

Counteralliance, as cost of allying, 44, 46

Defense, as alliance benefit, 43, 56, 63, 113

Delcassé, Théophile, 140, 154, 227, 268–72, 274, 295, 314, 354, 398n, 399n, 402n

Dependence, 30–32, 391n; in Austro-German alliance, 202–4, 205–6, 217, 236; balance of, 150, 179, 191; as determinant of alliance bargaining power, 166–68; elements in, 31, 166–67; in Franco-Russian alliance, 261–64; military, 167; in multipolar vs. bipolar systems, 38; political, 31; and restraint of ally, 321, 328; scope of, 168; symmetry of, 31, 38. See also Bargaining, bargaining power

Detente, 11,19

Deterrence, as alliance benefit, 43, 56, 63, 113; theory of, 180, 193, 338; in composite security dilemma, 196, 198

Diesing, Paul, 176n

Diplomacy, as interaction arena, 33–35

Disraeli, Benjamin, 95, 108, 136

Cornell Studies in Security Affairs

edited by Robert J. Art, Robert Jervis,
and Stephen M. Walt

Liberal Peace, Liberal War: America's Diplomatic Crises, 1794–1898, by John M. Owen

Bombing to Win: Air Power and Coercion in War, by Robert A. Pape

Inadvertent Escalation: Conventional War and Nuclear Risks, by Barry R. Posen

The Sources of Military Doctrine: France, Britain, and Germany between the World Wars,
   by Barry R. Posen

Dilemmas of Appeasement: British Deterrence and Defense, 1934–1937, by Gaines Post, Jr.

Crucible of Beliefs: Learning, Alliances, and World Wars, by Dan Reiter

Eisenhower and the Missile Gap, by Peter J. Roman

The Domestic Bases of Grand Strategy, edited by Richard Rosecrance and Arthur A. Stein

Societies and Military Power: India and Its Armies, by Stephen Peter Rosen

Winning the Next War: Innovation and the Modern Military, by Stephen Peter Rosen

Israel and Conventional Deterrence: Border Warfare from 1953 to 1970, by Jonathan Shimshoni

Fighting to a Finish: The Politics of War Termination in the United States and Japan, 1945,
   by Leon V. Sigal

Alliance Politics, by Glenn H. Snyder

The Ideology of the Offensive: Military Decision Making and the Disasters of 1914, by Jack Snyder

Myths of Empire: Domestic Politics and International Ambition, by Jack Snyder

The Militarization of Space: U.S. Policy, 1945–1984, by Paul B. Stares

The Nixon Administration and the Making of U.S. Nuclear Strategy, by Terry Terriff

Making the Alliance Work: The United States and Western Europe, by Gregory F. Treverton

The Origins of Alliances, by Stephen M. Walt

Revolution and War, by Stephen M. Walt

The Ultimate Enemy: British Intelligence and Nazi Germany, 1933–1939, by Wesley K. Wark

The Tet Offensive: Intelligence Failure in War, by James J. Wirtz

The Elusive Balance: Power and Perceptions during the Cold War, by William Curti Wohlforth

Deterrence and Strategic Culture: Chinese-American Confrontations, 1949–1958,
   by Shu Guang Zhang

Lightning Source UK Ltd.
Milton Keynes UK
UKHW01f1311140818
327039UK00017B/429/P